Information and Communication Technologies for Economic and Regional Developments

M. Hakikur Rahman
Sustainable Development Networking Programme, Bangladesh

T0325233

IDEA GROUP PUBLISHING
Hershey • London • Melbourne • Singapore

Acquisition Editor:	Kristin Klinger
Senior Managing Editor:	Jennifer Neidig
Managing Editor:	Sara Reed
Assistant Managing Editor:	Sharon Berger
Development Editor:	Kristin Roth
Copy Editor:	Julie LeBlanc
Typesetter:	Michael Brehm
Cover Design:	Lisa Tosheff
Printed at:	Integrated Book Technology

Published in the United States of America by
Idea Group Publishing (an imprint of Idea Group Inc.)
701 E. Chocolate Avenue
Hershey PA 17033
Tel: 717-533-8845
Fax: 717-533-8661
E-mail: cust@idea-group.com
Web site: http://www.idea-group.com

and in the United Kingdom by
Idea Group Publishing (an imprint of Idea Group Inc.)
3 Henrietta Street
Covent Garden
London WC2E 8LU
Tel: 44 20 7240 0856
Fax: 44 20 7379 0609
Web site: http://www.eurospanonline.com

Copyright © 2007 by Idea Group Inc. All rights reserved. No part of this book may be reproduced in any form or by any means, electronic or mechanical, including photocopying, without written permission from the publisher.

Product or company names used in this book are for identification purposes only. Inclusion of the names of the products or companies does not indicate a claim of ownership by IGI of the trademark or registered trademark.

Library of Congress Cataloging-in-Publication Data

Information and communication technologies for economic and regional developments / M. Hakikur Rahman, editor.
     p. cm.
  Summary: "This book includes evolution, planning, development, implementation and practical implications of diversified development practices around the world, focusing on socio-economic empowerment and regional developments through ICTs; it provides recommendations, success cases and failures of those practices that can be taken into consideration for future project preparation"--Provided by publisher.
  Includes bibliographical references and index.
  ISBN 1-59904-186-3 (hardcover) -- ISBN 1-59904-187-1 (softcover) -- ISBN 1-59904-188-X (ebook)
  1. Information technology--Economic aspects. 2. Technological innovations--Economic aspects. 3. Economic development. 4. Regional planning. I. Rahman, M. Hakikur, 1957-
  HC79.I55I53575 2006
  338.9'26--dc22
                              2006032170

British Cataloguing in Publication Data
A Cataloguing in Publication record for this book is available from the British Library.

All work contributed to this book is new, previously-unpublished material. The views expressed in this book are those of the authors, but not necessarily of the publisher.

Information and Communication Technologies for Economic and Regional Developments

Table of Contents

Preface... vi

Section I:
Learning Systems

Chapter I
ICTs and Educational Benefits in Regional Development.. 1
James J. Rennie, Simon Fraser University, Canada

Chapter II
Strategies for the Cooperation of Higher Education Institutions in ICT 22
Juha Kettunen, Turku Polytechnic, Finland

Chapter III
ICT-Based Learning: A Basic Ingredient for Socio-Economic Empowerment 39
Hakikur Rahman, SDNP, Bangladesh

Section II:
Applications of Technologies

Chapter IV
New ICTs for Conflict Prevention and Management.................................56
Ángela-Jo Medina, ConcienciAcción.org, USA

Chapter V
Technological Innovation, Trade and Development 79
Laura Márquez-Ramos, Universitat Jaume I, Spain
Inmaculada Martínez-Zarzoso, Universitat Jaume I, Spain
Celestino Suárez-Burguet, Universitat Jaume I, Spain

Chapter VI
Support Networks for Rural and Regional Communities....................... 102
Tom Denison, Monash University, Australia

Section III:
Information and Knowledge Management

Chapter VII
Developing a Global Perspective for Knowledge Management.......................... 122
Martin A. Schell, New York University, USA

Chapter VIII
Cultural Knowledge Management and Broadband Content
in Development: Open Content Platforms, Copyright and Archives.................. 148
David Rooney, University of Queensland, Australia
Elizabeth Ferrier, University of Queensland, Australia
Phil Graham, University of Queensland, Australia
Ashley Jones, University of Queensland, Australia

Chapter IX
Holistic Evaluation of the Role of ICTs in Regional Development...................... 166
Chris Keen, University of Tasmania, Australia
Dean Steer, University of Tasmania, Australia
Paul Turner, University of Tasmania, Australia

Chapter X
Role of ICTs in Socioeconomic Development and Poverty Reduction................ 180
Hakikur Rahman, SDNP, Bangladesh

Section IV:
Success Stories/Case Studies

Chapter XI
**A Dissemination Strategy for the Management of Knowledge
in Rural Communities** 221
Ken Stevens, Memorial University of Newfoundland, Canada

Chapter XII
**Role of ICT in Development Process: A Review of Issues and
Prospects in South Asia** 240
Dilip Dutta, University of Sydney, Australia

Chapter XIII
Potential Challenges of ICT Implementations in Sri Lanka 259
Kennedy D. Gunawardana, University of Sri Jayewardenepura, Sri Lanka

Chapter XIV
E-Government Practices in Regional Context: Turkish Case 282
Derya Altunbas, Canakkale Onsekiz Mart University, Turkey
Elif Karakurt Tosun, Uludag University, Turkey

Chapter XV
ICTs as Tools for Poverty Reduction: The Tanzanian Experience 305
Zaipuna O. Yonah, Tanzania Telecommunications Company Ltd., Tanzania
Baanda A. Salim, Sokoine University of Agriculture, Tanzania

Chapter XVI
**Management of New Genetic Knowledge for Economic and Regional
Development of Ethnic Minorities in China** 320
*Jan-Eerik Leppanen, International Institute for Asian Studies (IIAS),
The Netherlands*

About the Authors 336

Index 342

Preface

Emerging Issues

The information revolution has generated a tremendous arousing of new information and communication technologies (ICTs) that have completely transformed its approach towards the global development. In recent years, access to these technologies is spreading fast. It was estimated that, by the end of 2005 the number of Internet users in developing countries may cross the 500 million mark, surpassing industrial nations for the first time,[1] though ITU estimates that some 800,000 villages—representing around one billion people worldwide—still lack connection to any kind of ICT (ITU, 2006). By some other estimates, more than 75% of the world's population now lives within range of a mobile network. Yet the long-heralded promise of ICT remains out of reach for most of the developing world, and in reality for the information poor, economic and social gaps are widening both within and among countries.[2]

At the same time, the significance of information management in the developing nations needs no introduction; it is a well-established phenomenon in the development arena. Consequently, there is an urgent need to understand the technology perspective along with the pragmatic applications of it and to explore the potential of different types of knowledge that it may yield. In this context, synthesis on contents from computer science and theoretical physics to information science, communication studies and entomology need to be revisited with nascent eyes, focusing development of common people; the majority of the global community.

Concrete plan of action through streamlined activities can assist any country to build a people-centred, inclusive and development-oriented information society. One of the most important prerequisite in this aspect is to build a development community among the stakeholders, forming global, regional, national, and local partnership and networking. However, successful and dynamic development of any nation in this globalize information driven society depend on highly varied and diversified parameters that are intermingled over the network, to attain common goals and objectives.

To enable socioeconomic development through ICT, the following important parameters are needed to be taken into account[3]:

- **Accelerating Digital Inclusion:** Economic growth is built on technology but remains inaccessible to most of the global population. To improve the situation, acceleration of e-readiness needs to be focused.

- **Localizing IT Industries:** Use of ICT in government's instrument always generates more employments and provides greater opportunities for its growth and competitiveness. For better utilization of in house ICT resource, dispute in correlation between GDP Growth and ICT needs to be settled.

- **Transforming Education:** To play leadership roles in future economies, each of the community member need to have knowledge in ICT and it is as essential as reading, writing, and arithmetic. Systemic transformation of education system is expected to enable them for tomorrow's employment.

- **Bridging the Digital Divide:** Accessibility to the Internet is important for education and development (Dravis, 2003). The growing digital divide may be reduced by utilizing wireless broadband and next generation WiMAX, so that most of the remote areas can be taken into the Internet coverage. Improved information infrastructure can reduce the digital divide (WSIS, 2005).

ICT as an Enabler of Economic Development

Evidently ICT is becoming an increasingly powerful tool for enhanced participation of its stakeholders in the global market; promoting governance; improving the delivery of basic services; enhancing local development initiatives; and strengthening economic capacity. But without innovative ICT policies, many people in developing countries—especially the poor —will remain as marginal (Nicol, 2003). In this perspective, international organizations are assisting countries draw on expertise and best practices from around the globe to develop strategies that expand access to ICT and harness it for economic development.[4]

Since 1992, UNDP has been a pioneer in ICT4D (Information and communication technologies for development) action programs. It has gained substantial practical expertise and knowledge through global initiatives such as the Sustainable Development Networking Program (SDNP), the Small Islands Developing States Network (SIDSNet), and the Cisco-UNDP Network Academies program; regional initiatives such as the Asia Pacific Development Internet Program (APDIP) and the Internet Initiative for Africa (IIA); and national programs such as Ukraine's FreeNet, Egypt's Community Access Centers and Cameroon's SchoolNets, to mention a few.[5]

ICT Division in ESCWA (Economic and Social Commission for Western Asia) during the first half of 2004 focused on building the information society in Western Asia. In the form of a regional preparatory activity (UN–ESCWA, 2001) towards the second phase of the World Summit on the Information Society (WSIS-2, 2005) its outcome constitutes important material from the Second Western Asia Preparatory Conference 2004 in Beirut (UNDP, 2002).

The Partnership on Measuring ICT for Development 2004,[6] launched in Brazil aims to accommodate and develop further the different initiatives regarding the availability and measurement of ICT indicators at the national, regional and international levels. It provides an open framework for coordinating ongoing and future activities, and for developing a coherent and structured approach in advancing the development of ICT indicators globally, and in particular in developing countries. Its objectives are to:

- Achieve a common set of core ICT indicators, to be harmonized and agreed upon internationally, which constitutes the basis for a database on ICT statistics.

- Enhance the capacities of national statistical offices in developing countries and build competence to develop statistical compilation programs on the information society, based on internationally agreed upon indicators.

- Develop a global database on ICT indicators and make it available on the Internet.

Similarly, socioeconomic development is a key concern of countries of the South struggling to emerge from decades and even centuries of exploitation, political conflicts, and armed struggles. Today, opportunities offered by harnessing ICT for economic development are abundant. Trade and commerce, manufacturing, transport, banking, outsourcing, software development, and supply chain are those economic sectors that are heavily facilitated by ICT (World Bank, 2004a). Furthermore, ICT is essential for increasing competitiveness and efficiency of entrepreneurs, whether small, medium or large. Most importantly, the ICT sector, on its own, provides numerous opportunities for resource creation at the one end, and employment creation at the other.[7] Therefore, initiatives have to be taken for the diffusion of ICT in the social and economic fabric within the overall regional system.

Notwithstanding, the potential of ICTs that has been overlooked for some time because of their apparent de-materiality (Graham & Marvin, 1996) in the current information society, but in the globalizing economy and evolving democracy, ICTs are regarded as overwhelming determinants for the competitiveness of local areas, cities, and regions (Pollone & Occelli, 2005). The communication and information sector can enhance the development of adequate ICT policy environments, improve equity of access to ICT, strengthen localized content, develop capacity through knowledge management, and build the investigative capacity of common people in the developing countries (Gilhooly, 2005; NGLS, 2003).

Information/Knowledge Management and Development Dynamics

It is universally accepted that, in making the most effective use of any inadequate resources for nation building, access to knowledge and information by the marginal poor is crucial. There has been growing concern that urban research and development efforts have failed in many countries to achieve their full potential due to their ignorance to accommodate and enhance the knowledge and information systems for the poor. As a result, the program developed, policy initiated and experience gathered at the top level could not be widely disseminated and adopted by the marginal users.

Furthermore, information cannot be put as a supply driven process. Instead it should be demand driven, focusing the information need of the poor and marginal communities, with relevant sources and easier access to it. Information related to basic livelihood of common people creates a demand at the user end and fabricates contents to raise their knowledge and capacity. Utilizing in micro-usage pattern, contents in the form of information can produce immense impact on the overall social uplift (and technological development) of the community through coherent strategic planning and implementation. Hence, information and content can be termed as catalysts to generate knowledge.

Knowledge can be defined as information which has been internalized by individuals, a community or a society; frequently, this knowledge has been observed to be developed by them. Knowledge is a critical factor in concurrent development dynamics. Information is different in a sense that it can be shared or transmitted through communication media; people can consider it in the light of what they know already, and either accept to add it to their knowledge base, or reject it. Knowledge is seldom developed from a particular source of information: people tend to compare it obtaining from different sources, which could include the print media, broadcasting media, physical and virtual networking and other diversified media.

Knowledge management means developing, integrating, processing, utilizing, and managing organizations' structural knowledge resources. The system should carefully design all interfaces towards the tacit knowledge at both tactical and strategic levels. This may raise the efficiency and quality of knowledge based works, maintain and develop organizations' knowledge repository, and open new horizons for knowledge based services.[8]

Hence, creation of development dynamics through information and knowledge reiterates proper scientific research and management. Here, knowledge acts as a concept, wherein stakeholders contribute to it by ways of information sharing among retrospective domains to generate resources. Along the way, accumulated resources eradicate poverty; knowledge empowers them and ICT plays a major role in bridging the gap between these two. Knowledge or information could either be enhanced by establishing interactive communication among the stakeholders or through improved information dissemination. Knowledge science seems to be a new discipline of science that evolved within and around philosophy, technology and processes to enhance these abilities. Mainly there are two approaches to develop intelligence of social individuals; one is through management science and the other is through information science. Therefore, management of information and knowledge is of prime importance for the development of the masses.

Therefore, ICT for knowledge management in the context of socioeconomic development should focus on:[9]

- Building and sustaining knowledge-based resources.
- Collecting, processing, structuring and utilizing organizational knowledge,
- Strategic and tactical management of knowledge-bases,
- Tailoring ICT-based tools to enrich knowledge management models,
- Prototyping and Testing ICT-supported entities for standardization,
- Modeling and evaluating knowledge development practices.

Challenges

So far, modern ICTs could not able to play a major role in managing livelihood information to the urban poor and rural marginal communities. This portion of the society rarely have direct access to ICTs; a factor which should be emphasized to increase their inclusion in the mainstream. Though, ICTs have worked as the most thriving parameter in a number of pilot projects in many countries, including telecentres, community databases, community videos, radio and television, but their sustainability still remains as a challenge. Similarly, the assessment on the impact of information dissemination remains intricate, amongst others because information chains are unpredictably long, and often difficult to trait to a single intervention, within the context of a wholesome perspective.

Similarly, the role of ICT in rural development can be extremely crucial. ICT provides the technology for connectivity, but connectivity without content is futile. There are agencies and governments who have successfully utilized ICT to deliver local-specific demand-driven information to be used for day-to-day activities. However, due to intricate management issues, efforts of these natures could not get authenticated momentum at the outer peripheries. Information can become knowledge if it fits in with the receiver's pattern of learning, which also can be strengthened inter alias through different ICT usage.

Technological change is both a cause and a consequence of economic and social development (Mrad, 2002). Though, much has been reported and analyzed about the digital divide challenges and opportunities, but many regions have been mostly absent from the global technology revolution. By far, the impact of all the ICT acquisition on development in the area is a difficult issue to quantify, and in general not immediately noticeable. Some may argue that ICT have a negative impact on the regional economies through the high level of spending mainly on imported infrastructure products, services, and "gadgets." In addition, ICT have supplied more efficient marketing tactics for the international firms that competed with local and regional industry and taken over local markets more effectively. Even if part of this dark image is true, in reality the backwards countries have to compete, survive, and benefit from the globalization through various ICT tools and technologies (ESCWA-ILO, 2002a, 2002b).

No set of indicators on ICT impact in development are available and no such indicators would be sufficiently exhaustive for ICT impact for socioeconomic and regional developments to be universally acceptable. Regional variations, including socioeconomic and cultural divergence would render some factors as less important, even irrelevant, in a given country, while they may be of great importance in others (UN–ESCWA, 2001; Tongia, Subrahmanian & Arunachalam, 2004). Incidentally, some effects may remain as non-measurable, such as quality, impact or outcome, in shorter terms.

New research and development has created efficient ICTs that put corporations, communities and public institutions in a challenging situation. Bureaucracies may implement tools to integrate management of recourses, even at the level of knowledge, at least to a certain extent, but may remain as a challenge for quite a period of time.

However, the tools and routines for use of structural knowledge resources are often found to be inadequate. This may apply to searching, processing or mining contents, access structures, presentation and dissemination, integration with other tools and systems and so forth. Accessing the repositories at different times, situations, and locations when necessary is also remains as an unsolved challenge. Supporting organizational learning through use of the structured knowledge repository often proves to be challenging during routine operations, and too often leads to breaches in the organization's knowledge maintenance and the learning loop. Last, but not least at the tactical level many unsolved challenges accumulate within an organization's ability while contributing to its own knowledge repository.[10] For successful implementation, the main objective of any knowledge product activity in terms of regional developments should:

- Agree on a common set of core ICT indicators that are comparable at the international level (including all intermediary levels).
- Assist in setting up a global database for hosting data on core ICT indicators.

ICT as part of the new economy is supposed to create a lot of new jobs and in effect, may dismiss other professions. But the important aspect of it is the transformation of the old economy due to the breakdown of existing organogram and organization, leading to a completely new subset of the economic indicators. The main reason is the disappearance of delay and distance, which was a key obstacle to world trade in the old economy. Now, the digital convergence has changes the situation (Dimacali, 2002). Therefore, a number of specific dangers may threaten the developing countries, because of their lack of access to and knowledge of ICT. For instance:

- Developing countries will not experience the possible dynamo for growth and job creation that ICT as such could bring to them.
- Companies in developing countries will not be able to supply to the private sector in the industrialized part of the world, if their procedures/accounting systems/e-commerce facilities are not sufficiently developed. Their risks are not being part of the new value chain, but may also be severely prejudiced by dramatically increased global competition in the domestic economy created by introduction of the new electronic networks.
- New international capital will go to countries which have the facilities needed for the modern economy.
- Developing countries will not get access to the available knowledge that public, private and academic sectors make available publicly trough the Internet.
- The educational system could become outdated, not being able to take advantage of new technologies (European Parliament, 2001; Falk, 2001).

Consequently, further analysis is needed to better understand the demand for and production of ICT indicators, especially in poor countries. The lack of resources for statistical work may prove these countries' inability to respond to the contemporary digital access indicators. Though the existence of national ICT policies would indicate demand for these forms of indicators, but no information on indicators used in the national policies is available yet. Additional information such as the existence of inter-institutional working groups (composed by CSOs, authorities for ICT, and other line ministries), the presence of ICT authorities in the national statistical councils (where these are functional), the inclusion of ICT indicators in national statistical program (where these are in place) and the preparation of joint publications could give further insight into the level of demand for ICT indicators and the possible response to it by statistical institutions (UN ICT Task Force, 2005).

Where the Book Stands

A book focusing on management of information and knowledge utilizing technological and applied science for the development of common citizens can feed the society as a knowledge tool and guideline. It includes knowledge information system (KIS), knowledge management (KM) system, information management (IM) and other learning tools, their evolution, planning, development, and implementation, with other implications related to their successes and failures.

ICT application related to IM can become an integral part of the overall strategy for development. Fostering partnerships among government, civil society, the private sector and other development partners can effectively address economic, social, and cultural divides. Similarly, the society can take benefits from these sequences to create a domain of knowledge networking. ICTs have the potential to digitally link each and every member of the community to open up endless dimension of opportunities through information interchange.

This book also includes indicators, parameters, synthesis of contemporary learning utilities in the realm of knowledge and information management. These accommodate successful pilot initiatives, outstanding researches, pragmatic applications, and future research scopes in orienting human resources to form a knowledge ring along the outer peripheries of the society through information management and planning.

Life in rural areas is relatively complex than the metro areas and rural people, therefore, have a different range of information needs. It is not easy to epitomize those, except in rather general terms such as earnings or lodgings, though as such they may not comply with the general requirement to fulfill the demand at the marginal end (Mchombu, 2004). The specific needs vary among geographical disparities, cultural diversities, ethnicities, localities, and even within localities, and to address those adequately, inclusive investigation is necessary.

A book with essential elements containing management of information, policies of implementation, and technological aspects of implementation, operation and maintenance of technology-based outlets to fulfill the demand at the grass root communities deserves importance. Social networks are the foremost source of information for the marginal poor. But, without proper knowledge and management of the KIS pattern ultimate benefit out of it may not reach to the end users. Main objective of this book is to take on these issues and act as a delivery modality to the target users and stakeholders.

It has been found that a major obstacle in promoting an inclusive knowledge society is due to the lack of specific national policies and strategies to ensure easy access to information and to develop appropriate localized tools, technologies and methodologies in the ICT arena. The lack of policy support and political will is also due to deficit of awareness of the economic, political, and social benefits that ICT can bring (World Bank, 2004b). The level of awareness among professionals and decision makers in the developing countries about the role of ICT in development is generally low. This book will serve as a repository and guideline for the knowledge providers, development partners, academics, policy initiators, and general people.

Foremost, this book rationalizes the government's critical role in infrastructure development ensuring sustainability and community engagement with longer term strategy. At the same time, promotes the role of civil society organizations as the facilitators for community participation and capacity development. Academic institutions through their innovation and research, especially by harnessing the potential of distance learning techniques can assist in materializing these efforts. A multi-stakeholders partnership synergizing the efforts of government, private sector, civil society organizations, and local communities may then assist in building technology and content by providing physical infrastructure and technical assistance to local counterparts within the sphere of development.

Organization of the Book

The book is organized into 16 chapters. A brief description of each of the chapters follows:

Chapter I focuses on ICTs and their educational benefits in regional developments. It argues that ICTs can play an important role in improving public education, especially in rural regions. The effects of ICT use in schools can, in turn, bring surprising economic benefits to the region. Hence, ICT developers interested in building economies can use education as a sustainable and grassroots building block for future growth. Therefore, as long as ICTs are being recognized as pedagogical tools, they serve both the long-term economic and cultural needs of communities.

Chapter II analyzes the strategic planning of a few ICT centres, by forming a joint venture of higher education institutions. These higher education institutions (HEIs) try to focus their activities on specific fields of education and the needs of their geographical area. The strategies of focus and operations excellence are natural choices to define the strategic outlines for the centre, which aims to increase the economic growth of the region. The selected strategies are described in this chapter using the balanced scorecard approach, allowing the network of organizations to articulate and communicate their strategy to their employees and stakeholders upholding regional developments.

Chapter III has tried to critically analyze the effective role of ICT methods in learning and put forwards several success cases of learning systems that assisted in socioeconomic empowerment and at the same time, provided a few futuristic recommendations in establishing similar endeavors in potential economies. This chapter also concentrates on ICT mediated learning utilities for achieving the goal of education for all, and supports that ICT can act as an enabler in reducing the digital divide, reducing poverty and promoting social inclusion.

Chapter IV introduces the impact of new information and communication technologies (nICTs), specifically the Internet, on national and international conflict prevention and management. This analysis provides case studies on the use and examples of the prospective use of nICTs to counteract conflict as it undermines social and economic structures: public healthcare, education systems, employment, and so forth, and hinders regional development. This study reviews the specific application of nICT-related initiatives at the different phases of the conflict cycle: from addressing the root causes of conflict as a tool for prevention and management, through the reconciliation and reconstruction phase. It also demonstrates the application and potential of nICTs to complement activities that are already being carried out in the field to address the root causes of conflict, its prevention and management, as well as the fomentation of reconstruction and reconciliation.

Chapter V tests empirically to what extent technological innovation influences the international trade and studies its effect on different groups of countries according to their level of economic development. Different measures used in the literature to proxy for technological capabilities are reviewed and the estimation results show that technological innovation has a considerably high explanatory power on trade compared with other traditional determinants. Countries tend to trade more when they have similar technological capabilities and the development of technological innovation has lowered the effect of geographical distance on trade. According to the obtained results, investing in technological innovation leads to the improvement and maintenance of the level of competitiveness; therefore, a good economic policy in developing countries should invest in technological innovation.

Chapter VI examines the role of organizational networks in the success and failure of information and communications technology projects. Within a framework informed by the literature of information systems failure, the diffusion of innovation and social network analysis, it argues that information systems projects must take into account the social context in which they are being implemented. It further argues that, the people in a regional setting felt themselves to be in an extremely disadvantageous situation, because they typically lacked support from similar networks. The author hopes that highlighting the importance of such support networks will lead to a better understanding of failure and success of this system, and will contribute to improved policy formulation and practice.

Chapter VII argues that localization of a document or other product requires tacit knowledge of the target language and culture. It also argues that a key issue in economic and regional development (ERD) is the applicability of one region's successful program of development to another region. However, localization is becoming increasingly inadequate as a strategy for disseminating knowledge on the worldwide Web. Hence, the best way to maximize the accessibility of Web content is to make it more explicit, not more tacit. Although general solutions to universal problems (literacy, environmental awareness, AIDS prevention, sanitation, transportations, etc.) can be designed by nongovernmental organizations (NGOs) or other global entities, their actual implementation needs to be adapted to local culture and conditions, ideally with grassroots stakeholder participation.

Chapter VIII examines the possibility of creating online creative production archives to make locally and internationally sourced high quality video, audio, graphics, and other broadband content available to grassroots producers in developing economies. It also argues that in a global knowledge economy, cultural production is a major driver of economic growth. The creativity and culture needed for cultural production are plentiful in developing countries indicating that if technical and institutional conditions are appropriate, there is significant potential for developing economies to compete in the global economy. It is, therefore, desirable for local groups to be able to acquire, store, and deliver locally and internationally sourced content to stimulate local level cultural production.

Chapter IX examines the issues surrounding what is meant by ICT-related development in a regional context. It also explores the usefulness of multiple measures, as opposed to single measures, to describe what in reality is very complex. In this context the chapter outlines the preliminary development of, and the rationale behind, a holistic approach to evaluate the role of ICTs in regional development, based on insights generated from an ongoing research.

Chapter X looks into critical aspects of ICTs in raising socioeconomic development in under-developed countries and tries to illustrate success cases in developed countries that can be replicated in developing countries to reduce poverty. Furthermore, emphasis has been given to analyze the role of ICTs in poverty reduction processes upholding regional developments.

Chapter XI provides an outline of how ICTs have been used to re-shape education in a predominantly rural region, thereby preparing people for participation in the emerging knowledge-based economy. It also outlines the transition from traditional (face to face) to virtual teaching and learning environments in a small network of rural high schools. It argues, on the basis of research that, the introduction of e-learning in schools involves a shift from a closed to an open model of teaching and learning and the shift from closed to open teaching and learning has implications beyond the school in terms of regional development in Canada, as a case study.

In Chapter XII the author argues that the developing countries need to integrate ICT policies more closely into economic strategies, which can be done by strengthening the links between development and technology agencies via the organizational structure of policy-making bodies. The chapter focuses on ICT policy initiatives in a few developing nations, as a case study and make a comparison on how these initiatives are having their roles in the development processes in South Asia.

Chapter XIII offers a state-of-the-art review of the implementation of ICTs strategies in developing country with special reference to Sri Lanka as a case study. It also brings in a small number of empirical studies that serve to illustrate the practical use of the ICT to support development practices. The chapter focuses on potential challenges on ICT implementations in Sri Lanka and details out a comprehensive ICT based educational plan of the Sri Lankan government for national capacity development that will assist to face the challenges of the ICT implementations. Finally, it proposes a few strategies to restraint the challenge and to uplift the human capacity of Sri Lanka.

Chapter XIV introduces the importance of the ICTs on the regional development in Turkey, as a case study. It included a few regional programs of Turkey that are related with regional development and ICTs. Objective of this chapter is to point out improvements of information and communication technologies and importance of e-government programs in Turkey.

Chapter XV attempts to enhance the understanding and knowledge of ICTs in relation to the Tanzania National ICT Policy as a case study. It extensively explores these pervading technologies as ICTs impact on education, commerce, social, cultural, and economic life of the poor Tanzanian people. The chapter looks also on how Tanzania is coping with the issue of poverty eradication as one of the eight UN Millennium Development Goals (MDGs). It addresses the issue of digital divide and the role that ICTs can play in poverty reduction and Tanzania's efforts in embracing ICTs and the challenges facing the country.

In Chapter XVI the author has tried to give an overview on genetic sampling of ethnic minorities (minzu) in China and to the different claims companies and research ventures have on this industry. It looks at a question, like; how the new genetic knowledge—acquired by biobanking activities—could be turned into ethically sustainable, economic, and regional development of ethnic minorities in China, as a case study. The chapter focuses on the

Chinese genetic information management system and argues that there are a number of development needs among the ethnic people groups in East Asia, Southeast Asia, and in South Asia. However, nature of most of the regional and economic development conditions of these ethnic minorities remains transboundary.

Conclusion

Through the provision of information to support activities and decision-making for economic, social, and regional developments, ICT plays a major role. In addition, ICT can be a thriving parameter in the industrial sector for sustainable decent employment. In the most pessimistic assessment of ICT impact on development, the selective deployment of these technologies can be viewed as a loss minimizing strategy. True indicators of the impact of ICT on development are not universal and sometimes not measurable, especially those that are related to quality and convenience enhancement applications. ICT can only contribute to development, and is not the answer to all requirements and problems. Misleading ICT statistics in a country can sometimes lead to a wrong perception. Therefore, useful and productive ICT utilization is a challenging issue for all (Mrad, 2002; WTO, 1998; World Employment Report, 2001).

The evaluation of a complete, effective, and objective driven program with the development of ICT is a necessary condition for analyzing the current state of an economic sector, and working out effective measures to support and promote further development in regions. In addition, program should allow summarizing, analyzing and distributing the most effective methods of ICT development. Furthermore, programs should distribute ideas and values of the open information society and make them popular among the public, to involve more residents, state establishments and businesses in economic reforms implemented with ICT.[11]

Firstly, the promotion of ICT development in various fields of life will result in the reduction in budget expenses, saving of funds for the social sector (for example, for to the development of distance learning and telemedicine programs), and more effective interactions between community members and local governing bodies. Secondly, increased information support will attract the attention of local and foreign IT companies and investors. Thirdly, and probably most importantly, partnerships will enable regional entities to estimate the current state of ICT and the corresponding outlooks compared to other regions of the world, defining the set of necessary priority measures for supporting ICT development. Finally, the outputs will establish additional information base for a region's effective development.

Therefore, harnessing ICT in developing countries can have important impacts:

- In the fight against poverty; by improving sectors such as education, health, environment, rural development, and tourism.
- In empowering people in developing countries; particularly with respect to their economic situation, their ability to develop and participate in democracy by creating good governance and strengthening human rights.

- In extending support to already existing development strategies and programs through more effective delivery mechanisms, as well as improving the final result (European Parliament, 2001; O'Sullivan & Lloyd, 2004).

References

Dimacali, C. (2002). *Information technology enabled services* (ITES). Bangladesh: Carana Corporation, USAID.

Dravis, P. (2003). *Open source software: Perspective for development*. Washington: The World Bank.

ESCWA-ILO. (2002a, July). Findings from the World Employment Report 2001: Life at work in the information economy. In *Proceedings of the ESCWA-ILO Forum on Technology, Employment and Poverty Alleviation in the Arab Countries*, Beirut.

ESCWA-ILO. (2002b, July). E-Services: What? How? Challenges ahead. In *Proceedings of the ESCWA-ILO Forum on Technology, Employment and Poverty Alleviation in the Arab Countries*, Beirut.

European Parliament. (2001, March). *AS draft report on ICT in the developing countries. Committee on Development and Cooperation*, European Parliament.

Falk, I. (Ed.). (2001). *Learning to manage change: Developing regional communities for a local-global millennium*. Leabrook: National Centre for Vocational Education Research Ltd. (NCVER).

Gilhooly, D. (Ed.). (2005). Creating an enabling environment towards the millennium development goals. In *Proceedings of the Berlin Global Forum of the United nations ICT Task Force*, UN ICT Task Force, New York.

Graham, S., & Marvin, S. (1996). *Telecommunications and the city: Electronic spaces, urban places*. New York: Routledge.

ITU. (2006). *World telecommunication development report*. Retrieved June 27, 2006, from http://www.itu.int/newsroom/wtdc/2006/stats/index.html

Mchombu, K.J. (2004). *Sharing knowledge for community development and transformation: A handbook*. DLR International, Oxfam Canada.

Mrad, F. (2002). *On the ICT priority issues for the Arab Countries*, information and communications technologies division (ICTD) of the UN-ESCWA in Beirut.

Nicol, C. (Ed.). (2003). *ICT policy: A beginner's handbook*. Association for progressive communications. Johannesburg: STE Publishers.

O'Sullivan, J., & Lloyd, N. (2004). *Background papers*. European e-Skills Conference, 2004, Thessalonica, Greece.

Pollone, M., & Occelli, S. (2005, June 6-9). *Leveraging ICT for regional development: The case of Piedmont*. Paper presented at the International Conference, Digital Communities 2005, Benevento.

Tongia, R., Subrahmanian, E., & Arunachalam, V.S. (2004). *Information and communications technology for sustainable development: Defining a global research agenda.* Bangalore.

UN Non Governmental Liasion Service. (2003). T*he NGLS guide for NGOs, intergovernmental negotiations and decision making at the United Nations.* Geneva: UN Non Governmental Liasion Service.

UN ICT Task Force. (2005). *Measuring ICT: The global status of ICT indicators.* Partnership on Measuring ICT for Development, United Nations ICT Task Force, New York.

UNDP. (2002). *Information and communication technologies for development in the Arab States: Overview, considerations, and parallels with Asia.* UNDP regional Bureau for Arab States.

UN-ESCWA. (2001). *New technologies for enhancing competitiveness and productivity in selected sectors.* New York: UN-ESCWA.

World Bank. (2004a). *World development report 2005: A better investment climate for everyone.* Washington, DC: Author.

World Bank. (2004b). *Task managers' ICT toolkit: A route map for ICT components in World Bank projects.* Washington, DC: Author.

World Employment Report. (2001, March). International labour organization. Belgium.

World Trade Organization. (1998, July). *Background note on computer and related services.*

WSIS. (2005, November). *Creating transformations.* Intel Workshops at the "ICT 4 All" Exhibition.[a]

Endnotes

[1]   http://www.global-reach.biz/globstats/

[2]   http://topics.org/special/informationsociety/

[3]   http://www.developmentgateway.org/ict/rc/filedownload.do~itemId=1046992

[4]   http://sdnhq.undp.org/it4dev/

[5]   http://www.sdnp.undp.org/it4dev/docs/about_undp.html

[6]   http://www.itu.int/ITU-D/ict/partnership/

[7]   http://www.escwa.org.lb/wsis/meetings/apr04/main.html

[8]   http://www2.nr.no/documents/imedia/research_areas/work_in_future/ict_for_km_text.html

[9]   http://www2.nr.no/documents/imedia/research_areas/work_in_future/knowledge_management.html

[10]   http://www2.nr.no/documents/imedia/research_areas/work_in_future/ict_for_km_text.html

[11]   http://www.rbcnews.com/press_rev/press_rev150403_esp.shtml

Section I

Learning Systems

Chapter I

ICTs and Educational Benefits in Regional Development

James J. Rennie, Simon Fraser University, Canada

Abstract

ICTs can play an important role in improving public education in rural regions. The effects of ICT use in schools can, in turn, bring unexpected economic benefits to the region. ICT developers interested in building economies can use education as a sustainable, grassroots building block for future growth. While many development programs tend to focus on private models for ICT dissemination in remote regions (such as telecenters), public education embodies a spirit of universal accessibility that can bring global technologies into the daily lives of all world citizens. When ICTs are recognized as pedagogical tools, they serve both the long-term economic and cultural needs of communities.

Copyright © 2007, Idea Group Inc. Copying or distributing in print or electronic forms without written permission of Idea Group Inc. is prohibited.

ICT in a Globalized World:
Education and Economics Collide

Information and communication technologies (ICTs) have changed the way of thinking about the planet by transforming almost every field of human activity, from agriculture to entertainment, from government to education. While many rural regions of developing nations have yet to experience all of the benefits of a high-tech era, significant efforts are being made to bring ICT to all communities around the globe. However, building and maintaining the infrastructure of a networked world is no small undertaking, and many governments strain to justify the costs of bringing cutting-edge technologies to impoverished regions in the developing world. Furthermore, the technologies exported from developed nations seldom come without considerable ideological baggage concerning their usefulness, as well as their social and environmental impacts. If many communities around the world continue to struggle with basic necessities, it can certainly be asked whether or not an aggressive strategy of ICT development is really a universal priority.

Nevertheless, ICT's potential to bring about radical growth and development is difficult to dismiss. In regions where many development agencies continue to focus on providing clean water and protecting fundamental human rights, other development groups are exploring ICT dissemination as a useful tool in those same projects. Although ICT growth is often at odds with established programs of development, many innovative projects attempt to balance these two, seemingly contradictory sets of demands. ICT infrastructure is an extraordinary expense for many developing governments, but short-term costs must be considered in relation to long-term advantages. Communication networks allow remote regions to interact with urban centers, democratizing trade and protecting against widespread health crises. Telecenters and computer kiosks provide rural communities with increased access to government records and forms, improving democratic transparency and aiding with legal disputes.

Furthermore, and most importantly for this chapter, information and communication technologies radically transform public education, allowing students and teachers to bridge the gap between local communities and global issues. ICT development can introduce young learners to an incredible realm of information and culture, while at the same time allowing students to express their own identities to the world. Technical literacy, supported with the critical skills needed to protect cultural awareness, can open unimaginable possibilities for students, bringing the realities of a global knowledge economy to any schoolroom on the planet.

Accordingly, the international community has long held education as a fundamental and inalienable human right. Education helps to create citizens for the world in which they want to live, allowing individuals to develop their identities within a context of historical, cultural and ethical norms. As a result, education plays a pivotal role in development projects; as the Director-General of the United Nations Educational, Scientific and Cultural Organization (UNESCO), Koïchiro Matsuura, argues, "Education—in all its forms and at all levels—is not only an end in itself but is also one of the most powerful instruments we have for bringing about the changes required to achieve sustainable development" (UNESCO, 2004, p. 8). Education fosters development because it encourages learners to consider their own, local circumstances in a broader context. Furthermore, it promotes sustainable development by situating new perspectives within historical frameworks; whereas individual development

Copyright © 2007, Idea Group Inc. Copying or distributing in print or electronic forms without written permission of Idea Group Inc. is prohibited.

projects may bring about positive changes for a community, long-term initiatives must rely on local knowledges in order to sustain the growth and benefits of development. As a central site for nurturing and teaching local knowledges, schools are invaluable resources for development projects.

The challenge for ICT development programs is to recognize both the pedagogical and economic potential of ICT-enhanced education. Too often, ICT infrastructure is built for a specific set of predetermined functions, ignoring broader community needs and desires. Most ICTs, however, are inherently adaptable; to limit their use is to limit the abilities and outcomes of the people who use them. It is precisely through innovation and ingenuity that ICT finds its most important economic function: that of harnessing human knowledge as a creative, productive force. As Avgerou and Rovere (2003) argue, it is difficult to assign concrete financial value to ICT development, as "The significance of ICT innovation cannot be adequately captured in concepts of economic value; ICT is implicated in social changes that are not driven by norms of economic rationality" (p. 5). In order to achieve long-term economic success, it is in a government's best interests to allow ICT to develop on its own terms, relying on the individual and collective ingenuity of citizens to transform technological systems into productive industries.

At its best, ICT development can empower communities and individuals alike, allowing for unexpected applications and undiscovered abilities. At its worst, ICT development merely reinforces existing hierarchies of power, ignoring community and identity, subjugating all local knowledges to a singular, technical, expert knowledge. This chapter will attempt to show that when innovative technologies are introduced to communities through private industry, the potential for economic development is severely limited. However, if ICT developers place schools and students at the center of their communities, the resulting dissemination of technology will have an enormous benefit for everyone involved.

A Philosophy for Educational Development Initiatives: ICT in Context

Development projects often represent a fundamental conflict between local knowledge and perceived Western hegemony. Aid materials and social programs bring with them the underlying values, assumptions and beliefs of a distant culture, threatening the identities of individuals and communities alike. Programs of ICT development are further burdened with cultural and ideological baggage, as hardware and software are often designed and produced far from the site of dissemination. Development agencies must carefully consider these challenges before undertaking any project, particularly in a field as culturally specific as education. Whereas many economic activities in developing regions are directly tied to modern and colonial interference, education must continue to serve the values and purposes of local communities. These goals, however, need not be incompatible with the economic development of regions and nations. As Uma Kambhampati (2004) observes, "the process of education is seen to encourage self-discipline, hard work, and an achievement orientation, characteristics pinpointed by modernization theorists as being necessary for the transition from tradition to modernity" (p. 228). The recovery of traditional cultural practices and

Copyright © 2007, Idea Group Inc. Copying or distributing in print or electronic forms without written permission of Idea Group Inc. is prohibited.

identities can, therefore, take place inside increasingly modernized communities. Within this transformation, education represents the single most important site for the intersection of tradition and innovation in the developing world.

Tradition and innovation in teaching and learning methods, however, must be considered as only one part of education's role in community life. Thus, even though the challenges facing developing communities are often at odds with sound pedagogical practices, it is imperative that development organizations recognize the role that education can play in addressing broader social issues. UNESCO (2004) has recognized two fundamental characteristics of education and its role in sustainable development initiatives, the first being that "education is a fundamental human right that has its own intrinsic benefits for individuals" (p. 13). The second characteristic is less evident to many developers; as UNESCO argues:

... education is a tool for introducing the values, skills and competencies needed to address the challenges of today's world ... such as poverty, social and political conflicts, gender discrimination, violation of human rights, unsustainable patterns of consumption and production, environmental degradation and unsustainable use of natural resources, and the fight against HIV/AIDS and other infectious diseases, etc. (UNESCO, 2004, p. 13)

Despite the obscured visibility of education's second role, it is essential that developers keep this role in mind when creating and operationalizing projects.

It is equally important, however, to treat each specific development project as a unique set of circumstances and obstacles. Educational practices and curricula may be standardized across entire regions, but cultural and geographic varieties are unavoidable, as certain pedagogical goals are relatively universal: each community and society hopes to teach their children how to survive in the world; cultures sustain themselves by passing on to children the languages, customs, traditions, and values most important to the group. Students are encouraged to develop a sense of their identity, both personal and collective, as part of their general lifelong education. In order to achieve these educational goals, communities build schools, train teachers, and select appropriate educational content; although development projects can assist in each of these areas, it is imperative that developers recognize the cultural politics that exist at all three stages. If content is developed for local schools by educators who are not part of that community, the result will be an inevitable loss of local culture; no matter how good the intentions of foreign, "expert" educators may be, the value of local knowledge cannot be replaced. The success or failure of ICT initiatives in the developing world will greatly depend on a collective recognition of education's value in society, coupled with a global respect for local knowledge in all forms.

Although the increasingly global nature of development threatens community identities, it also reminds developers of the richness and vitality that are inherent to diversity. As individual citizens and organizations from developed countries carry out more and more projects, the impacts on remote communities are inseparable from the impacts on the developers themselves. External development groups working in the field of education may act as unwitting cultural crusaders in modern disguise, but they are also unacknowledged ethnographers, explorers, and innovators waiting to be taught. As John Fien of UNESCO observes:

Copyright © 2007, Idea Group Inc. Copying or distributing in print or electronic forms without written permission of Idea Group Inc. is prohibited.

Globalization is proving to be a particular challenge to education. Its economic impacts have been uneven and its cultural impacts threaten local ways of viewing the world. However, globalization has brought an awareness of the scale of the shared burdens we face and of ways of cooperating with others to address them. (UNESCO, 2004, p. 97)

The practices and priorities of development agencies are always open to renegotiation in the field, allowing for flexible, community-driven additions and revisions to stated developmental outcomes. What is most important is that education developers recognize globalization's inherent oscillation between universal aims and local realities.

In order to ensure that ICT development recognizes and confronts the various challenges posed by public education, it is imperative that governments and development organizations underpin their projects with appropriate philosophical paradigms. In concrete terms, this would require ICT development projects to thoroughly question their own motivations, assumptions, and ambitions. Epistemological issues might not seem to hold the same economic weight as technical issues of compliance and compatibility, but the broad and unforeseen effects of ICT dissemination necessitate serious consideration during the early stages of a program's development. Recognizing the educational (and thus long-term financial) benefits of ICT development strategies does not always come easily to the creators and vendors of specific technologies. It is, therefore, essential to any project's success that community members themselves play an active role in the development of ICT initiatives.

One possible strategy for ensuring such contribution in ICT development is to pursue programs and projects that are conducive to an inclusive arrangement of technology and humanity, such as "Community Informatics" (CI) or Clement and Shade's rainbow model. Michael Gurstein (2003) defines CI as "the application of [ICTs] to enable community processes and the achievement of community objectives including overcoming the digital divides both within and among communities"; more importantly, however, CI approaches can go on "to examine how and under what conditions ICT access can be made usable to the range of excluded populations and communities and particularly to support local economic development, social justice, and political empowering using the Internet" (p. 4). Initiatives grounded in the principles of CI may suffer many of the same pitfalls as any other program of ICT development, but the overarching belief that technology can bring excluded peoples into global economies should be the cornerstone of all ICT projects. Without this belief in the revolutionary potential inherent in ICTs, development projects are condemned to stagnate in their own inherent limitations.

Similarly, Clement and Shade (2000) have developed what they term the rainbow model of ICT infrastructure development, which is "an integrated model for analyzing and discussing access to network services" (p. 35). The rainbow's seven layers (Carriage Facilities; Devices; Software Tools; Content/Services; Service/Access Provision; Literacy/Social Facilitation; and Governance) must be considered as a unified whole, wherein each factor plays a significant role in the overarching success of ICT initiatives (p. 36). Like Gurstein's community informatics, the Rainbow model provides developers with an initial framework for development projects, ensuring that ICT infrastructure is developed in a sustainable, socially equitable manner. As Clement and Shade (2000) argue:

Copyright © 2007, Idea Group Inc. Copying or distributing in print or electronic forms without written permission of Idea Group Inc. is prohibited.

The design process must be broadly participative and dynamic. It must be carried out in the face of strong pressures from rapid technological change, ideological opposition, ignorance of technical possibilities and social implications, strained public resources and societal instability. (p. 49)

Both models recognize the importance of aligning development's long-term goals with the social and economic needs of communities and countries. Furthermore, both models stress the need to design ICT initiatives that recognize and respond to the marginalized voices in rural settings. Most importantly, by underpinning ICT development projects with models of this type, developers recognize and respect the essential difference between development and modernization; whereas the former seeks to assist societies in their own evolution and progress, the latter, "although it may affect certain groups ... is always induced; and it is the metropolitan society which derives the true benefits therefrom" (Freire, 2004, p. 161). Keeping pace with technological change may dominate the economic agendas of many ICT projects, but the long-term sustainability of such a narrow focus must now be seen as increasingly untenable.

When considered in greater detail, a model such as Community Informatics begins to generate more specific criteria for ICT development projects. In Gurstein's model, informatics can be understood to forward the following characteristics:

- A commitment to universality of technology-enabled opportunity including to the disadvantaged
- A recognition that the "lived physical community" is at the very center of individual and family well-being – economic, political, and cultural.
- A belief that this can be enhanced through the judicious use of ICTs.
- A sophisticated user-focused understanding of Information technology.
- Applied social leadership, entrepreneurship, and creativity.
- Networked linkages (particularly ethnic or cultural) in urban communities as compared to the more limited overlapping in rural communities. (Gurstein, 2003, p. 5)

It is worth noting that Gurstein's list recognizes both the economic and cultural wealth of communities, as well as ICT's ability to enhance or hinder both. Development projects that only consider the positive outcomes of ICT dissemination risk any number of unforeseen disturbances in community life. Similarly, development projects that only consider the economic benefits of ICT use can inflict long-term cultural damage, which can ultimately undermine the short-term economic gains of ICT development. By adopting a framework such as CI, developers are encouraged to see economic and cultural factors as inextricably linked.

The interplay of a community's cultural life with its economy is a delicate and complex connection, and any disruption of one will undoubtedly impact upon the other. ICT developers interested in assessing the health and wellness of this important balance would be well advised to use public education as a sort of barometer; schools are a natural space for the forces of culture and business to collide, as their very mandate is to develop future citizens

Copyright © 2007, Idea Group Inc. Copying or distributing in print or electronic forms without written permission of Idea Group Inc. is prohibited.

and workers. Providing attention and resources to public education is quite simply one of the easiest and most effective strategies for monitoring the status of community well being. If ICT developers want to know how effectively a new technology has been introduced to a community, they can start by gauging its impact on the local schools; if students are aware of the technology and are intrigued by its possible uses, there is a very good chance that the project will have a lasting impact on the community.

Constructive, sustainable development initiatives in the field of education must confront the twin forces of culture and economics, particularly with respect to actual curricular content. Although ICT development necessitates the addition of technical skills training in public education, the realities of rural communities necessitate the preservation of skills and values that are often perceived of us outdated in a globalized era. As Fien cautions:

Parents around the world are rightly keen that their children should do well at school and then get a job. However, job opportunities are increasingly difficult to find, especially in rapidly changing economies. Most students will make their living at home, in villages, on farms, working with their families using the resources of their local environment or in the informal or 'popular' economies in cities. Those who continue to higher levels of schooling may find employment in the formal sector, but they will still need knowledge and skills in order to help their communities make informed decisions. (UNESCO, 2004, p. 108)

Development initiatives, and particularly those that promote ICT hardware and solutions, must consider that the changing face of international business and communications will only affect most of the world's citizens peripherally. Thus, the breed of techno-fetishism, which currently consumes many in the developed world, might not be an appropriate export to developing communities in remote, rural regions. Many ICT applications bring with them enormous economic advantages, but some of these advantages are, in fact, culturally and politically specific. For example, ICTs designed to enhance productive efficiency in industrial settings are the result of a unique set of business demands. If developers unquestioningly extol the virtues of these technologies, they ignore the business demands that are unique to every other country and region in the world. This is because, as Kambhampati (2004) writes:

With most research and development being undertaken in capital-rich, labour-scarce Western economies, new technology is more likely to be labour-saving. International competition and the need for efficiency, together with the reliance on imported capital goods, have re-inforced the tendency to use the most up-to-date technology (usually labour-saving) even in labour-rich developing countries. (p. 39)

While the tools and techniques of most ICT initiatives in education are wholly different from the industrial technologies of the economic sector. This example of ideological assumptions and their potentially catastrophic consequences illustrates the dangers inherent in all ICT development projects. There is a pressing need for local solutions to problems, even when those problems recur from one community to the next. It is a mistake to believe that what works in one instance will work in all instances. Therefore, while educational reform is undoubtedly an urgent and ongoing struggle, it is essential that solutions are as

Copyright © 2007, Idea Group Inc. Copying or distributing in print or electronic forms without written permission of Idea Group Inc. is prohibited.

varied as the crises are numerous; developers gain nothing from the unquestioned mimicry of standardized reforms.

Current Approaches and Controversies: Telecenters, Kiosks, and the Need for Grassroots Consultation

Despite the enormous economic and social potential of ICTs for the developing world, current programs for ICT dissemination warrant a more critical appraisal; the telecenter model of ICT access, and how it has failed to properly consider the role of education in development initiatives, is an illustrative example. Broadly defined, telecenters are remote information kiosks that connect specific technologies (typically including phone lines, fax machines, computers, printers, scanners, digital cameras, and Internet access) to national and global information networks. A system of telecenters allows citizens in rural communities to access contemporary technologies from permanent sites in the region, thereby increasing technological literacy and simplifying the bureaucratic processes of centralized government offices. Many telecenters are built with the assistance of development agencies, in the hopes that increased access to ICTs will improve the daily living conditions of communities and citizens.

For example, in a district of Dhar in Madhya Pradesh, central India, a Rural Intranet Project established a network of "village information kiosks" in order to provide citizens with agricultural information, government forms, and public health announcements. In addition, the network allows public officials to learn of potential crises immediately, so that outbreaks of disease and environmental contamination can be contained (Bhatnagar, 2003, pp. 38-41). Many ICT kiosks in the developing world—such as those in the Dhar project—are operated as private businesses by local entrepreneurs, generating income from customers who can afford the services provided. In an alternate model, paid employees of a central organization, public or private, staff the telecenter networks, ensuring that the kiosks remain open whether there is substantial demand for the services or not. As Colle and Roman (2003) observe, both models depend on the usefulness of the applications provided for financial sustainability: "One of the biggest challenges telecenters face is providing relevant information and services for their stakeholders. To survive, telecenters must be substantially demand driven whatever their sources of income. This translates into the need to have relevant and useful content" (p. 83). ICT kiosks have the potential to connect rural communities with the global world of culture and trade; their potential, however, depends on universal access, reliable service, and above all grassroots content development. If community members are active participants in ICT dissemination, rather than passive recipients of mere tools and techniques, they will have a tangible interest in maintaining and expanding ICT networks.

Consequently, it is imperative that telecenter networks depart from their exclusive relationship with private industry. Despite the economic advantages of privatized telecommunications industries (as demonstrated by Henriques & Sadorsky, 2005, among others), privately owned telecenters dull the effectiveness of ICT networks in two important ways. Firstly, so long as ICT kiosks are operated for profit, they limit their usefulness in any community by attaching a price to information itself. Although many individual citizens may choose to

Copyright © 2007, Idea Group Inc. Copying or distributing in print or electronic forms without written permission of Idea Group Inc. is prohibited.

pay for certain conveniences (e.g. submitting government forms electronically in order to avoid travelling to a central office), the majority of citizens will be hard-pressed to justify the cost of casual ICT use. Instead of introducing the benefits of long-range communication, unlimited research opportunities, cultural expression and improved education, ICT risks becoming an expensive gadget for those that can afford its limited use.

The second problem that arises from privately owned telecenters is a broader issue of harnessing knowledge for purposes of control. When the kiosk operator rations out ICT use to individual customers, there is little opportunity for individual community members to learn how these technologies really work. Widespread technical literacy may develop over time, but actual hands-on experience is limited to paying customers. The kiosk operator, usually trained by the network owners, holds a monopoly of technical knowledge in the community. Although he or she may choose to share their skills with customers and community members, there is no necessary incentive to do so.

To avoid the problems raised by private ownership, telecenter networks need to be developed as part of a region's public infrastructure. The costs can be prohibitively high, but the long-term economic advantages are very real. Building and maintaining a system of ICT kiosks seems expensive, but what is the real cost of an illiterate, underemployed community? How expensive is a family that falls sick because they had no way to know that their water supply was contaminated? ICT development forces us to consider the real costs associated with social and economic progress. If ICT infrastructure is treated as an expensive addition to a nation's economy, it will continue to serve the narrow interests of select individuals and industries. If, however, ICT infrastructure develops in tandem with a nation's educational institutions, citizens and communities will be encouraged to adapt ICTs to existing needs and desires, thereby exploring the real and unexpected benefits of global technology.

It should be noted, however, that in many regions of the developing world, education and learning have long been at the core of economic and social planning. In a study of the Fast Reliable Instant Effective Network for Disbursement of Services (FRIENDS) project, Shirin Madon notes that the Indian state of Kerala, where FRIENDS introduced a network of "one-stop, IT-enabled payment counter[s]" for all government bills, has long benefited from the presence of village libraries (Madon, 2003, pp. 76-78). As Madon writes, "These libraries are now an established part of village life in Kerala, being used as centers for adult literacy and the venue for political meetings and youth events. Education has played a larger role in the evolution of Kerala's society by encouraging the growth of the print media and communication industry" (p. 76). Nevertheless, the FRIENDS project, aimed at simplifying a number of bureaucratic processes through ICT design, operated independently of the village libraries. Faced with the major investments in ICT infrastructure needed to establish the FRIENDS network, the decision was made to keep new technologies away from centers of learning. The failure to recognize this type of ICT dissemination as both educationally and economically advantageous to a region is symptomatic of ICT development projects throughout the world. Even in a state that actively encourages learning and education, the FRIENDS designers chose to build narrow-use telecenters, conceived of for specific bureaucratic functions. Had these ICT kiosks been developed in coordination with the village libraries, they may have proven to be of far greater value to communities.

In addition to recognizing and respecting the role played in communities by schools and libraries, ICT developers must understand that these educational institutions represent the unique identities of rural communities. Although there are a great many advantages to the

Copyright © 2007, Idea Group Inc. Copying or distributing in print or electronic forms without written permission of Idea Group Inc. is prohibited.

high-tech schools in developed nations, there are also a number of ongoing pedagogical debates surrounding the use of ICTs in these schools and, therefore, it is essential that these debates follow educational technologies, wherever they may be adopted. For example, it would be a mistake to assume that ICT-equipped schools can replace traditional, teacher-student models of learning. Although networked computer terminals can facilitate online learning, it does not follow that students in remote communities are best served by distance learning. Online and distance education have plenty of critics around the world, as these models place individual learners at the core of the education process. Introducing ICT-based learning to the developing world runs the risk of alienating students from their actual communities, threatening cultural survival and encouraging individuals to see themselves at global citizens first, community members second. As Bresnihan and Doyle (2004) argue, "virtual communities tend to be based purely on communities of interest leading to narrow discussions on mostly predefined topics which, while giving the contributors a sense of community, can in fact keep them dislocated from the real world" (p. 389). The online communities created by distance and ICT-enhanced learning promote global citizenship at the expense of the very real communities that students inhabit. There are, undoubtedly, significant benefits associated with online and distance-learning models, including improved access to education (particularly for students with physical disabilities or learning disorders) and standardized delivery of content, benefits that are harder to obtain with traditional methods of communications and teaching. As Quan-Haase and Wellman (2004) argue, "Although face-to-face and telephone contact continue, they are complemented by the Internet's ease in connecting geographically dispersed people, institutions, and organizations bonded by shared interests" (p. 123). Nevertheless, the potential for misuse (intentional or not) of these technologies must be acknowledged before introducing ICTs into the classrooms of the developing world.

The value of grassroots consultation simply cannot be overstated in development paradigms. Regardless of its economic outcomes, a successful development strategy will recognize local systems of knowledge as the foundation for any real progress. As George Dei (2000) argues in his analysis of African development:

For the idea of "development" to have any credibility at all, it must speak to the social, cultural, economic, political, spiritual, and cosmological aspects of local peoples' lives, as well as to their specific needs and aspirations. Debates about "development" must be situated in appropriate social contexts that provide practical and social meaning to the actors as subjects, rather than as objects of development discourse. (p. 73)

When development projects fail to appreciate the centrality of local culture and knowledge, they risk mimicking the colonial and imperialist adventures of the past. Development requires the community to acknowledge the limitations of their own beliefs and assumptions. As developers attempt to bring the benefits of modern ICTs to the rest of the world, it is imperative that they treat all knowledge systems as equal, valid, and enlightening. Furthermore, it is important to recognize the spectrum of educational differences that exist within countries, as not all regions and communities share common values and needs. As Gasperini and Lakin (2003) observe, "Most developing countries have a unitary, centrally determined curriculum, which is generally designed for pupils familiar with an urban environment and may contain

Copyright © 2007, Idea Group Inc. Copying or distributing in print or electronic forms without written permission of Idea Group Inc. is prohibited.

elements that conflict with local customs and beliefs" (p. 89). Promoting appropriate ICT use in local schools may therefore strengthen community autonomy and identity, as grassroots ICT applications can transform centralized practices and programs.

Developing communities can benefit from the educational benefits of ICT infrastructure in a number of ways, many of which occur outside of traditional classrooms. The increasing use of ICTs in their economic and cultural lives has seen an incredible growth in the field of adult literacy training. People who did not enjoy the benefits of public education in their youth are now adopting the model of the "lifelong learner" in order to keep pace in an increasingly technological world. As Fien argues, this form of literacy:

... is an essential skill for coping with the economic and social changes that are rapidly affecting traditional rural ways of living. Literacy and continuing education projects are needed to help rural people understand the 'what' and 'how' of production and the marketing of goods and services. ... Above all, adult education must help rural people suffering from poverty to develop positive attitudes and values that enhance their self-esteem and self-confidence. (UNESCO, 2004, pp. 119-120)

Adult literacy programs can introduce mature learners to the benefits and wonders of a networked planet, thereby opening an untold number of doors for future employment and expression. Nevertheless, ICT development projects need to differentiate between the goals of adult literacy programs and primary public education. Although it is economically responsible to *double up* ICT infrastructure in rural regions, it must be noted that technologies cannot always be shared among various groups with equal success. Public schools are the long-term caretakers of critical and technical knowledge, as they continue to share information and knowledge with each subsequent generation. Adult literacy must, therefore, be treated as a one-time project aimed at bringing entire communities into a knowledge economy, whereas public schools will ensure that future citizens will have the skills and knowledge necessary to survive and prosper. As the long-term economic benefits of ICT instruction are the responsibility of public education, it would be appropriate for efforts aimed at "doubling up" ICT infrastructure to concentrate their resources in schools. Teachers and students might, however, use ICT resources during regular school hours, and adult education programs could access the same facilities during evenings and weekends.

Certainly, there are a range of ICT applications that can benefit communities and individuals in developing regions. Projects such as FRIENDS, which emphasize bureaucratic processes and governmental business, might best be served by an independent network of telecenters. Had the FRIENDS kiosks been placed in public schools, for example, their usefulness would have been severely limited by their accessibility; had regular business hours overlapped with the school's schedule, their would have been a never-ending contest for use of the machines. Similarly, the Rural Intranet Project in Dhar could not function as an effective public health advisory system if news of a possible contagion first reached a young child in the classroom. Nevertheless, it is troubling that so many ICT development programs fail to consider the economic importance of public education. The immediate utility of bureaucracy-driven networks is undeniable, but it should not come at the expense of the long-term prosperity of a region.

Copyright © 2007, Idea Group Inc. Copying or distributing in print or electronic forms without written permission of Idea Group Inc. is prohibited.

Unless significant efforts are made to provide technical and critical training to communities, ICT development will quickly reach the limits of its own effectiveness. Warnings of this type tend to be dismissed as mere neo-Luddism, stemming from Western academics with their own personal axes to grind with all things technological. What should not be lost in the calls for cautious ICT development is the insistence on inclusive, sustainable practices that respect local knowledges in all forms. This is not a crude, Orientalist reverence for all things exotic and rural—the developing world is home to a multitude of voices that continue to be ignored in the dominant discourses of technology and progress. As Dei (2000) argues, "Leaders must include local people—particularly women and the poor, whose knowledge and power have been marginalized—at all stages of the conception, planning, implementation, and evaluation of development activities" (p. 83). If the marginalized voices are not accorded their inherent worth in development initiatives, local and regional economies will continue to be burdened by individuals and communities who cannot or will not participate in the productive activities that fuel economies. Education generally, and public schools specifically, represent the development movement's best chance at ensuring total, equal participation in local economies.

The single greatest obstacle for ICT development to address is the marked division between internal community needs and external perceptions of need. Newly introduced ICTs must meet some type of existing demand—consciously expressed or not—in order to play a meaningful role in community life. As Avgerou (2003) explains, "the socio-technical analysis suggests that the innovation process depends on the situated actors' capacity to make sense of the value of the new artefacts and organizing techniques, and to accommodate them in their historically-formed enactments" (p. 157). She goes on to warn that, "The risk—all too visible in the widespread 'failures' of IS projects in developing countries—is that technology-diffusion policies which push specific technologies as 'drivers' to desirable 'impacts' or business 'best practice' distort local economic activities and frustrate, rather than enable, improved performance" (p. 157). When development groups see ICT applications as "drivers" for specific outcomes they fail to recognize existing social and economic practices that constitute community experience. Worse still, prescriptive ICT solutions relegate local community members to passive roles in a networked world. As Paulo Freire (2004) warns, "In cultural invasion the actors (who need not even go personally to the invaded culture; increasingly their action is carried out by technological instruments) superimpose themselves on the people, who are assigned the role of spectators, of objects" (p. 180). Developers must recognize that their technological instruments have the same potential to become cultural invaders as they themselves do.

The inherently flexible nature of ICT tools and techniques is what encourages many groups to actively develop ICT infrastructure in a variety of communities (see, for example, Diane Nelson's, 1999, discussion of "Maya-hackers" in Guatemala). It is this same degree of flexibility that creates new opportunities for cultural expression and economic growth in communities, and that ensures a healthy balance between global perspectives and local identities. However, as Russell Bishop, a Maori scholar, writes, "When one curriculum, one set of knowledges and narratives is constructed as representing 'the truth' or 'the real,' and it obliterates or marginalizes alternative conceptions, it is an act of violence" (as quoted in O'Riley, 2003, p. 62). Constructive, successful development initiatives embrace the alternative conceptions that are characteristic of ICTs, because they recognize the short-sightedness of advancing pre -determined goals and outcomes.

Copyright © 2007, Idea Group Inc. Copying or distributing in print or electronic forms without written permission of Idea Group Inc. is prohibited.

Finally, although ICT development has become a priority for many governments and agencies, the enormity of the obstacles to ICT development must be confronted before any serious attempts at dissemination are undertaken. For example, an organization known as Learning and Development Kenya (LDK) is attempting to build ICT infrastructure that will benefit both the social and economic development of that country. Although the group considers education to be a central area for focus, there are a number of challenges to be faced: "Despite the fact that more educational opportunities have been created in the last decade, many children ages 6 to 13 years are still not in school. … The enrolment levels are compounded by high rates of dropouts, and the situation is becoming more complicated with high death rates of the parents due to HIV/AIDS" (p. 95); as Philip Ndeta (2003) notes, "This trend in not promising for the successful use of ICT by the majority of Kenyans" (p. 95). LDK's success is, therefore, inextricably linked to the health and social crises affecting entire communities in Kenya. Although specific ICT initiatives may bring economic benefits to select groups and individuals in Kenyan society, it is impossible to ignore the broader concerns of daily life and their impacts on development projects. Education initiatives are linked to food shortages, the spread of disease, and even to cultural norms and mores of specific regions; if ICT development projects are to achieve any real degree of effectiveness it is imperative that organizers and implementers pay attention to the greatest possible number of considerations.

General Recommendations

As this chapter has attempted to argue, ICT development in rural communities is most effective when it embodies the values and goals of local knowledges. One of the most effective methods for securing and institutionalizing this link is to build development projects around existing sites of public education. A few simple principles and practices can greatly enhance the effectiveness and sustainability of ICT projects; taken as a whole, the recommendations in this section can provide a sound foundation for future development initiatives. Nevertheless, it is important to recognize that this is only a first step; the world of development changes and evolves as quickly and unpredictably as the world of technology, and it is necessary that developers of all types continue to stay informed and alert.

The University and the Schoolhouse: Centralized vs. Localized Knowledges

For many ICT developers, it is tempting to devote significant resources to the most visible, influential sites of education in a country—the universities. For example, the Sudan Virtual Engineering Library—Sustainability Network (SudVEL-SKN) uses centralized resources in order to disseminate knowledge across ICT networks; as Anna McKenzie (2005) writes, "Databases such as these are needed in every country to draw out local material and ensure technology transfer from international sources into the curriculum of engineering students, material for researchers and professional development" (p. 438). Universities and colleges employ a large number of citizens as teachers and researchers, and they tend to be important

Copyright © 2007, Idea Group Inc. Copying or distributing in print or electronic forms without written permission of Idea Group Inc. is prohibited.

sites of research and development for ICTs, making them ideal hubs for future investment in ICT infrastructure. For example, in their study of sustainable development initiatives, Colle and Roman (2003) see Universities playing a key role in ICT development around the world. Universities, they argue:

- Conduct continual research on community information needs so that appropriate information resources can be developed.

- Convert their own research and academic knowledge into education, information, and training packages suitable for community use.

- Mobilize, interpret, integrate, and package information from external authoritative sources and tailor it to the needs of populations in surrounding communities.

- Design and execute ICT training programs for various community groups, especially those that are likely to be bypassed by conventional ICT training. (p. 85)

Despite these positive outcomes, universities currently occupy too much of the development movement's time and effort. Although universities are important resources for the economic and educational development of a country, their impacts are not always felt directly in rural communities. Public schools and local libraries benefit from actual grassroots involvement, allowing community members to participate in educational initiatives and to see the results firsthand. Universities tend to concentrate resources and personnel in large urban centers, distancing ICT infrastructure from the millions of citizens that the development movement hopes to serve. The SudVEL-SKN initiative, although a useful tool for Sudan's engineering students, draws out *local material* in order to support the advanced learning of a small group. While university staff and students may *design and execute ICT training programs* for use in rural communities, relying on such a centralized model of knowledge dissemination hardly seems practical or desirable. One need only consider the ill-fated notion of *trickle-down economics* in order to see the inherent limitations of a university-centered strategy for ICT development.

Additionally, and perhaps more importantly, the benefits of a university education tend to help individuals rather than communities, whereas primary and secondary schools benefit both groups. Education, generally speaking, benefits both individuals and communities. Although students alone receive formal education in school settings, the effects on the community are palpable and desirable; as Kambhampati observes, "The social returns from education can be higher than the private returns if education leads to technological progress not captured in the private returns to education, or if education produces positive externalities like a reduction in crime rates and social security pay-outs, or more informed political decisions" (p. 229). As primary education enhances the collective security and well being of communities, it is funded by local and national governments, which consider long-term social benefits to be a good investment. While similar collective gains are recognized at the level of secondary schooling, tertiary education (universities and colleges) represents a different set of costs and benefits. Thus, although "many empirical studies indicate that tertiary education has higher private than social benefit, and there is therefore a case for it to be privately funded," writes Kambhampati (2004), "most developing country governments spend more on it than its social benefits warrant" (p. 235).

Copyright © 2007, Idea Group Inc. Copying or distributing in print or electronic forms without written permission of Idea Group Inc. is prohibited.

Rather than treating universities as the educational and economic cores of a nation's school system, developers need to treat universities as important, centralized hubs for individual advancement in specific economic and cultural fields. Even though the tertiary educational sector generates and sustains a great deal of a nation's technical and historical knowledge, it should not receive a disproportionate share of a nation's ICT infrastructure. Universities have an important role to play in ICT development, but they must not overshadow the pivotal role of primary and secondary schools, which have a far greater potential to reach the entire population of a country.

Telecenters and the Private Sector: ICT and Profitability

Even though universities and colleges have received a disproportionate amount of resources and attention from ICT development initiatives, it can at least be argued that some portion of the resulting benefits have helped individuals and communities in impoverished regions. Privately operated telecenters and kiosks, however, continue to benefit only a narrow cross-section of any population. Before governments and development agencies begin to design massive ICT networks in remote rural settings, it is imperative that they appreciate what distinguishes rural ICT applications from their urban equivalents. As Bhatnagar (2003) thoughtfully observes:

Rural areas need to be serviced through low-cost, low-bandwidth solutions that have high reliability. This means that technology solutions will have to be adapted to local terrain and conditions. Demand for information services would have to be generated through aggressive marketing, and overheads kept low to serve a cost-sensitive market. Large organizations in the public or private sector are unlikely to be able to operate in this manner. (p. 51)

The question, then, is whether or not ICT infrastructure in rural regions can (or even should) be expected to generate any real profits. Bhatnagar suggests that large public organizations are unlikely to operate successfully in these economic confines; although this reflects the prevailing attitudes in many countries, the public sector nevertheless remains the only body capable of building and maintaining ICT networks in rural regions.

Whereas a private business model of kiosks and telecenters requires *aggressive marketing* and low overheads, a public model based on existing educational infrastructure does not. It is entirely possible that ICT solutions for rural regions cannot become sustainable investments for private businesses. However, if neither businesses nor governments can perceive benefits to offset investment losses, then ICT development will be mothballed indefinitely. What is needed is either a stabilization of rural markets in order to appeal to private firms, or an effective *doubling up* of community ICT infrastructure with existing government programs and institutions. If stabilization remains unlikely in the near future, then public schools offer an ideal site for additional investment and development, as the project of widespread, meaningful ICT use significantly overlaps the goals and values of public education. If young people are taught to read, write, and express themselves creatively using ICT tools and techniques, an entire generation of young citizens will be comfortable working with the knowledge tools of a globalized world.

Copyright © 2007, Idea Group Inc. Copying or distributing in print or electronic forms without written permission of Idea Group Inc. is prohibited.

The issue of staffing and maintaining ICT kiosks, too, becomes far less problematic if developers seek out existing institutions and organizations. In their discussion of telecenters and operating practices, Colle and Roman (2003) emphasize the importance of volunteers in maintaining the effectiveness of telecenters: "The challenge for telecenters is to move from largely spontaneous use and management of volunteers to developing an explicit strategic plan for recruiting, training, retaining, and rewarding volunteers" (p. 86). Such a strategic plan can be grounded in the community structures surrounding public schools, so that teachers and students themselves can play an active role in the community use of ICTs. Once ICT infrastructure is a part of school life, the nature of volunteer recruitment drives will be drastically different.

Culture and Language: Long-Term Investments

Although projects aimed at improving educational opportunities carry with them the inherent economic advantages of a well-educated populace, the preservation and promotion of local cultures and languages often seem less imperative than other, more technology-aligned aspects of ICT-enhanced education. Publicly funded initiatives are therefore essential to the success and sustainability of ICT development programs, because they recognize that many important projects cost far more money than they can immediately return. In Thailand, for example, the Inter-village Connectivity and Empowerment initiative introduced ICT to a number of rural areas, in order to "disseminate knowledge and information to support economic stability and increased international competitiveness" (UNESCO, 2005, p. 7). One of the initiative's projects was the translation of herbal medicine texts from a traditional, at-risk language, the Lanna script ("which only a few people in the [Ban Samkha] village can read and understand"), into modern languages, in order to preserve historical, cultural knowledge (p. 9). Similar programs include the "Chakma Language Preservation Project" in India and the "Pukllasunchis Primary School" project in the Andean region of Peru (King & Schielmann 2004, pp. 139, 217). These are costly, Labor-intensive ICT development programs with only a few financial incentives. Seen in a long-term perspective, however, the preservation of scripts and medicinal practices may bring enormous benefits, both cultural and economic, to the entire world.

The issue of language preservation is especially significant in development programs focused on ICT dissemination, because unless ICT applications are developed with grassroots consultation, they will tend to present themselves to communities in the dominant, hegemonic languages of international business and trade. In a list of conclusions drawn from multiple ICT development initiatives, UNESCO (2005) notes that:

Language becomes an important issue at the global and national levels because approximately 80 per cent of the world's websites are in English. Thus, English literacy is needed to access the global online information network. Likewise, literacy in the national language is necessary to read documents related to local and national programmes. (p. 31)

Copyright © 2007, Idea Group Inc. Copying or distributing in print or electronic forms without written permission of Idea Group Inc. is prohibited.

With this warning in mind, UNESCO (2005) goes on to note that:

There is a certain belief at all levels that ICT tools are something given by outside experts rather than developed locally. Although external support is essential for initiating new activities and updating knowledge and skills, local people need to develop a sense of ownership of their ICT programmes, including the technology itself. (p. 31)

It is imperative that the development movement recognizes the extreme sensitivity of the hundreds of distinct languages used in remote regions of the world. Although public education can be an effective site for the preservation and growth of cultural practices, ICT tools and applications themselves can greatly undermine these efforts if proper consideration is not given before their dissemination.

The Future of ICT and Education in Development Projects

Future ICT initiatives should begin to look for precedents that are widely regarded as both economically and pedagogically successful. Although it can be difficult to identify such successes, particularly in the short-term, there are several indicators that can alert researchers and developers to good practices and anticipated results. Firstly, developers should look for ICT projects that introduce technologies broadly, allowing local community residents to adapt and innovate as they see fit. For example, project organizers might be well served to consider one of the conclusions UNESCO draws from the connectivity initiative in Thailand: "If the use of ICT is linked to solving different community problems, and not restricted to learning in school, the villagers will realize its functional importance and become more interested in acquiring ICT skills" (UNESCO, 2005, p. 11). ICT development may help businesses, and it may also help schools, but it can also bring with it many unimagined opportunities for additional growth, so long as developers do not limit its use to one single sector. Secondly, it is equally useful to consider how ICTs can solve many, but not all, problems facing rural communities. In the same list of UNESCO's conclusions regarding the connectivity initiative in Thailand, they observe that, "ICT is one tool used to create a good learning environment in the community. So it is not necessary to start with ICT in every learning activity" (p. 11). When developers try to apply ICT solutions to every economic and educational crisis they perceive, the end result is usually far from what had been anticipated.

Thirdly, developers can identify successful ICT initiatives by their commitment to grassroots consultation. From the early planning of a project to ensuring and maintaining its ongoing sustainability, community members themselves—particularly the marginalized, the poor, and women—must play an active role in ICT development. Educational applications in particular must be developed locally, to ensure that local needs are not supplanted by centralized, national imperatives, or by international forces. As a useful template for future projects, Lavinia Gasperini and Michael Lakin (2003) list four guidelines for ensuring that educational content is developed properly:

Copyright © 2007, Idea Group Inc. Copying or distributing in print or electronic forms without written permission of Idea Group Inc. is prohibited.

First, the curriculum should relate to the local context, customs, livelihoods and rural de-
velopment activities. Second, it should take due account of the teachers' qualifications and
training (although ideally these should be in accord with the curriculum). Third, it should
make use of locally available skills, knowledge and other resources. Fourth, it should respond
to the expressed wishes of the community (i.e., be demand-driven). (p. 145)

Once curricular content is established along these guidelines, developers can begin to support and complement pedagogical practices with ICT tools and applications. If ICT becomes
a driver, rather than a useful navigational instrument, it risks wrenching control out of the
hands of communities and placing it in the hands of distant ICT *experts.*

A fourth consideration for ICT development initiatives in rural communities is particularly
important to public education, as it stresses the involvement of education's primary audience. Often ignored in grassroots consultations, children and youth must play a central role
in development programs focused on ICT applications in education. As UNESCO notes,
children offer creative input in a wholly unique manner, as "They can help to alter the
mindset of adults by coming up with some unusual, but effective, ways of doing things"
(UNESCO, 2005, p. 11). As ICTs allow young people to explore the networked world in
greater detail, developers should look to students for innovative ideas that remain grounded
in local communities. Therefore, as UNESCO suggests, "Encouraging children and youth
to become active partners in the process of community development is an effective way to
achieve a higher level of sustainability for both ICT and community development activities"
(p. 11). Grassroots consultations can no longer afford to ignore such a vital, fresh source of
inspiration and reflection.

Finally, ICT developers need to seek out models for infrastructure development that do not
limit their definition of ICTs solely to computers and computer technologies. In order to
sustain the benefits of increased connectivity and creative expression, development initiatives
should attempt to match community needs and desires with appropriate tools and techniques.
UNESCO's summary of findings from multiple projects indicates that, "Although many
countries believe that ICT means computers and the Internet, the use of other kinds of ICT
such as radio, television, and audio technology are worth further exploration. Some of these
media are more useful for raising awareness and also more cost-effective than computers"
(UNESCO, 2005, p. 31). Technologies that seem older and less attractive to Western development agencies may in fact be ideally suited to the immediate needs and desires of rural
communities in developing regions.

Conclusion

The project of ICT infrastructure development brings with it the promises and dreams of
a networked society, where every individual and community can play an active role in the
economic and cultural life of the planet. Remote communities and rural centers alike can
share the benefits of a connected world, humanized and democratized by the forces of
technology. This vision is, of course, still a long way off. Significant economic disparities
continue to handicap whole countries and regions, while fundamental issues of access and

Copyright © 2007, Idea Group Inc. Copying or distributing in print or electronic forms without written permission
of Idea Group Inc. is prohibited.

training prevent millions of citizens from participating in the hi-tech global community. If developers are to realize any form of a vision for the future, they need to begin by addressing the obstacles of access and disparity in the developing world. Public education is quite simply the single most important weapon for social progress in the world. When coupled with the radical transformative potential of ICTs, public education can become a site for economic, cultural, and personal growth on a previously unimagined scale.

For development groups interested in exploiting the potential of ICTs for economic growth, the most important lesson to learn is that economic growth cannot be sustained without a corresponding investment in education. ICT applications must be introduced to communities as tools and resources, and not simply as economic drivers for limited functions. The creative uses and applications of ICTs are bound only by the human spirit of imagination and ingenuity. Historical understandings of ICT use simply do not provide ample space for individuals and communities to develop real world solutions to existing problems. This is particularly true in education, where young minds and exciting technological opportunities can combine in an infinite number of possibilities. As Stephen Kerr (2001) observes of ICT use in schools, "We tend to see the future, as Marshall McLuhan noted, through the rearview mirror of familiar approaches and ideas from the past. In order to allow the potential inherent in educational technology to flourish, we need to shift our gaze and try to discern what lies ahead, as well as behind" (p. 164). It is time that ICT infrastructure developers look to what lies ahead. They should start in the classroom.

References

Avgerou, C. (2003). New socio-technical perspectives of IS innovation in organizations. In C. Avgerou., & R. Rovere (Eds.), *Information systems and the economics of innovation* (pp. 141-161). Cheltenham, UK: Edward Elgar Publishing.

Avgerou, C., & Rovere, R. (2003). Introduction. In C. Avgerou & R. Rovere (Eds.), *Information systems and the economics of innovation* (pp. 1-11). Cheltenham, UK: Edward Elgar Publishing.

Bhatnagar, S. (2003). Development and telecommunications access: Cases from South Asia. In C. Avgerou & R. Rovere (Eds.), *Information systems and the economics of innovation* (pp. 33-52). Cheltenham, UK: Edward Elgar Publishing.

Bresnihan, N., & Doyle, L. (2004). Sharing places, enhancing spaces: An investigation into the effects of mobile networking technologies on physical communities. In K. Morgan, C. A. Brebbia, J. Sanchez, & A. Voiskounsky (Eds.), *Human perspectives in the Internet society: Culture, psychology and gender* (pp. 387-396). Southhampton, Boston: WIT.

Clement, A., & Shade, L. R. (2000). The access rainbow: Conceptualizing universal access to the information/communications infrastructure. In M. Gurstein (Ed.), *Community informatics: Enabling communities with information and communications technologies* (pp. 32-51). Hershey, PA: Idea Group Publishing.

Copyright © 2007, Idea Group Inc. Copying or distributing in print or electronic forms without written permission of Idea Group Inc. is prohibited.

Colle, R. D., & Roman, R. (2003). Challenges in the telecenter movement. In S. Marshall, W. Taylor, & X. Yu (Eds.), *Closing the digital divide: Transforming regional economies and communities with information technology* (pp. 75-92). Westport, CT: Praeger Publishers.

Dei, G. J. S. (2000). African development: The relevance and implications of "Indigenousness." In G. J. S. Dei, B. L. Hall & D. G. Rosenberg (Eds.), *Indigenous knowledges in global contexts: Multiple readings of our world* (pp. 70-86). Toronto: University of Toronto Press.

Freire, P. (2004). *Pedagogy of the oppressed: 30th anniversary edition* (M.B. Ramos, Trans.). New York: Continuum International Publishing Group Inc.

Gasperini, L., & Lakin, M. (2003). Basic education in rural areas: Status, issues and prospects. In D. Atchoarena & L. Gasperini (Eds.), *Education for rural development: Towards new policy responses. A joint study conducted by FAO and UNESCO* (pp. 77-174). Paris: United Nations Educational, Scientific and Cultural Organization Publishing.

Gurstein, M. (2003). Perspectives on urban and rural community informatics: Theory and performance, community informatics and strategies for flexible networking. In S. Marshall, W. Taylor, & X. Yu (Eds.), *Closing the digital divide: Transforming regional economies and communities with information technology* (pp. 1-11). Westport, CT: Praeger Publishers.

Henriques, I., & Sadorsky, P. (2005). Risk and investment in the global telecommunications industry. In H. S. Kehal & V. P. Singh (Eds.), *Digital economy: Impacts, influences and challenges* (pp. 39-61). Hershey, PA: Idea Group Publishing.

Kambhampati, U. S. (2004). *Development and the developing world*. Cambridge, UK: Polity Press.

Kerr, S. T. (2001). Toward a sociology of educational technology. In D. H. Jonassen (Ed.), *Handbook of research for educational communications and technology* (pp. 143-169). Mahwah, NJ: Lawrence Erlbaum.

King, L., & Schielmann, S. (2004). *The challenge of indigenous education: Practice and perspectives*. Paris: United Nations Educational, Scientific and Cultural Organization Publishing.

Madon, S. (2003). IT diffusion for public service delivery: Looking for plausible theoretical approaches. In C. Avgerou & R. Rovere (Eds.), *Information systems and the economics of innovation* (pp. 71-85). Cheltenham, UK: Edward Elgar Publishing.

McKenzie, A. (2005). Changing hearts and minds: The role of education. In K. C. Hargroves & M. H. Smith (Eds.), *The natural advantage of nations: Business opportunities, innovation and governance in the 21st century* (pp. 430-444). London: Earthscan.

Ndeta, P. (2003). ICT integration in social and economic development: Kenya's perspective. In S. Marshall, W. Taylor, & X. Yu (Eds.), *Closing the digital divide: Transforming regional economies and communities with information technology* (pp. 93-100). Westport, CT: Praeger Publishers.

Nelson, D. M. (1999). *A Finger in the wound: Body politics in quincentennial Guatemala*. Berkeley, CA: University of California Press.

Copyright © 2007, Idea Group Inc. Copying or distributing in print or electronic forms without written permission of Idea Group Inc. is prohibited.

O'Riley, P. A. (2003). *Technology, culture, and socioeconomics: A rhizoanalysis of educational discourses*. New York: Peter Lang Publishing, Inc.

Quan-Haase, A., & Wellman, B. (2004). How does the Internet affect social capital? In M. Huysman & V. Wulf (Eds.), *Social capital and information technology* (pp. 113-132). Cambridge, MA: The MIT Press.

UNESCO. (2002, September 2-3). Educating for a sustainable future: Commitments and partnerships. In *Proceedings of the High-Level International Conference on Education for Sustainable Development at the World Summit on Sustainable Development*, Johannesburg, South Africa. Paris: United Nations Educational, Scientific and Cultural Organization Publishing.

UNESCO. (2005) *Information and communication technologies (ICTs) for community empowerment through non-formal education: Experiences from Lao PDR, Sri Lanka, Thailand and Uzbekistan*. A report by UNESCO's Asia-Pacific Program of Education for All (APPEAL). Bangkok: UNESCO Asia and Pacific Regional Bureau for Education.

Copyright © 2007, Idea Group Inc. Copying or distributing in print or electronic forms without written permission of Idea Group Inc. is prohibited.

Chapter II

Strategies for the Cooperation of Higher Education Institutions in ICT

Juha Kettunen, Turku Polytechnic, Finland

Abstract

This study analyzes the strategic planning of the ICT center, which is a joint venture of three higher education institutions. The strategies of focus and operations excellence are natural choices to define the strategic outlines for the center, which aims to increase the economic growth of the region. The selected strategies are described in this study using the balanced scorecard approach. It allows the network of organizations to articulate and communicate their strategy to their employees and stakeholders. The concept of the strategy map is used to describe the strategy. The decentralized efforts of separate organizational units would most likely fail without the network strategy and cooperation.

Copyright © 2007, Idea Group Inc. Copying or distributing in print or electronic forms without written permission of Idea Group Inc. is prohibited.

Introduction

Higher education institutions (HEIs) try to focus their activities to specific fields of education and the needs of their geographical area. Each HEI has its historical background and strengths. The educational institutions try to reinforce their strengths and improve their quality by focusing their resources on specific activities. Strategic choices are typically made to focus on the specific segments of knowledge creation and delivery.

Another strategy of HEIs emphasizes the operations excellence theme. Institutions try to reduce their costs and improve quality by doing operations more efficiently. The HEIs can achieve their desired objectives in ways other than traditional pure operational excellence. This study shows how the interests of various HEIs can converge in research and education in information and communication technology (ICT). The close cooperation of institutions has led to a partnership to build a joint ICT center, which produces better labor force and enhances the competitive advantage of the ICT companies in the region.

The various strategic approaches aim to move educational institutions from their present position to a desirable future position (Davies & Ellison, 2003; Fidler, 2002; West-Burnham, 1994; Wheale, 1991). The strategy of focus aims to direct activities to specific customer segments. This also leads to operations excellence and overall cost efficiency. These two strategies are essentially the competitive strategies by Porter (1990, 1996) applied to educational institutions.

The purpose of this study is to show that the balanced scorecard approach and the concept of the strategy map developed by Kaplan and Norton (2001, 2004) can successfully be used to describe and communicate the network strategy of the ICT center, which is a joint venture of HEIs. The communication of strategic objectives is important especially in a network project. The stakeholders have diverse backgrounds which increase the need for enhanced communication. The decentralized efforts of separate organizational units would most likely fail without the network strategy and cooperation. The approach helps to create a shared understanding about the planning and operation of the center. The balanced scorecard translates the center's strategy into tangible objectives and balances them into four different perspectives: customer, finance, internal processes, and learning.

The strategies typically reflect the structure of the organization for which the strategy has been planned. In such cases the implementation of the strategy is straightforward, because the strategies of different administrative units can be aligned with one another to obtain an effective plan for the whole organization. This study presents strategies which are not congruent with the structure of an existing organization but with the network of independent institutions. The strategies favor the cooperation of the institutions in an ICT center in order to increase their external impact.

In many regions there are typically several HEIs, which have their own unique strengths but much in common. In these regions no single HEI is solely responsible for the regional development nor is in complete control of it. Their strategies can, however, be aligned and linked in order to strengthen their external impact on the local community. This study uses the balanced scorecard approach to plan strategies for virtual organizations to achieve commitment to a common strategy. Thus, the strategy for a virtual organization involves multiple autonomous operators with their own activities.

Copyright © 2007, Idea Group Inc. Copying or distributing in print or electronic forms without written permission of Idea Group Inc. is prohibited.

The ICT center is a joint venture of the University of Turku, Åbo Akademi University, Turku Polytechnic and the Turku Science Park Ltd. As the owner of Turku Polytechnic and Turku Science Park Ltd, the City of Turku has had an active role in establishing the center. The ICT center was planned according to the educational policy outlined by the Ministry of Education in order to increase the external impact of HEIs in Finland.

This is a qualitative study based on the concepts of strategic planning and the balanced scorecard approach. The focus of the study is on the interpretation of how the participants make sense of the planning concepts. The focus is not in the numerical exactness, which is typically the strength of the quantitative research. When a qualitative study is conducted, qualitative data are used to clarify and illustrate the meaning of findings. Typically one case or a small number of cases are studied preserving the individuality of the analyzes.

This study is organized as follows: The next section presents the operational environment of the ICT center. The third section presents the strategic planning and the cooperation of educational institutions. The fourth section presents the balanced scorecard approach and the strategy maps, which are used to describe and communicate the strategy. It also presents the strategic initiative to build the ICT center. The results of the study are summarized and discussed in the concluding section.

The Operational Environment of the ICT Center

Economic Development of the Region

The strategic location of the ICT center is at the Turku Region situated in the county of Southwest Finland. The Turku Region is one of the largest growth areas of Finland and is the second largest growth area on the southern coast of Finland after the Helsinki metropolitan area. Turku has an excellent location right at the heart of an area comprising the Scandinavian countries, the Baltic countries and St. Petersburg. Turku has only 175,000 inhabitants, but about 30 million people live within an easy reach of Turku. This offers the business in Turku a clear potential for continuous economic growth.

The main clusters in Southwest Finland include ICT, biotechnology, and metal and maritime technology. These clusters are based on high technology, but they mix with low technology, manufacturing, and services. Porter (1998) defines clusters as geographic concentrations of interconnected companies, specialized suppliers, service providers, firms in related industries and associated institutions in particular fields that compete but also cooperate. Recent growth has particularly boosted the ICT and biotechnology. The traditional metal and maritime cluster provide the basis for new products in pharmaceutics, functional foods and life sciences, transport as well as printing technology and media.

The growth of industrial production in Southwest Finland has been particularly fast compared to the average development of the whole country. The value of production of electro-technical industry in Southwest Finland has increased more than tenfold during the last decade, while the growth rate of other industries has been 15%. Also many other industrial and service industries began to grow faster during the late 1990s. Particularly rapid growth is

Copyright © 2007, Idea Group Inc. Copying or distributing in print or electronic forms without written permission of Idea Group Inc. is prohibited.

expected to continue in transport and storage services, data communication, construction, and services provided for business life.

The fast growth of the electro-technical industry can also be seen in the production structure of the industry. The share of electro-technical industry has reached an all-time high in Southwest Finland. It accounted for 25% of all industrial production in Finland after being only less than 7% in 1990. The share of electro-technical production is the highest among the industries of Finland. The structural change has particularly affected the production in Southwest Finland.

The advantages of clusters involve location-specific factors and public goods. The clusters are supported by the public sector including educational institutions. The advantages of clusters include physical proximity, close cooperation, and access to information. Public investment in knowledge and specialized infrastructure benefit these clusters and increase their competitive advantage. HEIs located within clusters are able to more clearly and rapidly perceive new educational needs (Pfeffer, 1997).

The traditional universities and Turku Polytechnic are closely situated in the same district of Turku Science Park. The City of Turku established a holding and development company Turku Science Park Ltd. to develop the area. Turku Science Park comprises a five square kilometer area in Turku including properties for cluster-specific innovation activities. There are also three cluster-specific development companies ICT Turku Ltd., Bio Valley Ltd. and Turku Technology Center Ltd., which also operate in cooperation with education institutions, companies and other stakeholders.

Turku Science Park links together public and private investments, major construction companies and the companies of the Turku Region. It combines four HEIs, 13,500 employees, 25,000 students, 400 professors and 300 companies in a single location. It combines research, development, education and production involving public and private operators. Turku Science Park breeds the future products of digital mobile communication, biotechnology and bioinformatics, process engineering and transport technology.

The ICT center will increase the cooperation of HEIs and increase competitive advantage of ICT companies through the research and development and the quality of learning. The center is common ground for research, development and education of multinational telecommunication companies such as Nokia, Siemens, Eriksson, and TeliaSonera. The improved competitive advantage of the companies increases the economic growth of the region and provides employment opportunities for graduates.

Turku Polytechnic

Turku Polytechnic is located in Southwest Finland, which is the second largest economic area after the capital of Finland. Education, culture, and technology are engaged in Southwest Finland in mutually beneficial cooperation with commerce and industry. Regional development is one of the main objectives of Turku Polytechnic. The interaction is close with its operational environment. The purpose of the institution is to react to the changes in its environment in a flexible way. Turku Polytechnic was the first HEI which committed to build the ICT center.

Copyright © 2007, Idea Group Inc. Copying or distributing in print or electronic forms without written permission of Idea Group Inc. is prohibited.

Higher education is fragmented in Turku. There are three traditional universities, the main premises and activities of Turku Polytechnic, and three branch offices of three other smaller polytechnics. The universities include the University of Turku, Åbo Akademi University, and the Turku School of Economics and Business Administration. Åbo Akademi University provides education for the Swedish speaking population. Turku Polytechnic is the largest polytechnic in Finland. The smaller polytechnics Diaconia Polytechnic, Humanities Polytechnic, and the Sydväst Polytechnic have only a relatively small amount of students in Turku. There are plenty of good examples of cooperation between the higher education institutions in Turku.

Turku Polytechnic is a multidisciplinary higher education institution founded in 1992. The City of Turku owns the Polytechnic, which has 750 full time employees. Turku Polytechnic has seven fields of education and a Continuing Education Center. Technology, communication and transport, healthcare and social services, and business and administration are the largest fields of education. The Continuing Education Center has 6,000 participants in a year. The Polytechnic operates in six municipalities in Southwest Finland.

Turku Polytechnic has 8,300 students in 36 Bachelor's and Master's degree programs, and among them five programmes are taught in English. Internationalization is one of the focus areas of the institution. The objective is to improve the students' ability to work in global environment. Turku Polytechnic has a plenty of cooperating higher education institutions in Europe, Asia, and Americas.

Strategic Planning

Strategic Outlines for the Cooperation

The purpose of strategic management is to achieve the desired objectives in the future. The strategic management also involves the development of the organization and its present activities to achieve the objectives set in the strategic plan (Davies & Ellison, 2003; Fidler, 2002). According to Peters (1988), the strategy is used to create organizational capabilities to react to the changing environment. Educational institutions typically develop their internal processes and structures to meet the needs of the changing educational policy, society, and local community.

The competitive strategies were selected for the ICT center on the basis of the strategic outlines. These strategies presented by Porter (1990, 1996) were originally planned for business companies, but they are also applicable to educational institutions (Kettunen, 2002; Treacy & Wiersma, 1995). The strategy of focus was combined with the strategy of cost-efficiency and applied to the center.

The strategy of focus means that an organization selects a market segment and creates bonds with its customers. It knows the customer organizations and can plan the products and services to meet the needs of customers. The focus may also be on a geographical region, occupational group, and organizational level. The functional policy is to serve the selected

Copyright © 2007, Idea Group Inc. Copying or distributing in print or electronic forms without written permission of Idea Group Inc. is prohibited.

market segments particularly well. The focus strategy enables the HEIs to enhance their knowledge in their respective areas.

The strategy of cost efficiency means that the institutions deliver a combination of costs and quality that creates competitive advantage. Typically HEIs have unit-priced funding. They emphasize efficient internal processes and try to achieve high quality in their activities. The strategy of cost efficiency also makes it possible to eliminate overlapping activities and achieve cost reductions. The ICT center use shared premises and support activities to reduce costs.

Even though the focus strategy does not primarily aim to achieve low costs, it does also achieve cost efficiency. The HEIs can eliminate the overlapping activities, focus them, and direct the resources to improve their quality. Cost efficiency is a natural choice for the strategy of educational institutions, which typically have set annual budgets.

Strategic Themes Create Success

The balanced scorecard developed by Kaplan and Norton (1992, 1993) is a general framework for describing and implementing strategy. It can be used to describe a holistic model of the strategy linked to the vision of the future. The balanced scorecard translates the strategy into linked cause-and-effect objectives and measures, which can be used to communicate the strategy to organizational subunits and workers (Kettunen & Kantola, 2005). It helps to create a shared understanding about the efforts and needed steps for the change.

Balanced scorecards have been developed for business companies, but they are also applicable in public organizations. The balanced scorecards of HEIs look remarkably similar to those developed for profit-seeking corporations. They do not pay as much attention to the financial perspective, but emphasize more on the role of students and employees. Given that the financial result is not the primary objective for most of the non-profit organizations in the public sector, it is reasonable to place the recipient at the top of the hierarchy.

Measurement managed companies tend to have better teamwork at the top, better communication throughout the organization and better self-management at the bottom level (Lingle & Shieman, 1996). The results of the study by Frigio and Krumwiede (1999) show that the performance management systems which used balanced scorecard were significantly more effective compared to other systems.

The general strategic statement is that "the ICT center will strengthen the expertise of HEIs and increases the competitive advantage of the companies in the global markets." The improved competitive advantage of local companies increases economic growth, expands the employment opportunities of graduates and generates prosperity in the region. The success of the local company Nokia Mobile Phones Ltd. creates expectations for a wider range of flourishing companies.

Strategic themes describe what management believes must be done to succeed and achieve the desired outcomes (Kaplan & Norton, 2001). They describe the strategy of an organization in a concise way. Each organization has a unique set of strategic themes for creating value for customers. The strategy typically emerges from local initiatives and also within

Copyright © 2007, Idea Group Inc. Copying or distributing in print or electronic forms without written permission of Idea Group Inc. is prohibited.

the organizations (Kettunen, 2003, 2004; Minzberg, 1987). Usually, the strategic themes are tailored to a specific case and cannot necessarily be replicated in other regions.

The first strategic theme of the ICT center emphasizes that the HEIs have to focus their activities on their strengths in order to improve the quality of their activities. Each institution has its specific interest areas and strengths. The first theme describes the customer-oriented strategy to create distinct value for the ICT companies, students, and region.

The second strategic theme is to increase the cooperation of HEIs in order to improve cost-efficiency. The center aims to take advantage of the cooperation of HEIs in order to achieve cost-effective and high-quality operation. These themes reflect the generic competitive strategies which are applicable in many types of organizations. The strategy of focus is combined in this case with the strategy of overall cost efficiency.

The strategy of the ICT center can be written as follows:

- The ICT center will strengthen the expertise of HEIs and increase the competitive advantage of the companies in the global markets.
- Each HEI will focus on its strengths to serve its customers better.
- The increased cooperation of HEIs will enable cost-effective and high-quality activities.

The strategy for the joint ICT center describes the activities required in the center. Each HEI is then able to define its own strategic plan, where the overall network strategy is taken into account.

The first theme is a vertical strategic theme that accommodates the underlying drivers in the learning perspective that will lead to the desired strategic outcome in the customer perspective placed at the top of the hierarchy. It emphasizes the development of the existing strengths of each HEI. The focus on the strengths helps the HEIs to use their resources efficiently and improve the quality of their services. The efficient and high-quality services help the HEIs to serve their customers better.

The other theme is a horizontal strategic theme, which describes the activities in the internal processes perspective. It describes the cooperation of HEIs enabling cost-effective and high-quality activities. Reinforcing strengths and avoiding overlapping operations makes it possible to direct the resources to improved quality in research, development and education and provide regional development and customers with better service. For students this strategy means wider opportunities and higher quality of learning.

Porter (1996) emphasizes that the essence of the strategy is in the activities. The strategy is about selecting the set of activities in which an organization will excel to create a sustainable difference in the marketplace (Kaplan & Norton, 2004). The strategy requires an organizational theory of value creation. The first strategic theme is clearly linked to the activities and describes the value proposition for the customers. The second strategic theme describes the cooperation of different organizational units. The internal processes perspective actually describes the innovation chain, where each institution develops its strengths and cooperates with the others.

Copyright © 2007, Idea Group Inc. Copying or distributing in print or electronic forms without written permission of Idea Group Inc. is prohibited.

Cooperation of Educational Institutions

The University of Turku has a strong and internationally distinguished position as a multidisciplinary scientific university having 17,000 students. Åbo Akademi University offers the Swedish speaking population in Finland higher education in their mother tongue. It has 7,600 students. The Turku School of Economics and Business Administration provides research and higher education in the field of business science. It has 4,200 students. Turku Polytechnic is the largest polytechnic in Finland, having 8,300 students. All these HEIs are participating in the ICT center.

Table 1 presents the number of cooperation projects between HEIs in Turku. According to the results of the survey by Puustelli (2002) most cooperation is in teaching, where 72 examples are found. There are 37 projects of cooperation in research and development. In addition, there are 25 projects in other activities, which include mainly cooperation among support units. However, there are only a few examples of cooperation between the polytechnics. This can be largely explained by the fact that the units of The Sydväst Polytechnic, The Diaconia Polytechnic, and The Humanities Polytechnic are small.

The three universities have a joint network, the Turku Center for Computer Science (TUCS), which was started in 1994 to coordinate research and education in the field of information technology. Education is coordinated entirely by the departments up to the bachelor's level. The educational workgroups of the TUCS coordinate the master's level and postgraduate education.

Table 2 describes the education and research at the ICT center. The cooperation between the HEIs was strengthened starting in the 1990s when TUCS started the joint master's and postgraduate programmes. That also enabled the expansion of the cooperation in research and development. The ICT provides a joint and up-to-date learning environment for the institutions to expand their cooperation.

The traditional functions of the HEIs are to create new knowledge and deliver it. Research and development serves education, providing new contents and improving the quality of education. It also provides development projects, which can be combined with education. The University of Turku and Åbo Akademi University have basic and applied research laboratories within TUCS. Turku Polytechnic has applied research and development facilities. The development includes, for example, projects that develop entrepreneurship.

Table 1. The number of cooperation projects between higher education institutions

	Teaching	Research and development	Other activities
Between universities	39	31	16
Between polytechnics	4	1	4
Between universities and polytechnics	29	5	5
Total	72	37	25

Copyright © 2007, Idea Group Inc. Copying or distributing in print or electronic forms without written permission of Idea Group Inc. is prohibited.

Table 2. Activities at the ICT center

Focus:	Partners of the ICT center:		
	University of Turku	Åbo Akademi University	Turku Polytechnic
Research and development	Basic and applied research at research laboratories	Basic and applied research at research laboratories	Applied research and development
			Entrepreneurship
Educational programmes	Master's programme in information technology	Master's programme in software engineering	Degree programme in information technology (bachelor's degree)
	Graduate programme at TUCS Graduate School	Master's programme in electronic and mobile commerce	Degree programme in electronics (bachelor's degree)
		Graduate programme at TUCS Graduate School	

It has been observed that the cooperation between the HEIs is more active in information and communication technology than in other fields of study. An important reason that facilitates this cooperation is that the same subject is represented in all three universities and Turku Polytechnic. Another reason is that the HEIs are operating in the same district of Turku. The cooperation includes, for example, the consortium of digital media, exchange of students and teachers, international education, Master's program in software engineering in Salo, Center of Software Engineering, TUCS and data networks.

All the HEIs have different profiles in their degree programs. The universities have graduate programs at the TUCS Graduate School. The University of Turku has focused on information technology. Åbo Akademi University provides education for the Swedish-speaking population. It has focused on software development, electronic, and mobile commerce. Turku Polytechnic has two degree programmes in information technology and electronics.

The Balanced Scorecard Describes the Strategy

Perspectives of the Balanced Scorecard

Strategies are typically planned for the whole organization and also for its subunits. The plans reflect the structure of the organization for which they have been tailored. This study

Copyright © 2007, Idea Group Inc. Copying or distributing in print or electronic forms without written permission of Idea Group Inc. is prohibited.

shows that the balanced scorecard provides an approach where strategies have not been planned for a single organization or administrative unit, but the strategies can be shared to achieve the synergy of autonomous HEIs.

The planning of strategies for virtual organizations or networks of independent operators is notably different from that of other strategies, because there is no single organization which owns and implements the strategy or is evaluated against it. On their own the decentralized and overlapping efforts of HEIs would likely have a smaller effect on the economic growth of the region.

If the strategy cannot be described and communicated, it cannot be implemented. Here, the balanced scorecard can be used to translate the vision and strategy into tangible objectives and measures that can be communicated to the personnel and external stakeholders. Hence, a good measurement system should have a balanced mix of objectives and measures in the different perspectives to indicate the strategy.

The objectives and measures have to be defined for each of the four perspectives:

1. **Customer:** The customer perspective describes the value created for customers by the internal processes. The customer perspective also includes regional development.

2. **Finance:** The financial perspective describes the funding from central government and external funding, which are aligned with the cost-efficient internal processes.

3. **Internal processes:** The internal processes perspective describes the strategic priorities for internal processes and how value is created for customers.

4. **Learning:** The learning perspective describes the drivers for future performance and the learning which is required for the internal processes.

These perspectives have been found to be necessary and sufficient across a wide variety of organizations (Kaplan & Norton, 1996, 2001).

The customer-oriented process begins in a top-down fashion, defining the objectives of the customer perspective. It starts by asking, "Who are the target customers and how do we measure our success with them?" Then the process continues, "What funding is required?" and "What has to be done in the internal processes?" Finally the process asks, "What skill and knowledge is needed in the internal processes?"

The customers of HEIs include students, employers, and the local community. The Ministry of Education in June 2002 imposed a requirement that the Finnish HEIs should intensify their cooperation in order to increase their external impact. The first regional strategies were planned by the end of 2002 and updated in 2005. The Ministry of Education hopes that the HEIs will offer better integrated activities for the students and employers in the region. The Ministry hopes also that the increased cooperation enhances the cost efficiency of the institutions.

The ICT center can create synergies across the diverse HEIs by providing students with a broad set of courses and services. It is often reasonable to share the lecturers on basic courses and take advantage of scale effectiveness. This enables the concentrations of expertise in a broader set of specific high-quality courses, which offer students wider perspectives. The cooperation of the HEIs depends largely on the activeness of the professors and other members

Copyright © 2007, Idea Group Inc. Copying or distributing in print or electronic forms without written permission of Idea Group Inc. is prohibited.

of the personnel. The purpose is also to improve the competitiveness of the ICT companies. The needs of the companies are collected from the employers' advisory boards.

Education is financed by central government. The Ministry of Education also finances the joint development projects of HEIs that have a positive impact on regional development. The additional project-based funding for the ICT center expands the degree of cooperation, removes overlapping activities and increases the external impact of the HEIs. This study supports the findings by Tolbert (1985) and Gumport and Sporn (1999) that the activities and organizational structures follow the funding sources.

The additional financial support from the City of Turku maintained sufficient coherence and ensured that the needed decisions for the investment were taken. The meetings organized by the Mayor of Turku stimulated an intense management dialogue, which helped the partners to define their strategic outlines for the ICT center. The extra funding enabled them to share common premises and facilities. The value of the total investment is more than 50 million euros.

The internal processes of the ICT center include many different administrative units. Chandler (1990) describes how synergies across organizations and the economies of scale can be used to achieve cost-efficiency in the operations of smaller and focused organizations. The strategies of different organizational units should be aligned and linked to achieve cost-efficiency. The strategy provides the insight and direction to guide them to increase their strengths, eliminate the overlapping activities and improve the quality of activities.

The ICT center creates synergies across the separate HEIs that aim to increase economic growth and welfare in the local community. The departments of autonomous institutions have intensive interactions with each other. The degree programs of the HEIs benefit from synergies through the sharing of students and staff. They also share libraries, data networks and other facilities which reduce costs and enables higher quality.

The learning of knowledge and skills is the driver of an organization's success (Collis & Montgomery, 1995). Rucci, Kirn, and Quinn (1998) studied the drivers of the future performance of business companies. Their analysis reveals how improvements in training and employees' understanding of the business led to better outcomes. It has also been found that awareness of strategic objectives is one of the key driving forces.

The knowledge-based synergies among the different units enable the whole ICT center to be more valuable than the sum of its parts (Collis & Montgomery, 1995; Goold, Campbell & Alexander, 1994). Typically the strategies of various educational departments are rather similar so that they can be aggregated into larger entities. In this case the different ICT departments have their historical backgrounds and strengths. Their strategies can be combined into the cooperative network strategy of the ICT center.

The importance of cooperation was evaluated in a survey from the different perspectives of the balanced scorecard on the scale 1-5, where 1 is low and 5 is high (Kettunen, 2004; Puustelli, 2002). According to the perceptions of the respondents from the HEIs the cooperation is most important from the perspective of regional development (mean 4.4), customer (mean 3.9) and learning (mean 4.1). Joint ventures, data networks, problem-based activities, and science parks are the most important forms of cooperation from the perspective of regional development. The perspective of customer underlines the subject-related activities. Also the joint ventures and joint support units are evaluated to notably increase the customer value. A pleasing result is that learning is an important motivating factor for cooperation.

Copyright © 2007, Idea Group Inc. Copying or distributing in print or electronic forms without written permission of Idea Group Inc. is prohibited.

The finance and internal processes perspective have the lowest importance for cooperation according to the respondents (means 3.9). There are clear financial benefits only in data networks and research schools. These results are obvious, because the HEIs are able to benefit from economies of scale.

Strategy Maps Describe the Way to the Future

The strategy map is a visual representation of the cause and effect relationships among the components of an organization's strategy and a great insight to executives and stakeholders in understanding the strategy (Kaplan & Norton, 2001, 2004). It has been used in thousands of companies and other organizations. Strategy is a way to a better future described by the organization's vision. The strategy map is simply a graphical representation of the strategy. Strategy maps describe the essential characteristics of the strategy like a road map, but omit all the minor details. They help the employees and stakeholders of the organization to understand why the objectives of the organization have been set and how they can be achieved.

Strategy maps provide tools to describe the strategic themes and help the management of the organization to define the objectives in the different perspectives. Strategy maps describe the causal linkages between the objectives. They provide a comprehensive description of the functioning of an organization and provide an organizational theory, which communicates the organization's desired outcomes and how these outcomes can be achieved. The balanced scorecard approach was selected for the City of Turku and HEIs to provide them a common and understandable framework of indicators. The approach is used in many other cities and educational institutions in Finland.

Figure 1 presents the strategy map of the ICT center, which includes customer, finance, internal processes, and learning perspectives. The perspectives include objectives that have to be achieved in order that the final outcomes in the customer perspectives can be achieved. The objectives in the perspectives and the linkages between the objectives help to understand the strategy, which is necessary for the efficient implementation of the strategic plan. Cost efficiency and improved learning are obvious reasons for the cooperation, but it is difficult to quantify them.

The customer perspective contains two blocks describing the regional development and customer satisfaction. The objectives of the regional development are the competitive advantage of ICT companies and the economic growth of the region. The objectives of customer satisfaction include student satisfaction and employer satisfaction. High quality learning and employment opportunities are sources of student satisfaction. Employers are satisfied with skilled labor. Customer satisfaction provides feedback on how the ICT center is doing. The objectives in the financial, internal processes, and learning perspectives have to be achieved to achieve the desired outcome in the customer perspective.

The financial perspective includes the objectives of funding from central government, external funding and cost-efficiency. An important objective of the ICT center is to increase the cost efficient activities so that the HEIs can improve the quality and provide better service for companies. The external funding is primarily used to finance research and development. The funding from central government is used to finance education. The funding is a prerequisite for the internal processes but, on the other hand, the cost effective processes ensure sufficient funding.

Copyright © 2007, Idea Group Inc. Copying or distributing in print or electronic forms without written permission of Idea Group Inc. is prohibited.

The internal processes perspective includes the objective cooperation of HEIs. It also includes the sequential process of research and development and high quality learning. Each HEI identifies and develops its strengths. Overlapping activities are avoided and cooperation between the HEIs is carried out. The cost efficient organization of education makes it possible to increase the resources used in research and development.

The learning perspective includes the objective focused capabilities of each HEI. Each HEI has its own historical background. The ICT center provides shared premises, which afford better possibilities to develop and intensify the cooperation between the HEIs. The strengthening of the capabilities of the personnel is the driver for the objectives in the internal processes perspective.

The strategy map was used in a press conference by the representative of Turku Polytechnic. It helped the journalists to understand the objectives of the ICT center. The analytical presentation got plenty of publicity in the media (e.g., Karvonen, 2004; KunnallisSuomi, 2005). The strategy map was also used in many meetings arranged during the construction of the new ICT building. It helped the persons involved in the project to create a shared knowledge and joint understanding of the efforts and steps needed to reach the strategic objectives.

Figure 1. The strategy map of the ICT center

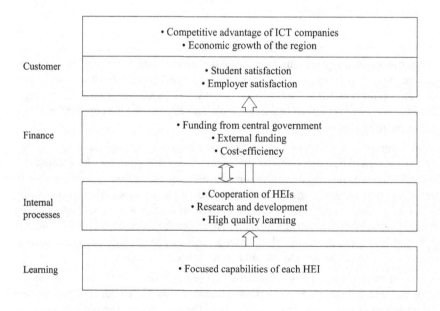

Copyright © 2007, Idea Group Inc. Copying or distributing in print or electronic forms without written permission of Idea Group Inc. is prohibited.

Strategic Initiatives to Implement the Strategy

Managers typically specify short-term milestones along the strategic path. Once targets for measures have been set, it is possible to assess whether the short or medium-term targets can be achieved by challenging resources in annual budgets to achieve them. If the managers conclude that by solving local problems for continuous improvement of the internal processes, the targets cannot be achieved, then there is a need for long-term development.

In order to satisfy customer needs and improve the competitive advantage of customers, the goal for the strategic initiative should focus on substantial cost reductions and quality improvements. In the longer run, managers should develop or reengineer processes that could be critical to the organization's strategic success, rather than merely applying process redesign where minor gains might be obtained. The managers should link the investment decisions to their strategic plans and long-term priorities. They should be committed to achieving the objectives and at the same time accountable for achieving the organizational vision by directing significant resources.

Strategic initiatives can be planned in a balanced way to effectively implement the strategy. All the necessary objects of the different perspectives must be taken into account. The essence of the strategic initiative is to develop the internal processes to achieve the desired strategic objectives and value for customers. However, sufficient funding is needed to develop internal processes. In addition, sufficient coherence and learning are needed to maintain strategic awareness and capabilities for the change.

The first plans to establish the center were made at the end of the 1990s in order to increase the competitive advantage of the ICT companies and economic growth in the region. The measures were planned in numerous meetings, where specific targets were described and agreed. Precise steps were gradually taken, and a timetable was planned and responsibilities were assigned to named groups and individuals.

Turku Polytechnic was the first institution to commit to the investment in 2002. Shortly after that the University of Turku and Åbo Akademi University made their decisions gradually so that the construction of the new building of more than 30,000 square meters of floor space could be started in 2004. A property developer, Kiinteistö Oy ICT, was established in 2004 to own the building and rent the premises to the HEIs. The construction work will be completed soon and the cooperation can be started from 2006.

Conclusion

For several years the various organizational units had a long planning process, which led to mutual understanding about the need to invest in the ICT center. The City of Turku played an active role in the planning of the ICT center to the area of the Turku Science Park, where the educational institutions are located. Each educational institution, however, made their own plans separately and took their own investment decisions following the mutual understanding and commitment to build the ICT center.

Copyright © 2007, Idea Group Inc. Copying or distributing in print or electronic forms without written permission of Idea Group Inc. is prohibited.

The strategy of cost-effectiveness combined with the strategy of focus is the basis for the overall strategy of the ICT center. According to the general strategic statement the center strengthens the expertise of HEIs and increases the competitive advantage of companies in the global markets, so that each HEI develops its strengths to better serve its customers and the increased cooperation of HEIs enables cost-effective and high-quality operations.

In this case, the balanced scorecard approach is a useful tool to describe and communicate the strategy. It can also be used to accomplish its strategic themes, objectives and measures for the partnership projects. It turns out that the balanced scorecard can also help the institutions to plan a common strategy for the several departments operating in the same center. It assists the senior executive teams of the educational institutions in specifying objectives and allocating resources to achieve the objectives.

The strategy map is a useful tool to translate the strategic statement and strategic themes into a graphic representation which clearly describes the objectives in the different perspectives of the balanced scorecard. Furthermore, the strategy map describes the linkages between the objectives and helps the personnel and external stakeholders to understand why the ICT center has been established and specific objectives have been set and how these can be achieved.

This study shows that the planning period of an investment may last for several years, but in this case it took only 4-5 years. However, sufficient time is needed to describe and quantify the different needs of educational institutions. It is paradoxical that the construction takes much less time than the planning. Unfortunately the balanced scorecard approach was found only at the very end of the planning period. The experiences of this study show that rigorous planning methodology is needed to shorten the planning period and fulfill the various needs of the cooperative partners.

References

Chandler, A. D. (1990). *Scale and scope: The dynamics of industrial capitalism*. Cambridge, MA: Belknap Press.

Collis, D. J., & Montgomery, C. A. (1995, July-August). Competing on resources: Strategy in the 1990's. *Harvard Business Review*, pp. 118-128.

Davies, B., & Ellison, L. (2003). *The new strategic direction and development of the school*. London: RoutledgeFalmer.

Fidler, B. (2002). Strategic management for school development. London: Paul Chapman Publishing.

Frigio, M. L., & Krumwiede, K. (1999, February-March). Balanced scorecard: A rising trend in strategic performance measurement, *Journal of Strategic Performance Measurement*, pp. 42-48.

Goold, M., Campbell, A., & Alexander, M. (1994). *Corporate-level strategy: Creating value in the multibusiness company*. New York: John Wiley & Sons.

Copyright © 2007, Idea Group Inc. Copying or distributing in print or electronic forms without written permission of Idea Group Inc. is prohibited.

Gumport, P. J., & Sporn, B. (1999). Institutional adaption: Demands for management reform and university administration. In J. C. Smart (Series Ed.), *Higher education: Handbook of theory and research, Vol. XIV* (pp. 103-145). New York: Agathon Press.

Kaplan, R., & Norton, D. (1992, January-February). The balanced scorecard: Measures that drive performance. *Harvard Business Review*, pp. 71-79.

Kaplan, R., & Norton, D. (1993, September-October). Putting the balanced scorecard to work. *Harvard Business Review*, pp. 134-147.

Kaplan, R., & Norton, D. (1996). *The balanced scorecard*. Boston: Harvard Business School Press.

Kaplan, R., & Norton, D. (2001). *The strategy-focused organization*. Boston: Harvard Business School Press.

Kaplan, R., & Norton, D. (2004). *Strategy maps*. Boston: Harvard Business School Press.

Karvonen, T. (2004, October 15). ICT-talo kokoaa alan opetuksen ja tutkimuksen Turussa, *Talous Sanomat, IT viikko*, p. 1.

Kettunen, J. (2002). Competitive strategies in higher education. *Journal of Institutional Research, 11*(2), 38-47.

Kettunen, J. (2003). Strategic evaluation of institutions by students in higher education. *Perspectives: Policy and Practice in Higher Education, 7*(1), 14-18.

Kettunen, J. (2004). The strategic evaluation of regional development. *Assessment and Evaluation in Higher Education, 29*(3), 357-368.

Kettunen, J., & Kantola, I. (2005). Management information system based on the balanced scorecard. *Campus-Wide Information Systems, 22*(5), 263-274.

KunnallisSuomi. (2005, January). Informaatioteknologia leimaa nykyaikaista oppimi-sympäristöä (Information technology characterized the modern learning environment), p. 20.

Lingle, J. H., & Shieman, W. A. (1996, March). From balanced scorecards to strategic gauges: Is measurement worth it? *Management Review*, pp. 56-62.

Minzberg, H. (1987, July-August). Crafting strategy. *Harvard Business Review*, pp. 66-75.

Peters, T. (1988). *Thriving on chaos: A handbook for management revolution*. London: Macmillan.

Pfeffer, J. (1997). *New directions for organizational theory*. New York: Oxford University Press.

Porter, M. (1990). *The competitive advantage of nations*. London: Macmillan.

Porter, M. (1996, November-December). What is strategy? *Harvard Business Review*, pp. 61-78.

Porter, M. (1998). *On competition*. Boston: Harvard Business School Press.

Puustelli, P. (2002). *Synergialla alueellista vaikuttavuutta, Selvitys Turun yliopistojen ja ammattikorkeakoulujen välisestä yhteistyöstä*, (Synergy creates external regional impact, A study about the cooperation of the universities and polytechnics in Turku)

Copyright © 2007, Idea Group Inc. Copying or distributing in print or electronic forms without written permission of Idea Group Inc. is prohibited.

(University of Turku, Pulbications of the Rector's Office)2/2002. Turku: University of Turku.

Rucci, A. J., Kirn, S. P., & Quinn, R. T. (1998, January-February). The employee-customer-profit chain at Sears. *Harvard Business Review*, pp. 82-97.

Tolbert, P. S. (1985). Institutional environments and resource dependence: Sources of administrative structure in institutions of higher education. *Administrative Science Quarterly*, 30(1), 1-13.

Treacy, M., & Wiersema, F. (1995). *The discipline of market leaders: Choose your customers, narrow your focus, dominate your market*. Reading, MA: Addison-Wesley.

West-Burnham, J. (1994). Strategy, policy, and planning. In T. Bush & J. West-Burnham (Eds.), *The principles of educational management* (pp. 77-99). Harlow: Longman.

Wheale, J. (1991). *Generating income for educational institutions: A business planning approach*. London: Kogan Page.

Copyright © 2007, Idea Group Inc. Copying or distributing in print or electronic forms without written permission of Idea Group Inc. is prohibited.

Chapter III

ICT-Based Learning:
A Basic Ingredient for Socio-Economic Empowerment

Hakikur Rahman, SDNP, Bangladesh

Abstract

ICT mediated learning provides utilities for achieving the goal of education for all, and in turn acts as an enabler in reducing the digital divide, reducing poverty, and promoting social inclusion. However, the integration of ICTs in education deserves considerable investment in time and resources. Consequently, during planning to integrate ICTs in evidence-based information for making sound decisions by the end users incorporate extensive research and sharing of critical information along different phases of planning. Furthermore, implementation of ICT based learning demands in depth analysis and intelligent feedback of the processes. Technology does not improve learning in a straight way and the fundamental question remains always unanswered, in assessing the effectiveness of ICTs or assessing the effectiveness of instructional treatments that were initially (and effectively) less than perfect. This chapter has tried to critically analyze the effective role of ICT methods in learning and put forwards several success cases of learning mechanisms that assisted in socioeconomic empowerment and at the same time, provided a few futuristic recommendations in establishing similar endeavors in promising economies.

Copyright © 2007, Idea Group Inc. Copying or distributing in print or electronic forms without written permission of Idea Group Inc. is prohibited.

Introduction

ICTs can increase access to information and this information helps communities to work more productively as well as in new opportunities. Increasing common people's access to ICTs should involve increasing availability of ICT infrastructure where most of them live. The infrastructure should be highly subsidized for at least a number of years so that the investment costs are not passed on to the end users (Mijumbi, 2002).

ICT can improve the learning process by making it faster, cheaper, and wider reaching that were not possible before. This form of learning can be treated as an interactive process among many entities and supporting the improvement of this process is expected to produce better results. However, innovative processes have to be incorporated both in terms of pedagogy and technology. Pedagogy should be universal and technology should give ubiquitous access with ambient intelligence.

In the area of education and training several hundred projects with thousands of participants around the globe have produced acceptable results in the areas of general education, specialized skill development training, and life long learning and have contributed positively to horizontal issues such as standards, metadata, interoperability, and sustainability.

Among them in 2001, an ambitious project, Prometeus, was built to establish a forum for expert opinions where participants from a wide range of countries, activities, professions, cultures, and languages productively interact towards the establishment of a community of cooperation in the field of educational technology and applications. All those contributions were taken into consideration and the contributors referenced in a position paper. Its aim was to bridge the gap between research and actual use of learning technologies, content and services, through direct contribution in a open consultation process (Bottino, 2001).

In 2002, Appeal launched a project on ICT Application for Non-Formal Education Programs with the support of the Japanese Funds-in-Trust. During its first phase, five countries (Indonesia, Lao PDR, Sri Lanka, Thailand, and Uzbekistan) implemented programs and activities to empower communities through the effective use of ICT.

However, in 2003 a study in this area entitled "Quality and e-learning in Europe training" was conducted and found that through a survey among 433 teachers and trainers from public and private sectors, about 61% felt that the quality of e-learning was fair or poor (Attwell, 2005). So, investment in this sector will remain a fair trade for many investors, including the development partners.

Therefore, the shift to the information society throws new challenges for learning processes and acquisition of knowledge through learning. In a society where information is becoming a strategic raw material and knowledge a value added product, how this resource is used is critical to the performance potential of each entrepreneur. The information and communication media provide necessary technologies to make knowledge available worldwide and transform the information society into a knowledge society. However, in response to individual needs, it is becoming increasingly important to harness appropriate information and systematize knowledge. A falling "half-life" of knowledge formulates life-long learning and up-to-date information becomes critical. Hence, in times of increasing globalization and networking, flexible access to information must be guaranteed at any place and at any time (Massey, 2003).

Copyright © 2007, Idea Group Inc. Copying or distributing in print or electronic forms without written permission of Idea Group Inc. is prohibited.

In this context, economic freedom plays an important role, in addition to technology update and information management. The 2006 Index of Economic Freedom measures 161 countries against a list of 50 independent variables divided into 10 broad factors in terms of economic freedom. The higher the score on a factor, the greater the level of government interference in the economy and the less economic freedom a country enjoys. In the ranking the top five countries (with lower scores between 1.28 and 1.74) are Hong Kong, Singapore, Ireland, Luxembourg, and United Kingdom, whereas North Korea, Iran, Burma, Zimbabwe, Libya, and Venezuela are among the bottom five (with higher scores between 5.00 and 4.16)[1]. This shows the level of ICT improvement in those countries, especially applicable to Hong Kong and Singapore in Asia.

The European Union has taken a lead role in reforming its member countries, improving their ICT situation, and establishing enhanced learning processes through ICT. The diverse e-learning visions, experiments and programs launched by individuals, organizations, institutions, nation-states of EU are found to be potentially more efficient in fostering flexible learning than traditional methods. The dominant view of e-learning has been, therefore, purely instrumental in legitimizing its *raison d'etre* as an ideal method to match the learner's choice and demand with more autonomy (Apollon, 2005).

The process of integrating ICT in the lower level of the education system involves a paradigm shift with new insights and new challenge facilitating new forms of understanding through earlier understandings to create new perspectives and interpretations. Integration should also incorporate an embedding of ICT in the institute's organizational structures and the organization of teaching (Walsh, 2002).

With the development of ICT a new brand of leaders are emerging, in instructional and transformational forms through commitment and enthusiasm for learning, working in partnership with colleagues across the curriculum to embed ICT into the learning process. These leaders have often come up very quickly through their ranks and subsequently their ICT skills have been learned on the job (Walsh, 2002).

At the same time, there is a growing interest with regards to ICTs being used to extend educational opportunities in developing countries. While many governments paid specific attention to integrate ICTs into compulsory schooling during the 1990s, more recently the focus has been shifted to post-secondary (K12) education. In essence ICTs need to be encouraged to make post-secondary teaching and learning more effective and more equitable by offering a diverse range of learning opportunities to a diverse range of learners in a convenient and cost-effective manner (Selwynn, 2003).

Henceforth, the ability to continue to learn throughout life is seen as a prerequisite to the development and sustainability of knowledge economies as countries, corporations, and communities require workers and citizens with flexible, *just-in-time* skills, competencies, and knowledge. Particularly the need for diverse and accessible learning opportunities has drawn policy makers in many countries towards the use of ICT as an educational delivery mechanism (Selwynn, 2003).

ICT-based learning can be formal (institutionally sponsored and structured), non-formal (non-credential but still institutionally-based and structured) or informal (happens incidentally or during everyday activities). This form of learning can, therefore, take place in the office, institution, home, or community, at different times for different purposes (Selwynn, 2003).

Copyright © 2007, Idea Group Inc. Copying or distributing in print or electronic forms without written permission of Idea Group Inc. is prohibited.

Hence, attempting to encourage full and effective participation of all stakeholders in ICT based education now forms a central part of current educational and economic policymaking in most developed countries (Selwynn, 2003). ICT in learning processes should not merely be used to acquire knowledge and skills; the processes should be more interactive and self-directed uses of ICTs should be encouraged so that the learners can actively construct new ideas, concepts, and meaning while transforming their existing knowledge (Rosen, 1998).

Background

Learning is the cognitive process of acquiring knowledge[2] or skill through study, experience, or teaching. It is a process that depends on experience and leads to long-term changes in behavior potential. Behavior potential describes the possible behavior of an individual (not actual behavior) in a given situation in order to achieve a goal[3].

ICT-mediated learning is a process used to acquire data, information, skills, or knowledge. It is a form of learning that enables learning in a virtual world where technology merges with human creativity to accelerate and leverage the rapid development and application of deep knowledge[4]. ICT-based learning covers a wide set of applications and processes such as Web-based learning, computer-mediated learning, virtual classrooms, and digital collaboration. It includes the delivery of content via Internet, intranet/extranet (LAN/WAN), audio and videotape, satellite broadcast, interactive TV, PDA, mobile phone, CD-ROM, and other available technologies[5]. This chapter, specifically focuses on ICT-based learning to enable empowerment and socioeconomic development.

Empowerment is the process and practice of deriving power from within the self, or assisting others to do so through power within[6]. It is the process of equipping communities with knowledge, skills, and resources in order to change and improve the quality of their own lives and their community. Empowerment may evolve from within or it may be facilitated and supported through external agencies[7]. However, in terms of knowledge acquisition, empowerment is a consequence of liberatory learning and created within the emerging praxis in which co-learners are also engaged. The theoretical basis of this process is provided by critical consciousness; its expression is collective action on behalf of mutually agreed upon goals. Empowerment through knowledge is distinct from building skills and competencies that are being commonly associated with conventional schooling. Education for empowerment differs from schooling both in its emphasis on collective participation (rather than individuals) and in its focus on cultural transformation (rather than social adaptation)[8].

Whereas, socioeconomics is the study of the social and economic impacts of any product or service offering, market promotion or other activity on an economy as a whole and on the entrepreneurs, organization and individuals who are its main economic actors. These effects can usually be measured in economic and statistical terms, such as growth in the size of the economy, the number of jobs created (or reduced), or levels of home ownership or Internet penetration (or number of telephones per inhabitant); and in measurable social terms such as life expectancy or levels of education[9]. This chapter provides emphasis on raising socioeconomic capacity of the economic actors through learning: information, content and knowledge; to lead into a knowledge-based economy.

Copyright © 2007, Idea Group Inc. Copying or distributing in print or electronic forms without written permission of Idea Group Inc. is prohibited.

Table 1. Initiatives taken by EC for ICT-based learning

Year	Groups/Councils	Strategies Taken
2000	Lisbon Council	To form the most competitive and dynamic knowledge-based economy
2001	Ministers of Education	To achieve coherent community cooperation in the fields of education and training
2001	Working Group on ICT in education and training	To work on indicators and benchmarks, exchanging good practices and peer review
2002	Standing Group on Indicators and Benchmarks	Indicators and benchmarks were developed to monitor the progress
2003	Working Group on ICT in education and training	Focused on policy practices aiming at better quality education through integration of ICT

A dynamic knowledge-based economy is capable of sustainable economic growth, but to achieve it, the economy not only needs a radical transformation within it, but also a modernized education system. The Lisbon Council of European Commission (EC) envisioned this in their March 2000 meeting, while in 2002 the EC stated that by 2010 Europe would be the world leader in terms of the quality of its education and training systems. To achieve this, a fundamental transformation of education and training has been taking place throughout Europe (European Commission, 2004). ICT-based education always demands a longer term strategy which the EC has initiated in 2000[10]. This strategy has been taken with a 10-year work plan to be implemented through an open method of coordination aiming at coherent community strategic framework of cooperation in the field of education and training. To support the implementation of the shared objectives for education and training systems at the national level through exchanges of "good practices," study tours, peer reviews, and so forth[11], EC has been working through twelve working groups since 2000.

Table 1 (*above*) shows a few initiatives taken by the European Commission to enhance the ICT-based learning in Europe. To date, the whole work has been carried out in four stages:

- First, decide upon key issues on which to focus future work.

- Second, focused on good practices and sharing policies to develop better quality education through ICT.

- Third, gather good policies and formulate recommendations learning from their problems.

- Fourth, gather examples to map those recommendations on good policy practices[12].

Integrating ICT in learning can mean anything from complete online training, with specific learning platforms using virtual microworlds and laboratories, to online access to and control of distant physical set ups such as cyber kiosks, or telecenters, or physics laboratories. This form of learning may also include a face-to-face situation in a laboratory with digital

Copyright © 2007, Idea Group Inc. Copying or distributing in print or electronic forms without written permission of Idea Group Inc. is prohibited.

Table 2. Non-Capital investment for learning in EU countries (Source: The Learning Citizen, 2003)

Items	Increase in 2001	Increase in 2002
Spending on training products and services	7%	7%
Raise in e-learning content	70%	50%
Growth rate of e-learning products expenditure	17%	23%

controls and computer-based mathematical tools. However, the question will remain: How is ICT-mediated learning taken into account by current school architecture decisions, or what are the priorities in setting up costly permanent establishments that will include such ICT-based activities?

Hence, the objectives for ICT based learning should be "to develop technologies to empower individuals and organizations to build competencies to explicit the opportunities of tomorrow's knowledge society. This is achieved by focusing on the improvement of the learning process for individuals and organizations, and of the intertwined learning process between individuals and organizations" (The Learning Citizen, 2003, p. 2).

Table 2 (*above*) illustrates a few figures on non-capital investment of the European Union (EU) for learning purposes.

In this way, the ICT (specifically, the WWW, or the Internet) offers itself as a tool to increase formal education as well as "ambient" learning that may be treated as electronic-mediated learning, or e-learning. During a survey done by the Oxford Internet Institute (OII), 78% of users say they use the Internet to look up a fact, while 47% say they look up the definition of a word. Nearly 40% of the respondents say they use the Internet to find information for school, and 20% of them use it for distance learning (OII, 2005).

Main Thrust

Given the critical changes in education and given the potential of ICT, it is vital that policies and strategies in the area of ICT be driven by long-term educational objectives, such as:

- ICT supported learning provisions in the services sector.
- ICT inclusive educational policies.
- ICT conducive research programs incorporating solutions to problem locale.
- Optimal use of ICT for educational purposes.
- Integrating ICT in bringing fundamental transformations in education.

Copyright © 2007, Idea Group Inc. Copying or distributing in print or electronic forms without written permission of Idea Group Inc. is prohibited.

Transformations with ICT can be limited to learner-centered multimedia learning, without changing the school curriculum and progressively invalidating the changes. Thus, school reform is not a spontaneous consequence of the introduction of ICT in education. Furthermore, as learners enter into education system with a growing ICT familiarity, the definition of basic skills, to be addressed by the educational integration of ICT, needs to embrace more and more higher-order thinking skills. Therefore, a global vision of ICT supported education has to be prepared for common citizens to actively take part in an increasing communication setting to improve their own values and thoughts. In this context, utilizing available utility software, exciting ICT-based e-learning materials can be developed with an absolute minimum of effort.

The main thrust of this chapter comprises of a few case studies that are being treated as success stories in the aspect of ICT mediated learning, and at the same time act as empowering tool in terms of socioeconomic development. Emphasis has been given to incorporate cases that involve ICT for community learning, and they have been portrayed with analytic approach. It is expected that these cases will be able to justify inclusion of ICTs in community learning and regional development.

Case Studies

Case 1

Asia Pacific Information Network (APIN)
> *A regional network working to achieve information for all*

Among key five areas of interests, one is to promote ICT literacy and the application of ICT in education, science, culture, and communication.

Broad aims are to:

- Encourage the development of strategies, policies, infrastructures, human resources, and tools for application of ICTs.
- Prepare policy advice to member states for use of ICT in national targets,especially for improvement of education, (APIN, 2004).

Specific focus areas are to:

- Promote ICT based learning opportunities for all.
- Enhance learning opportunities through access to diversified contents and delivery systems.
- Assist in establishing networks for learners and educators.

Copyright © 2007, Idea Group Inc. Copying or distributing in print or electronic forms without written permission of Idea Group Inc. is prohibited.

- Assist in promoting universal and equitable access to scientific knowledge.
- Support the development of code of practice involving scientific information chain by using ICT.
- Strengthen capacities for scientific research, information and knowledge sharing. (APIN, 2004)

Case 2

Adult Basic Education (ABE)

Integrates the use of ICT into teaching practices for organizational realignment and empowerment

Established in 1990, ABE provided ICT supported courses in the South Wales Valleys in UK that is a post-industrial area with low levels of education, widespread illiteracy and innumeracy in adult population and growing digital divide. The program has established

Table 3. ICT based ABE courses during 1997-2002 (Adapted from Harris, 2002)

Year and Duration of Courses	Courses	Activities
1997-98, 4 hrs/week	Internet Club	• Web browsing and searching • email • HTML authoring
1998-99, 6 hrs/week	Internet Club2	• Web browsing and searching • Email • HTML authoring • Computer graphics • 3D Animation
1999-2000, 8 hrs/week	Internet Club3 under network	• Web browsing and searching • Email • HTML authoring • Computer graphics • 3D Animation
2000-01, 16 hrs/week	• Computer Club • Creative Computation • Web workshops	• Web browsing and searching • Email • HTML authoring • Computer graphics • Digital Video • Computer Programming
2001-02, 24 hrs/week	• Computer Club • Creative Computation • Web workshops • Film workshops • DTP workshops	• Web browsing and searching • Email • HTML authoring • Computer graphics • Digital Video • Computer Programming • Desk Top Publishing

Copyright © 2007, Idea Group Inc. Copying or distributing in print or electronic forms without written permission of Idea Group Inc. is prohibited.

community based Open Learning Centres (OLCs) dedicated to teaching basic literacy, communication, and numeric skills to adult groups. It introduced a network of personal computers with broadband Internet since 1997 and gradually led to the design and development of many innovative courses utilizing multimedia technologies. This has created increased participation of learners, tutors, and volunteers resulting in changes to the structure of learning content and techniques acting as a catalyst among the adult communities (Harris, 2002).

Table 3 shows the ICT based courses that evolved since its inception in 1997. This table not only shows the necessary modification of courses to meet the demand of the community throughout this period, but also adjusted contents that show the development trend of ICT based courses.

Case 3

Gateshead Testbed Learning Communities (GTLC)

Demonstrates how communities and individuals develop through learning and share good practices in UK[13].

Priority areas are to:

- Build on success.
- Listen to local demands and needs.
- Recognize all aspects and levels of community learning.
- Recognize barriers and address them properly.
- Improve quality of life, not just qualifications.
- Unlock national digital resources.
- Encourage establishment of remotely based stations with subsidies.

Case 4

EdComNet (Humanistic Urban Communal Educational Net)[14]

Aims to enhance the participant's sense of autonomy and dialogical belonging

Based on Autonomy Oriented Education (AOE) for personal empowerment and personal growth, users of this network actively utilize Internet content and features for their learning processes to reflect and explore elements of self and the alternatives available. According to AOE, gaining knowledge is to learn as per a personal plan that stems from one's self knowledge, and it portrays one's personal interests, performance styles, and capabilities. EdComNet incorporates AOE principles and offers an empowerment tool for the European Citizen.

Copyright © 2007, Idea Group Inc. Copying or distributing in print or electronic forms without written permission of Idea Group Inc. is prohibited.

Case 5

EducaNext[15]

Supports acquisition of high skills as per demand of the European industry and need of the global market

This program supports the creation and sharing of knowledge between educators. It also enables collaboration among the participants by providing a complete package of services to support the exchange and delivery of learning resources. EducaNext acts as a collaboration facilitator and at the same time as a marketplace. It is primarily considered as a business-to-business service and enables partnerships among institutes of higher education and industry to provide the right expertise at the right time.

Case 6

Pan Asia Network (PAN) in Bhutan[16]

Establishment of ICT supported distance education

In 2003, PAN started a project supporting Bhutan's National Institute of Education (NIE) to establish ICT based distance education programme for educators. The project developed and tested appropriate ICT based learning support system and assessed whether ICTs improve the quality of and access to learning. The project aims to implement 16 distance education courses, including development of online tutorials, support services, counseling services, and multimedia contents. This project also emphasized the development of key performance indicators for distance educators, especially for those that may be replicated across the PAN regions (PAN, 2005).

Case 7

Scottish Workforce Empowerment for Lifelong Learners (SWELL) Project[17]

Promotes lifelong learning for working people in Scotland

The project has successfully facilitated new learning opportunities to more than 700 learners till May 2005 across Scotland's urban and rural labor markets. SWELL support has enabled partners to develop and deliver innovative learning solutions, by empowering "non-traditional" learners through offering new opportunities to the disadvantaged communities; learners that are remotely located, with disability, not adequately literate, and jobless. The organizational leadership has been carried out efficiently through innovation, transnationality, mainstreaming, empowerment and equal opportunity. The most successful SWELL activities have involved mainstreaming education providers to deliver a wide ranging and

Copyright © 2007, Idea Group Inc. Copying or distributing in print or electronic forms without written permission of Idea Group Inc. is prohibited.

high quality training provision. It has contributed to a "community of learning" by equality of learning opportunities through ICT (McQuaid & Lindsay, 2005).

Case 8

S2NET in EU Region[18]

ICT-based learning as a tool for social inclusion

The project prepared a guide to support the target groups in the design, delivery, and evaluation of training actions for disadvantaged individuals, provided directives to develop learners' meta-competencies and train them in order to sustain an empowered attitude towards their practical lives (Dondi, 2003).

Main objectives are to:

- Encourage use of e-learning for training educators and policy makers.
- Support innovation in training and education methods using ICT based learning.
- Promote good practices in the use of ICT for real life application.
- Raise awareness on e-learning to prevent social exclusion.

Case 9

e-learning for sustainable development by IGES (Institute for Global Environmental Strategies)

Promotes community-based learning for sustainability

This project provides community learning programme on sustainable development through ICT. E-courses are designed for teachers novice in computer-based learning and these courses act as stand alone training material replacing face-to-face trainings on community learning. The course content is built based on ten years experience of the Institute of Sustainable Communities, USA in Central and Eastern Europe, USA, and Japan[19].

Future Issues

The question about the quality of ICT based learning remains opaque and fraught with difficulties. These difficulties further compounded when it comes to evaluate the quality of the use of ICT for learning en masse. However, the development of ICT based learning products and opportunities are rapidly expanding in areas of education and skill development. The

Copyright © 2007, Idea Group Inc. Copying or distributing in print or electronic forms without written permission of Idea Group Inc. is prohibited.

media varies from intranet, Internet, multimedia, email, interactive TV, teleconferencing, video conferencing, or other computer mediated learning methods[20]. But, until now innovative approaches have been missing to evaluate the development, growth, impact, and potential of this form of education system. Despite global efforts in diversified platforms, distance education or e-learning, or ICT based learning has not attained a suitable state; governments remain hesitant (often mismanaged or misguided) in funding, private investors behave in unfamiliar ways, and development actors stay away from investing in this sector.

In the near future, education will be online or at least blended with online teaching and learning activities. However, the strategies should focus on constraints and normalization of educational interactions, without much restricting on initial investments. Similarly, standardization of education system should be object oriented and encouraging. Learning models should pass through technical and quality as standards, rather than just *industrialization* or *professionalization* and focus on extensive research to achieve fundamental educational objectives.

The opening to higher education should ensure better links between education and research. Higher education has to be at the forefront of knowledge production, management, and dissemination. Moreover, the use of ICT in education at all levels requires new pedagogical and organizational settings. Therefore, cross-partnership among education, social science, pure science and within different fields of research is needed.

Innovative e-learning should aim to empower the lifelong learners and vocational trainees. This form of ambient learning provides access to high quality learning materials suiting individual's demand and pace. To achieve this, ICT based learning should utilize multimodal broadband access and content management. Furthermore, the provision of content integration will allow access to new e-learning materials, as well as existing resources from those repositories (Paraskakis, 2005). There is a need to develop policies and action plans in using technological and non-technological means to address the social, economic, and cultural factors underlying educational problems. There are also clear needs to redevelop educational and pedagogical understandings on effective ICT across life long learning in its many forms (Selwynn, 2003).

Conclusion

Looking at the success cases around the globe, it is apparent that educational policy makers are tempted to deal with ICT based learning as a potent bridging method used to flexibilize individuals and make them adequate to the needs of the community, thus empowering them to act as an element of socioeconomic development. The main educational, social, and economic discourse related to new professional, social, and learning needs tends, therefore, to relapse recurrently into the flexibilization rhetoric, according to which the adaptability of the new demand evolves, if one adopts this perspective to a new flexibility of individual's desire (Apollon, 2005).

Copyright © 2007, Idea Group Inc. Copying or distributing in print or electronic forms without written permission of Idea Group Inc. is prohibited.

The development of e-learning up to this point has been largely demand driven, the two principal players being the technology and the content. Perhaps for this reason the majority of products developed in this sector have followed two basic and well-tried business models, by providing:

- Distance education to individuals, which is a technologically enhanced continuation of the previous correspondence course model;
- Online environments to permit existing educational institutions in extending their services through the use of virtual classroom.

The technology driven and network intensive nature of these *virtual classrooms* however, restricts the number of users to those who have specialist, up to date equipment and broadband access, shutting out the majority of marginal learners. Furthermore, in both models e-learning approaches are based on assumptions about the pedagogical focus and organizational structure of existing educational institutions, rather than potentially validated research (PROMETEUS, 2003).

Many recommendations floated around focusing the potential for development of more appropriate ways of learning through ICT, but at the same time suffered the lack of a solid framework of learning theory in providing a more comprehensive and less anecdotic understanding. Only in this way can it be ensured that many positive experiences taking place already across the globe can be reproduced in other countries. There are thousands of handbooks on e-learning but they lack good validated research. In this context, intensive analysis of e-learning processes is needed and particularly there is a need for a conceptual framework for lifelong learning, and for the development of models derived from non formal settings and self organizing communities of learners (PROMETEUS, 2003).

To realize that ICT is not another passing fad or innovation, which might or might not affect learning and to be able to change the way the institutions work accordingly, is perhaps one of the most important requisites for leaders in this field. Emphasis should be given in communicating the vision, and at the same time efforts should be given for skills development and involvement of all teaching and non teaching staff who might have come through the conventional system of learning (Walsh, 2002).

ICT based education and training leads to improved learning environment. However, as with most research on education and technology the effectiveness of ICT-based mass learning is still fragmented. It is also suggested that learning with ICT leads to a more reflective, insightful learning with more empowered and democratic diffusion amongst learners (Doubler, Harlen, Harlen, Paget & Asbell-Clarke, 2003; Jeris, 2002) as well as proving to be an attractive and motivating medium of learning with basic skills (Lewis & Delcourt, 1998). Furthermore, engagement in e-learning is also leading to wider educational outcomes, such as increases in learners' self-esteem and propensity to engage in further learning. Therefore, as Kennedy-Wallace (p. 49) reminds, "whether learning online in the workplace, in college or at home, e-learning is still about learning and culture, not just technology and infrastructure" is a true reflection of the transformation of communities in this respect.

Copyright © 2007, Idea Group Inc. Copying or distributing in print or electronic forms without written permission of Idea Group Inc. is prohibited.

References

APIN. (2004). *Report of the first statutory meeting of the Asia Pacific Information Network.* Retrieved June 17, 2006, from http://irandoc.ac.ir/apin/constitution.html

Apollon, D. G. (2005, May 10-20). The shape of things to come in learning and e-learning. *Conference on e-learning*, European Commission, Brussels.

Attwell, G. (2005). *Quality and the use of ICT for learning in SMEs, The Wales-Wide Web.* Retrieved June 17, 2006, from http://www.theknownet.com/writing/weblogs/Graham_Atwell/

Bottino, R. M. (2001, September). *PROMETEUS position paper to the open consultation process of the European Commission.*

Chinien, C., & Boutin, F. (2005, July 7-9). Framework for strengthening research in ICT-mediated learning. In *Proceedings of the ITHET 6th Annual International Conference*, Juan Dolio, Dominican Republic.

Dondi, C. (2003). E-learning-me included: How to use e-learning as a tool for social inclusion. *Leornado da Vinci Programme 2000-2006*, European Commission.

Doubler, S., Harlen, W., Harlen, W., Paget, K., & Asbell-Clarke, J. (2003, April 21-25). *When learners learn on-line, what does the facilitator do?* Paper presented at the American Educational Research Association Annual Conference, Chicago, Illinois.

European Commission. (2004, November). *ICT in education and training. Progress Report of Working Group C on Implementation of Education and Training 2010 Work Programme*, Directorate-General for Education and Culture, European Commission.

Harris, S. R. (2002). PD in Ponty: Design-by-doing in adult basic education. In A. Dearden & L. Watts (Eds.), *Proceedings of HCI2004: Design for Life* (Vol.2, pp. 41-44). Bristol: Research Press International.

Jeris, L. (2002). Comparison of power relations within electronic and face-to-face classroom discussions: A case study. *Australian Journal of Adult Learning, 42*(3), 300-311.

Kennedy-Wallace, G. (2002, April 16). E-learning is booming but the UK still lags behind. *Guardian-Education Supplement*, p. 49.

The Learning Citizen. (2003, April-June). *The knowledge citizen* (Forward by J. Christensen, Issue No. 5, p. 2).

Lewis, L., & Delcourt, M. (1998). Adult basic education students' attitudes toward computers. In *Proceedings of the SCUTREA 1998 Conference,* University of Exeter, Devon, UK (pp. 238-242).

Massey, J. (2003). *Lifelong learning: A citizen's views: Quality and e-learning in Europe.* Luxembourg: Office for Official Publication of the European Communities.

McQuaid, R.W., & Lindsay, C. (2005, May). *Evaluating the Scottish Workforce Empowerment for Lifelong Learners (SWELL) Project.* Final evaluation report and quarterly progress report, Employment Research Institute, Edinburgh.

Mijumbi, R. (2002, November 11-14). ICTs as a tool for economic empowerment of women: Experiences from the use of a CD ROM by rural women in Uganda. In *Proceedings*

Copyright © 2007, Idea Group Inc. Copying or distributing in print or electronic forms without written permission of Idea Group Inc. is prohibited.

of the Expert Group Meeting on Information and Communication Technologies and Their Impact on and Use As an Instrument for the Advancement and Empowerment of Women, Seoul, Korea. UN Division for the Advancement of Women (DAW).

OII. (2005). *The Internet in Britain: A survey report of the Oxford Internet Institute on the Oxford Internet Survey (OxIS)*. Oxford, UK: University of Oxford.

PAN. (2005, November). *Connecting people-changing lives in Asia: Pan Asia networking*. Retrieved June 17, 2006, from http://www.idrc.ca/IMAGES/ICT4D/PanAsia/PANA-SIAHTML/

Paraskakis, I. (2005). Ambient learning: A new paradigm for e-learning. In *Proceedings of Recent Research Developments in Learning Technologies*, Formatex 2005. Retrieved June 17, 2006, from http://formatex.org/micte2005/

PROMETEUS. (2003). *PROMETEUS position paper on pedagogical and organizational aspects*. Sixth Framework on Open Consultation Process, European Commission.

Rosen, D. (1998). Using electronic technology in adult literacy education. *The annual review of adult learning and literacy* (vol. 1). Cambridge, MA: NCSALL.

Selwynn, N. (2003, November 12-14). ICT in adult education: Defining the territory. In *Proceedings of the ICT in Non-formal and Adult Education: Supporting Out-of-School Youth and Adults, OECD/NCAL International Roundtable*, Philadelphia, Pennsylvania.

Walsh, K. (2002). *ICT's about learning: School leadership and the effective integration of information and communications technology*. UK: National College for School Leadership.

Endnotes

[1]   Index of Economic Freedom 2006, available at http://www.heritage.org/research/features/index/index.cfm

[2]   wordnet.princeton.edu/perl/webwn

[3]   en.wikipedia.org/wiki/Learning

[4]   www.mountainquestinstitute.com/definitions.htm

[5]   www.cybermediacreations.com/elearning/glossary.htm

[6]   www.soul-dynamics.com/glossary

[7]   www.quest-net.org/glossary.asp

[8]   http://www.trentu.ca/nativestudies/courses/nast305/keyterms.htm

[9]   http://en.wikipedia.org/wiki/socioeconomic

[10]   http://register.consillium.eu.int/pdf/en/01/st05/05980en1.pdf

[11]   http://europa.eu.int/comm/education/policies/2010/objectives_en.html

[12]   http://europa.eu.int/comm/education/policies/2010/objectives_en.html#information

Copyright © 2007, Idea Group Inc. Copying or distributing in print or electronic forms without written permission of Idea Group Inc. is prohibited.

13   http://www.gatesheadgrid.org/testbed/

14.   http://learningcitizen.net/download/LCCN_Newsletter_N5.pdf; http://www.calt. insead.edu/project/EdComNet/; http://www.isoc.org.il/docs/eva_anex1.pdf

15.   http://www.prolearn-project.org/links/list; http://projekte.l3s.uni-hannover.de/pub/ bscw.cgi/d37280/nejdl_learntec_prolearn.final.ppt http://learningcitizen.net/down-load/LCCN_Newsletter_N5.pdf

16.   http://www.pandora-asia.org/panprojects.php?main=panprojects_10.htm

17.   http://www.sfeu.ac.uk/

18.   http://www.menon.org/publications/HELIOS%20thematic%20report-%20Access. pdf

19.   http://cmp.iges.net/learn/faculties/courses/index.php?CMS_Session.html

20.   http://wiki.ossite.org/index.php?title=ICT_and_Learning_in_Small_and_Medium_en-terprises._The_issue_of_learners_needs

Copyright © 2007, Idea Group Inc. Copying or distributing in print or electronic forms without written permission of Idea Group Inc. is prohibited.

Section II

Applications of Technologies

Chapter IV

New ICTs for Conflict Prevention and Management

Ángela-Jo Medina, ConcienciAcción.org, USA

Abstract

This chapter introduces the impact of new information and communication technologies (nICTs), specifically the Internet, on national and international conflict prevention and management. This analysis provides case studies of the use and examples of the prospective use of nICTs to counteract conflict as it undermines social and economic structures and hinders regional development. This study reviews the specific application of nICT-related initiatives at the different phases of the conflict cycle: from addressing the root causes of conflict as a tool for prevention and management, through the reconciliation and reconstruction phase. The author intends this analysis to illustrate and contribute to the discussion of how the social and development-related application of nICTs can compliment existing conflict prevention and management reduction strategies.

Copyright © 2007, Idea Group Inc. Copying or distributing in print or electronic forms without written permission of Idea Group Inc. is prohibited.

Introduction

According to the United Nation's Development Program's Human Development Report the greater part of countries with limited human development, 22 of 32, have experienced violent conflict since 1990 (2005, pp. 149-179). Conflict undermines social and economic structures: public healthcare, education systems, employment, and so forth. Regional development is also one of its victims.

This chapter outlines the uses of new Information and Communication Technologies (nICTs) for the prevention and management of active and latent national and international conflicts. It will demonstrate the application and potential of nICTs to complement activities that are already being carried out in the field to address the root causes of conflict, its prevention and management, as well as the fomentation of reconstruction and reconciliation.

Some of the uses given within the structure of this analysis are the creation of a medium of coherent manifestation, the establishment of a basis for transparent governance, and the development of generic platforms of common interest. Case studies illustrate the actual and prospective use of nICTs in the different phases of the conflict cycle.

The term nICTs is used to designate the Internet individually and/or its conversion with other types of information communication technologies like community radios, television, mobile telephony, and so forth. In this case, however, for the most part, the Internet will be the focus. Nevertheless, later in the chapter, mobile telephony, another very important nICT, will be considered.

Background

Differences of opinion are commonplace and conflict is natural; neither of them is necessarily negative. The crux of the issue is finding and applying methods to prevent and manage these conflicts in a peaceful manner.

Today's intra and inter state conflicts[1] are difficult to analyze, thus difficult to solve. Since the end of the Cold War, the nature of global conflicts has significantly changed[2]. The ethnopolitical, structural, and social factors that cause and transform conflict constitute a complex, ever-changing web. The weakening and/or disintegration of state authority, the existence of third parties that benefit from strife and the many cases in which civilians are the target of violence are constants within this framework. As indicated by Timothy Shaw, "Prospects for regional development recede as conflicts both escalate and proliferate and 'off-budget' incomes and expenditures become priorities for regimes and leaders alike" (2003, p.7).

Society's evolution has expanded the variety of sources and scenarios of conflict and simultaneously increased the number of tools available to deal with them. New information and communication technologies are among these. To date, non-military studies about the impact of nICTs on conflict situations have been few[3]. This possibility results from the Internet which evolved from ARPANET, a military command and control center dating back to the 1960s (Sequeira Bolaño, 2001).

Copyright © 2007, Idea Group Inc. Copying or distributing in print or electronic forms without written permission of Idea Group Inc. is prohibited.

The public eye is quick to hone in on the dangers of the Internet: identity theft, digital crimes, child exploitation and pornography, as well as it being a potential virtual breeding ground for terrorists and insurgents, to name a few. Paradoxically, non-governmental organizations that address human rights, conflict transformation, governance, and development issues, however, have also been quick to adopt nICTs to support their work in the field (Naughton, 2001, pp. 147-168). Similarly, governments are increasingly sensitive to the possible importance of nICTs in official and grassroots interventions directed at preventing and managing ethno-political conflicts. Tony Rutkowsky, former senior Telecommunication Union Executive, has emphasized the potential of the Internet to compensate for many of the structural deficiencies within national and international governing bodies (1997). The Internet creates a common border-free information space where equality is inherent[4].

Issues

For Carment and Schnabel (2003) conflict prevention includes, "institutional mechanisms that prevent tensions from escalating into violent conflict, to employ early warning mechanisms that allow the international community to monitor relations between and within states, and to facilitate capacity building within conflict-prone societies" (p. 1).

Figure 1. The conflict cycle

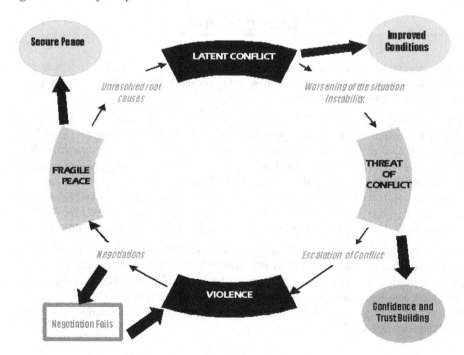

Copyright © 2007, Idea Group Inc. Copying or distributing in print or electronic forms without written permission of Idea Group Inc. is prohibited.

Conflict by nature is non-linear, yet in theory, the line between conflict prevention and conflict management is very distinct. In practice, however, and faithful to the fluctuating nature of conflict itself, this distinction becomes blurred. Figure 1 depicts this reality through an illustration of the conflict cycle. The possibility of diffusing conflict is present at every stage, as is the possibility of escalation.

This difference is even more distorted in the case of the relationship between nICTs and conflict. The problems, actors, and interests change over time because of society's changing dynamics, economies and policies (Vayrynen, 1991, p. 1-25). nICTs to be used in to assist both in the prevention of conflict as well as post-conflict reconstuction and reconcuilation. The room for action for nICTs spans every nuance that affects the conflict cycle and its potential outcome. As Jan Berting notes, information systems penetrate modern societies in all spheres of life (Berting, 1990, pp. 33-36). The line between social structures and technological systems has become increasingly difficult to define.

Conflict Prevention

According to the European Commission, conflict prevention spans from initiatives directed at reacting rapidly to emerging conflicts to those aimed at projecting long-term stability. International cooperation and development initiatives, institution building, and rapid-reaction mechanisms fall under this category. Identifying and addressing the presence of factors that are a breeding ground for conflict—undemocratic political systems, ethnic, cultural and religious tensions, the presence of refugees, a weak or non-existent welfare state, and unequal distribution of resources—in a timely manner is essential.

nICTs are useful in responding to some of these structural—governmental, social, and economic—deficiencies because they serve as a bridge between developed and developing countries. They provide alternative solutions to existing realities, act as a catalyst for social and economic change, and defy geographical limitations. The strategic use of nICTs can encourage existing relationships, foster subtle changes in existing paradigms and mobilize society to reinforce the social perspective towards a community goal or ideal. This approach enables opportunities for early alerts, and pre-emptive measures to deal with the potential sources of conflict.

Difficult socioeconomic conditions are among the root causes of conflict. UN Secretary General Kofi Annan has recognized that "peace and development remain inextricably linked —one feeding on the other, enabling the other and securing the other. The renunciation of violence as a means of gaining and holding power is only the beginning. Then must follow a renewed commitment to national development founded on sober, sound, and uncorrupted economic policies" (United Nations, 1998). The Secretary General says the proposal in his report on Africa requires new ways of thinking, of acting (1998, p. 3). The facts speak for themselves: 50% of the 45 poorest countries in the world have seen their social and economic foundations eroded by wars and other forms of violence ("Breaking the Conflict Trap," 2003). Poverty itself does not generate conflict, but it does generate pressure for change in countries in which there is an unequal distribution of resources. Because of this, the Swedish Cooperation Agency has noted that when development is lacking, countries become more susceptible to conflict.

Copyright © 2007, Idea Group Inc. Copying or distributing in print or electronic forms without written permission of Idea Group Inc. is prohibited.

According to Nobel Prize winner, Amartya Sen, poverty is not limited to lack of income, but includes the lack of skills or capabilities needed to be more productive and obtain higher income (2000). Some of these are basic education, health services, food security, and so forth. nICTs are useful in the development process because they supplement existing development initiatives. They also open new routes to address inequities and existing sources of structural violence. Electronic commerce (e-commerce) contributes to addressing these issues in many ways.

The Internet offers many possibilities for establishment of small and medium-sized businesses. The benefits it offers are immense, as it provides any business an avenue to enter into the global markets. Size and location have become issues of little relevance in finding markets that are receptive to the goods from any business (Heeks, 2002).

Ecosandals.com[5], a cooperative based in the shantytown of Korogocho in Nairobi, Kenya, is a successful example of the use of e-commerce in poverty and violence-stricken areas. This international business is the product of the Wikyo Akala Project, which educates, trains, and provides employment for the inhabitants of Kogorocho. They do this through the production and sale of sandals made from recycled tires that are sold throughout the world from the project's Web site.

PeopLink[6], and Mercado Global[7] are two nonprofit organizations that also seek to foment development and fair trade by helping artisans from remote areas around the world to sell their products via the Internet.

In these examples, e-commerce has dramatically reduced transaction costs, allowed artisans to reach larger numbers of customers, provided a means to build capacities in local communities and ensured the long-term sustainability of the projects. This approach has provided holistic solutions to development and poverty related dilemmas. Unfortunately, the digital divide related problems, such as infrastructure, access, and training (Bastos Tigre & O'Connor, 2002) as well as a lack of regulatory and legal frameworks have made banks and financial institutions reticent to assume a more active role in promoting e-commerce. Their participation, however, remains primordial in many countries to extend the reach and attractiveness of e-commerce and avoid fraud.

Another variable in the solution to the poverty problem is agriculture. It generates earnings for governments by raising the per capita income, foments a more equal growth and, if necessary, provides reparations for the less-fortunate segments of the population particularly when dealing with issues relating to agricultural reform and access to natural resources (Addison, 2005).

Regardless of location, farmers need access to certain types of information to maximize productivity and comprehend and take advantage of market trends. The Food and Agriculture Organization (FAO) of the United Nations' Global Information and Early Warning System[8] provides timely information on production, trade, stocks, food consumption, food aid requirements and the status thereof from each sub-region in the world. This enables governments, the international community, and other organizations to tailor their actions to existing situations and avoid potential crises.

Research has shown that wages increased by a worldwide average of 10% per year of schooling, and educated parents are more likely to have educated children. Education is an important key in breaking the inter-generational poverty cycle. Worldwide, there are one billion youth between the ages of 15-24, and 85% of them live in developing countries. Their

Copyright © 2007, Idea Group Inc. Copying or distributing in print or electronic forms without written permission of Idea Group Inc. is prohibited.

unemployment and under-employment rates tend to be much higher than that of the average population. Young people with limited education and employment opportunities fall prey to groups involved in violent conflict that seek to increase their numbers. This is particularly disturbing since, according to UNESCO, over 27 million children and youth that are in the midst of, or recovering from, conflict lack access to formal schooling (Roberts, 2005). In this situation, e-learning can be found very useful in providing learning opportunities for young people because of its flexible delivery method and can be easily adapted to the demands of their day to day lives. In rural areas, lacking formal educational centers, ICT and nICTs have been proven successful in facilitating the educational process. Such is the case of the African Virtual University[9] (AVU) based in Nairobi, Kenya.

AVU has over 34 learning centers in 17 African countries. It educates and supports economic development through the network of African institutions that work with internationally recognized universities. Learning is done via online materials, CD-ROMs, DVDs, and realtime chat sessions. The exchange between student and instructor takes place, for the most part, by e-mail and online discussions forums.

The use of nICTs provides the combination of distance education with traditional learning methods and allows access to high quality teaching materials that support and/or substitute poorly qualified teachers. Furthermore, initiatives of this nature not only train future employees, but also create human capital that is prepared to contribute to and take a leadership role in the development process.

In these contexts, legitimate institutions, strong civil society, and good governance have been found to play a central role in conflict prevention. States in danger of, or affected by, conflict tend to suffer crisis of legitimacy. Then the state gradually adopts an oppressive and predatory attitude vis-à-vis society and is undermined by strife and its gradual inability to carry out its duties. Faced with "failed" statehood, governments cannot respond to the needs and demands of its citizens, and violence becomes almost inevitable. nICTs can be used to intervene in this dynamic and aid in the correction of these deficiencies.

Through e-government and e-governance initiatives, nICTs contribute to the relationship between government institutions and citizens. The Gyandoot Project—implemented in India, and winner of the Stockholm Challenge IT Award in Public Services and Democracy in 2000 (Stockholm, 2000)—for example, has established kiosks throughout the rural, poverty-stricken area of Madhya Pradesh. This has been done to facilitate access to information pertaining to agricultural transactions, municipal affairs—such as the filing of complaints, registries and land titles—and governmental transparency[10]. The use of electronic media to complete public transactions has eliminated many of the economic, physical, and time constraints of traditional bureaucracy. Easy access to information and knowledge regarding political processes, services, and so forth, allows citizens to play a more active role in government, thus increasing government accountability, and promoting the open communication needed for state legitimacy. These are the mechanisms of democracy.

The manner in which the use of nICTs empowers citizens makes them a means for the poor, marginalized and disenfranchised to find their voice, organize grassroots movements, and demand governmental accountability. Such is the case of the ex-Yugoslavia in which local non-governmental organizations (NGOs) and student groups used the Internet and mailing lists to organize and overthrow Slobodan Milosevic (Cronnauer, 2004). Mailing lists of this nature often satisfy the psychological need for support that many individuals and groups

Copyright © 2007, Idea Group Inc. Copying or distributing in print or electronic forms without written permission of Idea Group Inc. is prohibited.

who feel traditional media fails to provide. Through the movement's use of the Internet, they realized that they were not alone and that there were people throughout the country and world that shared their messages. These forms of large-scale virtual mobilizations often manage to gather traditional media attention, and influence public institutions though public opinion.

nICTs allow timely monitoring of conflict indicators and adoption of measures to address the root causes of conflicts. Human rights violations, for example, are not only indicators of the imminent threat of conflict and the possibility of violence, but also a root cause of conflict. Thereby, human rights violations lead to massive refugee movements, which, in turn, increase the socio-political tensions that ultimately result in the long-term threat of the eruption of violence.

The World Organization Against Torture (OMCT) is the largest coalition of NGOs fighting against all forms of malicious and demeaning treatment for the protection of human rights. It became fully active in February 1997, resulting from the need for more effective action and efficient means of transmitting information in cases of possible violations. The SOS Torture network has 250 NGOs at its disposal as sources of information and urgent intervention. Through these networks, urgent actions reach over 90,000 state and non-state institutions, associations, and pressure groups. Since the rapid transmission of information is essential, the OMCT counts on over 90,000 correspondents ready to intervene if required. This permits the network-based monitoring of information pertaining to existing and potential human rights violations. Simultaneously, the analysis of the information might be used to predict and prevent human rights violations that may aggravate already tense situations and result in further violence.

In "Information Technology and Human Rights," Metzl (1996) emphasized the transnational nature of the relationship between human rights and the Internet by characterizing it as "having enormous consequences for the human rights movement as an aid to its efforts to collect, interpret, and disseminate information and to push for appropriate action in response to violations"[11] (p. 179). Here, digital technology plays a crucial role in developing issue networks that compel state and international actors to take action. In this way, digital networks remove national intermediary players that might otherwise hinder, censor, or conceal certain invaluable information. The Internet offers local occurrences and local groups the opportunity to gain the attention of the international transcendence that might have otherwise been denied. This often acts as a vital catalyst for action and essential to the spirit of their message. On Friday, March 9, 2001, Amnesty International[12] won the Revolution 2001 Award for the best use of e-mail and the Internet for Stoptorture.org, (Amnesty International, 2001) which went live on Wednesday, October 18, 2000, to mark the launch of its global campaign against torture. The site received over 10,000 hits from people in 146 countries in the 48 hours following its publishing (Amnesty International, 2000).

Amnesty International has harnessed the power of the Internet to improve its traditional letter writing method of campaigning. Among these improvements one finds increased momentum in human rights emergencies. The (Amnesty International Urgent Action) network activates rapid action for those who are in imminent danger of grave human rights violations. Urgent Actions circulate by e-mail and fax to Amnesty International sections worldwide who then distribute them to members of the UA network asking them to send appeals through the fastest channels available. It has been found that e-mail through the

Copyright © 2007, Idea Group Inc. Copying or distributing in print or electronic forms without written permission of Idea Group Inc. is prohibited.

UA network has facilitated networking at an international level, and each case sometimes generates between 3,000 and 5,000 appeals.

In any type of democracy, the Internet offers citizens and civil society an alternate source to obtain political legitimacy and at the same time strengthens the legitimacy of the system in which they operate. These opportunities are essential conduits for democracy and become vital when the plurality of opinions that circulate in a society can be channelled in a productive manner. However, their function and success are based on the normative commitment of the stakeholders towards the transformation of the existing system (Flichy, 2001).

Conflict Management

The independence of media from private and political interests is one of the important parameters among the European Commission's indicators for the prevention of conflict. This is clearly because they play an important role in the search for freedom of speech, human development, and movements for peace. They are important tools for shaping public thought and perceptions. Media has the ability to polarize communities or unite them; consequently, nICTs harbour great potential in moments of crisis.

When used properly, the Internet is a tool that can offer a panoramic and simultaneous view of situations in conflict. The methodology used by the human rights organization, Equipo Nizkor[13], facilitates this. The Vigía del Fuerte cases in Colombia demonstrates this perferctly (Equipo Nizkor, 2002).

As Diaz Dionis (2002) remarks on the FARC church incident that killed 90 people in which, official versions of the event omitted the action was intended to provoke the massive displacement of the population (p. 95). Twenty-four hours after the incident contact was re-established with clerics from the affected area through a religious group in Panama. They, in turn, transmitted information via the Internet every six hours. The official communiqués of the Archbishopship of Quibdo denouncing the incident were disseminated online in Spanish and English to over 18,000 human rights organizations, 5,000 activists and 40 list-serves, including a closed discussion list for jurists specialized in international tribunals. The information ultimately also reached 200 legal experts and the parliaments of 11 countries (Dionis, 2002, p. 96). The massive dissemination of information that Nizkor carried out, de-legitimized the official government version (Oficina en Colombia del Alto Comisionado de las Naciones Unidas para los Derechos Humanos, 2002) and forced the Colombian government to change from its position. Additionally, it enabled the application of the II Additional Protocol to the Geneva Conventions Relating to the Protection of Victims of Non-International Armed Conflicts ("Protocol Additional to the Geneva Conventions of 12 August 1949, and Relating to the Protection of Victims of Non-International Armed Conflicts [Protocol II]"). Therefore, the documental treatment of information pertaining to human rights issues and the monitoring of the situation in a particular locality via the Internet can help manage an existing crisis.

Modern conflicts articulate themselves in the communicative realm. The "Internet, War, and Peace in Colombia," project notes that "The narratives of war are strategies of the war itself, they are inscribed in its logic: lies and cover-ups are basic tactics to bring down the contenders" (Barón Porras, Corredor & Mancera, 2002, pp. 6-7). The use of symbolic

Copyright © 2007, Idea Group Inc. Copying or distributing in print or electronic forms without written permission of Idea Group Inc. is prohibited.

language, the environment, and the media produce the narrative of the war and create the discourse of public reality. During Colombia's 40 years of strife, the war has not only taken place in rural and urban settings, it has been fought in the collective imagery of the population. Colombian media were critical at various levels of the conflict. It became yet another actor, responsible for the polarization of society and in many cases the escalation of conflict (Barón Porras, et al., 2002).

In the past 10 years, along with the expansion of the use of nICTs around the country, "the citizen movement for peace," organized by civil society, has emerged. This group uses new and old ICTs to reach its goals (Barón Porras). Their use has had such a deep impact on the dynamics of the Colombian conflict that the belligerent parties—the government and the FARC—have favored nICTs to disseminate information, educate about the conflict, and involve civil society (Porras, 2002). Web sites open the way for public discourse and allow the parties involved to create meaning for their actions and reality. The Internet is playing vital role in their legitimacy. It has opened direct channels of communication with the national and international public. The actors engage in the negotiation process through their participation in the narration of the Colombian people's collective reality (Porras, 2002). Contextualizing the conflict gives it a political meaning and supplies information that enables actors to make informed decisions and join the peace process (Barón Porras).

Similarly, electronic conferences allow users to share their points of view, publications, or commentaries so that other users can read them and respond. The first recorded electronic conference organized to seek a solution to a war took place in 1991 during the war in the former Yugoslavia. Sponsored by the Swedish Association for Peace and Arbitration and the Association for Progressive Communications, it contained 5,000 messages, ideas, opinions, calls for action, and information on disappearances. As the cyber-Balkan communication center with messages from Switzerland, United States, Croatia, the Netherlands, Australia, Bosnia-Herzegovina, Germany, Finland, and so forth, it was also used to coordinate the aid received (Walch, 1999).

nICTs permit the immediate dissemination of local information and provide informational and communicative infrastructure services to millions of users and organizations worldwide. These types of networks facilitate an exchange of information that is otherwise impossible through traditional media. In fact, traditional media strictly regulates the fixed roles of the content providers and audience. On the other hand, the roles adopted by participants in a virtual environment are more fluid and involve participants from any corner of the earth, in a variety of capacities. Online publications are a resource for journalists that attract a readership of millions, but refuse to conform to the constraints of mass media. These are the authentic voices of cyberspace.

The blog[14] phenomenon which began circa 1994 is a recent, concrete example of this. Simply put, a blog is a journal that is updated periodically and is available on the Web. As Andrew Sullivan from Wired Magazine notes, "Blogs do two things that Web magazines like Slate and Salon simply cannot. First off, blogs are personal. Almost all of them are imbued with the temper of their writer. This personal touch is much more in tune with our current sensibility than were the opinionated magazines and newsarticles of old" (2005). The impact of blogging is such that Reporters without Borders (2005) recently released a Handbook for Bloggers and Cyberdissidents, arguing that, "Bloggers are often the only real journalists in countries where the mainstream media is censored or under pressure" (Create your own blog, 2005).

Copyright © 2007, Idea Group Inc. Copying or distributing in print or electronic forms without written permission of Idea Group Inc. is prohibited.

nICTs form a decentralized system that can mobilize any amount of information in web-like fashion. This can be used to strengthen the articulation of networks and interest groups. Technology 4 Peace[15] began its work in 1996 as a virtual based organization whose primary goal was to inform and recruit expatriate Greek and Turkish Cypriots to complement the need for structured, organized, and long lasting dialogue between the belligerent parties. As a focal point for information and peace-related activities, it fomented workshops, coordinated events, marches, and meetings between different bi-communal groups. In this context, the project designed and created a holistic infrastructure for individuals and groups interested in promoting peace.

Burmanet[16] and the Free Burma Coalition[17] have found nICTs to be the most important campaigning tool available. Thanks to the collaboration of international activists, they are able to coordinate activities beyond their national borders. Using the Internet, its members have created a virtual community that uses cyber diplomacy to pressure the State Law and Order Restoration Council peacefully. The Internet's role was essential in getting legislation passed in the state of Massachusetts condemning companies that do business with or within Burma. This is particularly the case since Massachusetts does not have a large Burmese electorate. This illustrates how the Internet can be a peaceful alternative to the violent transformation of repressive regimes through the search for consensus and public debate, regardless of where it takes place.

Electoral violence biases and shapes the ethno-political factors that contribute to violent conflict. In Sri Lanka, the Center for Monitoring Election Violence (CMEV) uses the Internet to hinder initiatives that intend to undermine the peaceful transformation of the conflict in Sri Lanka (Liyanaarachchi, 2003). It does this by releasing numerous updated reports daily on its Web site that publicly expose existing political violence and naming its perpetrators.

nICTs inform of events instantly as they occur. In May 19, 2002, Fiji suffered a *coup d'état* that brought on a political crisis. The Internet became an essential source of information during that crisis. Fijilive.com Web site was the first source to release news of the coup internationally (Baghwan Rolls, 2002). In fact, the BBC began its coverage of the event with a picture of the Web site because that was the only image available at that time.

Thus, the Internet empowers its users to partake in informational processes and the creation of public consciousness. It introduces new messages into the dominant message flow and creates alternative, horizontal means to reach people at large. It mobilizes the mind of the world.

Post-Conflict Reconstruction and Reconciliation

Although reconstruction may occur at different points during and after conflict, in general terms, it is characterized as taking place between the cessation of violent conflict and the return to normalization. Reconstruction provides an initial response as a tool for transformation, and fosters long-term sustainability through addressing the following issues: security; justice/reconciliation; social/economic well-being; and governance/participation (Center for Strategic and International Studies (CSIS) amd the Association fo the United States Army (AUSA), 2002).

Copyright © 2007, Idea Group Inc. Copying or distributing in print or electronic forms without written permission of Idea Group Inc. is prohibited.

Most of the time, violent confrontation destroys physical and social infrastructures, hinders development, and exacerbates already existing precarious conditions. Once violence has ceased, unaddressed, unmanaged, unresolved conflicts continue to be fertile ground for future confrontations. Therefore, certain measures and conditions become imperative to establish the foundations necessary to move beyond conflict. These include, but are not limited to, measures involving the:

- Protection of victims and survivors
- Reform of political and legal institutions
- Revitalization, restructuring of social and economic structures
- Management and return of refugees and internally displaced persons
- Promotion of reconciliation and facilitation of political participation

As mentioned earlier, initiatives like addressing the reform of political and legal institutions, social and economic revitalization, and promoting political participation become invaluable in reconstruction and reconciliation processes. Addison (2001) argues that, "conflict resolution and prevention require economic reform—independently of the need for reform to raise growth, reduce poverty and safeguard the environment. And infrastructure reconstruction (e.g. in rural areas) is ineffective if policies that depress its values to livelihood are retained" (p. 2).

On the other hand, long-term solutions are required to avoid relapses. They must aim to heal (Øberg, 1996) the:

- Bodies and psyches of the victims
- Social and economic structures
- Environment
- Loss of trust

These are the reasons for using nICTs in the prevention of conflict and at the same time are equally applicable for post-conflict reconstruction and reconciliation.

Similarly, the concept of *human security* recognizes the notions of conflict, health and their interdependence. It refers to the safety of individuals and groups to be freed from acts of violence. This includes human rights violations and terrorism, and non-violent threats, such as environmental degradation, economic crisis, infectious diseases, and natural disasters (Commission on Human Security, 2003). Apart from these, illnesses like tuberculosis, malaria, HIV/AIDS, and other sexually transmitted diseases affect and threaten the reality of the poverty and conflict-stricken.

Furthermore, extended periods of conflict not only undermine economic development, but also worsen the lack of sanitary measures. Humanitarian organizations often attempt to supplement this deficit with an influx of aid. In general, the main recipients of these services and goods are refugees, whose presence involuntarily increases the existing tensions in that

Copyright © 2007, Idea Group Inc. Copying or distributing in print or electronic forms without written permission of Idea Group Inc. is prohibited.

area. The resentment of local residents may arise under these circumstances, but in situations like this, health services can mitigate the displacement of population (Bunde-Birouste, Eisenbruch, Grove, Humphrey, Silove, Waller, & Zwi, 2004).

More importantly, in times of peace the use of nICTs can provide indications for its potential uses in post-conflict scenarios.

E-health[18] telemedicine and tele-health have an important impact on the supply of health services, knowledge sharing, access to medical information and research and training. Through an easy-access, combination of e-mail communication and Web-based medical databases can be made available to practitioners worldwide[19]. The India Health Project (Graves & Reddy, 2000) facilitates the work of rural health care providers by using nICTs to improve prevention programs and provide timely information to monitor, analyze, and plan urgent responses. Midwives, who are the primary care providers in India[20], use PDAs to process patient data, collect information, generate schedules, and so forth. Telemedicine is used in Ethiopia to connect rural clinics with the central hospital in Addis Ababa, and the Tigray regional hospital with a mobile physician. This aids the decision making process by allowing medical professionals in remote areas access to the knowledge and experience of urban doctors through interactive audiovisual and data applications (Lemma, Atnaf & Kassegne, 2004).

Tools of this nature when applied to conflict-ridden or conflict-prone areas could ease the load of medical personnel, while improving the health of the general population.

In "Towards Conflict Transformation and a Just Peace," Clements (2004) remarks that stable peace requires a deep analysis of the structural causes that underlie conflict. Determining the commonalities between traditional and budding social sources of power are complicated tasks, and that if not approached from an organic perspective they will worsen existing conditions or will create new confrontations. Thus, the task of promoting reconciliation is a multidimensional and extremely difficult challenge. This challenge can only be met if the warring factions can be moved beyond the confines of the reasoning and realities that led to the positions they adopted at the beginning of the conflict. Information and communication can act here as an essential element for dialogue initiation and confidence building.

Internet has minimized the distance factor and, despite the technological component, relationships do not cease to be human. According to Aguirre (1999), "behavioral sciences and, especially, psychological schools," have demonstrated that "the initial 'distance' Internet places between people, enables individuals to know that there are others with similar affinities in a faster, simpler way than in normal relationships."

Info-Share[21] is interactive software developed by a group of peace promoters in response to the September 2003 dwindling of the Sri Lankan peace process. Its purpose is to develop networks between the stakeholders of the peace process, so that instant communication —via messenger or chat—is available at all times. The project, which is sponsored by Groove Networks, USAID and the Academy for Educational Development, among others, is designed to be a platform that offers support for the creation of "shared spaces" in the public and private domain. V. Anandasangaree, the leader of the Tamil United Liberation Front commented that lapses in communication were extremely pernicious to the evolution of the peace process (Liyanaarachchi, 2003). Info-Share has bridged the communication gaps between the parties involved. For example, the tools available have assisted in finding the most appropriate strategic responses for the dissemination of information through early

Copyright © 2007, Idea Group Inc. Copying or distributing in print or electronic forms without written permission of Idea Group Inc. is prohibited.

alert systems and other more appropriate networks. Info-Share's Hattotuwa (2004) claims that the process of conflict transformation and management as well as peace-building are strengthened if the entities involved are connected through multi-sectoral networks and have open access to stored knowledge. The creation of this type of networks makes the positive impact of nICTs plausible and possible.

The importance of human contact in conflict transformation and peacebuilding should not be overlooked. It is essential to strengthen relationships and foment cooperation. The combinations of interpersonal communication and daily collaboration, however, have been proven to be the most appropriate and successful formal methods to reduce tension (Huntington, 1993).

Although the Israeli-Palestinian conflict has reached a new peak in terms of ethnic tensions and violence, the Project for Arab-Jewish Dialogue has made positive contributions to peacebuilding efforts in that area. Under the sponsorship of the Program in Conflict Resolution at Bar-Ilan University and its Palestinian counterpart, Al-Quds University in East Jerusalem, the project has organized virtual encounters between Israeli and Palestinian students. These virtual meetings are dialogues that revolve around finding the commonalities between Islam and Judaism. This is important because the religious element, considering the social structure of the communities involved, is essential to the characterization of these collectives. These similarities are intended to be the basis of future relationships (Mollov & Lavie, 2000). This platform helps to establish bonds of trust that are favorable to the implementation of the political agreements that arise from formal negotiations. It helps advance beyond the stereotypes and labels to identify with the "other."

A follow-up of these activities demonstrated that when face-to-face contact was complemented with virtual contact, it increased the level of intimacy and trust between both groups. It levelled the terrain for interaction on equal terms because both groups perceived they have something to teach and learn from each other. The success this project has had in meeting the objective of changing the perceptions and improving the quality of relationships between the groups indicates that the large scale implementation of these types of initiatives can facilitate negotiation, reconstruction, and reconciliation processes. The type of interpersonal exchanges and cultural respect promoted in this context is vital to reach a long-lasting peace.

Recommendations

Suggestions on the use of nICTs for conflict management and prevention in the future must first be pre-empted with a disclaimer of sorts regarding nICTs and their implications within the discourse of conflict. nICTs are by no means the end-all, be-all of conflict prevention and management.

The Internet offers the advantages of decentralization and participation, it merges the local with the global; it is a means to communicate and transmit information and empowers individuals who have access to it. Nevertheless, and due to great part of these same factors, the other side of the coin is as dangerous as the first one is full of advantages. Francisco Marín Calahorro (2004) notes both in times of peace and conflict the dissemination of content is

Copyright © 2007, Idea Group Inc. Copying or distributing in print or electronic forms without written permission of Idea Group Inc. is prohibited.

free, which is why the presence of information on crises, conflicts, subversive groups, and other types of national and international activities have proliferated (pp. 341-349). As per sociologist, Sherry Turkle, "the Internet is an 'ideal medium' to recruit small groups of people" (Guzman, 1997). Although this chapter has focused on the positive facets of nICTs in conflict situations, it is important to realize that in the same way that they empower citizens and assist in the promotion of the universal ideals of peace, human rights, equality, and social justice, Neo-Nazi and terrorist groups, like Al-Qaeda, also make use of nICTs to network, disseminate, and legitimize their messages.

From the communicative and informational perspective, the flux and immediacy of information through nICTs facilitates the transmission of reality as it occurs. One of the dangers or problems that arise when dealing with conflicts in a virtual setting is, however, the very characteristics of the medium itself: it is virtual and text-based. The lack of non-verbal cues might inhibit "speakers" from understanding the totality of the message being transmitted[22]. On one level, cyberspace requires a straightforward communicative style to determine the degree to which parties agree or disagree to avoid lapses and misunderstandings. On that same note, however, lack of tact or sensitivity could be lethal to the dialogue process. Since the Internet is a discursive medium, it is important to take into account the cultural and social context of the individuals who are communicating. This helps minimize the effect of the personal backgrounds of the negotiators or dialoguing parties that may contribute to the interaction. The goal is to avoid misunderstandings and maintain the fluidity and openness of the exchange.

Censorship and governmental monitoring are also issues that arise when discussing the application of nICTs for conflict prevention and management. Countries like China frequently restrict access to Web sites that are critical of their government, speak of human rights abuses, or denounce corrupt behaviour[23]. This content is considered subversive and illegal and is automatically blocked by governmental Internet filters (Zittrain & Edelman, 2003). These types of limitations inhibit the extent to which nICTs can be of use in many of the scenarios mentioned earlier in this chapter.

Additionally, the benefits that might arise from the use of nICTs are greatly hindered by the existence of the digital divide (The Economist, 2005). It is essential to realize that the advantages of the Internet can only be seen as such if one presupposes that this chapter relates specifically to individuals, populations, and countries that do not suffer, or suffer a lesser version of the digital divide. According to the Digital Divide Network, access to digital technology hinges on numerous factors: telecommunications infrastructure, national poverty index, the cost of the necessary technology, literacy rates and basic education. The digital divide and the development divide are practically the same. As Cynthia Hewitt de Alcántara (2001) notes:

The digital divide is an integral part of a much broader and more intractable development divide. The likelihood that people in low-income countries can improve their life chances is often sharply limited not only by their lack of access to modern means of communication and sources of information, but also by a complex network of constraints ranging from unresolved problems of poverty and injustice in their own societies to the structure and dynamics of the global economic system. (pp. 7, 30)

Copyright © 2007, Idea Group Inc. Copying or distributing in print or electronic forms without written permission of Idea Group Inc. is prohibited.

Populations that are on the losing end of the development divide will continue to have problems when it comes to using digital technology to improve their realities.

Furthermore, problems arise regarding the legal, fiscal, and regulatory frameworks of the political and policy environments in which nICTs are used[24]. It is because of this, that the role of nICTs in conflict is only complementary to other measures taken to prevent, manage, and bring conflict to a conclusion.

However, it is important to recognize that there are no solutions to the issue of the impact of nICTs on conflict prevention and management, but there are realities. Of those realities, only some of them, those relating to access, technology, infrastructure, and expertise can be addressed in a straightforward manner through policy and concrete national and international initiatives. For the other realities, which hinge on the nature of the medium itself and the content communicated, there are no quick fixes or easy solutions. They require an increased general awareness on the exchange of ideas and the potential for dialogue of the Internet, as well as knowledge to discern the quality and legitimacy of the information available.

In concluding this segment, in spite of limitations outlined, it is important for institutions addressing conflict prevention and management to incorporate the use of nICTs into the breadth of their work. Only then they will be able to take full advantage of the benefits and assistance they could afford from this technology.

Future Trends

The opportunities that technology affords can be practically endless. In the same way that software can search databases worldwide to predict the number of military war causalities (The Economist, 2005), it may well be used to project and find ways to avoid loss of civilian life.

The future for the use of nICTs in conflict prevention and management does not limit itself to the evolution of the realities and possibilities outlined above, but encompasses a variety of other scenarios and uses. Governments, international organizations, and financial institutions might consider investing increased time and funds in further studying their effects within this context. Also, it is important to extend research and foment the use of related indigenous innovations.

Unlike computer-based Internet and other more traditional ICTs, mobile telephony has the advantage that their use neither requires literacy nor a permanent electricity supply. Both on its own and merged with the Internet—mobile data services—mobile telephony has proven to be a useful political tool in the cases of Spain, the Philippines, the United States, India, and Hong Kong (Standage, 2001). In all these situations short message services have served as mediums to mobilize voters (Adelman, 2004). Furthermore, in terms of development, efforts such as the Grameen Bank's "telephone ladies" have proven their usefulness to the development cause (Buerk, 2005). Results in this respect have been such that it has been estimated that "that an extra ten phones per 100 people in a typical developing country increases GDP growth by 0.6 percentage points" (Bishop, 2005).

Copyright © 2007, Idea Group Inc. Copying or distributing in print or electronic forms without written permission of Idea Group Inc. is prohibited.

Attention should also be given to the use of nICTs to prevent the loss of life in road accidents, militia fights, kidnappings, ambushes, and so forth. The informational vacuum that exists between life in urban and rural areas, which often requires unprotected citizens to travel long distances on precarious roads, could be filled by providing information and news via mobile short message services, mobile data services and digital networks, where available. These tools would help maintain a functioning alternative back-end media infrastructure at times when traditional media collapses.

It would be extremely useful to compile information and centralize data repositories on the implementation of these mechanisms within different conflict contexts to determine typologies for action.

Conclusion

Conflict is a global phenomenon. Thanks to new and old ICTs, conflict now reaches beyond its immediate physical location and travels around the globe as information in the blink of an eye. The purpose of this article has been to explore the methods via which the nICTs can help to prevent and manage the globalized conflict. Within this framework, nICTs have been used to provide punctual specific, incidental sources of income generation and economic empowerment that compensate for deficits in social services, like health and education, and assist in local capacity building. Through initiatives and projects of this nature, international organizations, civil society, and governments can use nICTs to contribute to the correction of structural flaws that produce or aggravate some of the root causes of conflict.

From the communicative and informational perspective, nICTs can play as facilitators and catalysers of dialogue[25] is certain. Virtual communities have become one of the central axis of social mobilization in the information society. This confirms Wellman's affirmation regarding how computer networks unite individuals as much as they do machines and the manner in which this coincides with the emergence of social networks (1996). They emerge and develop in an environment that is very different from every day life: cyberspace (Tirado & Gálvez, 2002). Furthermore, they continue to be a forum for complete interaction. They create bridges between the parties involved in the conflict that complement the activities and negotiations taking place in situ. Foremost, they are important in the reconstruction of the communal concept of the "other" to overcome stereotypes and false assumptions.

These technologies have also proven valuable to:

- Predict and manage crises
- Create and manage solidarity of action networks
- Disseminate information.
- Plan and coordinate activities
- Mobilize citizens

Copyright © 2007, Idea Group Inc. Copying or distributing in print or electronic forms without written permission of Idea Group Inc. is prohibited.

In many cases, particularly relating to conflict management, one might argue that rather than offering any tangible support, messages are introduced into the flow of public discourse through the Internet. This newly integrated information then becomes a means to act on the imaginary collective of the conflict. Therefore, the communication process demands a collective course of action, but at the same time should invoke individual decision-making and enable contributions to the formation and revision of opinions.

In conclusion, it can be stated that the ultimate enduring success and sustainability of the effects of these initiatives are linked to the complementary use of nICTs processes that are already taking place in the field. They are meant to be another, but no less important, component of the holistic solutions that conflict—its causes and consequences—may require.

References

Addison, T. (2001). *Discussion article 2001/16 from conflict to reconstruction.* Retrieved June 17, 2006, from http://www.wider.unu.edu/publications/dps/dp2001-16.pdf .nsf/ c2fabb74f3f54c22ca256afc00097c53/ddc68095c9ab62b8ca256f6300760289/$FILE/ Issue_Article_I.pdf

Addison, T. (2005). *Agricultural development for peace.* Retrieved June 17, 2006, from http://www.wider.unu.edu/publications/rps/rps2005/rp2005-07addison.pdf

Adelman, J. (2004, July 12). U say u want a revolution. *TIME Asia Magazine*, 164(2). Retrieved June 17, 2006, from http://www.time.com/time/asia/magazine/article/0,13673,501040712-660984,00.html

Aguirre, A. (1999). *Relaciones humanas telematizadas (Telematic Human Relationships).* Retrieved June 17, 2006, from http://www.funredes.org/mistica/castellano/ciberoteca/ participantes/docuparti/esp_doc

Amnesty International. (2000). *Torture campaign: Electronic activism an outstanding success.* Retrieved June 17, 2006, from AI Index ACT 40/037/2000, http://www.amnesty.org

Amnesty International. (2001). *UK Amnesty International wins award for innovative campaigning.* Retrieved June 17, 2006, from AI Index EUR 45/005/2001, http://www. amnesty.org

Amnesty Internationl Urgent Actions Saves lives; sign up today!(n.d.) Retrieved June 15, 2001, http://webamnesty.org/pages/uaindex-eng

And now forecast war. (2005). *The Economist Technology Quarterly*, 376(8444), 22-23.

Barón Porras, L. F. (n. d.). *Guerra, drama y victimización: Conclusiones y alternativas. (War, drama and victimisation: Conclusions and alternatives).* Retrieved June 17, 2006, from http://ntci.cinep.org.co/conclusiones/con6.htm

Barón Porras, L. F. (n. d.). *Proyecto de Investigación: NTCI y Paz de la paz en Colombia. (Research Project: NICT and Peace in Colombia).* Retrieved June 17, 2006, from http://ntci.cinep.org.co/presentacion/nuestroproyecto.pdf

Copyright © 2007, Idea Group Inc. Copying or distributing in print or electronic forms without written permission of Idea Group Inc. is prohibited.

Barón Porras, L. F., Valencia Corredor, M., & Bedoya Mancera, A. (2002, October). *Noticias de guerra: la "extraña lógica" de la guerra y la paz en Colombia en prácticas de consumo de noticieros. (News of war: The "strange logic" of war and peace in Colombia and practices in the consumption of news broadcasts)*. Retrieved June 17, 2006, from http://ntci.cinep.org.co/presentacion/notiguerra.pdf

Bastos Tigre, P., & O'Connor, D. (2002, April). *Policies and Institutions for E-Commerce Readiness: What can developing countries learn from OECD Experience?* Retrieved October 28, 2006, http://www.ideas.repec.org/p/oec/devaaa/189-en.html

Berting, J. (1990). Technological impacts on human rights: Models of development, science and technology, and human rights. In C. Weeramantry (Ed.), *The impact of technology on human rights* (pp. 33-36). New York: United Nations University Press.

Bhagwan Rolls, S. (2002, November 15). *The impact of new information communication technology on the media: A community media perspective from the Pacific Island Region of women*. Paper presented at the United Nations Division for the Advancement of Women (DAW) Expert Group Meeting on Participation and Access of Women to the Media, and the Impact of Media on, and Its Use As an Instrument for the Advancement and Empowerment of Women, Beirut, Lebanon.

Bishop, M. (2005). Loose talk saves lives. *The International Development Magazine*, 31. Retrieved June 17, 2006, from http://www.developments.org.uk/data/issue31/loose-talk.htm

Blog. (2005, September 15). *Wikipedia: The free encyclopedia*. Retrieved June 17, 2006, from http://en.wikipedia.org/wiki/Weblogging

Boltz, L.C. (2002). I*nformation technology and peace support operations relationship for the new millennium*. Retrieved June 17, 2006 from Information Technology and Peace Support Operations: Publications: Virtual Diplomacy Initiative at http://www.usip.org/virtualdiplomacy/publications/reports/13.html

Buerk, R. (2005). *Telephone ladies connect Bangladesh*. Retrieved June 17, 2006 from http://news.bbc.co.uk/go/pr/fr/-/1/hi/world/south_asia/4471348.stm

Bunde-Birouste, A., Eisenbruch, M., Grove, N., Humphrey, M., Silove, D., & Zwi, A. (2004, December). *Health and Peacebuilding: Securing the Future*. Retrieved March 9, 2005, from The University of New South Wales Health and Conflict Project Web site: http://humansecurity-chs.org/finalreport/index.html

Carment, D., & Schnabel, A. (2003). *Conflict prevention: Path to peace or grand illusion*. Tokyo: United Nations University Press.

Center for Strategic and International Studies (CSIS) and the Assocation of the United States Army (AUSA) (2002, May). Retrieved October 28, 2006, from CSIS Reports: Post-Conflict Reconstuction Task Framework Report Web site: http://www.csis.org/media/csis/pubs/framework.pdf

Clements. K. (2004). *Towards conflict transformation and a just peace*. Retrieved December 12, 2004, from Berghof Handbook for Conflict Transformation Web site: http://www.berghof-handbook.net/uploads/download/clements_handbook.pdf

Copyright © 2007, Idea Group Inc. Copying or distributing in print or electronic forms without written permission of Idea Group Inc. is prohibited.

Commission on Human Security (2003, May 1). *Human Security Now.* Retrieved July 4, 2003, from Final Report of the Commission on Human Security Web site: http://www. humansecurity-chs.org/finalreport/index.html

Cronauer, K. (2004, April 4). Activism and the Internet: Recommendations for uses of electronic mailing lists. Retrieved October 28, 2004, from Activism and the Internet: Using electronic mailing lists for mobilization Web site: http://cs.ubc.ca/spider/cronauer/

Diaz Dionis, G. (2002). El Activismo de los derechos humans y el control politico-social a traves de las nuevas tecnologias. (Human rights activism and socio-political control through new technologies) In M. Agúndez Basterra (Ed.), *Derechos Humanos y Nuevas Tecnologías: Colección "Jornadas sobre Derechos Humanos"* (pp. 78-99). San Sebastian, Spain: Ararteko.

Equipo Nizkor. (2002, May). *Crisis humanitaria de Vigía de Fuerte* (Mayo de 2002). Retrieved June 30, 2002, from Colombia-Derechos Humanos-Informes Web site: http://www. derechos.org/nizkor/colombia/informes.html

Flichy, P. (2001). *L'imaginaire de l'Internet. (The imaginary of Internet).* Paris: La Découverte.

Fromkin, V., & Rodman, J. (1983). *An introduction to language.* New York: CBS College Publishing.

Guzman, D. (1997). *Racism and racial discrimination on the Internet.* Retrieved June 17, 2006, from Seminar on the Role of the Internet with Regard to the Provisions of the Internet Convention on the Elimination of All Forms of Discrimination at http://www. unhchr.ch/html/menu2/10/c/racism/guzman.htm

Graves, M., & Reddy, N.K. (2000). *Electronic support for rural healthcare workers.* Retrieved June 17, 2006, from http://unpan1.un.org/intradoc/groups/public/documents/APC-ITY/UNPAN019013.pdf

Hattotuwa, S. (2004). *Untying the Gordian knot: ICT for conflict transformation and peace building.* Retrieved June 17, 2006, from http://www.masternewmedia.org/news/2004/06/13/untying_the_gordian_knot_ict.htm

Heeks, R. (2002, June). *iDevelopment not e-development: ICTs and micro-/small enterprise. Development Gateway.* Interview with Richard Heeks. Retrieved June 17, 2006, from http://www.developmentgateway.org/node/133831/sdm/docview?docid=254666

Hewitt de Alcántara, C. (2001). *The development divide in a digital age: An issue article.* United Nations Research Institute for Social Development (UNRISD). Retrieved June 17, 2006, from http://www.unrisd.org/

Huntington, S. P. (1993). The clash of civilizations. *Foreign Affairs,* 72(3), 49.

Lemma, F., Atnaf, S., & Kassegne, S. K. (2004). *Survey of current efforts and potential in application of telemedicine in Ethopia.* Retrieved June 17, 2006, from Survey of Current Efforts and Potentials in Application of Telemedicine in Ethiopia, http://www. digitaladdis.com/sk/TeleMedicine_Ethiopia_Article1.pdf

Liyanaarachchi, Champika (2003, November 18). *Sri Lanka: As Peace Falters, Activists*

Copyright © 2007, Idea Group Inc. Copying or distributing in print or electronic forms without written permission of Idea Group Inc. is prohibited.

Turn to ICT to Build Bridges. Retrieved December 1, 2003, from One World South Adia Home/In Depth/War and Peace/Conflict Resolution/Sri Lanka Web site: http://southasia.oneworld.net/article/view/73045/1/975

Marin Calahorro, F. (2004). Nuevas tecnologías y conflictos en la era multimedia. (New technologies and conflicts in the multimedia era). In F.R. Contreras & F. Sierra (Eds.), *Culturas de Guerra: Medios de información y violencia simbólica* (pp. 341-349). Fuenlabrada, Madrid: Ediciones Cátedra (Grupo Anaya, S.A.).

Metzl, J. F. (1996). Information technology and human rights. *Human Rights Quarterly*, 18(4), 719.

Mollov, B., & Lavie, C. (2000). *Culture, dialogue and perception change in the Israeli-Palestinian conflict*. Retrieved June 17, 2006, from Culture, Dialogue and Perception Change In the Israeli-Palestinian Conflict, http://faculty.biu.ac.il/~steing/conflict/Articles/israelipalestiniandialogue.pdf

Naughton, J. (2001). Contested space: The Internet and global civil society. In H. Anheier, M. Glasius, & M. Kaldor (Eds.), *Global civil society 2001* (pp. 147-168). New York: Oxford University Press.

Øberg, J. (1996). *Conflict mitigation in reconstruction and development*. Retrieved June 17, 2006, from http://www.gmu.edu/academic/pcs/oberg.htm

Oficina en Colombia del Alto Comisionado de Naciones Unidas para los Derechos Humanos. (2002). *Informe sobre la misión de observación en el Medio Atra*to. Bogota.

The real digital divide. (2005, March 10). *The Economist Technology Quarterly*. Retrieved June 17, 2006, from http://www.economist.com/opinion/displayStory.cfm?story_id=3742817

Reporters without Borders. (2005). *Create your own blog, remain anonymous, and get round censorship!* Retrieved June 17, 2006, from http://www.rsf.org/article.php3?id_article=15083

Reporters without Borders. (2005). *Handbook for bloggers and cyberdissidents*. Retrieved June 17, 2006, from Handbook for Bloggers and Cyberdissidents, http://www.rsf.org/rubrique.php3?id_rubrique=542

Rutkowsky, T. (1997). *Seminar on the role of Internet with regard to the provisions of the International Convention on the Elimination of All Forms of Racial Discrimination, Item VI: Elements relating to conduct and good practices for Internet based materials*. Retrieved June 17, 2006, from http://www.unhchr.ch/html/menu2/10/c/racism.rutkowsl.htm

Sen, A. (2000). *Desarrollo y libertad. (Development as Freedom)*. Barcelona, Spain: Editorial Planeta.

Sequeira Bolaño, C. R., & de Santana Vasconcelos, D. (2001). Internet y la economía de la comunicación. (Internet and the communication economy). *Voces y Culturas*, 18, 73.

Copyright © 2007, Idea Group Inc. Copying or distributing in print or electronic forms without written permission of Idea Group Inc. is prohibited.

Shaw, T. (2003). *Conflict and peace-building in Africa: The regional dimensions.* Retrieved June 17, 2006, from http://www.wider.unu.edu/publications/dps/dps2003/dp2003-10.pdf

Standage, T. (2001, October 11). *The Internet, untethered.* Retrieved June 17, 2006, from The Economist http://www.economist.com/displayStory.cfm?Story_id=811934

Stauffacher, Daniel (Ed.)(2005). *Information and communication technology for peace: The role of ICT in preventing, responding to and recovering from conflict.* NY: United Nations Publications.

Stockholm Challenge. (n.d.). *Ecosandals.com: Wikyo Akala Project of Korogocho, Kenya.* Retrieved June 17, 2006, from Stockholm Challenge, http://www.stockholmchallenge.se/search_view.asp?IdNr=4303

Sullivan, A. (2005, May 10). *The blogging revolution.* Retrieved June 17, 2006, from Wired Magazine, http://www.wired.com/wired/archive/10.05/mustread.html?pg=2

Tirado, F.J., & Gálvez, A. (2002). *Comunidades virtuales, ciborgs y redes sociotécnicas: nuevas formas para la interacción social. (Virtual communities, ciborgs and socio-technical networks: New forms for social interaction).* Retrieved June 17, 2006, from Francisco Javier Tirado, Anna Gàlvez - Comunidades virtuales, ciborgs y redes socio-técnicas: nuevas formas para la interacción social, http:// www.uoc.edu/humfil/articles/esp/tiradogalvez0302/tiradogalvez0302.html

United Nations Development Program (UNDP) Human Development Report Office. (2005). *Human development report 2005: International cooperation at a crossroads.* New York: UNDP and Oxford University Press.

United Nations. (1998). *Secretary General says proposals in his report on Africa require new ways of thinking, of acting* (Press Release SG/SM/6524 SC/6503). New York: United Nations Information Service.

Roberts, B. (2005, March). *New minimum standards for education in emergencies aim at giving 50 million children a chance to learn.* Retrieved October 28, 2006, from Education Today Newsletter, July-September 2003-Saving lifes, saving minds Web site: http://portal.unesco.org/education/en/ev.php-URL_ID=38521&URL_DO=DO_TOPIC&URL_SECTION=201.html

United Nations High Commission for Human Rights (UNHCHR). (1997). *Protocol additional to the Geneva Conventions of 12 August 1949, and relating to the protection of victims of non-international armed conflicts* (Protocol II). Retrieved October 28, from the Higher Commissioner for Human Rights Web site: 2006, from http://www.unhchr.ch/html/menu3/b/94.htm

United Nations Press Service. (1998, April 16). *Secretary-General says proposal in his report on Africa requires new ways of thinking, of acting.* Retrieved June 17, 2006, from Press Release SG/SM/6524, http://www.un.org/News/Press/docs/1998/19980416.SGSM6524.html

Vayrynen, R. (1991). To settle or to transform? Perspective on the resolution of national and international conflicts. In R. Vayrynen (Ed.), *New directions in conflict theory: Conflict resolution and conflict transformation* (pp. 1-25). London: Sage.

Copyright © 2007, Idea Group Inc. Copying or distributing in print or electronic forms without written permission of Idea Group Inc. is prohibited.

Walch, J. (1999). *CMC under fire: The case of former Yugoslavia.* Retrieved June 17, 2006, from http://www.lhs.se/~jwalch/cmcuf.rtf

Wellman B., Salaff, J., Dimitrova, D., Garton, L., Gulia, M., & Haythornwaite, C. (1996). Computer networks as social networks: Collaborative work, telework, and virtual community. *Annual Review of Sociology*, 22, 213-238.

Zittrain, J., & Edelman, B. (2003). *Empirical analysis of Internet filtering in China.* Retrieved June 17, 2006, from http://cyber.law.harvard.edu/filtering/china/

Endnotes

[1]   The most common types of armed conflicts over the past 50 years have been liberation wars, civil wars, minority conflicts (ethnic groups seek to end oppression), and border disputes.

[2]   Of the 106 armed conflicts in the world that took place from 1989-1996, only six occurred between states. The remaining 86 were internal conflicts where over 80% of the directly affected populations were civilians.

[3]   For information regarding military studies see Boltz (2002). Since this chapter was written, the UNICTS Task force has also published Information and Communication Tecnologies for Peace: The Role of ICT in Preventing, Responding to and Recovering from Conflict by Stauffacher, Drake, Currion, and Steinberger (2005).

[4]   Reference is made to equality as the right to access available information once the technology is available.

[5]   Ecosandals.com, http://www.ecosandals.com.

[6]   PeopLink at http://www.peoplink.org.

[7]   Mercado Global at http://www.mercadoglobal.org.

[8]   Sistema Mundial de Información y Alerta, Food and Agriculture Organization at http://www.fao.org/WAICENT/faoinfo/economic/giews/spanish/index.htm.

[9]   African Virtual University at http://www.avu.org/.

[10]   The literacy threshold of the citizens in the area may, nevertheless, still be an important caveat to the total success of the Gyandoot Project as it may enable old gatekeepers to stay in control. The Organization for Economic Cooperation and Development's study on "Literacy in the Information Age" divides literacy into five levels. Level 1 (very easy text only) is the usual definition of literacy. Level 3 is needed to function within the Information Society, which includes the Internet. Level 3 approximately matches the skills acquired by completing secondary education. This research evaluated the literacy of individuals ranging from ages 16-65 in industrialized countries, and found an astonishing amount of population below level 3, for example, more than 40% in the USA, and 85% in Chile. OECD (Literacy in the Information Age, 2001).

[11]   nICTs are the tool of choice for disseminating information regarding human rights violations, toture, arbitrary detention, etc., that does not reach corporate media outlets.

Copyright © 2007, Idea Group Inc. Copying or distributing in print or electronic forms without written permission of Idea Group Inc. is prohibited.

[12]   Amnesty International, http://www.amnesty.org

[13]   http://www.derechos.org/nizkor/

[14]   Blogs can belong to individuals, groups of writers, corporations, media and political campaigns, and so forth. According to Wikipedia, "A Weblog, Web log or simply a blog, is a Web application which contains periodic posts on a common webpage. These posts are often but not necessarily in reverse chronological order. Such a website would typically be accessible to any Internet user. The term 'blog' came into common use as a way of avoiding confusion with the term server log" (Blog, 2005).

[15]   Tech4Peace at http://www.tech4peace.org.

[16]   http://www.ibiblio.org/freeburma/bnn/bnn.html. This is an e-mail-based newsgroup.

[17]   This is an activist network that includes Web pages, chats, news, grassroots campaigns, policy initiatives, and so forth. http://www.freeburmacoalition.org

[18]   This term refers to the use of computing, the creation of networks and communication as support mechanisms for medicine, nursing, pharmacology, and dentistry.

[19]   USAID financed, Managers Electronic Resource Center, exemplifies this.

[20]   The median is 5000 patients per midwife.

[21]   Info Share, http://www.info-share.org/.

[22]   Fromkin and Rodman (1983) claim that up to 90% of the meaning of a message is transmitted non verbally.

[23]   Dissident/democracy sites. Blocked sites include sites about democracy and human rights generally and sites specific to China. Of the top 100 sites returned by Google in response to a search for "democracy china," 40 were found to be blocked, while 37 "dissident china" sites were blocked, 32 were blocked for "freedom china," and 30 for "justice china." Specific blocked sites included Amnesty International, Human Rights Watch, the Hong Kong Voice of Democracy, the Direct Democracy Center, and dozens of Falun Gong and Falun Dafa sites.

[24]   This makes reference to regulation concerning industry standards.

[25]   Dialogue facilitators are neutral; their participation is limited to the fact that they maintain the flow of communication and channel information.

Copyright © 2007, Idea Group Inc. Copying or distributing in print or electronic forms without written permission of Idea Group Inc. is prohibited.

Chapter V

Technological Innovation, Trade and Development

Laura Márquez-Ramos, Universitat Jaume I, Spain

Inmaculada Martínez-Zarzoso, Universitat Jaume I, Spain

Celestino Suárez-Burguet, Universitat Jaume I, Spain

Abstract

This chapter tests empirically to what extent technological innovation influences international trade and studies its effect on different groups of countries according to their level of economic development. Different measures used in the literature to proxy for technological capabilities are reviewed and two of them are selected. The estimation results show that technological innovation has a considerably high explanatory power on trade compared with other traditional determinants. Countries tend to trade more when they have similar technological capabilities and the development of technological innovation has lowered the effect of geographical distance on trade. According to the obtained results, investing in technological innovation leads to the improvement and maintenance of the level of competitiveness, therefore a good economic policy in developing countries is to invest in technological innovation.

Copyright © 2007, Idea Group Inc. Copying or distributing in print or electronic forms without written permission of Idea Group Inc. is prohibited.

Introduction

In the last decades there have been important changes in the international environment, with an increasing number of countries that are closely linked to one another through international trade and foreign direct investment. Globalization, new technologies, and information flows play an important role in this worldwide interdependence. In this framework, trade theory highlights the importance of technological change in explaining the competitiveness of a country.

The main purpose of this chapter is to test empirically to what extent technological innovation influences international trade and to study its effect on different groups of countries according to their level of economic development.

In the next section, different measures used in the literature to proxy technological capabilities are presented. In a knowledge-based economy with high and increasing dependence on technology, information and human capital, the development of relevant indicators to measure the level of technological innovation across countries is a matter of great importance. For this purpose, three components of technological innovation are considered: creation of technology, diffusion of recent innovations and diffusion of old innovations (as measures of information technology), and development of human skills (as a measure of human capital).

The third section presents the estimated model and the empirical results. Empirical results show that technological innovation has a considerably high explanatory power on trade in comparison to other traditional determinants. Moreover, the view that countries tend to trade more when they have similar technological capabilities is supported. Results also show that the development of technological innovation has lowered the effect of geographical distance on trade, since long distances are less important nowadays than in the past. Therefore, investing in technological innovation could help to improve and maintain the level of competitiveness and this will increase the participation of the poorest countries in the world economy.

The fourth section includes a sensibility analysis where groups of countries with different levels of income are considered in order to test for the pooling assumption. Since the magnitude and sign of the explanatory variables depend on certain characteristics of the trading partners, the estimation results support the existence of important differences concerning the goodness of fit, and the significance and magnitude of the variable coefficients.

The fifth section includes three future perspectives for this research, related to the variables included in the model (distance as proxy of transport costs) and the improvement of the estimation methodology (division of countries in different groups and panel estimation). Finally, some conclusions of this research are presented in the last section.

Background

The interest in the study on the relationship between technological innovation and competitiveness dates back to the so-called "neo-technological trade theories" of the sixties (technology gap, product-cycle). Most of the research in this field was based on Schumpeter's analysis

Copyright © 2007, Idea Group Inc. Copying or distributing in print or electronic forms without written permission of Idea Group Inc. is prohibited.

of innovation and diffusion as the driving forces behind the competitiveness of firms. This author placed technological change and innovation at the core of economics.

The development of relevant indicators to measure the level of technological innovation across countries is a matter of great interest in a knowledge-based economy that is driven by high and increasing dependence on information technology and human capital. In recent years, important attempts have been taken to measure technology creation and diffusion, and human skills across countries. For example, Wakelin (1997) classifies different proxies for technological innovation used in the literature and points out that the main choice of technological innovation proxies has been between using an input to the innovation process, such as R&D expenditure or the number of scientists and engineers employed in research departments, and an output, such as number of patents. In a more recent study, Keller (2004) states that technology is an intangible parameter that is difficult to measure directly and he proposes that three indirect approaches can be used to measure it. This can be done through the measurement of inputs (research and development), outputs (patents) and the effect of technology (higher productivity). From a different point of view, Archibugi and Coco (2005) review several synthetic indexes that are used to assess the impact of technological capabilities on economic and social indicators. These authors also recommend considering individual indicators and sub indexes to understand how and why countries differ. The use of composite indices is criticised by Grupp and Mogee (2004), since composite scores and country rank positions can vary considerably depending on the selection process and alternative methods of calculation.

Table 1 shows six different composite indices that measure countries' endowment of technological innovation and that have been recently developed by some institutions and individuals. Most of the indices take into account several dimensions (3 or 4) that include variables

Table 1. Measurement of technological innovation with composite indices

Variable	Description	Source
ArCo	This index takes into account three dimensions: **Creation of technology** *(number of patents, number of scientific papers)*, **diffusion of technology** *(Internet penetration, telephone penetration, electricity consumption)* and **development of human skills** *(gross tertiary science and engineering enrolment, mean years of schooling, adult literacy rate)*.	Archibugi and Coco (2004)
European Innovation Scoreboard	This index takes 17 indicators into account. The aspects of the innovation process measured by the scoreboard are: **Availability and use of people with the right skills, creation of new ideas, innovation by firms,** and a **range of issues**. From these indicators a so-called "tentative summary innovation index" (SII) is constructed. The index is normalised to the interval [-10, 10]. An index of zero represents the European Union average (Grupp and Mogee, 2004).	European Commission (2005)
ITR	The "Internet Traffic Report" monitors the flow of data around the world. The index takes values between zero and 100. Higher values indicate faster and more reliable connections.	ITR[1] (2004)

Copyright © 2007, Idea Group Inc. Copying or distributing in print or electronic forms without written permission of Idea Group Inc. is prohibited.

Table 1. Continued

ICT	The Index of Information and Communication Technology (ICT) diffusion consists of two dimensions: **Connectivity** *(Internet hosts, PCs, telephone mainline,s and cellular subscribers)* and **access** *(Internet users, literacy, GDP per capita, and cost of a local call).* Moreover, a third dimension (**policy**) is presented separately.	Biggs, UNCTAD (2003)
TAI	The "Technology Achievement Index" is built up of four dimensions: **Creation of technology** *(number of patents granted to residents, receipts of royalty, and license fees from abroad),* **diffusion of recent innovations** *(Internet hosts, exports of high technology and medium technology products),* **diffusion of old innovations** *(number of telephones, electricity consumption)* and **human skills** *(mean years of schooling, gross tertiary science enrolment ratio).*	UNDP (2001)
NRI	The "Network Readiness Index" measures the degree of preparation of a nation or community to participate in and benefit from Information and Communication Technology (ICT) developments. It is built up of three dimensions: **Environment** offered by a country or community, the **readiness** of the community's key stakeholders, and the **usage** of ICT.	WEF, World Bank, and INSEAD (2004)

related to the creation, the diffusion and the use of new technologies and the development of human skills and new ideas. However, the correlation coefficient among these indices is high and the availability of the data varies considerably.

Table 2 shows a selection of 20 papers that have used single variables to proxy technological innovation. More than half of them have selected the innovation process as an input and only a few have chosen it as an output measure.

Among all the indices available in the literature, the technology achievement index (TAI), developed by the United Nations Development Program (UNDP, 2001), and the ArCo technology index, introduced by Archibugi and Coco (2004), have been selected to be used in this study. The selection has been made in order to analyse as many countries as possible. The TAI is available for 72 countries, but it is not comparable across time because the maximum and the minimum observed values used to calculate the index can change over time. The ArCo technology index is available for 162 countries. The authors fix an identical time period for a maximum and a minimum value (1987-1990 and 1997-2000) to allow symmetrical time-series comparisons. These indicators are also more complete compared to others, as they take into account a wider array of variables related to technological innovation.

The effect of the technological innovation dimensions on international trade is analysed, and each of the components of the TAI was included separately in the regression analysis. A detailed description of the components of the selected indices is presented in Martínez-Zarzoso and Márquez-Ramos (2005).

Copyright © 2007, Idea Group Inc. Copying or distributing in print or electronic forms without written permission of Idea Group Inc. is prohibited.

Table 2. Proxies for technological innovation

Variable	Description	Source
Proportion of non-managers using computers	Measures the impact of computers on productivity	Black and Lynch (2004)
R&D expenditure Workers in R&D and innovation sectors Number of researchers	Indicators of R&D and innovation	Caballero, Coca, and Escribano (2002)
Expenditure on innovation per worker	Indicators of innovation	Calvo (2002)
Imports of computer equipment	Proxy for technological adoption	Caselli and Coleman (2001)
Foreign R&D capital stock	R&D *spillovers*	Coe, Helpman, and Hoffmaister (1997)
Variable related to the stock of past research effort and the stock of human capital in countries	Level of technology	Eaton and Kortum (1997)
R&D expenditure	Input measure of investments in new technologies	Fagerberg (1997)
Absolute difference between the ArCo of the two trade partners	Proxy for technological distance	Filippini and Molini (2003)
Internet *hosts*	Measures the Internet development in a country	Freund and Weinhold (2004)
International patents	National innovative output	Furman and Hayes (2004)
Telecommunications and Internet consumption	Indicators of Information and Communication Technology (ICT)	García Castillejo (2002)
Total factor productivity (TFP)	Output measure of investments in new technologies	Gustavsson, Hansson, and Lundberg (1997)
Firms introducing an innovation (preceding year) Innovation expenditure	Indicators of innovation in firms	Lachenmaier and Woessmann (2004)
Average number of patents *per capita*	Proxy of innovative output	Moreno, Paci, and Usai (2004)
R&D expenditure Inputs assigned for basic research Information and Communication Technology (ICT) expenditure	Indicators of R&D and ICT	SáncheUsaz, López, Cervantes and Cañibano (2000)
R&D expenditure	Identifies industries where countries tend to have relatively efficient technology	Torstensson (1996)
R&D expenditure Number of patents	Input measure of investments in new technologies Output measure of investments in new technologies	Verspagen and Wakelin (1997)
Total factor productivity (TFP)	Output measure of investments in new technologies	Wolff (1997)
Equipment investment per person engaged in production	Proxy for technological change	Wolff (2002)
Telephone call traffic	Proxy for "disembodied" idea flows	Wong (2004)

Copyright © 2007, Idea Group Inc. Copying or distributing in print or electronic forms without written permission of Idea Group Inc. is prohibited.

Estimated Equation and Empirical Results

To evaluate the empirical effects of technological innovation on international trade, a gravity model, augmented with technological variables and a transport infrastructure index is estimated. The theoretical framework is taken from Suárez-Burguet, Martínez-Zarzoso, and Márquez-Ramos (2005). These authors analyse the role played by cross-country differences in both relative factor endowments and relative country size when determining the volume of trade. They developed a model based on Helpman and Krugman (1996) and introduced trade barriers, and "hard" and "soft" investment in infrastructure as determinants of the volume of trade. The model supports the notion that comparative advantage determines international trade, adding factors with a positive influence on production factors: "hard" (transport infrastructure) and "soft" (technological innovation) investment in infrastructure. Although the gains of increasing trade are attenuated by the resistance imposed by geographical barriers, infrastructure endowment also determines countries' specialisation and trade flows.

Based on this theoretical framework, an empirical model is derived to test the influence of technological innovation on trade. Integration dummies are included to take into account the impact of trade agreements on international trade. A number of dummies representing geographical and cultural characteristics are also added. The model is expressed in additive form using a logarithmic transformation.

The estimated equation is:

$$\ln X_{ij} = \alpha_0 + \alpha_1 \cdot \ln Y_i + \alpha_2 \cdot \ln Y_j + \alpha_3 \cdot \ln P_i + \alpha_4 \cdot \ln P_j + \alpha_5 \cdot Adj_{ij} + \alpha_6 \cdot Isl + \alpha_7 \cdot Land +$$
$$+ \alpha_8 \cdot CACM + \alpha_9 \cdot CARIC + \alpha_{10} \cdot MERC + \alpha_{11} \cdot NAFTA + \alpha_{12} \cdot CAN + \alpha_{13} \cdot UE +$$
$$+ \alpha_{14} \cdot \ln Dist_{ij} + \alpha_{15} \cdot Lang_{ij} + \alpha_{16} \cdot TAI_i + \alpha_{17} \cdot TAI_j + \alpha_{18} \cdot Inf_i + \alpha_{19} \cdot Inf_j + u_{ij} \qquad (1)$$

where ln denotes natural logarithms.

The model is estimated with data from 62 countries available in 1999 and a total of 3782 (62*61) bilateral trade flows are obtained (see Figure 1). The presence of missing/zero values in the bilateral trade flows data reduces the sample to 3126 observations. An Ordinary Least Squares (OLS) estimation on the double log specification is performed as given in Equation (1).

X_{ij} denotes the value of exports from country $_i$ to $_j$; Y_i and P_i are income and population in the exporter's country; Y_j and P_j are income and population in the destination market; Adj_{ij} is a dummy that takes a value of 1 when countries share the same border and zero otherwise; Isl takes a value of 1 when the exporter or the importer are an island; $Land$ is a dummy for landlocked countries; CACM is a dummy that takes a value of 1 when both countries belong to the Central American Common Market; CARIC is a dummy that takes a value of 1 when both countries belong to the Caribbean Community; MERC is a dummy that takes a value of 1 when both countries belong to Mercosur; NAFTA takes a value of 1 when countries are members of the North American Free Trade Area; CAN is a dummy representing Andean Nations Community members; and UE takes a value of 1 when countries are members of the European Union. Since direct measures of trade costs are unavailable, geographical distance between countries is often used as a proxy for transport costs in gravity equa-

Copyright © 2007, Idea Group Inc. Copying or distributing in print or electronic forms without written permission of Idea Group Inc. is prohibited.

tions, so $Dist_{ij}$ is the geographical great circle distance in kilometres between the capitals of country i and j. $Lang_{ij}$ is a dummy for countries sharing the same language, and TAI_i and TAI_j are technological variables measuring technological innovation in the exporter and the importer countries. Inf_i and Inf_j are infrastructure variables measuring the level of transport infrastructures in the exporter and the importer countries. Finally, u_{ij} is independently and identically distributed among countries.

Table 3 shows the results for the baseline model and the contribution of the dimensions considered in the TAI (creation of technology, diffusion of recent innovations, diffusion of old innovations, and human skills) to trade flows. Model 1 presents the OLS results,

Table 3. Determinants of international trade. Baseline model and augmented gravity model (technological innovation differentiated by 4 dimensions)

Variable	Model 1	Model 2	Model 3	Model 4	Model 5
Constant term	-10.42***	-10.84***	-11.62***	-22.8***	-16.69***
	(-11.94)	(-13.84)	(-17.64)	(-37.41)	(-26.49)
Exporter's income	0.27***	0.15***	0.08***	0.02**	0.06***
	(13.22)	(11.15)	(8.75)	(2.16)	(7.79)
Importer's income	0.22***	0.14***	0.09***	0.04***	0.07***
	(11.47)	(9.31)	(7.34)	(3.09)	(6.38)
Exporter's population	0.70***	0.71***	0.77***	1.03***	0.94***
	(23.08)	(29.37)	(39.42)	(57.95)	(48.66)
Importer's population	0.51***	0.53***	0.57***	0.77***	0.69***
	(15.79)	(21.36)	(26.41)	(37.38)	(34.71)
Adjacency dummy	-	0.44**	0.49***	0.37**	0.17
		(2.36)	(3.15)	(2.23)	(1.18)
Island dummy	-	-0.4***	-0.27***	-0.45***	-0.23***
		(-3.58)	(-3.01)	(-5.32)	(-2.61)
Landlocked dummy	-	-1.08***	-1.16***	-0.75***	-0.84***
		(-10.48)	(-13.47)	(-9.54)	(-10.21)
CACM dummy	-	0.93***	1.22***	2.38***	2.17***
		(2.89)	(4.92)	(9.96)	(8.04)
CARICOM dummy	-	2.99***	4.44***	2.88***	4.37***
		(2.91)	(4.65)	(2.86)	(4.65)
MERCOSUR dummy	-	2.52***	3.12***	1.74***	2.55***
		(8.56)	(10.09)	(5.54)	(5.81)
NAFTA dummy	-	3.07***	0.47	1.42***	1.53***
		(7.41)	(1.11)	(2.96)	(2.69)
CAN dummy	-	0.67	1.68***	0.71*	0.76
		(1.4)	(3.9)	(1.74)	(1.36)
UE dummy	-	0.51***	0.17*	-0.05	-0.17*
		(4.33)	(1.75)	(-0.53)	(-1.66)
Distance	-1.38***	-0.98***	-0.97***	-0.98***	-1.12***
	(-31.19)	(-20.82)	(-23.32)	(-26.53)	(-27.92)
Language dummy	-	0.67***	0.72***	0.88***	0.73***
		(6.12)	(7.43)	(10.58)	(8.51)
Exporter's creation of technology	-	4.89***	-	-	-
		(19.98)			
Importer's creation of technology	-	3.04***	-	-	-
		(10.59)			
Exporter's diffusion of recent innovations	-	-	5.78***	-	-
			(33.17)		
Importer's diffusion of recent innovations	-	-	3.88***	-	-
			(21.44)		
Exporter's diffusion of old innovations	-	-	-	7.07***	-
				(39.27)	
Importer's diffusion of old innovations	-	-	-	4.95***	-
				(30.38)	
Exporter's human skills	-	-	-	-	6.46***
					(41.31)

Copyright © 2007, Idea Group Inc. Copying or distributing in print or electronic forms without written permission of Idea Group Inc. is prohibited.

Table 3. Continued

Importer's human skills	-	-	-	-	4.52***
					(27.35)
Exporter's infrastructure	-	1.23***	0.82***	0.72***	1.03***
		(24.21)	(17.18)	(19.31)	(26.6)
Importer's infrastructure	-	0.98***	0.72***	0.58***	0.83***
		(17.76)	(13.9)	(13.09)	(17.99)
R-squared	0.407	0.637	0.719	0.786	0.761
Adjusted R-squared	0.406	0.634	0.717	0.785	0.759
S.E. of regression	2.511	1.971	1.733	1.511	1.598
Number of observations	3126	3126	3126	3126	3126

Notes: ***, **, *, indicate significance at 1%, 5%, and 10%, respectively. T-statistics are in brackets. The dependent variable is the natural logarithm of exports in value (current U.S. dollars). Income, population, and distance are also in natural logarithms. The estimation uses White's heteroscedasticity-consistent standard errors.

Model 1: *Baseline model;* **Model 2**: *Augmented gravity model. Contribution of the creation of technology dimension on trade;* **Model 3**: *Augmented gravity model. Contribution of the diffusion of recent innovations dimension on trade;* **Model 4**: *Augmented gravity model. Contribution of the diffusion of old innovations dimension on trade;* **Model 5**: *Augmented gravity model. Contribution of the human skills dimension on trade.*

excluding technological and transport infrastructure variables. The coefficients on income are both positive, as expected, and the income elasticities are below one for the exporter and the importer. The coefficients on population are positive and significant – a higher market fosters trade, thus indicating the presence of economies of scale. However, since countries with different levels of development are included, the sample should be divided according to the specialisation patterns in order to analyse the effect of demographic variables on trade[2]. Developed countries can be considered as manufacturing exporters and developing countries can be seen as non-manufacturing exporters. The elasticity of demographic variables might have a different sign and dimension across the two groups of countries (Filippini and Molini, 2003). The coefficient of distance has a negative sign, as expected, because lower distances imply lower transport costs and a higher amount of goods traded.

Models 2, 3, 4, and 5 consider the gravity model augmented with technological variables: creation of technology, diffusion of recent innovations, diffusion of old innovations, and human skills. These variables are significant and have the expected sign, although some differences in the magnitudes of the coefficients and in the significance of variables can be observed, depending on the dimension included in the gravity equation. For example, adjacency is not significant when human skills are considered and some coefficients and signs on integration dummies are also different. Moreover, income coefficients are lower when technological diffusion or human skills are added than when the creation of technology index is added. The reason could be that the two former variables are capturing part of the positive effect of income on trade. Results show a higher explanatory power when including technological variables for exporter countries than when including them for importer countries. Then a higher technological innovation in the exporter country leads to greater exports. When the diffusion of old innovations index is included as a proxy for technological innovation, a higher variability of the bilateral export flows is experienced.

In the quest of the differential effect of investing on each one of the four dimensions, the variability between the maximum and the minimum values of the indices is analysed. It has been found that the variability in the indices is 61.9% for creation of technology, 79.35%

Copyright © 2007, Idea Group Inc. Copying or distributing in print or electronic forms without written permission of Idea Group Inc. is prohibited.

for diffusion of recent innovations, 87.86% for diffusion of old innovations and 89.72% for human skills. Therefore, those countries that do not reach a basic level of technological innovation should invest in old innovations and education for fostering international trade.

Table 4 shows estimation results when the technological variables included are the TAI index (Models 6, 7, and 10) and the ArCo index (Models 8, 9, and 11). Technological variables are found to be significant and positive, as expected. A higher technological innovation endowment fosters international trade, although the magnitude of the estimated coefficient for TAI is higher than the estimated coefficient for ArCo.

In Models 7 and 9, a different way to add technology in the trade equation is considered: the variable included is the technological distance between trading partners (Filippini and Molini, 2003). This is defined as the absolute difference between technological indicators in the exporter and the importer countries. This variable indicates that two countries can be far away from each other not only geographically, but also from a technological perspective. Technological gaps can deter trade since similar countries trade more. Therefore, a negative correlation between this new variable and the export flows is expected. In Models 7 and 9, the TAI and the ArCo indices, respectively, have been used to construct the technological distance variable. Technological distance has been found to be significant in both models and it increases the explanatory power of the regressions. Therefore, results support the view that countries tend to trade more when they are "closer" from a technological point of view.

In order to determine the relative importance of the different variables included in the augmented gravity model, the beta coefficients are calculated (see Table A.2). They are used by some researchers to compare the relative strength of the various predictors within the model. Since the beta coefficients are all measured in standard deviations they are comparable when the explanatory variables are expressed in different units. The estimates of Model 6 imply that the highest beta coefficients are, in absolute value, for technological variables (0.504 for TAI in the exporter and 0.359 for TAI in the importer country). This means that a standard deviation increase in the endowment of technological innovation in the exporter country would lead to a 0.504 standard deviation increase in the logarithm of exports, whereas a standard deviation increase in the endowment of technological innovation in the importer country would enhance a 0.359 standard deviation in the logarithm of exports. Clearly, this indicates that technological variables are important determinants of international trade flows. Beta coefficients for technological innovation are also the highest in Model 7 (0.506 for TAI in the exporter country and 0.357 for TAI in the importer country). However, when beta coefficients for geographical and technological distance are compared, geographical distance appears to be a more important determinant of international trade flows since this variable may be capturing the effects of trade barriers that is different than transport costs such as cultural proximity, a shared history and information costs.

Freund and Weinhold (2004) fail to show evidence of the role played by the Internet in altering the effect of geographical distance in trade patterns. They use a dummy variable (LONGDIST), which equals one if the distance between trade partners exceeds the average distance between all countries. Then, they interact it with the growth in the number of Internet hosts in each country. In the process of comparing the results in this research with those obtained by these authors, the same interaction variable is added in the estimated equation. As in Freund and Weinhold (2004), the coefficient of this variable is not significant. It could be that a more general proxy for technological innovation would be better to measure this effect. In Model 10, the technological variable TAI is interacted with the dummy

Copyright © 2007, Idea Group Inc. Copying or distributing in print or electronic forms without written permission of Idea Group Inc. is prohibited.

Table 4. Determinants of international trade. Augmented gravity model

Variable	Model 6	Model 7	Model 8	Model 9	Model 10	Model 11
Constant term	-15.38***	-15.72***	-19.24***	-19.36***	-14.37***	-17.01***
	(-25.71)	(-27.04)	(-31)	(-32.05)	(-21.18)	(-24.41)
Exporter's income	0.02***	0.02**	0.05***	0.04***	0.02**	0.04***
	(2.62)	(2.53)	(6.35)	(5.69)	(2.34)	(5.61)
Importer's income	0.04***	0.04***	0.06***	0.05***	0.04***	0.05***
	(3.72)	(3.61)	(5.21)	(4.64)	(3.51)	(4.65)
Exporter's population	0.89***	0.89***	0.97***	0.98***	0.89***	0.98***
	(49.34)	(51.41)	(53.45)	(55.1)	(49.5)	(53.6)
Importer's population	0.66***	0.67***	0.71***	0.72***	0.67***	0.72***
	(34.92)	(35.64)	(36.5)	(37.46)	(34.66)	(36.43)
Adjacency dummy	0.43***	0.32**	0.38**	0.24	0.31**	0.13
	(2.89)	(2.15)	(2.34)	(1.52)	(2.03)	(0.8)
Island dummy	-0.46***	-0.47***	-0.27***	-0.31***	-0.46***	-0.28***
	(-5.64)	(-5.77)	(-3.17)	(-3.72)	(-5.58)	(-3.26)
Landlocked dummy	-0.86***	-0.83***	-1.04***	-0.97***	-0.86***	-1.02***
	(-11.34)	(-10.99)	(-13.82)	(-12.92)	(-11.29)	(-13.68)
CACM dummy	1.95***	1.99***	2.41***	2.39***	1.74***	1.95***
	(8.08)	(8.56)	(9.27)	(9.55)	(6.96)	(7.22)
CARICOM dummy	4.29***	4.17***	4.07***	3.91***	4.24***	3.99***
	(4.49)	(4.38)	(4.03)	(3.89)	(4.44)	(3.95)
MERCOSUR dummy	2.58***	2.49***	2.91***	2.76***	2.56***	2.85***
	(7.66)	(7.73)	(8.72)	(8.5)	(7.18)	(7.62)
NAFTA dummy	0.71	0.83	1.12*	1.2	0.81	1.31*
	(1.16)	(1.36)	(1.65)	(1.51)	(1.31)	(1.85)
CAN dummy	1.22***	1.05**	1.06**	0.89*	1.26***	1.14**
	(2.61)	(2.24)	(2.22)	(1.87)	(2.69)	(2.4)
UE dummy	-0.24**	-0.35***	-0.11	-0.26**	-0.22**	-0.09
	(-2.54)	(-3.76)	(-1.1)	(-2.45)	(-2.36)	(-0.89)
Distance	-1***	-0.95***	-0.95***	-0.91***	-1.12***	-1.2***
	(-26.72)	(-25.44)	(-24.82)	(-24.13)	(-20.55)	(-21.8)
Language dummy	0.92***	0.87***	0.91***	0.83***	0.93***	0.93***
	(11)	(10.49)	(10.41)	(9.81)	(11.16)	(10.78)
Exporter's TAI	9.12***	9.17***	-	-	9.01***	-
	(46.46)	(47.61)			(42.97)	
Importer's TAI	6.39***	6.35***	-	-	6.2***	-
	(30.7)	(31.09)			(27.19)	
Technological distance (TAI)	-	-1.73***	-	-	-	-
		(-9.43)				
Exporter's ArCo	-	-	7.71***	8.04***	-	7.48***
			(46.75)	(48.74)		(43.72)
Importer's ArCo	-	-	5.44***	5.68***	-	5.21***
			(30.08)	(32.69)		(26.8)
Technological distance (ArCo)	-	-	-	-1.93***	-	-
				(-11.61)		
Exporter's infrastructure	0.68***	0.68***	0.91***	0.88***	0.67***	0.88***
	(17.65)	(18.26)	(25.06)	(24.89)	(17.34)	(23.63)
Importer's infrastructure	0.57***	0.57***	0.74***	0.71***	0.56***	0.71***
	(12.57)	(12.89)	(17.45)	(16.94)	(12.31)	(16.51)
LONGDISTi	-	-	-	-	0.21	0.59***
					(0.99)	(2.75)
LONGDISTj	-	-	-	-	0.36	0.59**
					(1.53)	(2.52)
R-squared	0.788	0.793	0.781	0.789	0.788	0.783
Adjusted R-squared	0.786	0.792	0.779	0.788	0.786	0.782
S.E. of regression	1.506	1.484	1.529	1.499	1.505	1.522
Number of observations	3126	3126	3126	3126	3126	3126

*Notes: ***, **, * indicate significance at 1%, 5%, and 10%, respectively. T-statistics are in brackets. The dependent variable is the natural logarithm of exports in value (current U.S. dollars). Income, population, and distance are also in natural logarithms. The estimation uses White's heteroscedasticity-consistent standard errors.*

Model 6: *Augmented gravity model (technological innovation measured by TAI);* **Model 7**: *Augmented gravity model and estimation of the effect of technological distance on trade (technological innovation measured by TAI);* **Model 8**: *Augmented gravity model (technological innovation measured by ArCo);* **Model 9**: *Augmented gravity model and estimation of the effect of technological distance on trade (technological innovation measured by ArCo);* **Model 10** and **Model 11**: *Augmented gravity model and estimation of the effect of technological innovation on geographical distance and, therefore, on trade.*

Copyright © 2007, Idea Group Inc. Copying or distributing in print or electronic forms without written permission of Idea Group Inc. is prohibited.

LONGDIST, instead of using Internet hosts, obtaining LONGDISTi (LONGDIST*TAIi) and LONGDISTj (LONGDIST*TAIj). If technology and the advance of information and knowledge have reduced (increased) the impact of geographical distance on trade, then the coefficient on the interaction term should be positive (negative). However, though these coefficients have been found to be positive but they seem to be non-significant.

Finally, ArCo is used instead of TAI in Model 11 to analyse the effect of the knowledge-based economies on trade (LONGDISTi and LONGDISTj are interacted with TAIi and TAIj). Since the coefficient of LONGDISTi and LONGDISTj are both positive and significant, results in this research offer partial evidence showing that the information and knowledge advances have reduced the effect of geographical distance on trade. This result supports the inference to take into account different dimensions of technology, such as creation and human capabilities, and not only diffusion.

Model Extensions

Sensibility Analysis

To understand whether there exists a differential behaviour concerning the determinants of trade flows for developed (high-income) and developing (low-income) countries, the 62-country sample is divided into three groups according to their level of economic development: countries with high GDP per capita, medium GDP per capita, and low GDP per capita. Countries are ordered from higher to lower income levels, and then an upper level of GDP is composed by calculating the average of the first half of the sample, and an inferior level is set by calculating the average of the second half (see Martínez-Zarzoso & Márquez-Ramos, 2005).

Table 5 shows the main results of the augmented gravity model for developed and developing countries. Results are only presented for two groups instead of three in a way to have a higher contrast between them[3].

Model 12 presents the OLS results for the augmented gravity equation in the richest countries. Results show that income variables, adjacency, island and landlocked dummies, geographical distance, exporter's TAI, and exporter's transport infrastructure are significant. These variables have the expected sign, although island dummy presents a positive coefficient indicating that, when the richest economies are islands, they export more. Demographic variables (population of the countries) are not included since they are highly correlated with income in this group. The language dummy is not significant in this group of countries, proving that to share an official language with other high- income countries is not an important determinant of bilateral exports. However, it is positive signed and significant when trade among medium-income countries is analysed (see Table A.3)[4]. Variables in this model explain 87.8% of the variability in exports.

In Model 13, the augmented gravity model is estimated for low income countries. Exporter's and importer's population, being landlocked, geographical distance, the language dummy, and the exporter's and importer's TAI are significant and have the expected sign. Demographic

Copyright © 2007, Idea Group Inc. Copying or distributing in print or electronic forms without written permission of Idea Group Inc. is prohibited.

Table 5. Determinants of international trade. Estimation results for high and low income countries.

Variable	Model 12	Model 13	Model 14	Model 15
Constant term	-24.11***	-12.78***	-24.41***	-17.16***
	(-13.68)	(-4.63)	(-12.88)	(-4.85)
Exporter's income	0.81***	-0.01	0.81***	-0.02
	(15.82)	(-0.22)	(14.63)	(-0.36)
Importer's income	0.82***	-0.08	0.82***	-0.09
	(17.81)	(-1.15)	(16.79)	(-1.27)
Exporter's population	-	1.22***	-	1.32***
		(11.04)		(11.09)
Importer's population	-	0.62***	-	0.73***
		(5.24)		(5.08)
Adjacency dummy	0.43**	0.36	0.44**	0.13
	(2.3)	(0.72)	(2.32)	(0.27)
Island dummy	0.27*	1.91	0.28**	3.48
	(1.96)	(0.58)	(1.99)	(1.02)
Landlocked dummy	-0.36***	-1.12***	-0.35**	-0.91**
	(-2.81)	(-2.77)	(2.59)	(-2.08)
CACM dummy	-	-	-	2.57***
				(3.35)
NAFTA dummy	-	-	-0.09	-
			(-0.28)	
UE dummy	-	-	0.02	-
			(0.18)	
Distance	-0.94***	-1.36***	-0.94***	-1.17***
	(-12.17)	(-7.22)	(-10.13)	(-6.01)
Language dummy	-0.06	1.23***	-0.06	1.18***
	(-0.34)	(2.89)	(-0.34)	(2.73)
Exporter's TAI	2.39***	5.37**	2.73***	4.13*
	(2.88)	(2.39)	(2.61)	(1.81)
Importer's TAI	1.02	6.73***	1.36	5.48**
	(1.1)	(2.91)	(1.25)	(2.24)
Technological distance (TAI)	-	-	-0.65	-1.58
			(-0.61)	(-0.54)
Exporter's infrastructure	0.21***	-1.34	0.19***	-2.53
	(3.04)	(-0.36)	(2.76)	(-0.66)
Importer's infrastructure	-0.03	-1.88	-0.04	-3.08
	(-0.54)	(-0.51)	(-0.61)	(-0.82)
R-squared	0.886	0.694	0.886	0.708
Adjusted R-squared	0.878	0.668	0.876	0.678
S.E. of regression	0.716	1.731	0.722	1.702
Number of observations	182	165	182	165

*Notes: ***, **, * indicate significance at 1%, 5%, and 10%, respectively. T-statistics are in brackets. The dependent variable is the natural logarithm of exports in value (current U.S. dollars). Income, population, and distance are also in natural logarithms. The estimation uses White's heteroscedasticity-consistent standard errors. For the richest countries, income and population variables are highly correlated; only income variables are included in the gravity equation for this group of countries.*

Model 12: *Determinants of trade in developed countries;* **Model 13:** *Determinants of trade in developing countries;* **Model 14:** *Determinants of trade in developed countries and estimation of the effect of technological distance on trade (integration dummies are included);* **Model 15:** *Determinants of trade in developing countries and estimation of the effect of technological distance on trade (integration dummies are included).*

Copyright © 2007, Idea Group Inc. Copying or distributing in print or electronic forms without written permission of Idea Group Inc. is prohibited.

variables for exporters have a positive relation with trade, indicating that greater availability of cheap labour force for industries in developing countries fosters trade. This model has a lower explanatory power (66.8%) than the model for the richest economies, which could be due, in part, to the data for developed countries' being of higher quality.

In Model 14 and 15, the technological differences variable is included. Results show that, when trade is among countries with a similar level of development, technological endowments are more important for trade than the technological gap existing among these countries. Integration dummies are considered for the richest and the poorest countries, although they are only significant for the latter group.

In relation to the income coefficients, Garman, Petersen, and Gilliard (1998) analyse economic integration in a number of developing countries and support the notion that the costs and benefits of integration are unevenly distributed among members of an integration agreement in favour of the richest countries. They found that the income coefficients for Latin American countries have a smaller magnitude than those reported in other studies of European trade. Table 5 shows that income coefficients are negative signed and low in magnitude for the poorest economies; however, as income coefficients are not significant for these economies, the obtained results do not show clear evidence about this issue.

Technological and transport infrastructure variables are expected to have a positive influence on trade. Results show that they are non-significant for importers when trade is among high-income countries, and transport infrastructure variables are not significant for low-income economies. One explanation could be the non-arrival at a minimum level of infrastructure in developing countries.

Testing the Pooling Assumption

To improve the understanding of the differential behaviour concerning the determinants of trade flows for developed and developing countries, equation (1) is estimated by interacting the exogenous variables (except integration dummies) with a dummy (DP)[5] that takes the value of one when trading partners are richer than the simple average in the 62-country sample. DP takes the value zero when trading partners are poorer than the simple average in the sample. In Model 16, an OLS estimation is performed on the double log specification.

The Wald test is used in order to check whether both the exogenous variable and its interaction with the dummy representing developed countries present a different coefficient. The null hypothesis on equality of the coefficients in the two sub-samples (developed and developing countries) cannot be accepted. Table 6 shows the estimation results.

Model 16 presents the results for low-income and high-income countries, with the inclusion of iteration dummies. Results in this model can be compared to those obtained in Model 9. The results from the Wald test show that the poolability assumption is indeed rejected for bilateral exports and that the estimated parameters are not identical across bilateral relationships. In this research, the DP dummy has also been included as independent variable, to analyse whether the different behaviour of the determinants of trade in groups of countries can be found in the constant term and not only in the slope coefficients. Estimation results show that this dummy is not significant.

Copyright © 2007, Idea Group Inc. Copying or distributing in print or electronic forms without written permission of Idea Group Inc. is prohibited.

Table 6. Determinants of international trade. Testing the pooling assumption.

Variable	Model 16
Constant term	-22.11*** (-28.97)
Exporter's income	0.04*** (5.01)
DP*Exporter's income	0.48*** (2.97)
Importer's income	0.04*** (3.74)
DP*Importer's income	0.57*** (3.6)
Exporter's population	1.08*** (51.81)
DP*Exporter's population	-0.76*** (-4.26)
Importer's population	0.78*** (35.43)
DP*Importer's population	-0.66*** (-3.89)
Adjacency dummy	0.66*** (3.12)
DP*Adjacency dummy	-0.45* (-1.76)
Island dummy	-0.38*** (-3.42)
DP*Island dummy	0.11 (0.79)
Landlocked dummy	-0.85*** (-8.98)
DP*Landlocked dummy	0.12 (0.99)
CACM dummy	2.24*** (7.72)
CARICOM dummy	3.92*** (3.87)
MERCOSUR dummy	2.16*** (5.55)
NAFTA dummy	1.31*** (3.17)
CAN dummy	0.18 (0.38)
UE dummy	0.13 (1.56)
Distance	-0.97*** (-19.55)
DP*Distance	0.25*** (3.69)
Language dummy	1.04*** (10.63)
DP*Language dummy	-0.53*** (-3.12)
Exporter's ArCo	9.77*** (38.05)
DP*Exporter's ArCo	-5.67*** (-12.46)
Importer's ArCo	7.15*** (26.49)
DP*Importer's Arco	-5.48*** (-12.12)
Technological distance	-3.09*** (-13.82)
DP*Technological distance	1.91*** (4.58)
Exporter's infrastructure	0.92*** (18.57)
DP*Exporter's infrastructure	-0.24*** (-3.45)
Importer's infrastructure	0.8*** (12.62)
DP*Importer's infrastructure	-0.41*** (-4.86)
R-squared	0.808
Adjusted R-squared	0.806
S.E. of regression	1.437
Number of observations	3126

*Notes: ***, **, *, indicate significance at 1%, 5%, and 10%, respectively. T-statistics are in brackets. The dependent variable is the natural logarithm of exports in value (current U.S. dollars). Income, population, and distance are also in natural logarithms. The estimation uses White's heteroscedasticity-consistent standard errors. DP is a dummy that takes the value of one when trading partners are richer than the simple average in the 62-country sample and takes the value zero when trading partners are poorer than the simple average in the sample.*

The income variable is more relevant for developed countries. A 1% increase in own GDP increases exports from developed countries by 0.52% (0.04+0.48), and by only 0.04% when exports are from developing countries. Very similar coefficients are obtained for foreign GDP. Since the gravity equation is an accepted methodology to analyse the effects of economic integration on trade flows, a lower magnitude obtained in the elasticities of income may indicate that the costs and benefits of integration and globalisation are unevenly distributed among different economies depending on their level of development and it goes in favour of the richest countries (see Garman et al., 1998).

The coefficients for population variables present positive signs, but with a very low magnitude for developed countries and a magnitude close to unity for developing countries. As

Copyright © 2007, Idea Group Inc. Copying or distributing in print or electronic forms without written permission of Idea Group Inc. is prohibited.

developing countries are more specialised in labour intensive exports, the results indicate that greater availability of cheap labour force in developing countries fosters trade, whereas in developed countries the trend of population growth is stable and almost close to zero (see Filippini and Molini, 2003).

The magnitude of the distance coefficient is lower for developed, -0.72 (-0.97+0.25), than for developing countries (-0.97). The adjacency dummy coefficient falls 68% (-0.45/0.66) for developed countries, and also the language dummy is reduced 50% (-0.53/1.04) when countries are developed. Therefore, the responsiveness of trade to adjacency falls by about 36% {[exp(-0.45)-1]*100} and to language by 41% {[exp(-0.53)-1]*100}.

Summarizing, results show that trade flows are more sensitive to geographical and cultural variables (adjacency, geographical distance, and language) for developing than for developed economies. Since developing countries face higher transport costs, higher institutional and informal barriers, and more limited access to market information they tend to trade more with neighbouring countries. The result that language links have an impact on international trade has also been found by other authors, such as Guo (2004) who shows that language influences on trade are more significant in China (a developing country) than in the U.S. (a developed country).

The estimated coefficients for technological innovation and transport infrastructure variables are significant and higher in magnitude for developing countries. Moreover, results show that trade flows are more sensitive to technological distance in developing than in developed economies and suggest that technological innovation investments are a good economic policy for developing economies.

Future Trends

Future developments for this research are related to the variables included in the model and to the improvement of the estimation methodology.

Concerning the first issue, distance between country capital cities has been used in this chapter as a proxy for transport costs, assuming that $tij = tji$. Better transport costs measures could be investigated and included in gravity models instead of distances. Since transport costs tend to be fixed according to the supply and demand conditions applying in the market, the endogeneity of the transport cost variable in the gravity equation could also be investigated.

Concerning the second issue, a further extension of the current research could be not to impose *a priori* by dividing countries into developed and developing economies, but to estimate both the number of "regimes" and their positioning.

Finally, the sample could be extended to more countries and years and a panel data analysis could be undertaken, in order to investigate whether trade is beneficial for all countries in a dynamic environment. Nowadays, information flows, new technologies, regionalisation and globalisation are strengthening the interconnection and dependence among all countries.

Copyright © 2007, Idea Group Inc. Copying or distributing in print or electronic forms without written permission of Idea Group Inc. is prohibited.

Conclusion

The recent changes attended in international trade patterns and the growing interest in technological innovation claim for a better understanding of the relationship between both variables.

In this chapter, a gravity equation augmented with technological innovation and transport infrastructure variables is estimated in order to analyse their impact on trade. Geographical (distance, adjacency, being an island, and being landlocked) and social variables (integration agreements among countries and sharing a language) are also considered.

When the 62-country sample is considered, variables included have the expected sign and are significant, excluding some integration variables. Distance has a considerably low explanatory power on trade compared with transport infrastructure and technological innovation. Importers' technology has a lower effect on trade than exporters' technology and a higher technology endowment in the exporter country leads to greater exports. Moreover, results support the hypothesis that countries tend to trade more when they are "closer" from a technological point of view.

In a further step, it is analysed whether technology has any effect on geographical distance in a more globalised and integrated world. The results partially support that the development of technological innovation has lowered the effect of distance on trade, since its development means that long distances are less important nowadays than in the past.

To infer whether there is a differential behavior among countries, the components of the 62-country sample are divided according to their level of economic development. For the high-income countries, the model has a higher explanatory power than for the low-income countries. Geographical factors are always relevant, but geographical distance and being landlocked have higher elasticities for poorer countries than for richer ones. Technological and social factors also seem to be more important for developing economies. Furthermore, technological endowment in each group of countries seems to be more important for trade flows than technological differences among the countries in the same group.

Finally, the pooling assumption has been tested. This chapter shows that the coefficients of the explanatory variables are not the same for all the trading patterns and that the magnitude and sign of the explanatory variables depend on certain characteristics of the trading partners.

A common result is obtained in all regressions. Technological innovation and transport infrastructure can be considered as barriers to trade for those countries with lower endowment levels; thus, investing in these variables could foster international trade and increase the participation of developing economies in a more globalised and integrated world. Results obtained in this chapter advise authorities of developing economies to promote investments in traditional information technologies and human capital, since these variables are a good starting point to improve technological innovation and international competitiveness.

Copyright © 2007, Idea Group Inc. Copying or distributing in print or electronic forms without written permission of Idea Group Inc. is prohibited.

References

Archibugi, D., & Coco, A. (2004). A new indicator of technological capabilities for developed and developing countries (ArCo). *World Development, 32*(4), 629-654.

Archibugi, D., & Coco, A. (2005). Measuring technological capabilities at the country level: A survey and a menu for choice. *Research Policy, 34*(2), 175-194.

Biggs, P. (2003). Information and Telecommunication Technology (ICT) development indices (Document: WICT-40E.). Paper presented at the 3rd World Telecommunication/ICT Indicators Meeting. UNCTAD.

Black, S.E., & Lynch, L.M. (2004). What's driving the new economy? The benefits of workplace innovation. *The Economic Journal, 114* (493), 97-116.

Caballero, M., Coca, P., & Escribano, R. (2002). La transferencia de tecnología al tejido empresarial valenciano: Diagnóstico de la situación. *Revista Valenciana de Economía y Hacienda, 5*, 47-63.

Calvo, J. L. (2002). Innovación tecnológica y convergencia regional. ¿Se amplía o se cierra la brecha tecnológica entre las CCAA españolas? *Economía Industrial*, 347, 33-40.

Caselli, F., & Coleman, W.J. (2001). Cross-country technology diffusion: The case of computers. *American Economic Review, 91*(2), 328-335.

Central Intelligence Agency (CIA). (2003). *The world factbook.* Retrieved June 17, 2006, from http://www.odci.gov/cia/publications/factbook

Coe, D.T., Helpman, E., & Hoffmaister, A.W. (1997). North-south R&D spillovers. *The Economic Journal, 107*(440), 134-149.

Eaton, J., & Kortum, S. (1997). *Technology and bilateral trade (NBER Working Chapter 6253). 70*(5), 1741-1779.

European Commission. (2005). *European innovation scoreboard.* Retrieved June 17, 2006, from http://www.cordis.lu/innovation-smes/scoreboard/home.html

Fagerberg, J. (1997). Competitiveness, scale and R&D. In J. Fagerberg, P. Hansson, L. Lundberg & A. Melchior (Eds.), *Technology and international trade* (pp. 38-55). Cheltenham, UK: Edward Elgar.

Filippini, C., & Molini, V. (2003). The determinants of East Asian trade flows: A gravity equation approach. *Journal of Asian Economics, 14*(5), 695-711.

Freund, C.L., & Weinhold, D. (2004). The effect of the Internet on international trade. *Journal of International Economics, 62*(1), 171-189.

Furman J.L., & Hayes, R. (2004). Catching up or standing still? National innovative productivity among "follower" countries, 1978-1999. *Research Policy, 33*(9), 1329-1354.

García Castillejo, A. (2002). El consumo de servicios de telecomunicaciones e Internet por las empresas españolas. *Economía Industrial,* 343, 111-130.

Garman, G., Petersen, J., & Gilliard, D. (1998, Summer). Economic integration in the Americas: 1975-1992. *Journal of Applied Business Research, 14*(3), 1-12.

Great circle distances between cities. (2003). Retrieved June 17, 2006, from http://www.wcrl.ars.usda.gov/cec/java/lat-long.htm

Copyright © 2007, Idea Group Inc. Copying or distributing in print or electronic forms without written permission of Idea Group Inc. is prohibited.

Grupp, H., & Mogee, M.E. (2004). Indicators for national science and technology policy: How robust are composite indicators? *Research Policy, 33*(9), 1373-1384.

Guo, R. (2004). How culture influences foreign trade: Evidence from the U.S. and China. *The Journal of Socio-Economics, 33*(6), 785-812.

Gustavsson, P., Hansson, P., & Lundberg, L. (1997). *Technical progress, capital accumulation and changing international competitiveness.* In J. Fagerberg, P. Hansson, L. Lundberg, & A. Melchior (Eds.), Technology and international trade (pp. 20-37). Cheltenham, UK: Edward Elgar.

Helpman, E., & Krugman, P.R. (1996). Market structure and foreign trade. Increasing returns, imperfect competition, and the international economy. Cambridge, MA: MIT Press.

Internet Traffic Report. (ITR). (2004). Retrieved June 17, 2006, from http://www.internettrafficreport.com/main.htm

Keller, W. (2004). International technology diffusion. *Journal of Economic Literature, 42*(3), 752-782.

Lachenmaier, S., & Woessmann, L. (2004). Does innovation cause exports? Evidence from exogenous innovation impulses and obstacles using German micro data. CESifo Working Paper Series No. 1178. Available at SSRN: http://ssrn.com/abstract=540982

Martínez-Zarzoso, I., & Márquez-Ramos, L. (2005). Does technology foster trade? Empirical evidence for developed and developing countries. Atlantic Economic Journal, 33, 55-69.

Moreno, R., Paci, R., & Usai, S. (2005). Spatial spillovers and innovation activity in European regions. *Environment and Planning A, 37*(10), 1793-1812.

Sánchez, M.P., López, A., Cervantes, M., & Cañibano, C. (2000). *El capital humano en la nueva sociedad del conocimiento.* VI Premio Círculo de Empresarios. Madrid: Círculo de Empresarios.

Suárez-Burguet, C., Martínez-Zarzoso, I., & Márquez-Ramos, L. (2005). *The non-linear specification of the gravity model: An empirical application on international trade* (PD-ECO 2005/1). Castellón, Spain: Universitat Jaume I.

Torstensson, J. (1996). Technical differences and inter-industry trade in the Nordic countries. *Scandinavian Journal of Economics, 98*(1), 93-110.

United Nations Development Program (UNDP). (2001). *Human development report.* New York: Oxford University Press.

Verspagen, B., & Wakelin, K. (1997). *Technology, employment and trade: Perspectives on European integration.* In J. Fagerberg, P. Hansson, L. Lundberg & A. Melchior (Eds.), Technology and international trade (pp. 56-74). Cheltenham, UK: Edward Elgar.

Wakelin, K. (1997). *Trade and innovation.* Theory and evidence. Cheltenham, UK: Edward Elgar.

World Economic Forum (WEF), World Bank, and INSEAD (2004). *The global information technology report 2003-2004: Towards an equitable information society.* New York: Oxford University Press.

Copyright © 2007, Idea Group Inc. Copying or distributing in print or electronic forms without written permission of Idea Group Inc. is prohibited.

World Trade Analyzer (2001). *The International Trade Division of Statistics of Canada.*

Wolff, E. N. (1997). *Productivity growth and shifting comparative advantage on the industry level.* In J. Fagerberg, P. Hansson, L. Lundberg & A. Melchior (Eds.), Technology and international trade (1-19).Cheltenham, UK: Edward Elgar.

Wolff, E. N. (2002). The impact of IT investment on income and wealth inequality in the postwar US economy. *Information Economics and Policy, 14* (2), 233-251.

Wong, W. K. (2004). How good are trade and telephone call traffic in bridging income gaps and TFP gaps? *Journal of International Economics, 64* (2), 441-463.

World Bank (2001). *World Development Indicators.* Washington.

Endnotes

[1] In 2004, this measure only considers three routers in South America. However, 4 routers measure ITR in Australia, there are 13 routers in Asia, 22 in Europe and 58 in North America. In 2006, the ITR considers 6 routers in South America, 7 routers in Australia, 7 routers in Asia, 25 in Europe and fifty in North America. A lower number of routers has an adverse effect on Internet data flows.

[2] This is carried out in the next section.

[3] Results for medium GDP per capita countries are presented in the Table A.3 (Appendix).

[4] Two trading countries that speak a same language trade a 197% [exp(1.09)-1]*100 more than the rest of country pairs in this group of countries.

[5] **Developed countries:** Belgium-Luxembourg, United States, Norway, Iceland, Switzerland, Canada, Ireland, Denmark, Austria, Japan, Australia, Netherlands, Germany, Finland, France, Sweden, Italy, United Kingdom, Hong Kong, Singapore, Cyprus, Israel, Spain, Portugal, Republic of Korea, Greece, Czech Republic, Argentina, and Slovak Republic.

Developing countries: South Africa, Uruguay, Costa Rica, Chile, Poland, Mexico, Trinidad and Tobago, Croatia, Brazil, Turkey, Panama, Colombia, Dominican Republic, Bulgaria, Algeria, Peru, Syrian Arab Republic, Paraguay, El Salvador, China, Jamaica, Egypt, Honduras, Nicaragua, India, Ghana, Pakistan, Sudan, Senegal, Nepal, Kenya, Mozambique, and Tanzania.

Copyright © 2007, Idea Group Inc. Copying or distributing in print or electronic forms without written permission of Idea Group Inc. is prohibited.

Appendix

Data, Sources, and Variables

Table A.1 shows a summary of the data used in the analysis. With respect to technological and infrastructure variables, some additional explanations are needed. Values for TAI have been calculated using the same criteria followed by the United Nations Development Program. The classification obtained is slightly different from the Human Development Report classification for 2001 because the arithmetic averages are calculated for Organisation for Economic Cooperation and Development (OECD) member country indicators and then they are used to fill the gaps of missing data for some OECD countries, thus increasing the sample size. Results are able to be summarised in a ranking (see UNDP, 2001; also see Martínez-Zarzoso & Márquez-Ramos, 2005).

Transport infrastructure variables are calculated with data on kilometres of paved roads and kilometres of motorways per square kilometre, taking into account the quality of the roads. Equation (A.1) is used to calculate the index.

$$Infrastructure\ variable = \frac{((0.75 \cdot paved\ roads\,(km)) + motorways\,(km))}{Land\ area\,(km^2)} \quad (A.1)$$

The dependent variable is the natural logarithm of exports in value (current U.S. dollars). Income, population, and distance are also in natural logarithms. The estimation uses White's heteroscedasticity-consistent standard errors. For the medium income countries, income and population variables are highly correlated; only income variables are included in the gravity equation for this group of countries.

Figure 1. Selected countries

Copyright © 2007, Idea Group Inc. Copying or distributing in print or electronic forms without written permission of Idea Group Inc. is prohibited.

Table A.1. Variable descriptions and sources of data

Variable	Description	Source
X_{ij} : Exports from i to j	Nominal value of bilateral exports	Statistics Canada (2001)
Y_i : Exporter's income	Exporter's GDP, PPP (current international $)	World Bank (2001)
Y_j : Importer's income	Importer's GDP, PPP (current international $)	World Bank (2001)
P_i : Exporter's population	Total population in the exporter's market	World Bank (2001)
P_j : Importer's population	Total population in the importer's market	World Bank (2001)
Adj_{ij} : Adjacency dummy	Dummy variable = 1 if the trading partners share a border, 0 otherwise	CIA (2003)
Isl: Island dummy	Dummy variable = 1 if the country is an island, 0 otherwise	CIA (2003)
Land: Landlocked dummy	Dummy variable = 1 if the country is landlocked, 0 otherwise	CIA (2003)
CACM dummy	Dummy variable = 1 if the trading partners are members of CACM, 0 otherwise	
CARICOM dummy	Dummy variable = 1 if the trading partners are members of CARICOM, 0 otherwise	
MERCOSUR dummy	Dummy variable = 1 if the trading partners are members of MERCOSUR, 0 otherwise	
NAFTA dummy	Dummy variable = 1 if the trading partners are members of NAFTA, 0 otherwise	
CAN dummy	Dummy variable = 1 if the trading partners are members of CAN, 0 otherwise	
UE dummy	Dummy variable = 1 if the trading partners are members of European Union, 0 otherwise	
$Dist_{ij}$: Distance	Great circle distances between country capitals of trading partners (km)	Great circle distances between cities (2003)
$Lang_{ij}$: Language dummy	Dummy variable = 1 if the trading partners share the same official language, 0 otherwise.	CIA (2003)
TAI_i : Exporter's TAI	Technological variable	UNDP (2001), author's calculations
TAI_j : Importer's TAI	Technological variable	UNDP (2001), author's calculations
$ArCo_i$: Exporter's ArCo	Technological variable	Archibugi and Coco (2004)
$ArCo_j$: Importer's ArCo	Technological variable	Archibugi and Coco (2004)
Inf_i: Exporter's infrastructure	Transport infrastructure variable	CIA (2003), authors' calculations
Inf_j : Importer's infrastructure	Transport infrastructure variable	CIA (2003), authors' calculations

Note 1: The first column lists the variables used for empirical analysis, the second column outlines a description of the variables, and the third column shows the data sources.

Note 2: UNDP denotes United Nations Development Program and CIA denotes Central Intelligence Agency.

Copyright © 2007, Idea Group Inc. Copying or distributing in print or electronic forms without written permission of Idea Group Inc. is prohibited.

Table A.2. "Beta coefficients" of the variables included in the augmented gravity model

	Beta Coefficients in Model 6	Beta Coefficients in Model 7
Exporter's income	0.0183443	0.016847
Importer's income	0.0385702	0.037293
Exporter's population	0.4261248	0.4307026
Importer's population	0.3156517	0.3216922
Adjacency dummy	0.0245367	0.0180214
Island dummy	-0.0533542	-0.054391
Landlocked dummy	-0.0967349	-0.0929241
CACM dummy	0.0370647	0.0379439
CARICOM dummy	0.0333055	0.0323905
MERCOSUR dummy	0.0489882	0.0473729
NAFTA dummy	0.0095025	0.0111667
CAN dummy	0.0094735	0.0081441
UE dummy	-0.0172897	-0.0255349
Distance	-0.2706165	-0.2572081
Language dummy	0.1000771	0.0942539
Exporter's TAI	0.5036714	0.5065245
Importer's TAI	0.359052	0.3571144
Technological distance	-	-0.0817619
Exporter's infrastructure	0.1562054	0.1565873
Importer's infrastructure	0.1290454	0.1297312

Copyright © 2007, Idea Group Inc. Copying or distributing in print or electronic forms without written permission of Idea Group Inc. is prohibited.

Table A.3. Determinants of international trade. Estimation results for medium income countries.

Variable	(1)	(2)
Constant term	-30.36***	-30.18***
	(-18.06)	(-17.83)
Exporter's income	0.97***	0.97***
	(24.13)	(23.98)
Importer's income	0.77***	0.77***
	(18.79)	(18.73)
Adjacency dummy	0.99***	0.78***
	(4.34)	(3.92)
Island dummy	-1.12***	-1.15***
	(-6.47)	(-6.44)
Landlocked dummy	-0.94***	-0.96***
	(-6.78)	(-6.68)
MERC dummy	-	1.07**
		(1.96)
UE dummy	-	-0.2
		(-1.42)
Distance	-0.88***	-0.91***
	(-15.05)	(-14.15)
Language dummy	1.1***	1.09***
	(7.93)	(7.81)
Exporter's TAI	5***	4.95***
	(11.47)	(10.32)
Importer's TAI	2.18***	2.15***
	(3.95)	(3.81)
Technological distance (TAI)	-	0.39
		(0.76)
Exporter's infrastructure	0.75***	0.77***
	(9.53)	(9.4)
Importer's infrastructure	0.52***	0.54***
	(7.16)	(7.22)
R-squared	0.781	0.782
Adjusted R-squared	0.777	0.777
S.E. of regression	1.335	1.334
Number of observations	736	736

*Notes: ***, **, * indicate significance at 1%, 5% and 10%, respectively. T-statistics are in brackets.*

Column (1): Determinants of trade in medium income countries; Column (2): Determinants of trade in medium income countries and estimation of the effect of technological distance on trade (integration dummies are included). The dependent variable is the natural logarithm of exports in value (current U.S. $$). Income, population and distance are also in natural logarithms. The estimation used White's heteroscedasticity-consistent standard errors. For the medium-income countries, income and population variables are highly correlated, then only income variables are included in the gravity equation for this group of countries.

Copyright © 2007, Idea Group Inc. Copying or distributing in print or electronic forms without written permission of Idea Group Inc. is prohibited.

Chapter VI

Support Networks for Rural and Regional Communities

Tom Denison, Monash University, Australia

Abstract

Using a case study approach, this chapter examines the role of organizational networks in the success and failure of information and communications technology projects. Within a framework informed by the literature of information systems failure, the diffusion of innovation and social network analysis, it argues that information systems projects must take into account the social context in which they are implemented. To be successful such networks require a mix of extended and locally based support networks, because they provide access to much needed resources, including innovations, strategic advice, training, and support at the appropriate level. It further argues that the people who are working in a regional setting felt themselves to be in an extremely disadvantageous situation because they typically lacked support from similar networks. The author hopes that highlighting the importance of such support networks will lead to a better understanding of systems failure and success, and will contribute to improved policy formulation and practice.

Copyright © 2007, Idea Group Inc. Copying or distributing in print or electronic forms without written permission of Idea Group Inc. is prohibited.

Introduction

Quite often it is assumed that the mere implementation of technology and some initial guidance and training in its use will result in successful projects and their ongoing effective use. Time after time this has been found to be insufficient. The literature on information systems failure deals with the multiple causes of this phenomenon, but the intention of this chapter is to focus on one aspect that is particularly important in the context of rural and regional development: the role and type of support networks that are needed to properly plan, implement, and sustain information and communications technology (ICT) projects.

The starting point will be a brief overview of the literature on information systems failure, highlighting recent research that seeks to emphasise the importance of understanding the social context in which systems are implemented and the impact that can have on their success or failure. This will be followed by an introduction to the literature on the diffusion of innovation and social network analysis. Then it will provide a broad theoretical background that can be used to examine the characteristics of organisations as nodes in broader networks, the nature of the relationships they establish within those networks and the importance of those relationships in providing access to information, skills, and resources. These theoretical concerns will then be illustrated by drawing upon a selection of case studies available in the literature, as well as practical experience the author gained when implementing information systems in Vietnam.

The case studies have been chosen because they provide examples of the theoretical issues in rural or regional settings. While some, such as the attempt to implement geographic information systems in India (Barratt, Sahay & Walsham, 2001), serve to illustrate the extent of the problems that can arise when a lack of local knowledge and infrastructure is not addressed, most of the studies illustrate more positive outcomes and act to reinforce insights derived from the theory. As a whole, they demonstrate that network relationships are essential for development in rural and regional areas because they provide access to new ideas and innovations, strategic advice, training and support, as well as a host of other necessary resources. They also demonstrate that some resources, such as access to new ideas, should typically continue to be provided through extended networks, but successful and sustainable projects require the development of a localised infrastructure capable of harnessing resources in a trusted environment.

Information Systems Failure

There is a significant body of literature that has been found discussing the causes of information systems failure from a project management perspective, for example, the work of Lyytinen and Hirschheim (1987), Keil, Cule, Lyytinen, and Schmidt (1998), and Schmidt, Lyytinen, Keil, and Cule (2001). These have tended to focus on management issues, such as the lack of top management commitment to the project, failure to gain user commitment, misunderstanding the requirements, lack of adequate user involvement, lack of required knowledge/skills in the project personel and lack of frozen requirements (Schmidt et al., 2001) although recently there has been significant interest in concepts such as learning

Copyright © 2007, Idea Group Inc. Copying or distributing in print or electronic forms without written permission of Idea Group Inc. is prohibited.

organizations (Lyytinen & Robey, 1999) and their role in nurturing projects. The main thrust of the literature, however, relates to the ability of large organisations to successfully undertake new systems development.

Given its importance, the focus of this chapter is to assist those who seek to implement information systems in regional areas, specifically in the creation of the infrastructure or framework necessary for the successful diffusion and sustainability of technology. It complements the work of others such as Kling (2000) and Orlikowski (2000) who, having recognised that technology is not socially neutral, have attempted to broaden the understanding of the factors that contribute to systems failure by considering the social context in which information systems are implemented. The importance of such an approach has clearly been recognised by the United Nations Development Program (UNDP) Evaluation Office which identified six generic challenges that critically affect ICT for development initiatives: awareness; politics; access; relevancy and meaningful use; sustainability; and coordination (UNDP, 2001).

The work of Heeks (2002) is also important in this context, as he has attempted to model the implementation of information systems in developing countries in such a way as to identify the potential for failure, including what he terms "sustainability failure." He identified "design-actuality differences" as a powerful contributor to systems failure and suggested that systems which allow "contingent improvisation" – that is the ability to accommodate design changes and adapt to local needs – are more likely to be successful, and proved to be sustainable. As he notes, however, the success of this approach is based on environments in which the necessary skills and resources to adapt and successfully implement systems are available locally. This raises the question, then, of just what skills and resources are required, and how access to them can be provided. In this respect, this chapter provides significant insights relating to the diffusion of innovation and to network analysis.

Diffusion of Innovation and Network Analysis

The literature on the diffusion of innovation is dominated by Rogers (2003), who defines innovation as "an idea, practice, or object that is perceived as new by an individual or other unit of adoption" (p. 12). He describes five attributes of innovations: relative advantage, compatibility, complexity, trialability, and observability. According to Rogers, the way in which these attributes are perceived by those who are the beneficiaries of the innovation determines both the speed of adaptation and the degree to which a specific innovation is adopted, modified or ignored. This framework has been successfully used to model the diffusion of innovation in a wide range of studies, for example, Grover and Teng's (1992) study on the take-up of database technology, and Garrison's (2001) study on the adoption of online technology by news organisations.

Studies on the diffusion of innovation have been enriched by adding insights derived from social network analysis which, as Wellman (1988) explains, is based on the relationships between units, rather than the categorisation of those units into predefined categories, and on interpreting behavior in terms of structural constraints on activity rather than in terms of inner forces. In this theory, networks structure collaborative and competitive activities in order to secure scarce resources including information, support, and power. So, to understand the

Copyright © 2007, Idea Group Inc. Copying or distributing in print or electronic forms without written permission of Idea Group Inc. is prohibited.

behavior and capabilities of those units it is necessary to consider the relationships between all groups and individuals in their immediate environment. These relationships are important to innovation, because it is through them that many of Rogers' five attributes are realised.

A highly influential work in this field is that of Granovetter (1973), whose work centered on the strength of weak ties, defined as a casual or infrequent connections between two people or organisations. He emphasised the importance of social networks in the distribution of information and resources, arguing that those with networks of weak ties are best placed to receive new information and resources, since they can act as bridges to the broader community. He also found that the longer linked the network – that is the more links required to establish a connection between two people or units – the less effective it is.

In contrast, Coleman (1988) studied dense closed networks—those with multiple strong internal links but few weak links—finding them to be important for the enforcement of social norms, obligations, and expectations. These, he argued, are important in facilitating effective action. He further argued that those with limited ties to external communities have structural holes that, if they are not closed, can result in a lack of access to the information and resources necessary to facilitate action, particularly innovation. Burt (2000), building on this, argued that all networks can have structural holes and that those who can arrange relationships spanning across those holes may achieve a competitive advantage because they are best placed to obtain new ideas, information, support, and other resources. In this view, network closure is about maintaining the status quo while brokerage is about change. However, a number of researchers (Aldrich & Zimmer, 1986; Kadushin, 2002) have found that both brokerage and cohesion networks are required for the successful diffusion and exploitation of resources.

Considering the issues relating to brokerage and cohesion networks in more detail, Aldrich and Zimmer (1986) emphasised that the maintenance of effective networks requires the continual creation of weak ties so as to prevent a few strong ties from closing them to opportunities and alternatives, while Kadushin (2002) argued that "safety drivers," which act against change, are common when the costs of interaction are low, visibility is high, and moral obligations are more salient—a situation typical of rural and regional networks. And, in work of special significance for the diffusion of innovation, Valente (1995, 2005) found that a significant difference between effectiveness (brokerage) networks and safety (cohesive) networks is the location of trust, which is an important factor in the realisation of Rogers' (2003) five attributes.

Others have attempted to identify issues that relate to the development and success of regional groupings, and their work has obvious implications for developments in rural and regional areas. For instance, Hakansson (1990) suggested that networks are a new organisational form necessary to supplement internal competencies and that this implied a mutual dependence between government and business, particularly in regional areas where location has a strong impact on the availability of resources. Steward and Conway (2000) examined the conflicting goals and cultural variations that are likely to exist between organizations with extended supply chains, and identified that differences in culture, language, and business practices at the levels of individuals and organizations are potential sources of tension.

Finally, Furst, Schubert, Rudolph, and Spieckermann (2001) related the concepts of cohesion and brokerage to the complementary categories of stationary and mobile social capital. In their view, regional networks need a high degree of stationary capital to ensure self gover-

Copyright © 2007, Idea Group Inc. Copying or distributing in print or electronic forms without written permission of Idea Group Inc. is prohibited.

nance but also need to be able to lock in mobile social capital in order to bring in new ideas and the flexibility needed for development. Bebbington (1997) provided a clear example of this in the author's study on communities in the Ecuadorian and Bolivian Andes that had managed to improve their local economies, reversing trends in both migration and environmental protection, via a program of agricultural intensification based on the use of new technology. He demonstrated that this could not have been achieved without a broadening of support networks and the access to ideas, contacts, and resources they bring, nor without the involvement of strong local community groups that helped create the pre conditions to take advantage of those networks and opportunities when they were presented.

In summary, the successful diffusion of technology, particularly in rural and regional areas, is in large part dependent on the flow of resources and the capacity for local improvisation. Organizations and communities seeking to implement technologically based change, require both brokerage and cohesion networks: brokerage networks because they provide access to opportunities, innovation, strategic advice, new skills and support; cohesion networks because they provide a trusted environment in which to operate, harness local capacity and manage "contingent improvisation."

Case Studies

There are a significant number of case studies in the literature that explore these issues, but for the purposes of this chapter it will be sufficient to highlight five. The first, a study by Sherry (1998), illustrates a straightforward analysis of a technology diffusion program, using Rogers' (1995) framework to evaluate IT training programs in regional school districts in the United States. In the second, an ambitious, three year longitudinal study by Barratt, Sahay, and Walsham (2001), the efforts of the Indian Ministry of Environment and Forests (MoEF) to apply geographic information systems (GIS) technology to forestry management and wasteland reclamation are examined. Issues of trust are explored in some depth, as are the types of problems can arise when local conditions and expertise are not adequately acknowledged, themes that are further developed in an Australian study by Terziovski and Howell (2001). They examine network linkages connecting multiple stakeholders, demonstrating that interaction between government, business, and the community is important in facilitating new initiatives, particularly if trusted local connections can be harnessed.

An extended examination of the author's experiences in implementing a series of information systems in regional Vietnamese university libraries is then provided. This is a prime example of a project that was struggling to succeed because the technology was implemented without regard to the local context, but which was revitalised when gaps in local infrastructure were identified and the need to establish local support networks recognized (Johanson, Denison & Otis, 2004). This is complemented by the final case study, that of Gibb and Adkihary (2000) on the work of non-government organisations (NGOs) in South Africa. They explore the nature and role of NGOs as network brokers capable of supporting external interventions by using their relationships to assist in the development of local stakeholder networks.

Copyright © 2007, Idea Group Inc. Copying or distributing in print or electronic forms without written permission of Idea Group Inc. is prohibited.

Training and the Diffusion of Skills: Boulder Valley Internet Project

Sherry (1998) used Rogers' (1995) framework for studying the diffusion of technology to evaluate the Boulder Valley Internet Project (BVIP), a five-year collaborative venture between the University of Colorado at Boulder and the Boulder Valley School District (BVSD). The project was funded by the National Science Foundation (NSF) and aimed to incorporate Internet-based technologies and strategies into the teaching program of the District, by developing training programs and integrated telecommunications throughout.

Commencing in 1992, the project used a trainer-of-trainers model to create a core group of 26 teachers. Their mission was to become proficient in the use of e-mail and in investigating Internet resources, and experienced in integrating these into school curricula, so as to pass on their skills to other teachers within the district. Using a participatory design model, the bulk of the training concentrated on the needs of classroom teachers. Workshops and classes were given in BSVD classrooms, using the very platforms that the teachers would use once their classrooms were connected. Sherry found that the program achieved considerable success and that, as of January 1996, there were 435 teachers on the BSVD network who logged in regularly. However, she also reported that the project later lost much of its momentum when it lost the support of the school administrators and key policy makers at the district level.

She made the following points with respect to the level of success that was achieved:

- Rogers' (1995) framework emphasises the role of change agents in influencing their clients' behavior, and their ability to help them realise change. In this case, the project used BSVD teachers drawn from the district as change agents rather than relying on outside experts that could have been drawn from the project's partner organizations. This ensured a significant level of client/agent empathy.

- By focusing on providing an authentic context (dealing with real issues in an actual work environment) in which situated learning could take place, the project presented the opportunity for clients to observe the benefits of the technology firsthand, another critical factor in Rogers' (1995) model.

- The self-reflection involved in the participatory design process ensured that trainers and trainees explored the issues, dealt with conflicts and solved problems together, contributing substantially to the success of the training program.

- At least in its initial stages, the district as an organization ensured that the effort was aligned with district-wide visions and policies and integrated into the established telecommunications channels. As a result, the project had strong grassroots support from the local teachers who were the primary participants in the training program.

As Sherry (1998) noted, however, the project was not a complete success. The reason for this was that, as the project evolved, the attitudes of the policy makers became more conservative and the project gradually ceased to address the needs of all stakeholders, specifically the school administration and the district's policy making bodies. As a result, it

Copyright © 2007, Idea Group Inc. Copying or distributing in print or electronic forms without written permission of Idea Group Inc. is prohibited.

received a lower priority and stalled. Sherry concluded that "If there was a single lesson to be learned from the BVIP experiment it is … [that] information technology interventions cannot be separated from their ecological contexts or from the educational activities that they enhance" (p. 141).

Rogers' (1995) model postulates five stages that a successful intervention must pass through. They are: (a) seeking information about the innovation's existence and some understanding of how it functions; (b) forming a favourable or unfavourable attitude towards it; (c) engaging in activities that lead to a choice to either adopt or reject the innovation; (d) putting the innovation to use; and (e) seeking reinforcement of an innovation decision that has already been made (Sherry, 1998). In the case of the BVIP project, it can be seen that external linkages (brokerage networks) were used to successfully introduce new technology as in step (a), while the strong peer-to-peer (cohesive networks) represented by the teachers within the district assisted steps (b) to (d). However, the ultimate failure of the project was due to the poor management of its broader internal stakeholder network, allowing Kadushin's (2002) "safety drivers" to take affect, thereby cutting off access to the required resources and external support needed to reinforce the innovation as in step (e).

The Role of Trust in Local Adaptation: GIS Systems in India

Barratt et al. (2001) also undertook an in depth case study of a technology diffusion program. It was a three-year longitudinal study of the efforts of the Indian Ministry of Environment and Forests (MoEF) to apply geographic information systems (GIS) technology in the areas of forestry management and wasteland reclamation. For their analysis they used a framework strongly influenced by both Giddens (1990, 1991) and Kling (2000) to explore the types of problems that can arise when local conditions and expertise are not adequately acknowledged and utilised during the introduction of new systems.

The project commenced in 1991, initiated by the U.S. Agency for International Development (USAID), which also provided seed money, training, and software. Phase 1 of the project aimed to establish the technical feasibility of using GIS in eight scientific institutions. Phase 2 envisaged the subsequent transfer of those systems to local district offices. Although Phase 1 was completed in 1993, by the end of the research period only minimal progress had been made in transferring the technology to district level and it is this failure that the analysis focuses on.

While acknowledging variable management support that affected the enthusiasm with which the project was undertaken in different districts, Barratt et al. (2001) identified a number of specific issues that contributed strongly to the failure of Phase 2:

- There was no work culture based around the use of IT because there was no history of access to technology. At the same time, the social structure, organizational forms, and existing work arrangements were not taken into consideration. The pressure for change had come from external sources—governmental agencies and international bodies such as the World Bank and the United Nations (UN). These pressures confronted strong existing traditions and systems of work, but while the process of technology

Copyright © 2007, Idea Group Inc. Copying or distributing in print or electronic forms without written permission of Idea Group Inc. is prohibited.

transfer was useful in providing know how, technology, and funding, it promoted western values and management techniques that were often incompatible within the context of a developing country. The difficulties caused by these unresolved tensions hampered the development of the restructured and standardised work practices required to introduce GIS at the local level.

- Compounding the problems mentioned in the first point, the technology itself was not neutral. GIS systems were built on western notions of rationality and coordination, while the depiction of space as an objective was a value-free reality. Assuming the widespread use of maps and knowledge of spatial planning concepts, the new systems required a reorientation from planning based on non-spatial parameters such as development schemes and households, as was the existing practice, to planning based on spatial criteria, such as "watershed units" and "wasteland distributions." These concepts were in conflict with local practice and, as a consequence, the system was perceived to be less relevant to local need.

- There was a lack of relevant professional skills. The effect of the first two points may have been ameliorated had more attention been given to providing support and building local expertise and capacity. Forestry officials needed to develop new conceptual skills to translate their forestry related problems into the spatial terms required by the GIS models, but they also needed the skills to adapt those models to local conditions in order to facilitate contingent improvisation. The professional skills that were locally available enabled the achievement of success in Phase 1, but not in Phase 2. However, the models developed in Phase 1 reflected the view of the institutes as scientific research and development centers by placing little emphasis on other important socioeconomic variables in the context of the districts, for example population and livestock data.

- Regarding professional skills requirements, it was recognized by a number of the institutes that there would be problems in transferring the technology to the districts, because they considered that their technical resources and the skills of institute staff were inadequate to provide sustained support in the field. They lacked a core group of people with GIS expertise who could nurture the projects over time and, in any case, many scientists considered that their institutional mandate was limited to developing the technology, not its transfer to the district level.

As can be seen, this was an intervention that required significant changes in professional culture, technical skills, and work practices. Remote organizations were encouraging the take up of the technology, and although the project provided support networks sufficient to ensure implementation by the scientific institutions, the networks that were provided were inadequate to ensure the transfer of skills and the conditions required to effectively exploit the technology at the local level.

The analysis by Barratt et al. (2001) is also of interest because of the way in which it uses Giddens' (1990, 1991) theories to explore notions of trust, the lack of which they consider contributed to the problems that arose. Giddens identified two types of trust, distinguishing between situations in which the actors are face-to-face and those in which they are not. In this case, a typical situation in which information systems are implemented for the first time, it is a prime example of the latter, and required reconciliation between traditional and new knowledge systems and the development of new trust systems. However, the effectiveness

Copyright © 2007, Idea Group Inc. Copying or distributing in print or electronic forms without written permission of Idea Group Inc. is prohibited.

of these processes depended on the manner in which the technology was introduced and the nature of support provided and, in this case, these were inadequate to the task. As a result, the disembedding of traditional practices of forestry management did not occur, and made it difficult for standard methodologies to be modelled, codified, and applied.

The introduction of GIS technology also exposed workers at all levels to new networks of people, required to introduce and support the technology. For the project to be successful, they needed to develop trust in these new networks. But this could not happen in conditions where an unresolved tension existed between local requirements and the introduced system.

Barratt et al. (2001) argued that the project was not successful because it attempted to impose a new professional and technological framework without taking local conditions into account. There seems to have been little provision for local contingency in design, and little recognition of the types of support and support networks that would be required to implement and sustain the new environment. Significantly, there seems to have been little recognition of the need to develop trust in this new environment or the impact that that might have on the success of the project. Their final comment, noting that "the entry of the private sector into government GIS projects is one factor that can potentially lead to more rapid changes in the future" (2001, p. 15), clearly indicated an important issue. This comment is significant because it recognises that the private sector represents a means of providing additional expertise and support, localised in a way that enhances trust.

The Role of Trust in Technology Diffusion: E-Commerce in Regional Australia

The issue of trust also arises, albeit in a slightly different form, in an Australian study by Terziovski and Howell (2001). Reviewing a series of e-commerce projects undertaken by local government in regional Victoria, they found that while network linkages connecting external stakeholders were important to drive new initiatives, trusted local connections were also essential for their proper implementation and ongoing exploitation.

The scheme in question, VEEM (Victorian E-Commerce Early Movers) Scheme, was funded by the state government with the aim of identifying linkages that could aid and support local government usage of e-commerce and its subsequent take up by local industry and the wider community. A number of local government areas were funded to develop a range of projects, including promotional events such as e-commerce business planning workshops and regional expos, and more specific activities such as the development of regional business portals and the development of business plans to enable local businesses to adopt online fulfilment and procurement.

Feedback from participants confirmed that the scheme was a success, with e-commerce being embraced by business and communities alike. They also noted that, as the project progressed, many of the activities had been customised to better fit community and private sector expectations, reflecting the flexibility that had been built into the scheme, and the willingness of the responsible government agency to work with local government in a meaningful way.

Terziovski and Howell's (2001) report highlighted several strategies that were critical to this success, but noted that to achieve sustainability it was necessary for participants to develop

Copyright © 2007, Idea Group Inc. Copying or distributing in print or electronic forms without written permission of Idea Group Inc. is prohibited.

their own expertise, and it was important that strategies had been framed with that end goal in mind. Specifically, they commented that:

- Participants recognized that the projects would not have been undertaken without the stimulus provided by the state government, nor would they have been seen as a high priority for local government without that support, which provided credibility, resources, and a secure working environment.

- While participants acknowledged the important role of the state government, they also understood that, in order to ensure meaningful participation, it was essential to devolve decision making to local government and communities. In this context, local government saw its role as seeding community or industry based networks, and providing infrastructure support and training.

- As local small businesses were intensely focused on their own immediate needs, it was considered far more effective to use local experts to talk to local people, maintaining the focus on their needs rather than those identified by external stakeholders. These grassroots champions were seen as important because they could provide examples of success and act as marketing agents for uptake of technology. These are important factors in reducing local indifference. It was also considered more effective to have a number of champions, drawn from different business sectors, who had existing relationships with other local centers of influence such as banks, accountants, and community business groups. For example, one local government office sponsored six business champions from three targeted industry sectors – transport/distribution, manufacturing, and services industries – and was instrumental in connecting them to the economic development in the region by providing better access to its networks.

- While it was recognized that external expertise was essential to the success of the diffusion process, and that that expertise would be required on an ongoing basis, it was also recognized that much expertise could, and should, be localised. To facilitate this, the report recommended that the state government should fund an ICT Center in each regional area, using a local body such as part of the council or a university or the local e-commerce association, to deliver information, training, and so forth. These centres could not only provide trusted support, but could also strengthen the relationship between the State Government, local councils, and the community, thereby providing a sound foundation for future programs.

- Finally, it was recognized that something as simple as a database of service providers could be invaluable in assisting both local government and local businesses, by preventing duplication of time and resources when identifying and evaluating existing service providers.

Reflecting these considerations, the report proposed a model of best practice based on a tripartite relationship between state and local government, and local government and the community. In this model, the state government provides the vision, policies, initiatives, and funding, while local government provides a leadership role to facilitate e-commerce diffusion, working with local businesses and the community to address real needs.

Copyright © 2007, Idea Group Inc. Copying or distributing in print or electronic forms without written permission of Idea Group Inc. is prohibited.

All of the strategies adopted by the project built on existing networks and relationships to facilitate the successful diffusion of e-ommerce, using them to establish and reinforce existing trust systems and to develop strong relationships on a regional, business and individual basis. The creation of support (brokerage) networks that facilitate a flow of information, skills and resources was absolutely essential, but it was recognised that these would only be useful if they were combined with the strengths and resources of the local community (cohesion networks). As in the MoEF project (Barratt et al., 2001), trust in the ability of those managing the project to understand local needs and conditions was identified as a significant factor, but unlike the MoEF project, trust was harnessed and the project achieved its goals.

Building Support Networks: University Library Systems in Vietnam

Many of the themes and issues raised in this chapter found practical application in a series of projects in which the author participated, involving the diffusion of new technology among regional universities in Vietnam. In this case, which has been documented by Johanson et al. (2004), the NGOs managing the project not only brokered networks to support the initial diffusion of technology and distribution of resources, but also assisted in the development of more localized networks capable of exploiting the technology on an ongoing basis.

The first of these projects began in 1999, after Atlantic Philanthropies (AP), a US based NGO, decided to contribute to the educational infrastructure of Vietnam by developing a series of Learning Resource Centers (LRCs) in collaboration with regional universities in Da Nang, Hue, Can Tho, and Thai Nguyen. Each project involved the design and construction of a modern library facility based on western models and standards of information service, together with the provision of state of the art technology, and high quality teaching and learning facilities.

The initial project, the Da Nang University Information Resource Center (IRC), was completed in 2001 with high expectations. Staff had received training in the form of a short study tour to Australia and an introduction to the use of library management systems. The initial collection included 10,000 monograph and serial titles, in both English and Vietnamese, and access to a range of electronic resources. A Vietnamese company was contracted to provide both a local area network and an integrated library management system (ILMS) to manage housekeeping and public access functions. Although well resourced in comparison with other university libraries, it quickly became apparent that it was under utilized. Management decided not to circulate material and, partly in consequence of that decision, staff used only a fraction of the functionality of the ILMS. Further, without a support contract for either the communications infrastructure or the ILMS, there were ongoing problems with the stability of the technology.

AP was surprised by this result and delayed work on the remaining LRCs while a review was conducted. That review, undertaken by RMIT University Vietnam, found that strong and committed management had been provided and, although there were a number of resourcing issues, the most significant problems related to the fact that the IRC was operating without the supportive infrastructure that its western counterparts take for granted:

Copyright © 2007, Idea Group Inc. Copying or distributing in print or electronic forms without written permission of Idea Group Inc. is prohibited.

- The proposed operating environment of the IRC was essentially new to academic libraries within Vietnam and, although there was a training program for staff, it was both limited in scope and had no provision for ongoing support. There were only a few librarians with whom they could discuss ideas and share experience. The library schools were not producing appropriate graduates and the limited number of similar libraries were scattered throughout the country. Somehow, with little advice from the scanty professional infrastructure, traditional tasks such as cataloguing fared well, but new areas such as circulation, the use of IT, and the identification, acquisition, and use of electronic resources, did not.

- Also, apart from the inability to obtain immediate practical advice at a local level, the overall professional library infrastructure within the country was underdeveloped. There was little support for activities such as the adoption and promotion of national standards, the nurture of a national professional association or the encouragement of local systems vendors. That made it difficult for management to obtain strategic advice.

- Neither staff nor vendors had the experience to develop procedures that would allow them to incorporate the automated system into the new style of operation, nor to identify problems with the system that would allow them to recommend appropriate modifications. There was little capacity for local adaptation.

- Modern western libraries make intense use of IT, relying on a shared infrastructure that allows them to reduce the real costs of that technology as well as the resources required to manage it. Typically, that infrastructure includes consortia to support the purchase of electronic resources, the shared development of IT strategies and applications, interlibrary loan networks, and shared cataloguing. None of this was available to the IRC.

- The decision on how to proceed with acquiring an ILMS was crucial to the successful operation of the IRC. At that time the available choices were limited to importing an international system or developing one locally. Importing one had the advantage that it could be expected to be fully functional and would comply with the relevant standards, but there would also be several disadvantages: none had a Vietnamese language version; none provided local support; and none provided support in Vietnamese. Furthermore, the cost of the initial purchase and of ongoing maintenance was unaffordable. Eventually, a Vietnamese company was commissioned to develop an ILMS for the IRC. The chosen company was new to libraries and although it learnt quickly, the system it initially delivered had a number of serious problems.

- There were, and there still are, serious limitations in the national infrastructure with regard to the availability of trained IT staff, particularly in the regions where, although the number of IT staff is growing, there remains a shortage because there is an increasing demand for their services from other developing industries.

AP had come to realise that developing a sustainable service required a significantly broader perspective than that was at first apprehended. One other thing they recognised was that the LRCs not only had to be effective in themselves, but also they had to be integrated within the broader educational and professional communities. To advance their interests it was necessary to work within the already established framework in the country, putting

Copyright © 2007, Idea Group Inc. Copying or distributing in print or electronic forms without written permission of Idea Group Inc. is prohibited.

emphasis on those aspects that had been identified as being important to the LRC projects and their further development. The profession within Vietnam had already instigated work on a program of modernization but had been hampered by lack of funds. AP sponsored a workshop to discuss further on the adoption of standards at a national level. That workshop also explored issues of cooperative and collaborative activity, including the possibility of developing a national organisation of professional librarians and library educators, as well as recommending a national strategy for the development and acquisition of library management systems within the country. Working closely with the profession, AP subsequently initiated projects in a number of these areas.

From the view point on the diffusion of innovation and Rogers' (2003) framework, this intervention was strong enough in terms of relative advantage, but at the same time was weak in terms of compatibility, complexity, trialability, and observability. It became obvious that the success of the first IRC was dependent on the broader national infrastructure and it could not be considered successful if it was treated as self-contained. It could only be considered successful if it was treated as a first stage in the overall development of services within the country. In their analysis, Johanson et al. (2004) argued that support networks were essential to the success of these projects because they provided access to strategic advice, skills transfer, and an ongoing professional culture. Hence, the LRCs could not achieve their full potential until stakeholder communities had themselves progressed to the stage where they could provide the required additional support. In network terms, the first IRC had been created with numerous structural holes that could not be effectively closed until a shorter linked brokerage network and a stronger internal (cohesive) network had been established. Therefore, the other elements of Rogers' (2003) framework could come into play until that had been done.

The project is also of interest from the point of view of developing local capacity in order to support local adaptation or contingent improvisation. As mentioned earlier, the library management system was plagued with problems and the resolution of these problems was beyond the reach of the staff of the IRC and the vendor. An outside expert was called in to evaluate the system and to work with both parties to recommend improvements so that the resultant system would at least provide the necessary core functionality and meet international standards. This strategy resonates well with the views of Heeks (2002) because it allowed the staff of the local vendor and the IRC to build up the expertise required to take future development of the system under their own control. In this case, even though the need for local adaptation had been recognized, the capacity to undertake it was only achieved when the relevant support networks had been established.

Concluding their analysis, Johanson et al. (2004) reported that these issues were addressed directly in the development of the subsequent LRCs. They found that not only were the subsequent projects more successful, but that their success contributed to a revitalization of the Da Nang IRC.

Copyright © 2007, Idea Group Inc. Copying or distributing in print or electronic forms without written permission of Idea Group Inc. is prohibited.

Using NGOs to Build Support Networks:
The CEFE Network in South Africa

A common question running through these case studies is the question of how best to maximise the effectiveness of external interventions. The work of Barratt et al. (2001) highlights some of the problems that can occur, and although Terziovski and Howell (2001) describe a more successful case, they are clearly considering a technically potent and culturally homogenous environment. The projects documented by Johanson et al. (2004) are useful in that they provide examples of a successful intervention in a developing country, but a more general consideration of the issues is provided by Gibb and Adkihary (2000) who examine the role of NGOs in this process. In their view, NGOs can provide a useful mechanism for promoting the diffusion of innovation and development because they are more likely to be embedded in their communities and, as a consequence of that, are more likely to be capable of helping to develop the networks of trusted stakeholders that lead to sustainable outcomes.

They studied the Competency-based Economies through the Formation of Enterprise (CEFE) Network, an alliance of six NGOs in South Africa. In South Africa, the role of small business is seen as critical in supporting government policy, in meeting targets for new job creation, and as an effective means of redistributing income and opportunity to the indigenous population. NGOs, such as those of the CEFE Network, are important because they are seen as a means of delivering financial and business development services, including training and consultancy, and establishing the necessary support structure for small businesses to thrive. CEFE is important because it forms part of a national grouping of NGOs operating with a broader stakeholder group comprising major national players, including government organizations and public funding sources, national and international, private businesses (large and small), professional service companies, local and regional government, business representative organisations, and the media. Thus, it is in a position to broker a wide range of services.

Gibb and Adkihary (2000) chose the CEFE Network to study because, since its inception in 1995, it had successfully met a number of challenges, including the need to deliver services over a broad geographic area by focusing on local need and underpinning sustainability. As a result, it had been successful in helping its member NGOs to distribute resources and provide training, while developing a more standardised range of services that allowed them to mesh better with national priorities. By studying their experience, Gibb and Adkihary aimed to identify and promote new forms of partnerships and governance that could be used to assist the development of small and medium enterprises (SMEs) more generally.

They found that NGOs can play an important role in this type of activity because they are essentially bottom-up organizations which are more likely to be embedded in their communities and are thereby more likely to reflect local needs. Not only that, but they also have the ability to act as brokers, capable of connecting those communities to the support networks that can provide them with the access to external expertise and the resources they require to meet their needs. In this way, they can act to identify the local needs and close structural holes.

Gibb and Adkihary also recognised that NGOs are not without potential problems, though they are intrinsically connected with their strengths. For example, NGOs often have a weak resource base, and as a result, can fall into the trap of expending their energies on chasing

Copyright © 2007, Idea Group Inc. Copying or distributing in print or electronic forms without written permission of Idea Group Inc. is prohibited.

funding to ensure their continued existence rather than on fulfilling local needs. By focusing more on the requirements of their funding bodies, they react more to supplier needs rather than those of the community they seek to serve. Another potential problem is that, because of their commitment to meeting local needs, they may find it difficult to standardize service delivery by harming their ability to fit into national networks and to align with national priorities.

Gibb and Adkihary observed that, to be successful in helping their communities, NGOs must develop strategies to neutralise those problems. To that end, they proposed a Stakeholder Assessment Model (SAM) of NGO effectiveness, based on a series of key evaluation questions, including:

- To what degree the overall focus of the NGO on meeting the needs of the stakeholders?
- How well is the NGO known by the stakeholders?
- How clear is the mission/objectives of the NGO to the stakeholders?
- How well is the NGO perceived by the stakeholders to be meeting its objectives?
- To what extent does the NGO undertake joint ventures in partnership with stakeholders?
- Are these initiatives perceived as being successful? (Gibb & Adkihary, 2000, p. 145)

The model as developed, focuses on the requirements of NGOs as organizations at the center of stakeholder networks that need a clear understanding of their own missions and the needs of their various stakeholders. Gibb and Adkihary observed further that, if used correctly, the model can not only ensure a focus on client needs, but also can help in setting management objectives by contributing to NGO sustainability.

The study concluded by reporting that the CEFE Network was continuing to deliver successful programs and gain greater acceptance from government. By increasing its range of strategic alliances, it was also improving its ability to broker new services. Gibb and Adkihary's (2000) examination of the CEFE network demonstrates that, despite the potential problems, NGOs that focus on the issues identified in their SAM model can successfully act to facilitate network development and achieve the mutual support that derives from bringing local groups and external stakeholder communities together.

Future Trends

International agencies that are involved in development projects, for example the World Bank, are including social capital measurements in their analyses and are starting to acknowledge the role of social factors in their strategies for systems development (UNDP, 2001). Significant research is being undertaken in the areas of technology diffusion, social capital and network analysis. However, despite the examples provided in this chapter, much of it

Copyright © 2007, Idea Group Inc. Copying or distributing in print or electronic forms without written permission of Idea Group Inc. is prohibited.

relates to the role of business and the corporate world, which are generally seen as the most important drivers of economic growth. Furthermore, much of the work in regional areas is actually undertaken through the agency of NGOs, and therefore, there needs to be more intensive research into characteristics, role, and operating culture of NGOs.

This is particularly important in developing countries and there are a growing number of organizations working to explore those issues, for example, the research being undertaken by the Institute for Development Policy and Management at Manchester University, which focuses on policy formulation and implementation, and organisational design (Baark & Heeks, 1998; Madon, 2000). The emergent field of community informatics is also making a strong contribution in this context. For example, two recent conferences focusing on technology for development, and framing the issues in terms of sustainability and the social appropriation of technology, are of special relevance to the issues raised in this chapter (Erwin, Taylor, Bytheway, & Strumpfer, 2005; Johanson & Stillman, 2004).

Conclusion

The projects discussed in this chapter demonstrate that an over-emphasis on technology and technology-based services, and their development in isolation from the communities that they are intended to serve, will not lead to successful and sustainable outcomes. Successful, sustainable projects are the result of a careful interplay of controlled variables, many of which may need to go through a complex iterative process based on changing stages of organizational culture. Projects targeted at rural and regional communities must address the real needs of the communities they aim to serve. That requires not only long term commitment and strategic funding, but also, meaningful participation and proper consideration of all influences within and between the affected communities.

This chapter has used a framework provided by the diffusion of innovation within a network environment to highlight how necessary resources can be provided to make such developments a sustainable reality. Successful, sustainable projects require access to a complex infrastructure maintained by a range of stakeholders. Network relationships are essential in both the development and maintenance of such infrastructure because they provide access to new ideas and innovations, strategic advice, training, technical support, and a host of other resources. While some of these resources, such as access to new ideas, typically should continue to be provided through extended networks, successful and sustainable projects require a localized infrastructure capable of localizing and harnessing resources in a trusted environment. Specifically, it is important to recognise this sort of support network in rural and regional areas, and even more so in developing countries, because it is precisely these network structures that they lack.

The case studies examined, particularly those of Johanson et al. (2004) and Gibb and Adkihary (2000), highlight the fact that those networks are often brokered through the agency of NGOs, who provide access to contacts and resources that would otherwise be inaccessible to local communities. And while it could be argued that broad networks could be established without NGOs, the case studies emphasise that their importance derives from the fact that they are more often embedded within their communities, so that they can make use of existing trust

Copyright © 2007, Idea Group Inc. Copying or distributing in print or electronic forms without written permission of Idea Group Inc. is prohibited.

systems and local links to identify and close structural holes which would otherwise deny those communities access to much needed resources and expertise.

Acknowledgment

This chapter is based on research supported by the Australian Research Council.

References

Aldrich, H., & Zimmer, C. (1986). Entrepreneurship through social networks. In D. Sexton & R. Smilor (Eds.), *Art and science of entrepreneurship*, 3-23. Cambridge, MA: Ballinger,

Baark, E., & Heeks, R. (1998). Evaluation of donor-funded information technology projects in China: A lifecycle approach. *Development informatics working chapter series*. Manchester: Institute for Development Policy and Management, University of Manchester.

Barratt, M., Sahay, S., & Walsham, G. (2001) Information technology and social transformation: GIS for forestry management in India. *The Information Society, 17*, 5-20.

Bebbington, A. (1997). Social capital and rural intensification: Local organizations and islands of sustainability in the rural Andes. *The Geographical Journal, 163*(2), 189-197.

Burt. R. (2000). The network structure of social capital. *Research in Organizational Behavior, 22*, 345-423.

Coleman, J. (1988). Social capital in the creation of human capital. *American Journal of Sociology, 94,* S95-S120.

Erwin, G., Taylor, W., Bytheway, A., & Strumpfer, C. (Eds.). (2005, August 23-26). CIRN2005: *The Second Annual Conference of the Community Informatics Research Network, Cape Town, South Africa.*

Furst, D., Schubert, H., Rudolph, A., & Spieckermann, H. (2001). Regional actor networks between social capital and regional governance. *Connections, 24*(1), 42-67.

Garrison, B. (2001). Diffusion of online information technologies in newschapter newsrooms. *Journalism, 2*(2), 221-239.

Gibb, A., & Adhikary, D. (2000). Strategies for local and regional NGO development: Combining sustainable outcomes with sustainable organizations. *Entrepreneurship & Regional Development, 12*, 137-161.

Giddens, A. (1990). *The consequences of modernity*. Cambridge: Polity Press.

Giddens, A. (1991). *Modernity and self-identity: Self and society in the late modern age.* Cambridge: Polity Press.

Copyright © 2007, Idea Group Inc. Copying or distributing in print or electronic forms without written permission of Idea Group Inc. is prohibited.

Granovetter, S. (1973). The strength of weak ties. *The American Journal of Sociology, 78*(6), 1360-1380.

Grover, V., & Teng, J. (1992) An examination of DBMS adoption and success in American organizations. *Information Management, 23*(5), 239-248.

Hakansson, H. (1990). Technological collaboration in industrial networks. *European Management Journal, 8*(3), 371-379.

Heeks, R. (2002) Information systems and developing countries: Failure, success, and local improvisations. *The Information Society, 18*(2), 101-112.

Johanson, G., Denison, T., & Otis, N. (2004, September 29-October 1). Building sustainable learning communities in Vietnam. In G. Johanson & L. Stillman (Eds.), *Sustainability and community technology: What does this mean for community informatics?* Monash Prato Colloqium, Prato, Italy. Available at http://www.ccnr.net/?q=node/5. Accessed Jan. 30, 2006

Johanson, G., & Stillman, L. (Eds.). (2004, September 29-October 1). *Sustainability and community technology: What does this mean for community informatics?* Monash Prato Colloqium, Prato, Italy.

Kadushin, C. (2002) The motivational foundation of social networks. *Social Networks, 24*, 77-91.

Keil, M., Cule, P., Lyytinen, K., & Schmidt, R. (1998). A framework for identifying software project risks. *Communications of the ACM, 41*(11), 76-83.

Kling, R. (2000) Learning about information technologies and social change: The contribution of social informatics. *The Information Society, 16*, 217-232.

Lyytinen, K., & Hirschheim, R. (1987). Information Systems failures – A survey and classification of the empirical literature. *Oxford Surveys in Information Technology, 4*, 257-309.

Lyytinen, K., & Robey, D. (1999). Learning failure in information systems development. *Information Systems Journal, 9*(2), 85-101.

Madon, S. (2000). International NGOs: Networking, information flows and learning. *Development informatics working chapter series*. Manchester: Institute for Development Policy and Management, University of Manchester.

Orlikowski, W. (2000). Using technology and constituting structures: A practice lens for studying technology in organisations. *Organization Science, 11*(4), 404-428.

Rogers, E. (1995). *Diffusion of innovations* (4th ed.). New York: The Free Press.

Rogers, E. (2003). *Diffusion of innovations* (5th ed.). New York: The Free Press.

Schmidt, R., Lyytinen, K., Keil, M., & Cule, P. (2001) Identifying software project risks: An international Delphi study. *Journal of Management Information Systems, 17*(4), 5-36.

Sherry, L. (1998). An integrated technology adoption and diffusion model. *International Journal of Educational Telecommunications, 4*(2/3), 113-145.

Steward, F., & Conway, S. (2000). Building networks for innovation diffusion in Europe: Learning from the SPRINT Programme. *Enterprise and Innovation Management Studies, 1*(3), 281-301.

Copyright © 2007, Idea Group Inc. Copying or distributing in print or electronic forms without written permission of Idea Group Inc. is prohibited.

Terziovski, M., & Howell, A. (2001). *e-Commerce best practice: A review of the Victorian e-Commerce early movers* (VEEM) scheme in Victorian local councils. Report prepared for Multimedia Victoria, State and Regional Development.

UNDP. (2001). Information communications technology for development. *Essentials*, 5. Available at http;//www.undp.org/eo/documents/essentials_5.PDF. Accessed Jan. 30, 2006.

Valente, T. (1995). *Network models of the diffusion of innovations*. Cresskill, NJ: Hampton Press.

Valente, T. (2005). Models and methods for innovation diffusion. In P. Carrington, J. Scott, & S. Wasserman (Eds.), *Models and methods in social network analysis*. Cambridge: Cambridge University Press.

Wellman, B. (1988). Structural analysis: From method and metaphor to theory and substance. In B. Wellman & S. Berkowitz (Eds.), *Social structures: A network approach* (pp. 19-61). Cambridge: Cambridge University Press.

Copyright © 2007, Idea Group Inc. Copying or distributing in print or electronic forms without written permission of Idea Group Inc. is prohibited.

Section III

Information and Knowledge Management

Chapter VII

Developing a Global Perspective for Knowledge Management

Martin A. Schell, New York University, USA

Abstract

Localization of a document or other product requires tacit knowledge of the target language and culture. Although it is promoted by many activists, localization is becoming increasingly inadequate as a strategy for disseminating knowledge on the World Wide Web (WWW). The 21st century has already seen dramatic rises in the numbers of Internet users in nearly every country, making it unlikely if not impossible for any translation effort to accommodate all of the 347 languages that claim at least 1 million speakers. The best way to maximize the accessibility of Web content is to make it more explicit, not more tacit. This means developing a global perspective and writing English text clearly so that nonnative speakers can easily understand it. Global English *is characterized by simpler sentence structure, less jargon, and no slang, thereby making it a viable global language for countless Web users whose native language is not considered important enough to merit a localization effort.*

Copyright © 2007, Idea Group Inc. Copying or distributing in print or electronic forms without written permission of Idea Group Inc. is prohibited.

Introduction

A key issue in economic and regional development (ERD) is the applicability of one region's successful program of development to another region. Although general solutions to universal problems (literacy, environmental awareness, AIDS prevention, sanitation, roads, etc.) can be designed by nongovernmental organizations (NGOs) or other global entities, their actual implementation needs to be adapted to local culture and conditions, ideally with grassroots stakeholder participation.

In addition to the traditional top-down approach of applying general principles to local situations, there is increasing recognition of the importance of a bottom-up approach in which one region's developmental success is seen as a potential model for other regions. The generalization of a locally successful program into an exemplar that can then be adapted to other localities poses a major problem in communication, or rather two problems: The local knowledge must be articulated, and then it must be disseminated.

The implementation of information and communication technologies (ICT) has made huge strides in the first five years of the 21st century, and the number of people who have access to the Internet is now over 1 billion. In order to optimize ICT as a means for knowledge dissemination, it is necessary to have something to disseminate—specifically, knowledge that has been articulated. Therefore, the development of ICT needs to be accompanied by the development of human infrastructure, especially the ability to express oneself clearly to audiences who do not share one's cultural background.

This chapter explains how English can be written more clearly so that it functions better as a global language, not only between native and nonnative speakers but more importantly between nonnative speakers from diverse linguistic backgrounds. The explanation extends into a discussion of how to streamline Web content. Thus, the chapter addresses a point of intersection between the two issues of articulation and dissemination, which are essential to the sharing of any region's success so that it can benefit more of the world's people.

Background Concepts

It is often said that human beings learn in three general ways: by hearing or reading words, by seeing images, and by doing. Although students, teachers, and other people who engage in a lot of verbal communication tend to consider the first of these three methods to be the most important, learning by doing has primacy in the sense of developing earliest in an infant. As noted by Nonaka and Takeuchi (1995), "A child learns to eat, walk, and talk through trial and error" (p. 10).

Learning by doing involves empathy and intuition, as well as trial and error. When a child learns to tie shoelaces, for example, these processes enable him or her to acquire a skill that is rarely if ever learned through words, images, or a combination of both. Such *tacit knowledge* can be contrasted with *explicit knowledge* (Nonaka & Takeuchi, 1995, p. 8), *focal knowledge* (Sveiby, 1997), *codified knowledge* (Stiglitz, 1999, p. 11), or *formal knowledge*

Copyright © 2007, Idea Group Inc. Copying or distributing in print or electronic forms without written permission of Idea Group Inc. is prohibited.

(Jarboe, 2001, p. 2). All four expressions of this fundamental dichotomy in human knowing are derived from the theories of Polanyi (1962, 1966).

Jarboe (2001) observes that learning by doing is facilitated by the "web of relationships and connections" that constitutes social capital (p. 3). This type of learning often involves imitating other people—not only family, friends, and coworkers, but also strangers within one's community (who may, for example, unintentionally teach a person how to get on an escalator without hesitating). Learning by doing can also happen without guidance, which is how most video games and computer simulations are played.

Tacit knowledge can be operationally defined as knowledge that is demonstrated but not explained; it tends to be absorbed rather than grasped. It is acquired through learning by images and words, as well as learning by doing. For example, while growing up, people learn how to tell which colors will match acceptably when selecting a blouse and skirt (or jacket and pants) combination. Another example: Most gold shops in southeast Asia do not sell any items that are less than 18 karat (75% pure); the lack of a market for such items is not because customers in this region crave greater value or purity than Europeans or Americans do, but because they have tacit knowledge that higher karat gold looks better on darker skin.

In *Aspects of the Theory of Syntax*, Chomsky (1969) describes how native speakers tacitly understand their own language in ways that they often cannot explain:

Obviously, every speaker of a language has mastered and internalized a generative grammar that expresses his knowledge of his language. This is not to say that he is aware of the rules of the grammar or even that he can become aware of them, or that his statements about his intuitive knowledge of the language are necessarily accurate. Any interesting generative grammar will be dealing, for the most part, with mental processes that are far beyond the level of actual or even potential consciousness; furthermore, it is quite apparent that a speaker's reports and viewpoints about his behavior and his competence may be in error. Thus a generative grammar attempts to specify what the speaker actually knows, not what he may report about his knowledge. (p. 8)

For example, people who are fluent in English know that *Clifford is a big red dog* is correct but *Clifford is a red big dog* is incorrect. If a student of English as a foreign language (EFL) asks a native speaker why the second sentence is wrong, the latter will realize how difficult it is to turn syntax into an explicit form of knowledge. He or she may even devise an erroneous rule such as "The color adjective always comes last," which fits *long black hair* but not *blue suede shoes*.

Complementarity and Conversion

In comparing his ideas to those of Polanyi, Sveiby (1997) notes that we can recall the meaning of a message after reading it, but we rarely remember its exact words. Sveiby explains:

Copyright © 2007, Idea Group Inc. Copying or distributing in print or electronic forms without written permission of Idea Group Inc. is prohibited.

The focal and tacit dimensions are complementary. The tacit knowledge functions as a background knowledge which assists in accomplishing a task which is in focus. That which is tacit varies from one situation to another. For instance, when reading a text, words and linguistic rules function as tacit subsidiary knowledge while the attention of the reader is focused on the meaning of the text. (Tacit and Focal Knowledge section, para. 2)

With a moment's effort, anyone who is literate can shift between subsidiary awareness and focal awareness while reading. This happens when an unfamiliar word catches one's attention, prompting a pause to search a dictionary; alternatively, one can simply stare at an individual word, letter, or numeral. The process of learning to read involves familiarizing oneself with the shapes of characters and then recognizing combinations of them as words until one achieves the ability to scan a sentence without focusing on them. Becoming literate basically means converting explicit knowledge into tacit knowledge, a process that Nonaka and Takeuchi (1995) call *internalization* in their socialization, externalization, combination, and internalization (SECI) model (pp. 62-70), which is summarized in Table 1.

Tacit knowledge has been defined in diverse ways in knowledge management (KM) literature, leading to ambiguous KM terminology and confusion (Bouthillier & Shearer, 2002; Sveiby, 2001). Researchers seem to agree that a major goal of KM programs is to convert tacit knowledge into explicit knowledge in order to share it throughout an organization. Nonaka and Takeuchi (1995) call this type of conversion *externalization* and see it as the key to knowledge creation. Tacit knowledge can often be made explicit by articulation: drawing a map to guide a guest to one's home, or telling an audience how to sell successfully.

Table 1. Four modes of knowledge conversion (After Nonaka & Takeuchi, 1995, pp. 70-72)

Mode	Conversion	Trigger (Input)	Process	Contents (Output)
Socialization	Tacit to Tacit	Building a Field of Interaction (Self-Organizing Team)	Share Experiences by Empathy and Intuition	Sympathized Knowledge (exchange of technical skills and mental models)
Externalization	Tacit to Explicit	Dialogue or Collective Reflection (Brainstorming)	Articulate by Metaphor and Analogy	Conceptual Knowledge (creation of new knowledge)
Combination	Explicit to Explicit	Linking New Ideas with Existing Ones (Networking)	Systematize by Analyzing and Organizing	Systemic Knowledge (crystallization of ideas into new system, service, or prototype)
Internalization	Explicit to Tacit	Learning by Doing	Embody by Applying Documents and Procedures	Operational Knowledge (implementation of policy or mass production as routine)

Copyright © 2007, Idea Group Inc. Copying or distributing in print or electronic forms without written permission of Idea Group Inc. is prohibited.

There is a tendency in KM to conflate *unarticulated* with *hidden*, as Jarboe (2001) does when he exhorts economic development organizations to use information technology (IT) and "knowledge creation tools" that can "capture ... knowledge hidden within the organization" (p. 2). However, uncovering a seed of knowledge which can be disseminated does not prove that such knowledge was tacit. Suppose a project leader discovers that a team in another department recently developed some software which can expedite the leader's project. The project leader will rejoice in finding a hidden resource (hidden from his or her viewpoint, that is) but the team who coded the software already articulated those ideas into explicit knowledge. Such a "discovery" is a good example of networking, but not knowledge creation; Nonaka and Takeuchi (1995) would label it *combination*.

Tacit knowledge can be disseminated very widely by *socialization* (Nonaka & Takeuchi, 1995) without ever being articulated into explicit form. For example, charcoal is nearly always used as a base for growing orchids in southeast Asia. Perhaps this technique was discovered intuitively or accidentally by someone in Thailand, which has long been famous for its orchids. Countless amateur horticulturists adopted the technique by imitation ("It works!") without ever receiving an explanation about why charcoal is better than soil. An explicit reason could be codified or formalized by a botanist, but it is not necessary for the propagation of the idea.

Data, Information, Knowledge, and Wisdom

As NCR Corporation's overseas market expanded in the 1970s, their headquarters began receiving complaints from customer support representatives about confusing terminology that resulted in mistaken translations of end-user manuals. NCR had the foresight to accumulate the complaints and assign a senior technical writer, Charles "Ted" Brusaw, to look for patterns and provide guidelines.

Brusaw (1978) traced the translation errors back to misunderstandings caused by word choice in the original English text. He and his team identified a large number of common English words that have multiple meanings which are tacitly understood by native speakers but can easily confuse nonnative speakers. The team compiled the *NCR Fundamental English Dictionary*, consisting of 1,175 clearly defined root words printed in boldface plus hundreds of problematic words interspersed alphabetically in regular font (each followed by a suggested substitute in parentheses).

Although NCR's database about language problems predated the concept of KM, one could say that their knowledge repository belonged to the *IT track* in the KM model formulated by Sveiby (2001). The information technology track is characterized by seeing knowledge as quantifiable objects (e.g., a list of specific words that have been mistranslated), in contrast to the *people track* which views knowledge as processes (e.g., general awareness of how ambiguity results in mistranslation).

Sveiby (2001) emphasizes the differences between the two tracks in order to highlight the need for investment in intangible assets, especially human infrastructure, but the two orientations are complementary. In the NCR case, the back-and-forth flow was like this:

Copyright © 2007, Idea Group Inc. Copying or distributing in print or electronic forms without written permission of Idea Group Inc. is prohibited.

Accumulation of specific mistranslation incidents led to an awareness of general patterns, which led to the production of a list in a tangible book, which was distributed to employees as an informal training tool to increase their awareness.

Quantification facilitates digitalization, which has become the preferred method for recording, storing, and transmitting huge amounts of data without loss or distortion. Information and communication technologies have been developed and implemented to handle the technical aspects of information management (IM). While ICT strives to preserve the integrity of data and IM organizes it into information, KM operates at a higher level of abstraction. KM creates, combines, and communicates expertise (tacit knowledge) and ideas (explicit knowledge).

An underlying assumption in the collection and transmission of data is that it is worth retaining and disseminating. The maxim *garbage in, garbage out* (GIGO) applies here: "If invalid data is entered into a system, the resulting output will also be invalid. Although originally applied to computer software, the axiom holds true for all systems, including, for example, decision-making systems" (Jupitermedia, 2001). Therefore, when making economic and regional development decisions, it is essential to have confidence that one's data is reliable.

Although completeness is an important characteristic of data integrity, it can be a drawback at the level of information. In describing how the Internet can be used for ERD, Jarboe (2001) mentions online databases that link small businesses to "a myriad of sites" which provide information about finance, accounting, marketing, and so forth (p. 13). However, a Web site that contains dozens or hundreds of links can be time-consuming and even bewildering to navigate. It can also become a source of frustration if many of the links lead to sites that do nothing more than list links. As Jarboe himself notes, "There is an enormous need to be able to quickly distinguish between what information is relevant and what is irrelevant" (p. 2).

When the level rises from information to knowledge, the concept of GIGO becomes even more complex because subjective aspects must be taken into account. Instead of garbled data resulting from signal noise, or extraneous information manifesting as circular Web links, distortion becomes a matter of inaccurate reporting due to selective perception. For example, a TV camera can only record the scene that it is focused on. If a crew is filming a riot, the camera cannot show whether people who live a couple of blocks away remain undisturbed, unless the person behind the lens decides to seek a broader perspective.

At the level of wisdom, we recognize that our mental models may prevent us from determining what is useful and what is not. Nonaka and Takeuchi (1995) affirm the subjective nature of innovation, insisting "The key to knowledge creation lies in the mobilization and conversion of tacit knowledge" (p. 56). Development of a new idea, method, or invention means we are creating something that does not yet exist—the creative process has an intuitive element that leads us beyond what we already know. Therefore, no aspect of tacit knowledge should be rejected in advance as irrelevant, because no one can say for certain what the articulation of that aspect might bring (or help come into being). This state of receptivity is acknowledged in KM's people track with phrases like "build environments conducive to sharing of knowledge" and "create innovation enhancing environments" (Sveiby, 2001).

Copyright © 2007, Idea Group Inc. Copying or distributing in print or electronic forms without written permission of Idea Group Inc. is prohibited.

Inherent Weaknesses of the IT Track

The quest for quantifiable "knowledge objects" characterizes the IT track of KM, which focuses on capturing and distributing discrete items that are considered to be essential components of expertise. The act of counting objects assumes that they are identical members of a set (e.g., *one tree, two trees*, not *a mahogany tree, a teak tree*); consequently, the quantification of knowledge has an inevitable tendency to overlook diversity. As T. S. Eliot (1952) lamented, "Where is the wisdom we have lost in knowledge? Where is the knowledge we have lost in information?" (p. 96).

Imagine, for example, a man walking into a building. An observer from the U.S. Federal Bureau of Investigation (FBI) photographs him and records the location, date, and time, thereby producing data. By noting that a meeting of the Communist Party is being held in the same building, the FBI observer creates information with a certain context. The FBI then builds a dossier for the man, which includes the knowledge that he is probably a Communist. With the wisdom of hindsight, it is easy to see how this "knowledge" is fraught with unproven assumptions that facilitated the transformation of a single observation into a supposed pattern of behavior.

New software and hardware have enabled a vast acceleration of the tendency to see people as statistics rather than as lives, an abstraction process that has been used by administrators of large populations for millennia. The proverb "You can't see the forest for the trees" can apply to economic development in a literal way: Logging a rainforest is often justified in terms of providing jobs. Data about annual income is presented, analyzed, and evaluated, thereby producing economic information about the people who dwell in the forest, which in turn leads to the knowledge that they are benefiting from the removal of its trees.

However, as the proverb warns, focusing on details can prevent a person from seeing the whole picture. Awareness of the indigenous knowledge (IK) possessed by the forest people would lead the development specialist to look at tradeoffs. How many people have been gaining sustenance from the rainforest, for how many generations? How many people will be earning money from logging, and how many years will those jobs last? How will logging impact renewable resources (foods, medicines, and other materials) that indigenous people currently can obtain without using money?

The limited context of the original analysis would then be expanded to recognize long-term sustainable processes of obtaining food based on indigenous techniques of agroforestry, such as those outlined by Grenier (1998, p. 3). This broader perspective would lead to the collection of data that counts cashless providers (tacit income) as well as paid workers (explicit income). The new economic information would describe livelihoods, a concept that is more inclusive than jobs. Thus, the initial claim by government officials that they "know" that logging's benefits outweigh its drawbacks would need to be revisited, and perhaps exposed as erroneous.

Of course, the IT track provides many benefits, too. Initiatives on the Web include the Computer Systems Policy Project (CSPP), the Virtual Souk (http://www.southbazar.com), and the ICT Stories Project that was started by infoDev and the International Institute for Communication and Development (IICD). CSPP (1998) offers a 23 question online assessment to help communities gauge their readiness for electronic commerce. The Virtual Souk

Copyright © 2007, Idea Group Inc. Copying or distributing in print or electronic forms without written permission of Idea Group Inc. is prohibited.

(Hazan, 2002), developed in Egypt with NGO assistance, is itself an e-commerce project that connects local artisans and shopkeepers in North Africa with global markets. The Virtual Souk's story is one of the regional successes that are recounted at the ICT Stories Web site in order to facilitate their global dissemination (IICD, 2003).

Nevertheless, the rapid growth of the IT track (Sveiby, 2001) calls for criticism of its assumptions about KM before they become too ingrained. The remainder of this chapter challenges some IT-track ideas about producing and distributing documents, particularly on the World Wide Web. Respective sections address how assumptions about language, infrastructure, and culture impact the dissemination of knowledge. The author offers suggestions for expanding one's awareness to a global perspective, which hopefully will lead the reader to attain a greater degree of wisdom about how to manage ERD knowledge so that it becomes available to everyone on our planet.

The Limits of Localization

Most Web sites that aim for multinational audiences *localize* their content by translating it into languages spoken by major groups of Internet users: Spanish, Chinese, Russian, and so forth. The Switzerland-based Localization Industry Standards Association (LISA, 2005) defines *localization* as "taking a product and making it linguistically and culturally appropriate to the target locale (country/region and language) where it will be used and sold."

In August 2003, the software developer Mas i Hernàndez (2003) tallied the presence of several dozen languages on the Web to determine the relative standing of his native Catalan. By inputting keywords specific to each language, he found that English was the dominant language of the text on 1,280 million pages, followed by German (182 million), French (100 million), and then a cluster of four languages in the 65-70 million range: Japanese, Spanish, Chinese, and Korean. As the president of a Web translation agency, Hopkins (2002) agrees with the principle of multilingualism. However, he recognizes that localization is not needed on each page because most Web content is global information that can be translated directly without adapting it to the audience's culture (What is a Multilingual Website? section, para. 3).

Localizing every page of a Web site is not only "too much" but also "too little." By itself, localization can never succeed in reaching a worldwide audience because its purpose is to serve specific groups of users. Adding up a handful of regional groups—or even a few dozen local groups—does not equal a global audience. There are presently 6,912 living languages, including 347 that have over 1 million speakers each (Gordon, 2005d). It is not feasible to localize content into all of them. How often do you see sites that offer the option of viewing pages in *Bangla* (Bengali), Gujarati, Marathi, Panjabi, Telugu, or Vietnamese, each of which has over 40 million native speakers?

A common explanation for excluding these languages from Web site localization efforts is that they are spoken in areas that "do not have enough users to make localization worthwhile" (Nielsen, 1999, p. 315). However, the number of Internet users nearly tripled worldwide during the first five years of this millennium: from 361 million at the start of 2001 to 1,018 million at the end of 2005. Doubling or tripling occurred on every continent and in nearly

Copyright © 2007, Idea Group Inc. Copying or distributing in print or electronic forms without written permission of Idea Group Inc. is prohibited.

all countries that began the 21ˢᵗ century with only a small fraction of the population having Internet access (Internet World Stats, 2005c).

The rapid increases in Internet penetration worldwide suggest that localization is a short-term strategy for global dissemination, because its coverage of the world's online population will become less complete as time goes on. The number of Internet users who speak "minor" languages is rising, making a comprehensive localization effort more costly and unwieldy. During 2005, Internet penetration reached 13.9% in Turkey, 12.8% in Thailand, and 11.3% in the Ukraine (Internet World Stats, 2005c), each of which has a national language that is spoken by over 40 million people.

In developing countries, many people who lack a computer at home access the Internet via cyber cafes. This sharing of hardware is analogous to older forms of pass around reader-ship, such as joining a library or renting a video instead of buying it. Statistics about total Internet users in such countries are often based on multiplying the number of Internet service provider (ISP) accounts by a sharing factor.[1] Because this factor is only an estimate of the actual situation, one should view user statistics (as well as most other statistics related to the Internet) with some skepticism.

Nevertheless, the shortage of Web pages in many languages is obvious to people who are native speakers of those languages. If a Web site does not consider their language important enough to merit localization, these users are likely to access the English version of the site.[2] At cyber cafes in Indonesia, for example, a few people will gather around a single user whose English is fluent enough to comprehend Web pages in that language. He or she will provide impromptu translation for the others while they surf as a group.

And there is evidence that people who speak English as a second language sometimes choose the English version even though the Web site offers pages in their native language. A survey conducted by Research & Research found that only 8% of Hispanic American Internet users prefer Spanish-language Web sites but 41% prefer English-language sites. The remaining 51% said they are bilingual and read Web content in either English or Spanish. In other words, 92% of Hispanic American Internet users feel comfortable with English-language Web sites, despite the fact that 63% of this market segment were born outside the United States (Romney, 2000).

A Census 2000 brief (Shin, 2003) lists the top 20 languages other than English spoken in the U.S. in 1990 and 2000. The category "all other languages" accounted for about 10% of "total non-English" in both years, rising to 1.7% of the total U.S. population in 2000 (p. 4, Table 1). In other words, a localization effort that includes the top 20 languages would exclude about 4.5 million speakers of "all other languages" (1.6 million of whom speak English less than "very well").

The incompleteness of localization is even more dramatic in the global arena: Translating a document into each of the 83 languages that has more than 10 million speakers would fail to serve 20.5% of the world's population (Gordon, 2005d). In terms of the world's Internet users, 20.4% would be neglected by a localization effort devoted to the top 10 languages spoken by the online population (Internet World Stats, 2005a). Clearly, using a global lan-guage is an essential part of worldwide outreach.

Copyright © 2007, Idea Group Inc. Copying or distributing in print or electronic forms without written permission of Idea Group Inc. is prohibited.

Using English Globally

LISA (2005) defines *internationalization* as "generalizing a product so that it can handle multiple languages and cultural conventions without the need for redesign" and calls this process the "forerunner of localization" (question 3) because internationalization is often implemented by editing a document before translation. Another way to express the complementarity of the two processes is to say that internationalization aims to make text as explicit as possible for a global audience, while localization aims to evoke a local audience's empathy by appealing to tacit aspects of their culture.

Among the major languages of the world, English is the closest to being a global language. In *The Future of English?* Graddol (2000) lists 12 "major international domains of English" including international organizations and conferences, scientific and technical publications, global advertising and mass culture, aviation and maritime communications ("airspeak" and "seaspeak"), international tourism, universities, and the Internet (p. 8, Table 2). More than 60 countries publish at least some of their books in English (p. 9, Figure 2). And the vast majority of German scientists in eight fields reported that they use English as their working language, ranging from 72% of the scholars in sociology and in medical science to 98% of the physicists (p. 9, Table 3).

It certainly seems that producing a document in English is the best way to reach a global audience. However, the English spoken by Americans, Canadians, British, Australians, New Zealanders, Indians, Nigerians, Singaporeans, Jamaicans, and others is not itself a global language. Each nation speaks and writes its own variety, full of local idioms and slang: American English, Queen's English, and so forth.

In order to serve a worldwide audience (as in *World Wide Web*), it is necessary to use *Global English*—English which is written in such a way that it can easily be understood by non-native speakers, as well as by native speakers in diverse parts of the planet. Global English lacks slang; it also has simpler sentence structure, less jargon, and fewer idioms than the English that is typically spoken and written in the "inner circle" (Kachru, 2005, pp. 13-14) of countries that were settled by the British.

It is well known in the field of international development that a communications gap is likely to arise between bureaucracies (or stakeholder groups) and the public "when the decision-making process is either surrounded by secrecy or obscured in technical language" (Reinicke & Deng, 2000, as quoted in Waddell & Allee, 2004, p. 4). In this light, LISA's (2005) promotion of "techspeak" such as the abbreviations *G11n*, *I18n*, *L10n*, and *T9n* for the terms *globalization*, *internationalization*, *localization*, and *translation*, respectively, seems misguided. It is not obvious that each abbreviation's embedded numeral indicates the number of omitted letters; therefore, everyone needs a brief initiation when encountering this alphanumeric jargon for the first time. A more serious problem is that the abbreviations tend to confuse the reader's eye because the numeral *1* is similar to uppercase *I* or lowercase *l* in many fonts.

The NCR dictionary produced by Charles Brusaw (1978) was one company's early attempt to encourage its writers to globalize their English in order to make "technical documents easier to read and use by NCR employees and customers around the world." One category of words found to be problematic for translators was "jargon that was understood only by the initiated few" (p. 1). Idioms were discouraged and slang was strongly discouraged.

Copyright © 2007, Idea Group Inc. Copying or distributing in print or electronic forms without written permission of Idea Group Inc. is prohibited.

Eliminating the use of slang in written documents and online content is more than a matter of improving readability for a global audience. A report by Stanford University's Persuasive Technology Lab (Fogg et al., 2002) listed "writing tone" among the top 10 factors that users mentioned when describing the trustworthiness of a Web site. "People generally said that sensationalism or slang hurt a site's credibility, while a straightforward, friendly writing style boosted credibility" (p. 43).

It is also important to avoid the use of idioms and slang when participating in an online discussion. This may seem counterintuitive because chatting is a way to open up and express oneself with few restrictions. Indeed, instant messaging can be so fast and fluid that it seems like speech instead of writing. However, it lacks the nonverbal clues of face-to-face chatting (or even phone conversations), and so it is prone to misinterpretation, especially when participants are from diverse cultural backgrounds.

The moderator of an online discussion group should remind members that clarity is important. Pointing out incomplete sentences and gently discouraging the use of the latest slang may slow the action, but such emphasis on explicit language will make a multicultural discussion more inclusive. Although casual Internet English is great for communicating with friends, relying on tacit linguistic habits is too parochial for a chat room, Web site, or blog that aims to attract a worldwide audience.

How to Write Global English

Besides its lack of slang and scarcity of idioms, Global English is characterized by the avoidance of jargon and buzzwords. All four of these types of diction hinder inclusiveness by making it harder for uninitiated people to read a document. Consider the following sentence that ends a paragraph promoting an online clothing store:

Which is just the right feature for users who want what works.

This type of colloquial English is easy for a native speaker to understand. However, the incomplete sentence can confuse nonnative speakers, many of whom would expect the sentence to end in a question mark.

Changing the initial *which* to *this* might decrease the sentence's trendiness in the American or British market, but it would greatly increase the number of people who could understand the sentence in the global market. In addition, the word *just* and the idiom *what works* should be modified, resulting in:

This is exactly the right feature for users who want efficient online shopping.

The "coolness" of Web content often depends on using the latest buzzwords and slang. However, many nonnative speakers became fluent in English while studying or working in the U.S., UK, or Canada 20 or more years ago. After they returned to their native countries, they retained their fluency but their tacit knowledge of English slang eventually

Copyright © 2007, Idea Group Inc. Copying or distributing in print or electronic forms without written permission of Idea Group Inc. is prohibited.

became outdated. For example, they might not know that an expression like *It sucks* is now inoffensive enough to appear in mainstream media and dictionaries.

Colloquial usage is not the only tacit aspect of language that can undermine successful global communication. Many of the words that anglophones consider ordinary have multiple meanings (and even different parts of speech) that can create ambiguity in a reader's mind, particularly if he or she is less than fully fluent in English.

Ambiguity makes a translator's work harder, slower, and less accurate (N. Hoft, personal communication, September 6, 2005; G. Fletcher, personal communication, September 9, 2005). Writing the original text in Global English means making every paragraph, sentence, and word as explicit as possible. This process includes internationalizing the document so that it is "as culturally and technically 'neutral' as possible," which will save time and money when the document is translated from English into one or more other languages (LISA, 2005, question 3).

Here are two examples of ambiguity that most native speakers of English would read without hesitation. However, a nonnative speaker might become confused by them. And even a good translator might render one of these words into a phrase that is ambiguous or incorrect in the target language.

The word *once* can be confusing as a conjunction, because some readers might misinterpret it as an adverb meaning "one time." For example:

Once the prompt appears, enter the course title.

Some people might think the prompt appears only once, regardless of the number of course titles. It would be better to write:

After the prompt appears, enter the course title.

A similar type of confusion can occur if *since* is used as a conjunction, because it can be misinterpreted as an adverb or preposition meaning "after":

Keep a log, since the use of this device can produce momentary fluctuations in the supply of power to other electrical equipment in the room.

Someone might think that the log does not need to be started until a fluctuation occurs. To remove the ambiguity, use *because* as the conjunction:

Keep a log, because the use of this device can produce momentary fluctuations in the supply of power to other electrical equipment in the room.

After finishing a document's final draft, the writer or editor should reread its entire text, seeking points of ambiguity. Any words or phrases that could hinder comprehension or

Copyright © 2007, Idea Group Inc. Copying or distributing in print or electronic forms without written permission of Idea Group Inc. is prohibited.

translation should be replaced. However, the writer or editor cannot anticipate everything that might seem unclear to the document's readers or translators.

A people-track approach to removing ambiguity is to build redundancy into one's writing. This does not mean reiterating each sentence with a subsequent one that starts with *In other words* or a similar phrase. It is not necessary to be that blunt. Simply write in a way that provides some overlap between sentences, so they support each other and create a clear context for all of the paragraph's ideas. For example:

We recommend the purchase of this factory because it is a good medium-term investment. If our company buys the manufacturing facility this year, we will be able to upgrade it by the middle of next year. After we modernize the equipment, we will have additional production capacity to help us meet the increase in demand for our products that is expected two years from now.

Note the repetition of concepts in this example: *purchase ... buy, factory ... facility, upgrade ... modernize*. In addition, the time frames are in chronological order and support the use of *medium-term*.

Although some redundancy can be useful, most writing can be improved by making it more concise. A lot of writers repeat themselves unnecessarily and use extraneous phrases. Corporate and economic development reports tend to use double negatives and hedges that cloud their meaning. Here is an example of verbosity:

The other day, during our annual meeting, when most of us were thinking about the company's future, we heard, for the first time, some forecasts which, you will agree, were not discouraging.

The meaning could be made a lot clearer by splitting this run-on sentence into two shorter ones, such as:

Most of us were thinking about the company's future during our annual meeting. We heard new forecasts that were encouraging.

In "Standards for Online Content Authors," McAlpine (2005) emphasizes conciseness and clarity. She recommends that writers aim to limit sentences to a maximum of 21 words and paragraphs to 65 words (Style section, bullets 4 and 5). Indeed, it is generally less tiring to read sentences that have fewer words, as well as paragraphs that have fewer sentences. When a writer simplifies a document's syntax in order to achieve these targets, the content usually becomes clearer, too.

The principle that smaller "bundles" of information facilitate reader comprehension also operates at the level of document design. In *Designing Web Usability*, Nielsen (1999) advises keeping Web pages short so that they are "optimized for online readers who frequently scan

Copyright © 2007, Idea Group Inc. Copying or distributing in print or electronic forms without written permission of Idea Group Inc. is prohibited.

text." If a topic contains a lot of information, the primary page should be narrowly focused and "secondary information relegated to supporting pages" (p. 15).

Streamlining a text in all of the ways mentioned in this section will not restrict one's writing style much, but it will greatly expand the document's potential audience by making the content easier to understand. Many people who are not completely fluent in English can read the language more easily than they speak it. They can also reread a written document or Web page at their own pace with a dictionary, but such review is very awkward while engaging in a conversation or listening to a lecture.

Logistical Considerations

After knowledge has been articulated in Global English, the next consideration is: How can it be shared to the widest possible extent? If one chooses to use the World Wide Web to maximize the dissemination of economic and regional development knowledge, it is necessary to think about the logistics of Internet access before uploading the Web content.

Although digital subscriber line (DSL), cable, wireless, satellite, and other fast connections have become well established in industrialized economies, a significant fraction[3] of users rely on older ways to access the Internet. Many Web site visitors are likely to use an integrated services digital network (ISDN), or even 56 Kbps modems. Connection rates and speeds can be low, particularly during business hours in their countries when heavy Internet traffic overloads local ISPs. Therefore, it would be a mistake to design a Web site that only works smoothly when it is accessed via a broadband connection.

In addition, it is important to consider that Internet time is often charged by the minute, as is telephone time. People who visit a Web site might be paying their ISP and telecom company a dollar or more per hour for online access. Local utility costs can severely impact the success of a site that aims to disseminate knowledge globally.

Therefore, streamlining the online content is a key to reaching and retaining a worldwide audience. It is wise to reduce the loading time of every page on a Web site in order to make access smoother and cheaper. The site's Webmaster can provide feedback about page-view failures and also advise how to make pages easy to re-access if a visitor's connection unexpectedly fails.

In the "Response Times" section of his second chapter, Nielsen (1999) describes three thresholds of attention span:

1. A delay equal to 0.1 second is the limit for most users to feel that the system is reacting "instantly."

2. A delay of 1 second is the limit for feeling that one's flow of thought is uninterrupted (for example, after clicking on a link to read another page of text).

3. A delay of 10 seconds is the maximum for keeping a user's attention on the display screen while a page is loading.

Copyright © 2007, Idea Group Inc. Copying or distributing in print or electronic forms without written permission of Idea Group Inc. is prohibited.

Allowing for a half-second of latency in the system's responsiveness, Nielsen (1999) cautions that the 10-second limit for maintaining a person's attention on a Web page is reached with only 34 kilobytes (KB) for modem connections and 150 KB for ISDN connections (p. 48). Any page over these limits is likely to seem slow when loading on the screen, thereby becoming an unintended test of the user's patience.

Connection speed does not matter much for text-rich Web pages, which rarely exceed 10 KB. However, the Web designer needs to be careful about delays in loading time due to the inclusion of photos, music, or animation on a page. A digital photo in .jpg format is likely to exceed 34 KB, and a .wav file of instrumental or vocal music is typically 5-10 KB per second of playing time.

When planning a Web page, check the size of every multimedia file that will be part of it. Take all moving images off the page by providing a link to their .mov file ("Click here to see the video") instead of embedding the file in the page itself. Reduce the use of sound and carefully consider the visual quality of each photo in relation to its file size. A page that totals 500 KB is likely to take more than half a minute to appear on a user's screen if it is accessed via an ISDN connection, and longer if via a modem.

One should make the text as independent of the images as possible, even when it refers directly to a photo. Here is an example of dependent text that forces the reader to wait until the image loads:

Look at the photo on the left.

By adding a few words to describe the photo, one can make the text independent of it and free the reader to scan past it if he or she cannot see it immediately. For example:

Look at the photo of a traditional village in Africa (left).

It is also a good idea to ask the designer or Webmaster to insert the ALT attribute in the HyperText Markup Language (HTML) code for each page that includes an image. This attribute enables the display of descriptive text in the box that outlines a photo while its image is loading on the user's screen.

Tables and graphs should be planned carefully to accommodate their translation into other languages. German, for example, typically expands the length of the equivalent English text by about 30% (Nielsen, 1999, p. 318). Therefore, localization can cause problems in a table's appearance if the Web designer neglects to make the column widths flexible enough.

Transcending Cultural Preferences

Articulation and accessibility are not enough; knowledge must also be acceptable to local stakeholders so they become motivated to adopt and adapt it. Allee (2000) emphasizes the

Copyright © 2007, Idea Group Inc. Copying or distributing in print or electronic forms without written permission of Idea Group Inc. is prohibited.

importance of community participation in Web-based knowledge dissemination projects. "People usually don't follow a process or formula or steps. They want to tweak it or put their own spin on it. People, however, will support what they help create" (Experts are Everywhere section, para. 2).

Relating this aspect of KM to ERD in general, Stiglitz (1999) agrees that local "doers of development" need to adapt knowledge and "make it their own" when adopting it. He then notes that this type of active learning promotes self-reliance and supports group identity. "It is not just a matter of being 'open' or 'closed' to outside knowledge; it is a matter of being open to outside knowledge in a way that reaffirms one's autonomy" (p. 9).

Web pages and other documents that accompany ERD efforts should be conducive to autonomy, or at least not undermine it. Recall that LISA's (2005) definition of internationalizing a document includes the goal of making it "culturally neutral" (question 3). Removing cultural biases before producing a globalized document streamlines the subsequent localization process (if any) and reduces the possibility that the content will alienate some readers. The following examples reveal a few ways that we can broaden our minds to accommodate other worldviews.

In 1986, I edited a speech by a Japanese businessman who asked, "Why does the term *classical* always refer to Europe? If we want to refer to the traditional arts and culture of other regions, we must insert an extra adjective: classical *Japanese* music, classical *Indian* dance, classical *Chinese* calligraphy." Although two decades have passed, the unqualified term *classical music* still refers to a period in European history, and *Classics* is the name of a field of study that focuses on ancient Greece and Rome.

One cannot anticipate every point of sensitivity, but a little research can go a long way toward reducing the intercultural friction that might accompany a document's publication. For example, it would be unwise to refer to Hinayana Buddhism when discussing the role of religion in economic and regional development in southeast Asia because *Hinayana* is a pejorative term coined by self-declared Mahayana Buddhists in order to contrast themselves with Theravada Buddhists (Lie, 2005).

People say, "History is written by the victors," but there are exceptions to this cliché; Genghis Khan never lost a battle but his reputation is not good. If a country wins a war of independence, its people date their sovereignty from the year of declaration, not the year of the subsequent peace treaty; for the United States, it is 1776 rather than 1783. However, most Western history books ignore the August 17, 1945 declaration of independence by Indonesia and refer to The Hague conference late in 1949 instead.

The national languages of Indonesia (*Bahasa Indonesia*) and Malaysia (*Bahasa Melayu*) are often combined into *Malay* in lists of the world's largest languages (Graddol, 2000, p. 8, Table 1; also, p. 27, Table 7). When tallying speakers who have Internet access, the online marketing company Global Reach (2004) states, "Malay is the same language that is spoken in Indonesia" but indicates that most of this market segment lives in Indonesia (footnote 26). A reader in Jakarta might therefore wonder why this "single" language is not called Indonesian instead of Malay. The confusion is due to the conflation of modern Malay with the older language of the same name, which gave birth to it and its sister Indonesian (Gordon, 2005b)—a situation analogous to combining Romanian and French into *Romance language speakers* and then saying "Romance is the same language that is spoken in France."

Copyright © 2007, Idea Group Inc. Copying or distributing in print or electronic forms without written permission of Idea Group Inc. is prohibited.

Other cultural assumptions are unrelated to artistic, religious, political, or linguistic favoritism; they lead to embarrassment or confusion without arousing national pride. In his chapter about designing Web pages to serve a global audience, Nielsen (1999) shows a banner ad for Apple Computer that asked users to turn on a virtual light switch by clicking it. However, the switch was in the down position, which *is* the "on" position in many countries. Nielsen says the variation of this type of tacit knowledge is rarely mentioned in guidebooks that tell how to internationalize software or Web sites, but it can be discovered by testing the image on a sample of users overseas before uploading to the World Wide Web (p. 315).

The Rise of Mandarin

Is another language likely to replace English as the global language? When the British Council published the first edition of Graddol's *The Future of English?* in 1997, the mass media began sounding an alarm that English was being surpassed by "Chinese" (Lovgren, 2004). Graddol (2000) divided English speakers into three categories: those who speak it as a first language (native speakers, or L1), those who speak it fluently as a second (or third, etc.) language (L2), and those who are learning English as a foreign language (EFL) but are not yet fluent in it (p. 10).

Graddol (2000) estimated that there are 375 million L1, 375 million L2, and 750 million EFL speakers of English (p. 10, Figure 4). Although this rounded L1 figure is well above his estimates for Hindi (316 million) and Spanish (304 million), it is very far below the 1,113 million for "Chinese" (p. 8, Table 1). The popular press echoed these estimates without asking why the separation of L1 and L2 speakers was being applied to English but not to "Chinese."

Most linguists do not recognize a monolithic language called "Chinese" that is spoken as a first language throughout the People's Republic of China (PRC). "Chinese" consists of several large languages that have a common system of writing but are mutually unintelligible when spoken (C. Hurd, personal communication, December 5, 2005). In linguistic classification, it is considered a subfamily within the Sino-Tibetan family (Columbia, 2001; Gordon, 2005a). However, due to "social, cultural, or political factors," (Gordon, 2005c, The Problem of Language Identification section, para. 1), politicians tend to displace linguists as the authorities who determine whether two or more languages are equivalent (thereby promoting national unity) or distinct (thereby promoting ethnic identity).

Mandarin is the official language of the PRC and the standard language of instruction in its public schools. In these respects, it is analogous to other national languages that were created to unify diverse populations (e.g., Filipino in the Philippines and Indonesian in Indonesia). In its *Ethnologue* encyclopedia of world languages, SIL International (formerly the Summer Institute of Linguistics) states that 70% of the people in China speak Mandarin as their native language (Gordon, 2005a), which would yield an L1 of 910 million among the present population of 1,300 million.

However, in May 2005, the PRC's Xinhua news agency reported a survey by the National Language Commission which found that only 53% of the population can speak Mandarin, and many of them "are not frequent Mandarin users, preferring their local dialect" ("Half of all Chinese," 2005). This yields a combined L1+L2 of 689 million. If one adds in all

Copyright © 2007, Idea Group Inc. Copying or distributing in print or electronic forms without written permission of Idea Group Inc. is prohibited.

of the L1+L2 Mandarin speakers among the 23 million Taiwanese and 34 million (Liren, 2002) to 55 million (Seagrave, 1996, p. 14) overseas Chinese, Mandarin's total probably comes within the margin of error for Graddol's (2000) combined L1+L2 estimate of 750 million English speakers.

In *Asian Englishes: Beyond the Canon*, Kachru (2005) suggests a much higher L1+L2 total for English, based on estimates that one third of his native India uses English, as do 200 million people in the PRC, yielding 533 million L2 speakers in those two countries combined. However, these figures assume that people who have had only three years of English instruction in school are "users of the language" (pp. 206-207). When I lived in Tokyo, I frequently encountered Japanese who had studied English for six or more years and were reluctant to speak it; however, they had the potential to become L2 speakers. After conversing with many Japanese of varying levels of English fluency during 1984-1987, I observed that those who were L2 generally had lived at least six months in an L1 country such as the U.S. or UK.

Regardless of the numbers, there are two solid reasons why Mandarin will not become popular as a global language: It is hard to speak and hard to write. Tones in speech and ideograms in writing make it virtually inaccessible as a second language to the majority of the world's people. Adults whose native language is a tonal one such as Thai, Lao, or Vietnamese sometimes learn Mandarin by overhearing conversations or watching movies, but speakers of non-tonal languages have a lot more difficulty doing so and need twice as much time in an immersion setting such as Automatic Language Growth (J.M. Brown, personal communication, 1990). Learning enough ideograms to read a newspaper requires a long-term diligent effort.

One benchmark of a global language is whether it is used as a lingua franca between two nonnative speakers from separate countries, neither of whom knows the other's L1. For example, a Japanese who is working on a development project in Mozambique would be likely to use English to communicate with a Swede working on a project in Laos. This example is basically an extension of Kachru's (2005) definition of "a 'standard' English-knowing bilingual" in south Asia (p. 215), applying it as a touchstone for anglophones throughout the world. That is, a Global English speaker is someone who is intelligible not only to native speakers of English but also to nonnative speakers from diverse backgrounds.

Although Mandarin is used as an international lingua franca, its scope remains regional; people outside Taiwan, Singapore, and other Chinese-majority areas study the language primarily to communicate with citizens of the PRC. Its recent rise in popularity as a language for international commerce has been at the expense of Cantonese (Yue), not at the expense of English. One impulse for the shift was the reabsorption of Hong Kong in 1997. In addition, Mandarin language schools began to operate openly in Indonesia after the dictator Suharto resigned in 1998.

The Future of Global English

Graddol's (2000) report contains much more than a tally of speakers at various levels of fluency. He suggests that English will remain globally dominant but it will be influenced by nonnative speakers, leading to "new hybrid language varieties" (p. 36). A harbinger of this

Copyright © 2007, Idea Group Inc. Copying or distributing in print or electronic forms without written permission of Idea Group Inc. is prohibited.

hybridization is Singapore, which has four official languages: English, Mandarin, Malay, and Tamil. English is the default language when two Singaporeans of different ethnicity make each other's acquaintance, earning it an L2 (p. 11, Table 5). This L2 "Singlish" is flavored with words and structures from three non-Indo-European language families, making it a notable variety despite its narrow geographical range.

In addition, Graddol (2000) foresees "migration toward L1 use of English" by middle-class professionals and university students who use it "as a primary means of social communication" in L2 countries (p. 58). Such migration has been going on for more than half a century in India, where the large anglophone sector supports the creation of literature in their own variety of English, dating back to the 1938 publication of Raja Rao's pioneering novel *Kanthapura* (Kachru, 2005, p. 137).

It is widely recognized that the globalization of American movies, music, and fast food make English trendy among millions, even billions, of people who are not fluent in it. This "wave" of popular culture is augmented by a socioeconomic "wave" in developing countries, some of whose governments now require English to be taught as a foreign language in primary schools. It remains to be seen whether the critical mass of L1+L2 speakers attained by Singapore and India will be replicated by dozens of other countries, each of them thereby developing its own variety of English.

To test the ability of anglophones to understand each other's varieties, Smith (1992) recorded conversations between five pairings of fluent speakers from the U.S., UK, China, India, Japan, Taiwan, the Philippines, Indonesia, and Papua New Guinea. He played the audiotapes to three groups of anglophones who were studying in Hawaii in 1986: 10 Japanese, 10 Americans, and 9 people of various nationalities (mostly Asian L2). Smith found that the L1 British and American speakers were not always the most easily understood (p. 88). Graddol (2000) cites this finding to support his speculation that an "Asian standard English" (p. 56) may someday codify the similarities that already exist among the varieties of English spoken in east Asia.

A related finding of Smith's (1992) pilot study has a more immediate implication. Smith saw the skill of the listeners in the group of mixed nationalities as "evidence that familiarity with several different English varieties makes it easier to interpret cross-cultural communication in English" (p. 83). Both findings support this chapter's call for action: When used as a global language, English should be spoken in a way that is recognizable to anglophones all over the world; and Global English needs to be neutral enough to accommodate the phonologies and lexicons of all varieties of English, not only those in the traditional L1 countries that were settled by the British.

Kachru (2005) describes the interaction of diverse forms of English in terms of *pluricentricity*, the concept that "world Englishes have a plurality of centres" (p. 18). These centers provide norms and models for English language acquisition, regional codification, and literature. He places Singapore, India, Sri Lanka, and the Philippines in the *norm-providing group*, distinct from China, Taiwan, Japan, South Korea, and Thailand in the *norm-dependent group* (p. 19).

If the reader will permit a coinage, I propose the term *colingual* (analogous to *coworker*), which refers to people who *speak a language with each other*. People who converse in a common language are colinguals in that language. Although two native speakers of a lan-

Copyright © 2007, Idea Group Inc. Copying or distributing in print or electronic forms without written permission of Idea Group Inc. is prohibited.

guage are colinguals in their L1, they might not be colinguals in a shared L2. For example, two Japanese could both be colinguals in English with their American acquaintance but not with each other, because Japanese people tend to speak English only when communicating with non-Japanese. However, Singaporeans are likely to be colinguals in English with each other, even if they have the same L1.

This neologism is helpful for understanding Kachru's (2005) separation of anglophone countries into norm-providing and norm-dependent (p. 19). His division correlates with the answer to a question that tests the internal colingual level among an L2 country's English speakers: Do compatriots communicate with each other in English when no foreigners are present? In the norm-dependent group, the answer is "rarely;" however, in the norm-providing group, the answer is "often enough to create a critical mass of colinguals that generates its own norms."

Although Kachru (2005) makes an excellent case for a regional variety called South Asian English that is spoken in seven countries, he says nothing about the extent to which norm-providing Singapore has radiated its lexical influence to Malaysia and Indonesia (e.g., the coinage *handphone* to refer to a mobile telephone), nor whether the Philippines has provided syntactical models to Vietnam or Thailand. So, it is unclear why the Singaporean and Philippine varieties of English should be called centers rather than national varieties. Regional codification of the kind seen in South Asian English has yet to be evidenced in southeast Asia (Crystal, 2003, p. 57).

Given that the number of national and regional hybrid Englishes is likely to increase, what is the future of mutual intelligibility? A Japanese acquaintance told me about an experience she had while teaching her native language to Indonesians in North Sumatra. One day, the students invited her to go hiking, pronouncing the word in Japanese fashion (*haikingu*) as part of a Japanese sentence. Etsuko was confused when they said everyone would gather in the evening, because she understood *haikingu* to be a day trip on level ground or in low hills. Instead, the students trekked up a small mountain, arriving at the peak in time for sunrise. In Indonesian, the borrowed word *hiking* refers to an activity that Japanese think of as mountain climbing.

This anecdote illustrates how the expansion of English as a global language may undermine itself. To preserve mutual intelligibility, we should recognize common ground, not repress diversity. Therefore, Global English will become more essential in the future, as a way for speakers of divergent forms of English to communicate with each other. In this light, the implementation of ICT requires the development of human infrastructure as well as physical infrastructure. We must learn to express ourselves clearly to audiences who do not share our cultural background and the concomitant tacit aspects of our speech and writing. In addition to making English more explicit on the Internet, we should promote the use of Global English in education and business.

Graddol (2000) uses a pyramid diagram (p. 12, Figure 6) to explain how the expansion of an Indian citizen's viewpoint from home to village to state to nation is accompanied by shifts in language. At the base of the pyramid are local languages used within families and learned by infants as L1. A step higher are languages of wider geographical scope, which are used in media broadcasts and primary schools. Another step higher are state languages (e.g., Malayalam in Kerala), which are used in government offices and secondary schools.

Copyright © 2007, Idea Group Inc. Copying or distributing in print or electronic forms without written permission of Idea Group Inc. is prohibited.

At the top are Hindi and Indian English, which are used nationally and in universities. I propose that Global English is a step beyond the top of this pyramid, serving as a lingua franca for international communication and online education (e-learning).

Conclusion

Localization is very important in marketing and other fields that rely on tacit knowledge of a target language and culture. However, it is incomplete as a global strategy because it can never accommodate everyone. The limits of localization are becoming more apparent in the 21st century, with over 1 billion people now having access to the Internet and numbers increasing dramatically in virtually every country. Localizing a Web site into all 347 languages that each claim at least 1 million speakers is not a feasible approach to the global dissemination of knowledge.

To make the Web truly a worldwide medium, it is necessary to write English text in an explicit way that can be easily understood by nonnative speakers: simpler syntax, less jargon, fewer idioms, no slang. Writing a Web page or other document in Global English is the best way to ensure that people from all linguistic backgrounds have a reasonable chance of comprehending it. Global English will become more important in the near future, both online and in hardcopy; it may prove to be essential for maintaining English as a lingua franca if the growth of anglophones leads to a proliferation of new varieties of the language in diverse cultures throughout our world.

References

Allee, V. (2000, Fall). *e-Learning is not knowledge management*. Retrieved November 20, 2005, from LiNE Zine, http://www.linezine.com/2.1/features/vaenkm.htm

Bouthillier, F., & Shearer, K. (2002). Understanding knowledge management and information management: The need for an empirical perspective. *Information Research*, *8*(1), paper no. 141. Retrieved September 9, 2005, from http://InformationR.net/ir/8-1/paper141.html

Brusaw, C. (1978). *NCR fundamental English dictionary*. Dayton, OH: NCR Corporation.

Chomsky, N. (1969). *Aspects of the theory of syntax*. Cambridge, MA: MIT Press.

Columbia University. (2001). Chinese language. In *The Columbia electronic encyclopedia* (6th ed.). New York: Columbia University Press. Retrieved December 6, 2005, from http://www.bartleby.com/65/ch/Chinese.html

Computer Systems Policy Project. (1998). *The CSPP readiness guide*. Retrieved November 28, 2005, from http://www.cspp.org/projects/readiness/23ques.htm

Crystal, D. (2003). *English as a global language* (2nd ed.). Cambridge, UK: Cambridge University Press.

Copyright © 2007, Idea Group Inc. Copying or distributing in print or electronic forms without written permission of Idea Group Inc. is prohibited.

Eliot, T. S. (1952). Choruses from "The Rock." In *Complete poems and plays: 1909-1950*. New York: Harcourt, Brace & World, Inc.

Federal Communications Commission. (2005, June 10). *Frequently asked questions (FAQs) about FCC form 477 (local telephone competition and broadband reporting)*. Retrieved October 2, 2005, from http://www.fcc.gov/broadband/broadband_data_faq.html

Fogg, B. J., Soohoo, C., Danielson, D., Marable, L., Stanford, J., & Tauber, E. R. (2002, November 11). *How do people evaluate a Web site's credibility?* Stanford, CA: Persuasive Technology Lab, Stanford University.

Global Reach. (2004, September 30). *Global Internet statistics: Sources & references*. Retrieved May 24, 2005, from http://www.global-reach.biz/globstats/refs.php3

Gordon, R. G., Jr. (Ed.). (2005a). Chinese, Mandarin: A language of China. In *Ethnologue* (15th ed.). Retrieved December 6, 2005, from http://www.ethnologue.com/show_language.asp?code=cmn

Gordon, R. G., Jr. (Ed.). (2005b). Indonesian: A language of Indonesia (Java and Bali). In *Ethnologue* (15th ed.). Retrieved December 6, 2005, from http://www.ethnologue.org/show_language.asp?code=ind

Gordon, R. G., Jr. (Ed.). (2005c). Introduction to the printed volume. In *Ethnologue* (15th ed.). Retrieved December 6, 2005, from http://www.ethnologue.com/ethno_docs/introduction.asp

Gordon, R. G., Jr. (Ed.). (2005d). Statistical summaries: Summary by language size. In *Ethnologue* (15th ed.). Retrieved May 23, 2005, from http://www.ethnologue.com/ethno_docs/distribution.asp?by=size

Graddol, D. (2000). *The future of English?* (2nd ed.). London: The British Council.

Grenier, L. (1998). *Working with indigenous knowledge: A guide for researchers*. Ottawa, Canada: International Development Research Centre.

Half of all Chinese people can't speak Mandarin: Report. (2005, May 23). *Taipei Times*. Retrieved May 24, 2005, from http://www.taipeitimes.com

Hazan, M. (2002, March 25). *Virtual souk: E-commerce for unprivileged artisans*. Retrieved November 26, 2005, from http://www.iconnect-online.org/Stories/Story.import5014

Hopkins, R., Jr. (2002). *Multilingual Websites: Benefits you can count on, headaches you can avoid*. Retrieved December 12, 2005, from http://www.weblations.com/eng/articles/art_2.htm

International Institute for Communication and Development. (2003). *Welcome to ICT-stories*. Retrieved November 29, 2005, from http://www.iicd.org/stories/lbd

International Telecommunication Union. (2003). *Technical notes*. Retrieved May 24, 2005, from http://www.itu.int/ITU-D/ict/statistics/WTI_2003.pdf

International Telecommunication Union. (2005, April 26). *Economies by broadband penetration, 2004*. Retrieved May 24, 2005, from http://www.itu.int/ITU-D/ict/statistics/at_glance/top20_broad_2004.html

Internet World Stats. (2005a, December 31). *Internet users by language*. Retrieved January 22, 2006, from http://www.Internetworldstats.com/stats7.htm

Copyright © 2007, Idea Group Inc. Copying or distributing in print or electronic forms without written permission of Idea Group Inc. is prohibited.

Internet World Stats. (2005b). *Internet World Stats surfing and site guide*. Retrieved December 11, 2005, from http://www.Internetworldstats.com/surfing.htm

Internet World Stats. (2005c, December 31). *World Internet users and population stats*. Retrieved January 22, 2006, from http://www.Internetworldstats.com/stats.htm

Ipsos. (2005, March 2). *The majority of global Internet users using a high-speed connection*. Retrieved May 26, 2005, from http://www.ipsos-na.com/news/pressrelease. cfm?id=2583

Jarboe, K. P. (2001, April). *Knowledge management as an economic development strategy*. Washington, DC: Economic Development Administration, U.S. Department of Commerce.

Jupitermedia Corporation. (2001, December 3). What is garbage in, garbage out? In *Webopedia computer dictionary*. Retrieved October 7, 2005, from http://www.webopedia. com/TERM/g/garbage_in_garbage_out.html

Kachru, B. (2005). *Asian Englishes: Beyond the canon*. Hong Kong, China: Hong Kong University Press.

Lie, K. A. (2005). *The myth of Hinayana*. Retrieved November 3, 2005, from http://www. lienet.no/hinayan1.htm

Liren, Z. (2002, September 12). *Distribution of the overseas Chinese population*. Retrieved January 15, 2006, from http://www.library.ohiou.edu/subjects/shao/databases_popdis. htm

Localization Industry Standards Association, The. (2005). *Frequently asked questions about LISA and the localization industry*. Retrieved September 28, 2005, from http://www. lisa.org/info/faqs.html

Lovgren, S. (2004, February 26). *English in decline as a first language, study says*. Retrieved May 23, 2005, from http://news.nationalgeographic.com/news/2004/02/0226_ 040226_language.html

Mas i Hernàndez, J. (2003, September 2). *La salut del català a Internet*. Retrieved May 25, 2005, from http://www.softcatala.org/articles/article26.htm

McAlpine, R. (2005). *Standards for online content authors*. Retrieved September 5, 2005, from http://www.webpagecontent.com/arc_archive/177/5/

Nielsen, J. (1999). *Designing Web usability: The practice of simplicity*. Indianapolis, IN: New Riders.

Nonaka, I., & Takeuchi, H. (1995). *The knowledge creating company: How Japanese companies create the dynamics of innovation*. New York: Oxford University Press.

Polanyi, M. (1962). *Personal knowledge: Towards a post-critical philosophy*. Chicago: University of Chicago Press.

Polanyi, M. (1966). *Tacit dimension*. Garden City, NY: Doubleday & Co.

Romney, L. (2000, January 6). The cutting edge: Survey looks at online habits of U.S. Latinos. *Los Angeles Times*. Retrieved May 29, 2005, from http://www.latimes.com

Copyright © 2007, Idea Group Inc. Copying or distributing in print or electronic forms without written permission of Idea Group Inc. is prohibited.

Seagrave, S. (1996). *Lords of the rim: The invisible empire of the overseas Chinese*. London: Transworld Publishers.

Shin, H. (2003). *Language use and English-speaking ability: 2000* (Rep. No. C2KBR-29). Washington, DC: U.S. Census Bureau.

Smith, L. (1992). Spread of English and issues of intelligibility. In B. Kachru (Ed.), *The other tongue: English across cultures* (2nd ed., pp. 75-90). Urbana: University of Illinois Press.

Stiglitz, J. (1999, December). *Scan globally, reinvent locally: Knowledge infrastructure and the localization of knowledge*. Keynote Address at the First Global Development Network Conference, Bonn, Germany. Retrieved November 28, 2005, from http://www.iucn.org/themes/ceesp/Publications/CMWG/Stiegliz-local-knowledge.PDF

Sveiby, K. (1997). *Tacit knowledge*. Retrieved October 1, 2005, from http://www.sveiby.com/articles/Polanyi.html

Sveiby, K. (2001, April). *What is knowledge management?* Retrieved October 1, 2005, from http://www.sveiby.com/articles/KnowledgeManagement.html

Waddell, S., & Allee, V. (2004, January 20). *Global action networks and the evolution of global public policy systems*. Paper presented at the International Conference on Systems Thinking in Management conducted at the University of Pennsylvania, Philadelphia. Retrieved November 20, 2005, from http://www.gan-net.net/pdfs/ICSTM.pdf

Web Site Optimization. (2005, February 19). *January 2005 bandwidth report*. Retrieved December 11, 2005, from http://www.Websiteoptimization.com/bw/0501/

Endnotes

[1]   The International Telecommunication Union (ITU, 2003) explains how the total number of Internet users is estimated: "Countries that do not have surveys generally base their estimates on derivations from reported Internet Service Provider subscriber counts, calculated by multiplying the number of subscribers by a multiplier" (p. 4).

ITU's World Telecommunication Indicators database shows that these were some of the multipliers used in 2004: Myanmar 2; Argentina, Bahrain, Bangladesh 3; Nepal 4; El Salvador, Syria 5; Costa Rica 8; Latvia 9; Honduras 10; and Uganda 25 (E. Magpantay, personal communication, December 13, 2005). Other countries had more complex estimation methods, with the sharing factor sometimes varying even within a single city (E. de Argaez, personal communication, December 11, 2005).

The multiplier attempts to compensate for undercounting that results from several members of a household sharing a single Internet account. Internet World Stats (IWS, 2005b) reports various standards for tallying children, including "The ITU subscribes to the definition of an Internet user as someone aged 2 years old and above, who went online in the past 30 days" (Internet Usage section, para. 2).

Copyright © 2007, Idea Group Inc. Copying or distributing in print or electronic forms without written permission of Idea Group Inc. is prohibited.

However, the multiplier exacerbates overcounting that is related to an individual having more than one account (e.g., at work or school, as well as at home). Even so, the growing popularity of cyber cafes, which have extremely large ratios of users to accounts, probably outweighs the distortion that is due to multiplication of over-counts.

[2] Compare the estimated 750 million people who speak English as their first or second language (L1+L2) in Graddol's (2000) report (p. 10, Figure 4) with the estimated 1,125 million who access Web pages in English more often than pages in other languages (Internet World Stats, 2005a). Internet World Stats assigns only one language to each person, based on the following method: "The keywords they search for determine the language they use to surf" (E. de Argaez, personal communication, January 22, 2006).

[3] For most of the 21st century, South Korea has had the world's highest proportion of Internet users who subscribe to broadband. According to ITU figures for the country, 11.9 million of 31.6 million Internet users subscribed, resulting in a penetration of less than 38% at the end of 2004 (W. Yasandikusuma, personal communication, May 27, 2005).

However, "broadband penetration" figures are calculated in different ways, showing perhaps the greatest variance of all Internet statistics. The term *broadband* is sometimes applied to speeds less than the ITU minimum of 256 kilobits per second in both directions (V. Gray, personal communication, May 26, 2005). For example, the Federal Communications Commission (FCC, 2005) of the United States defines *broadband* as a connection that "enables the end user to receive information from and/or send information to the Internet at information transfer rates exceeding 200 kilobits per second (kbps) in at least one direction" (question 5).

In addition, the term *penetration* is defined in several ways. Some surveys divide a country's total number of broadband subscribers by the total number of inhabitants. Although the United States had the most broadband subscribers as of December 2004, the ITU (2005) ranked it only 16th globally on the basis of 11.4% penetration of its general population, compared to 24.9% for South Korea.

Other surveys divide the total number of households or users who have broadband capability installed (but might not actually subscribe) by the total number of "active Internet users." For example, over 69.4 million American households had the capability as of December 2004, yielding a penetration of 54.7% for home users according to Web Site Optimization (WSO, 2005). The inflated WSO figure is exaggerated even more in the "Face of the Web 2004" study by Ipsos-Insight, which claims that 68% of the entire world "accessed" the Internet via broadband in October 2004 (Ipsos, 2005).

Copyright © 2007, Idea Group Inc. Copying or distributing in print or electronic forms without written permission of Idea Group Inc. is prohibited.

Appendix: Suggested URLs

- http://www.12manage.com/methods_nonaka_seci.html (Tom De Geytere's summary of Nonaka and Takeuchi's SECI model, including a diagram of the knowledge spiral)

- http://www.algworld.com/history.htm (Automatic Language Growth and the work of J. Marvin Brown at AUA Language Center in Bangkok)

- http://www.anglistik.tu-bs.de/global-english/GE_Was_ist_GE.html (A list of links to online articles that use the term Global English)

- http://www.globalenglish.info/globallyspeaking/index.htm (Tips on intercultural communication in the Internet age)

- http://www.globelanguage.com (Translation company co-owned by George Fletcher)

- http://www.ik-pages.net/about-ik.html (List of indigenous knowledge characteristics)

- http://www.oecd.org/document/60/0,2340,en_2649_34225_2496764_1_1_1_1,00. html (Organization for Economic Co-operation and Development's broadband statistics for 2001-2004, based on ITU data)

- http://www.pulpchat.com/faq/faq215.php (List of chat room slang)

- http://www.research-research.com (Research & Research)

- http://www.sveiby.com/articles/TacitTest.htm (Karl-Erik Sveiby's hands-on exercise, "Test Your Tacit Knowledge")

- http://www.useit.com (Jakob Nielsen's Web site about usability)

- http://www.world-ready.com/academic.htm (A list of links offered by Nancy Hoft, a consultant in "world-readiness")

Copyright © 2007, Idea Group Inc. Copying or distributing in print or electronic forms without written permission of Idea Group Inc. is prohibited.

Chapter VIII

Cultural Knowledge Management and Broadband Content in Development:
Open Content Platforms, Copyright and Archives

David Rooney, University of Queensland, Australia

Elizabeth Ferrier, University of Queensland, Australia

Phil Graham, University of Queensland, Australia

Ashley Jones, University of Queensland, Australia

Abstract

This chapter examines the possibility of creating online creative production archives with which to make locally and internationally sourced high quality video, audio, graphics, and other broadband content available to grassroots producers in developing economies. In particular, the possibility of Cultural Knowledge Management Systems and the use of innovative Creative Commons copyright licenses are explored. It is argued that in a

Copyright © 2007, Idea Group Inc. Copying or distributing in print or electronic forms without written permission of Idea Group Inc. is prohibited.

global knowledge economy, cultural production is a major driver of economic growth. The creativity and culture needed for cultural production are plentiful in developing countries indicating that if technical and institutional conditions are right there is significant potential for developing economies to compete in the global economy. It is, therefore, desirable for local groups to be able to acquire, store, and distribute locally and internationally sourced content to stimulate local-level cultural production.

Introduction

In this chapter the authors argue that the recognized potential for social, cultural, and economic benefits that accrue from widespread participation in the production of cultural materials, as it has been discussed in developed countries such as Australia and the United Kingdom (Cutler, 2003; DEST, 2002; National Broadband Taskforce, 2004), and in the academic literature (Florida, 2002; Rooney & Graham, 2004), is equally applicable in developing countries. Recent discussions about cultural industries in the developed world show a concern for digital cultural production modes in the context of the Internet and broadband infrastructure. This chapter, therefore, discusses key aspects of capacity building for developing economies to take advantage of these new conditions. The kinds of capacities discussed are concerned with infrastructure, industry, creative expression, and cultural maintenance and renewal capacities. Furthermore, working on the assumption that culture is an expression or mode of enacting knowledge (Holden, 2002; McCarthy, 1996; Rooney & Schneider, 2005), the authors argue that such capacity building will be conducive to the emergence of developing countries as knowledge societies and economies.

In particular, this chapter is concerned with how cultural knowledge management in a digital broadband environment, and innovative copyright developments from Creative Commons (Creative Commons, 2003) have assisted in the creation of an "open" cultural content commons. This commons can develop into a global network of Internet accessible digital archives that collect, hold, and diffuse materials for use in creative production (for commercial or noncommercial purposes) in ways that increase the capacity for independent cultural production in developing countries.

Why Cultural Production?

Beyond the purely economic, there are important though less tangible benefits related to widespread participation in cultural life. Mumford (1934) identifies a civilizing aim that should reside at the centre of all economic endeavours:

The essential task of all sound economic activity is to produce a state in which creation will be a common fact in all experience: in which no group will be denied, by reasons of toil or deficient education, their share in the cultural life of the community, up to the limits of their personal capacity. (p. 430)

Copyright © 2007, Idea Group Inc. Copying or distributing in print or electronic forms without written permission of Idea Group Inc. is prohibited.

There are very practical reasons for taking such a stance in respect of economic goals. These include the health of democratic participation through sophisticated media practices; the economic and cultural benefits that flow from a vibrant, active, and innovative culture of creativity; the proven net economic benefits of a knowledgeable, educated, and intellectually active population; the decentralization of media power; diversification of sources and forms of media content; the maintenance and promotion of local, regional, and national identities; and the widespread personal fulfilment that comes from active and visible participation in the life of a culture. In more general terms, cultural participation assists in resisting the worst aspects of the Western tendency to instrumentalism and technocracy that impoverish culture, make authentic expressions of grassroots culture invisible and devalued, and make it difficult for non-Western countries to compete in the global creative or cultural economy.

One simplistic explanation for the disparity in cultural economic power of the U.S. is that its media corporations hold a global "monopoly" on distribution channels and key production enabling resources, and forcefully impose unfair protectionist trade barriers in the form of oppressive IP rights frameworks (Drahos & Braithwaite 2002). While other factors are always at play, such monopolies are strong and recognizable forces in the historical distribution of economic and cultural power.

Broadband distribution networks and new copyright innovations challenge the mass media patterns that emerged in the twentieth century and as such have the potential to create new opportunities for developing countries. This technological change brings historically low and diminishing costs for global distribution of cultural content (Rooney, 1997). Simultaneously, rapid developments in digital production technologies have led to lower costs of production, thereby making it possible for a much broader range of people than ever before to work as multimedia content developers at a commercially viable level. There is unprecedented demand for digital media content. This demand has stimulated media organizations, telcos, and governments to position themselves to capitalize on broadband technologies and media convergence, and compete to attract consumers to online services. Just as cultural forms and artifacts from non-Western countries have found global metropolitan markets (e.g., Japanese *anime* and *manga*, Chinese martial arts films, and postcolonial literatures), distinctive media content from developing countries has the potential to appeal to mass and niche audiences across the world. As a result of these trends, significant new opportunities are emerging. In short, the rise of widely accessible global distribution networks, greatly lowered costs of production technologies, heightens potential rates of involvement in production activities, and increased demand for digital media content (particularly distinctive content with appeal to multicultural metropolitan audiences). Furthermore, a policy willingness to embrace the potentials indicated by the above mentioned developments means that people who in the past have worked on the periphery of global cultural production may gain socially, culturally, and economically in the emerging online environments. While there are barriers in achieving this success in the form of poor infrastructure, the dominance of the English language on the Internet, lack of skills and training, low levels of investment, and so forth, the potential for mobilizing grassroots creativity that has direct economic and cultural benefits, in contributing to notions of civility and citizenry, in fostering artistic dialogue across cultures, and in exploring the democratizing potentials that a diversified media environment offers cannot be ignored.

Copyright © 2007, Idea Group Inc. Copying or distributing in print or electronic forms without written permission of Idea Group Inc. is prohibited.

Looking more closely, it can be observed that the mass media industry structures that developed throughout the twentieth century are premised on high-capital costs (e.g., large television, recording, and film studios); highly specialised divisions of labor (specialised divisions of labor in audio, music, cinematography, animation, pre and post-production, etc); long and expensive development times for content; heavy reliance on advertising revenues; highly integrated distribution networks; and highly restricted access to those networks through electromagnetic spectrum licensing regimes. As recently as a decade ago, the cost of plant and equipment required to create high-quality audio and video productions was a prohibitive barrier to entry for the majority of people regardless of their talents. Capital outlays required to finance the global distribution of multimedia works were even more prohibitive. As few as six companies have dominated global mass media broadcast networks (Bagdikian, 1997; McChesney, 2000; Schiller, 1999).

Today, however, the tools to create high-quality multimedia productions are widely and inexpensively available (Graham, 2005). In some cases, high-quality multimedia production tools can be legally downloaded by users at no cost. As a means of distributing creative content, broadband networks are becoming more common and efficient, with over 100 million people now subscribing to broadband services (De Argaez, 2004). Data transfer rates are increasing, the cost of broadband access is falling almost daily, and in some cases access is provided at no cost (National Selection Committee, 2004).

Combined with the above trends, and facilitated by new digital production tools, a blurring of roles and functions in creative labor processes has begun to replace the fairly rigid historical divisions of labor characteristic of mass media industries. Using basic consumer technologies, it is possible for a person to film, edit, compose music, produce, and globally distribute their multimedia productions. Moreover, collaborative content creation programs and tools enable teams and networks of people to participate in co-creation online, and pooling of resources and skills. An aspect of these emerging production arrangements are new content "customizing" practices, such as the modification, personalization, "remixing" and "repurposing" of existing content. An interesting result of these changes is that the participants now involved in content creation include fans and hobbyists who might not identify themselves as content producers. Such grassroots practices exemplify the blurring of boundaries between production and consumption that is characteristic of new media environments and which open up opportunities for developing countries.

Consequently, a new, much larger group of people is now engaged in the production and global distribution of high quality multimedia productions. This presents as a benefit in relation to the creative development of culture because it enables societies to renew their knowledge of themselves, to have new insights about their own condition, and to have new things to communicate about themselves. Thus, it is important that cultural innovation comes from the bottom up; in other words from the grassroots. With this constant cultural renewal there are social and economic benefits.

As suggested above, aesthetic innovation emerging from the grassroots has significant social and economic benefits. The new means and forms of production, distribution and exhibition available to grassroots content creators facilitate experimentation and innovation. As the independent sectors in the cultural industries have demonstrated, low-budget productions often afford a higher level of creative control to artists than they have when involved in large commercial productions. The finished product is more likely to be innovative and diverge from established formats and genres.

Copyright © 2007, Idea Group Inc. Copying or distributing in print or electronic forms without written permission of Idea Group Inc. is prohibited.

Further, there are local, national and global markets for grassroots stories, local knowledge and cultures, and hybrid content forms produced in developing countries. Independent film and television production sectors in a range of countries (such as Nigeria, Taiwan, and France) illustrate the way that low budget productions, made from the margins (independent of the major media companies), can hold wide appeal, representing cultures and subcultures to local and global audiences, different to those usually seen in mainstream cinema. Public television networks such as the UK's Channel 4, or Australia's SBS, have tapped into their respective independent production sectors (which Leadbeater and Oakley [1999] call "the missing middle" in the creative industries) to generate diverse, innovative, high-quality content that has succeeded in reaching national and international audiences (Ferrier & Lawe-Davies, 2002). If one makes a distinction between the independent and the grassroots sectors, the potential and diversity of the independent production sector in developed economies can be seen as indicative of the value of grassroots digital content production in developing countries (Ferrier, Bruns, Rooney & Graham, 2004; Ferrier & Lawe Davies, 2002). What is identified here as the "grassroots" content production sector – emergent, rapidly growing, informal and dispersed – can be thought of as "the missing grassroots" (Bruns, Ferrier, Graham & Rooney, 2005), and it is even less visible to many policy makers, governments and media corporations than the independent sector, yet is arguably a richer and more sustainable source of diverse media content. As the enormous success of discussion lists, online chat, Web site development, blogs, and wikis demonstrates, online grassroots or amateur content creation and consumption are thriving, emergent phenomena. At the very least, these conditions demonstrate that amateur media content regularly reaches large global audiences through the Internet. At best, it can be argued that when appropriate infrastructure for cultural production is available commercial producers will be able to access larger markets. However, significant penetration of those markets is not automatic and as will be shown later gaining access requires attention to content (storage, retrieval, and diffusion) management and copyright.

The "Grassroots" and the Economic Future of Genre

There are four main reasons why this chapter emphasizes grassroots production efforts. First, most approaches to developing broadband content have so far depended on principles and assumptions developed in older media environments. The most fundamental policy and regulatory frameworks designed to guide the development of broadband services are often developed and managed by national broadcasting authorities, applying "old media" logic to radically different converged new media environments (Young, 2004). Consequently, in developed countries there have been enormous losses associated with broadband content initiatives, as exemplified by the largest quarterly loss in U.S. corporate history by AOL-Time Warner in January 2003 (Keegan, 2003). The "dotcom bubble" notwithstanding, the impetus for the AOL-Time Warner merger, as well is the unparalleled losses the merged entity sustained in 2003, were in large part a function of Time Warner executives wrongly believing that transferring their print, movie, and music offerings to the broadband environment would automatically result in new markets and increased profits (Rushkoff, 2002). The faulty working assumptions underpinning the above failures are analogous to the assumptions underpinning the many failed early attempts to develop television by transferring the production principles, or "genres," used in radio (Twitchell, 1999).

Copyright © 2007, Idea Group Inc. Copying or distributing in print or electronic forms without written permission of Idea Group Inc. is prohibited.

Content types from older media, usually defined as "genres" of one sort or another, have been the main focus of attention in developed countries attempting to define and stimulate the broadband content agenda in the domains of policy, research, and industry (e.g., DCITA, 2003a, b). However, by definition the term "genre" refers to well established, relatively stable, and predictable media forms (Graham, 2001). A focus on genre is a focus on what has been successful in older media environments. However, entirely new types of content will flourish in broadband environments. These new types of content are unlikely to develop within the multinational mass media institutions for the reasons stated above. It is among grassroots producers that real innovation is likely to be found, precisely because of their distance from the centralized institutions of mass media. This situation suggests that by virtue of their distance from the core global production institutions the potential for developing countries to find competitive advantages in this new media environment is excellent.

Second, there is a vast difference between the "push" principle of broadcast mass media and the "pull" principle of Internet media. The "push" principle works on the assumption that relatively few people will participate in the production of mainstream mass culture while the majority of people will passively "consume" what the few produce. The "pull" principle operates on the assumption that people will, if given the opportunity, participate in the production of culture as well as actively seek attractive content to "consume." A recent Pew Internet survey found that 44% of Internet users in the US "have created content for the online world" sharing ideas, Web sites, photographs, video, and music (Lenhart, Horrigan & Fallows, 2004). Extrapolating from that figure, and given that broadband subscriptions have recently exceeded the 100 million mark globally, there are presently 44 million people with access to broadband infrastructure who are actively creating and sharing content. Even if these numbers were halved, this represents an enormous amount of creative energy with significant economic and cultural potential. These trends indicate a potential inversion of the economic model that underpins mass media – rather than a relatively small number of people and organizations controlling production and distribution networks for cultural content, many millions of people now have a potential audience of many millions. Again, the potential for developing countries to gain a foothold in the global production arena is clear.

By way of cautioning against over-optimism and of the need for concerted political and strategic effort, this is not to suggest all the content produced by broadband users will be successful or even of high quality, but if access to suitable infrastructure is provided in developing countries it is almost a statistical certainty that a sustainable proportion of people will learn to produce material that realizes economic, social, and cultural benefits, whether directly or indirectly. This can be seen as a similar process to that which resulted from the advent of cheap printing (following Gutenberg's innovations) and growing literacy rates, which combined to assist the emergence of a sustainable publishing industry.

Third, there are significant social, cultural, and economic benefits for regional, remote, and community-based initiatives (National Selection Committee, 2004). According to the National Selection Committee, broadband can bring economic revival to remote and regional communities by continuing the practice of leveraging "the high level of grassroots activism" evident in these communities (ITU 2003 in National Selection Committee, 2004). Remote regions are rich in cultural tradition and "broadband offers new possibilities for maintaining or reviving traditional cultures and languages as well as new opportunities for innovative cultural expression" by weaving the local –whether rural, remote, or urban – into the global (National Selection Committee, 2004, p. 7). It also "provides new ways for cultural industries,

Copyright © 2007, Idea Group Inc. Copying or distributing in print or electronic forms without written permission of Idea Group Inc. is prohibited.

visual and performing arts groups, museums, and other cultural institutions to reach their audiences" (p. 7). As the Time-Warner-AOL debacle demonstrated, the broadband environment is not amenable to being merely another conduit for mass media industries. Rather, it is a platform for the unique, the exotic, and the unusual. Cultural materials with these characteristics cannot be mass produced: they require grassroots participation at the local level. In turn, "distant" communities and cultural producers can reap the economic benefits of a global audience regardless of where they are. UNESCO's Creative Content e-Platform (http://creativecontent.unesco.org) is an example of an Internet-based attempt by producers from the fringes to reach out to a wider audience. This multicultural repository contains "challenging" productions by independent producers from Africa, the Asia-Pacific region, and South and Central America. While not focussed on creative content, the United Nations Development Program's Asia-Pacific Development Information Program (APDIP) (www.apdip.net) and Malaysia's United Nations Institute for Training and Research (UNITAR) (www.unitar.org) use online knowledge management systems to provide "open" access to such things as linguistic, cultural, health, educational, and software resources in ways that are designed to be responsive to their core users needs.

Fourth and finally, as Mumford (1934) has already pointed out above, closely linked to the potential for economic benefit and cultural preservation is an ethical imperative underpinning economic development more generally. While Mumford's words may be interpreted by the hardened cynic as a value-laden "motherhood" statement, there are very practical reasons for taking such a stance regarding economic goals. Indeed, central to the Declaration of Principles governing the WSIS are these very ideas (WSIS, 2003). To reiterate, these include: the health of democratic participation through sophisticated media practices; the economic and cultural benefits that flow from a vibrant, active, and innovative culture of creativity; the proven net economic benefits of a knowledgeable, educated, and intellectually active population; the maintenance and promotion of local, regional, and national identities; and the personal fulfilment that comes from active and visible participation in the life of a culture.

At this point it is worth investigating a little deeper the economic value of broadband content in the global economy. The following quote is typical of emerging attitudes in policy circles in developed countries but they could be applied to policy imperatives in developing countries as well:

Broadband take-up and availability of compelling content are inextricably linked. The level of broadband take-up is likely to remain relatively low unless there is sufficient compelling content available. Since the majority of content is generated overseas it is essential to promote local content that reflects Australians' values, identity, and character. It is also important that distribution channels work effectively with Australia's content industries. (Alston, 2003)

This set of policy imperatives can be read from the perspective of the "knowledge consumption services" sector, which derives from the applied social and creative disciplines (business, education, leisure and entertainment, media and communications) and represents 25% of economic activity in OECD economies (OECD, 1998). In fact all modern economies are consumption driven (e.g., 62% of U.S. GDP) and the social technologies that manage consumption all derive from the social and creative disciplines.

Copyright © 2007, Idea Group Inc. Copying or distributing in print or electronic forms without written permission of Idea Group Inc. is prohibited.

Worldwide, the creative industries sector has been among the fastest growing of the global economy. Several analysts point to the crucial role they play in the new economy, with growth rates better than twice those of advanced economies as a whole (Cunningham, 2005; Howkins, 2001; Jeffcutt, 2005). Creative production has become the model for new economy business practice (highly outsourced; producer model; project management within just-in-time teams, etc.). Rifkin (2000) claims that cultural production will ascend to the first tier of economic life, with information and services moving to the second tier, manufacturing to the third tier and agriculture to the fourth tier. This is a global economic structural change that developing countries should seek to participate in and benefit from.

Digital Production Technologies

The authors would like to discuss here, how digital production and postproduction technologies are able to change cultural production dynamics in favour of grassroots producers. Specifically, this section outlines the cultural knowledge management technologies that are central to being able to take advantage of recent changes and that will assist in reducing barriers to production of local content and the broadcast of cultural expression, the diffusion of knowledge, and assist in maintaining the cultural and epistemic integrity of content produced in, by, and for developing countries.

To understand how broadband can best be harnessed to increase economic, social, and cultural benefit requires an appreciation of enabling infrastructures such as new and emerging production processes; archival technologies and multimedia databases; metadata practices for distributed production processes; and education and literacy strategies for new media environments. These environments are characterized by digital re-use and re-mixing of cultural expression, using cut and paste, and file sharing practices in a distributed, collaborative production processes. Therefore, the even more participatory and collectivist nature of grassroots production demands appropriate (enabling) knowledge management, technical, and organizational platforms. In particular, archival technologies and multimedia databases including middleware are essential. These include culturally dynamic metatagging systems, or metadata that can be relevant to members of multiple and diverse cultures; robust middleware initiatives that enable collaborative creation over different temporal and geographical spaces;[1] and, most importantly, flexible licensing and copyright regimes that simultaneously reflect creative design practices, national and international laws, and encourage openness while protecting ownership rights. Initiatives such as Creative Commons (Creative Commons, 2005) have helped create a legal environment that achieves these important criteria.

Open Source Content Licensing:
A Legally Safe Open Sharing Environment

Perhaps the most critical aspect of open cultural production environments is the provision of intellectual property licensing arrangements designed specifically to stimulate creativity by accommodating open collaboration in a global "creative commons" (Creative Commons,

Copyright © 2007, Idea Group Inc. Copying or distributing in print or electronic forms without written permission of Idea Group Inc. is prohibited.

2005). This is a particular concern for open online repositories that mediate in the collection and diffusion of creative content, a process that is outside the value system of multinational media businesses. Furthermore, because of the development concerns of this chapter, such open copyright arrangements should not only be open but must also be flexible enough to account for differences between Western and non-Western or indigenous cultural intellectual property. Therefore, the focus in this part of the discussion is on Creative Commons copyright licenses that are designed specifically to provide this kind of flexibility. To this end, it is important to note that Creative Commons licenses have been adapted in many different countries including Argentina, Australia, Austria, Belgium, Brazil, Bulgaria, Canada, Chile, China, Croatia, Finland, France, Germany, Ireland, Israel, Italy, Japan, Jordan, Mexico, Netherlands, Philippines, Poland, Slovenia, South Africa, South Korea, Spain, Sweden, Switzerland, Taiwan, England and Wales, and Scotland.

In developed countries like Australia that have indigenous communities suffering significant inequalities, it has already been argued that creatively oriented broadband infrastructure is a way to bring social, cultural, health, and economic benefits. *The Island Watch* and *Cape York Digital Network* infrastructure programs are examples of what is being done in this respect in Australia. The Australian experience also highlights how traditional Aboriginal laws, and cultural and spiritual practices are at odds with the inflexible all rights reserved structure of orthodox copyright. Australian Aboriginal experience highlights how copyright (and attitudes among creators to issues of ownership and rights that are ingrained through the dominant discourse on IP) struggle to deal with the products of cultural expression in ways other than as exclusive private property and economic commodities (Hunter, 2003; Johnson, 1996; Kleinert & Neal, 2000). Therefore, placing indigenous cultural intellectual property rights on a sound legal footing is not necessarily easy to do (Joseph & Ayres, 2005). Yet it is only the limits of imagination that prevent the development of more flexible copyright licenses that will simultaneously respect indigenous cultural values and enable commercial activity on global markets. In respect of development, indigenous cultural production systems are key cultural innovation systems. In developing economies these innovation systems can be regarded as having particular importance for innovation and cultural policy. After all, indigenous systems of innovation are equal to Western systems of innovation even if they are different (Joseph & Ayres, 2005). Licenses already exist that acknowledge a range of rights (both economic and noneconomic); that go beyond the concept of exclusive private property and moral rights; that conceive of rights in ways that simultaneously enable the commercial and cultural handling of works of art while giving creators choices in how their works are accessed by different groups. Already at an advanced stage of responding to these issues, Gilberto Gil, Brazil's Minister of Culture and a practicing musician, has led a drive to provide freely available (online) locally produced cultural content using Creative Commons licenses (de Castro, 2004). However, before looking more closely at Creative Commons, it is possible to examine some larger questions related to copyright so as to frame Creative Commons licensing as a clear response to some important debates about the creative, social, cultural, and economic efficiency of copyright and IP law generally. Open content licensing is also an issue in education, software, health, linguistic and scientific archives, most notably in the UNITAR site.

Not only are there questions about the capacity of copyright to function effectively for economic reasons (Heller, 1998), there are persistent doubts about its effectiveness in fa-

Copyright © 2007, Idea Group Inc. Copying or distributing in print or electronic forms without written permission of Idea Group Inc. is prohibited.

cilitating what is often thought to be its central purpose: fostering creative and innovative work (Whale, 1971). As Bently and Sherman (2004) have observed:

Despite the prominent role that creative labour played in pre-modern intellectual property law, as the law took on its modern guise it shifted attention away from the labour that was embodied in the protected subject matter to concentrate more on the object in its own right. (p. 4)

Put another way, recognition of creativity as an activity or as a performance of value has been subverted to the extent that it is the economic value and communication of the finished work that modern copyright is primarily concerned with, while the activities, intentions, and values of the producer are now secondary considerations at best. The natural balance between equitably valuing the economic and social worth of creative work and creative workers has, therefore, been upset. Moreover, with this historical shift not only has there been a movement away from concern about protecting the rights and creative needs of the creative "laborer," there has been a shift in emphasis more towards protecting the financiers of creative work (Drahos & Braithwaite, 2002). This is a fundamental distortion of copyright, and one that is not helpful to creators—particularly those in developing countries. Most of the protected financiers controlling industrialized creative activities are organized into multinational media corporations. For this reason, the orthodox copyright framework favours developed countries rather than developing countries. Consequently, the copyright regimes of developed countries are a disincentive or barrier to cultural production, expression, and diffusion in developing countries. This is unhelpful because, while such cultures might be short of financial resources, two resources they have in plenty are culture and creativity. In other words, the raw materials for cultural development are present but the right institutional framework (particularly in terms of IP) may not be.

The open-source software licensing movement has shown that innovation can flourish outside the traditional IP framework (Goldman & Gabriel, 2004), Linux is just one example of this. In particular, questions are now being asked about how efficacious overly restrictive (or strong) intellectual property regimes are as stimulants to the creative mind and worker (Drahos, 2005; Lessig, 2004; Mandeville, 1996). In this light, it is highly significant that Kretschmer (2005) found modern digital cultural production is now conducted in such a way that the reuse of copyright content in new productions is the norm. These work practices are an affront to the monopoly and exclusivity logic of orthodox copyright. Consequently, Kretschmer (2005) also notes that with those new practices (and attendant technologies), a more complex legal, work and business context has been created in which many independent producers either deliberately or through ignorance, routinely break the law or compromise the creative quality of their work. One of his conclusions, therefore, is that traditional copyright hinders rather than helps these producers.

As mentioned above, one attempt to modernize copyright and to give creative producers more flexibility and choice are the licenses devised by Creative Commons. Researchers at Stanford Law School's Creative Commons (CC) (Creative Commons 2003) have developed what they describe as "a spectrum of rights" that fall between the extremes of copyright and public domain (www.creativecommons.org). Creative Commons licenses are designed to promote the sharing of intellectual property and creative works to further stimulate creativity

Copyright © 2007, Idea Group Inc. Copying or distributing in print or electronic forms without written permission of Idea Group Inc. is prohibited.

in the context of contemporary digital arts practices. In doing this the aim is to overcome the tendency of artists to "hoard" their work under an "all rights reserved" model, despite the advantages that a more open approach to sharing can bring to both the individual artist and the community as a whole. Creative Commons seeks to provide a flexible "some rights reserved" framework in which producers have more choices.

Importantly, the Creative Commons licenses are designed to accommodate both commercial and non-commercial uses of digital resources. They are based on the assumption that innovations and new ideas are fundamentally and necessarily extensions and elaborations of existing ones and that creative work should be possible in collaborative arrangements. This spectrum includes licenses in the form of:

- **By attribution:** a creator allows others to copy, distribute, display, and perform copyrighted work (and derivative works based on it) but only if they give the author credit.

- **Noncommerical:** creators allow others to copy, distribute, display, and perform their works (and derivative works based on it) but only for noncommercial purposes.

- **No derivative works:** creators allow others to copy, distribute, display, and perform only verbatim copies of their work and not derivatives based on it.

- **Share and share alike:** creators allow others to distribute derivative works only under a licence identical to the licence that governs the original work.

Once a licence has been assigned to a work by a creator it will take three forms: (1) a Commons Deed, written in plain language; (2) Legal Code, written in formal legal language that will be usable in court; and (3) Digital Code, written in machine readable form to help with archiving, searching and identifying creators' works. Authors are able to attach to their works the creative commons "some rights reserved" symbol (rather than the standard copyright symbol) (see Figure 1). The licenses can be used singly (e.g., By Attribution) or combination (e.g., By Attribution and Noncommercial) and therefore offer an extremely flexible regime of copyright suited to modern digital broadband production environments.

As noted above, the licenses have been written according to local law in many countries and there is a need to write "purpose built" licenses for developing countries. It is not only the local differences in law that are significant here. The main point about Creative Commons is its potential flexibility for individual producers and groups. Choices could be made by different individual and groups of producers in response to, for example varying spiritual beliefs, cultural values related to individual and collective ownership, and assumptions about how to distribute wealth.

Figure 1. Creative Commons symbol

Copyright © 2007, Idea Group Inc. Copying or distributing in print or electronic forms without written permission of Idea Group Inc. is prohibited.

By providing a unique and diverse set of resources, and by encouraging derivative and open usage of those resources for the production of new creative works, open content repositories will help lay the foundations for new and alternative business and creative practices suited to broadband environments through which grassroots producers can benefit from. Equally important is that open content archives can be established to create a legally safe and culturally sensitive framework for individuals and organizations to work with multimedia resources in an open content environment.

Open Source Archive Model

Nigerian producer and director, Amaka Igwe, says; "Our dream is to sell Africa to the world. It's going to be a display of our thoughts and an avenue to market ideas about Nigeria and products about Nigeria" (Balogun, 2005). She also points out that copyright, infrastructure, and distribution problems are holding the Nigerian industry back. The "open" provision of archives and their content, along with digital production and postproduction software will provide new opportunities to creative workers for whom such material would be beyond usual budgetary constraints. In this environment, a country like Nigeria can begin to address issues such as those identified above. To begin addressing these constraints creative workers can "recycle" high-quality archival materials into new broadband content and commercial and noncommercial cultural materials using the kinds of technical infrastructures described earlier. This open framework will lower barriers to entry in the cultural production sector thereby providing incentives for employment and new business creation. Commercial cultural producers will no longer be geographically tied to the locations of major production houses.

The provision of relevant open resources has already begun. In particular, there is a growing collection of Internet accessible multimedia content and software resources, much of which is available under Creative Commons and similar licenses. For example, content is available from:

- **UNESCO Creative Content E-Platform:** http://creativecontent.unesco.org This is an online, multicultural catalogue of/for independent producers and broadcasters. It contains a variety of high quality recent video productions with a focus on Africa, the Asia-Pacific, and South America. This site uses standard copyright and is therefore restricted as a grassroots production resource.

- **ACRO:** www.acro.edu.au This is an archive of free content in the form of video, music, and photographs that use open source copyright licences.

- **Internet Archive:** www.archive.org This is a massive archive containing a historical record of the World Wide Web and other resources such as movies, music, computer games, cartoons, newsreels, and more.

- **Prelinger Archive:** www.archive.org/movie/prelinger.php This is an archive within the Internet Archive containing over 4,000 movies, TV ads, educational films, and other interesting moving images.

Copyright © 2007, Idea Group Inc. Copying or distributing in print or electronic forms without written permission of Idea Group Inc. is prohibited.

- **BBC Motion Gallery:** http://www.bbcmotiongallery.com/customer/index.jsp The BBC Motion Gallery contains lots of old BBC footage from news, sports, natural history, wildlife, news, locations, art, music, celebrities, politics, culture, and the performing arts. Materials come from the BBC and CBS news archives.

- **The Freesound Project:** http://freesound.iua.upf.edu/whatIsFreesound.php This is a searchable archive for downloadable sound files.

- **Creative Commons:** www.creativecommons.org There are a range of resources here including links to open content resources of all types and software to assist in searching for such content on the Internet.

In addition open (post) production software tools available include:

- Avid DV; Free http://www.avid.com/freedv/
- Audacity audio editor; http://audacity.sourceforge.net/
- Gimp photo editing software; http://gimp-win.sourceforge.net/
- PhotoPlus; http://www.freeserifsoftware.com/serif/ph/ph5/index.asp
- Zwei-Stein video editor; http://www.thugsatbay.com/tab/?q=zweistein
- STOIK Video Converter; http://www.stoik.com/
- AviSplit Classic video editor; http://www.bobyte.com/
- DubIt; http://www.hitsquad.com/smm/programs/DubIt/
- Soliton audio editor; http://www.snapfiles.com/get/soliton.html
- DeepBurner Free DVD burner; http://www.deepburner.com/?r=download
- Swarm DVD encoder/authoring tool; http://www.free-codecs.com/download/DVD_Swarm.htm

In addition, Google and Yahoo (see http://creativecommons.org/find/) search Internet engines are now able to conduct searches for Creative Commons licensed materials across the Internet.

To finish this chapter it is useful to discuss how the authors have attempted to provide an Internet-accessible creative production (rather than finished product) archive of mostly locally produced open content to provide ideas for others to consider. Australian Creative Resources Online (ACRO) is an online repository for a wide range of material and provides the opportunity to share content otherwise treated as waste or junk by mass media agencies. This "junk" is video footage and film; audio tracks and interviews; and still images. ACRO is designed to make this content available to producers with broadband access. ACRO, therefore, provides the capacity to support a new class of cultural producers who under the rigid framework of traditional commercial mass media and copyright structures would have only limited opportunities to produce content. Importantly, new producers can include teachers, students, and members of local communities. It is also important to note that there would be benefits in creating a network of such archives internationally. Each node would focus on developing local content for local and international producers.

Copyright © 2007, Idea Group Inc. Copying or distributing in print or electronic forms without written permission of Idea Group Inc. is prohibited.

A quick practical example of how production can be stimulated and efficiencies can be increased through open content infrastructure is when a documentary maker shoots 300 hours of nature footage to make eight one-hour documentaries for television. At the end of the series, the producer has precisely 292 hours of footage that will remain unused. Much of it will be of very high quality. Normally, this "waste" material would go into a personal archive, perhaps to be discarded unused years later. However, when the material is digitised and made accessible on broadband networks, it can, for example, be used by teachers and students in multimedia courses, by budding documentary makers, by children learning how to make digital content in schools, or by cultural groups or communities to produce commercial and noncommercial works.

While much of ACRO is comprised of material originally intended for the traditional mass media, there is a new group of producers emerging. Producers who may come from outside the traditional commercial and educational structures can benefit from the provision of low cost, high quality content and production tools. Resource like ACRO will encourage a better understanding of the process of technology use and the role of ICT in economic and social development and in doing so will assist in building the skills necessary to develop new media production industries. In Brazil community telecenters using free software to enabling users to set up roaming accounts, and the use of wireless networking in Africa (APC, 2006) are examples of technological change in developing countries that can facilitate the construction of creative industries based around the benefits of digital multimedia technologies.

Conclusion

New work practices facilitated by new digital production tools and the blurring of roles and functions in creative labour processes have begun to replace the fairly rigid divisions of labour characteristic of traditional mass media industries. Using basic consumer technologies, a person or group of people can film, edit, compose music, produce, and globally distribute their multimedia productions. The new practices in interactive content production and consumption that have emerged in this environment challenge boundaries between production and consumption. Consequently a new, much larger group of people can now be engaged in the production and global distribution of high quality multimedia works. Creative development of culture can enable societies to renew their knowledge of themselves, to remix or repurpose "received" content to suit their own needs, to have new insights about their own condition and to have new things to communicate about themselves. Cultural innovation in such networks must come from the bottom up; in other words from the grassroots. With this constant cultural renewal there are social and economic benefits for developing communities. Open content provisions should boost activities in cultural production that will lead to cultural and economic development. In the context of knowledge-based economies the importance of building this kind of capacity cannot be underestimated (Rooney, Hearn, et al., 2003; Rooney & Mandeville, 1998). If culture is knowledge (Holden, 2002; McCarthy, 1996), then, cultural production is an obvious way for developing countries to gain a

Copyright © 2007, Idea Group Inc. Copying or distributing in print or electronic forms without written permission of Idea Group Inc. is prohibited.

foothold on a central pillar of the knowledge-based economy. It is important though that the combination of technology (archives and digital production tools), institutions (Creative Commons licenses) and creative workers (including their norms and work practices) are seen as a whole system in which none of the parts are neglected.

References

Alston, R. (2003). *Australia's broadband connectivity: The broadband advisory group's report to government.* Canberra: NOIE.

Association for Progressive Communications (APC). (2006). *Announcements from APC.* Retrieved June 17, 2006, from http://www.apc.org/english/index.shtml

Bagdikian, B. H. (1997). *The media monopoly.* Boston: Beacon Press.

Balogun, S. (2005). *Nigerian movies make "Outcast" stars.* Retrieved June 17, 2006, from The Sun News Online, http://www.sunnewsonline.com/Webpages/features/show-time/2005/feb/18/showtime-18-02-2005-002.htm

Bently, L., & Sherman, B. (2004). *Intellectual property law.* New York: Oxford University Press.

Bruns, A., Ferrier, E., Graham, P., & Rooney, D. (2003, October). *Mapping the missing grassroots: Online content creation and consumption.* Paper presented to Center for Social Research in Communication, University of Queensland.

Creative Commons. (2003). *Licenses explained.* Retrieved June 17, 2006, from http://creativecommons.org/learn/licenses

Cunningham, S. (2005). Knowledge and cultural capital. In D. Rooney, G. Hearn, & A. Ninan (Eds.), *Handbook on the knowledge economy* (pp. 93-101). Cheltenham: Edward Elgar.

Cutler, T. (2003). *Research and innovation systems in the production of digital content and applications: Report for the National Office for the Information Economy.* Melbourne: Cutler & Co.

DCITA. (2003a). *Australia's broadband connectivity*: The broadband advisory group's report to government. Canberra: NOIE.

DCITA. (2003b). *Film and digital content.* Retrieved June 17, 2006, from http://www.dcita.gov.au/Collection/CollectionPage/0,,0_1-2_2-3_471,00.html

De Argaez, J. (2004). *Broadband usage keeps growing.* Retrieved June 17, 2006, from Internet World Stats: Usage and Population Statistics, http://www.Internetworldstats.com/articles/art030.htm

de Castro, H.C. (2004). It's Brazil's time. Retrieved June 17, 2006, from *Linux Magazine*, http://www.linux-magazine.com/issue/45/International_Open_Source_Forum_Brazil.pdf

Copyright © 2007, Idea Group Inc. Copying or distributing in print or electronic forms without written permission of Idea Group Inc. is prohibited.

DEST. (2002). *Frontier technologies for building and transforming Australian industries: Stimulating the growth of world-class Australian industries using innovative technologies developed from cutting-edge research*. Canberra.

Drahos, P. (2005). Intellectual property rights in the knowledge economy. In D. Rooney, G. Hearn, & A. Ninan (Eds.), *Handbook on the knowledge economy* (pp. 139-154). Cheltenham: Edward Elgar.

Drahos, P., & Braithwaite, J. (2002). *Information feudalism: Who owns the knowledge economy?* London: Earthscan.

Dspace. (2003). *Dspace: Durable digital repositories*. Cambridge: MIT. Retrieved June 17, 2006, from http://www.dspace.org

Ferrier, E., & Lawe Davies, C. (2000, December). *In the shadow of Channel 4: SBS independent*. Paper presented at the Television: Past Present and Future Conference, University of Queensland.

Florida, R. (2002). *The rise of the creative class: And how it's transforming work, leisure, community and everyday life*. New York: Basic Books.

Goldman, R., & Gabriel, R.P. (2004). *Innovation happens elsewhere: Open source and business strategy*. San Francisco: Morgan Kaufmann.

Graham, P. (2001). Space: Irrealis objects in technology policy and their role in the creation of a new political economy. *Discourse & Society, 12*(6), 761-788.

Graham, P. (2005). Issues in political economy. In Albaran et al. (Eds.), *Handbook of media*

Heller, M.A. (1998). The tragedy of the anticommons: Property in the transition from Marx to markets. *Harvard Law Review, 111*(3), 621-668.

Holden, N.J. (2002). *Cross-cultural management: A knowledge management perspective*. Harlow: Ft Prentice Hall.

Howkins, J. (2001). *The creative economy: How people make money from ideas*. London: Penguin.

Internet2. (2003). *Shibboleth project*. Michigan: Author.

Jeffcutt, P. (2005). The organization of creativity in knowledge economies: Exploring strategic issues. In D. Rooney, G. Hearn, & A. Ninan (Eds.), *Handbook on the knowledge economy* (pp. 102-117). Cheltenham: Edward Elgar.

Johnson, V. (1996). *Copyrites: Aboriginal art in the age of reproductive technologies*. Sydney: National Indigenous Arts Advocacy Association and Macquarie University.

Joseph, S., & Ayres, A. (2005). Current indigenous arts law issues. *Media International Australia, 114*, 54-60.

Kalantzis, M., & Cope, B. (2001). Multiliteracies as a framework for action. In M. Kalantzis & B. Cope (Eds.), *Transformations in language and learning: Perspectives on multiliteracies* (pp. 19-32). Australia: Common Ground.

Keegan, V. (2003). *United we fall*. Retrieved June 17, 2006, from The Guardian, http://www.guardian.co.uk/economicdispatch/story/0,12498,875908,00.html

Kleinert, S., & Neal, M. (Eds.). (2000). *The Oxford companion to aboriginal art and culture*. Melbourne: Oxford University Press.

Copyright © 2007, Idea Group Inc. Copying or distributing in print or electronic forms without written permission of Idea Group Inc. is prohibited.

Kress, G. (2001). Issues for a working agenda in literacy. In M. Kalantzis & B. Cope (Eds.), *Transformations in language and learning: Perspectives on multiliteracies* (pp. 33-52). Australia: Common Ground.

Kretschmer, M. (2005). *Artists' earnings and copyright: A review of the British and German music industry data in the context of digital technologies*. First Monday, 10. Retrieved June 17, 2006, from http://www.firstmonday.org/issues/issue10_1/kretschmer/index.html

Lankshear, C., & Knobel, M. (2003). *New literacies: Changing knowledge and classroom learning*. Buckingham: Open University Press.

Leadbeater, C., & Oakley, K. (1999). *The independents: Britain's new cultural entrepreneurs*. London: Demos.

Lenhart, A., Horrigan, J., & Fallows, D. (2004). *Content creation online*. Retrieved June 17, 2006, from Washington, DC: Pew Internet & American Life Project, http://www.pewInternet.org

Lessig, L. (2004). *Free culture: How big media uses technology and the law to lock down culture and control creativity*. New York: Penguin.

Mandeville, T. (1996). *Understanding novelty: Information, technological change and the patent system*. Norwood: Ablex Publishing.

McCarthy, E.D. (1996). *Knowledge as culture: The new sociology of knowledge*. London: Routledge.

McChesney, R.W. (2000). The political economy of communication and the future of the field. *Media, Culture & Society, 22*(1), 109-116.

Mumford, L. (1934). *Technics and civilization*. New York: Harcourt Brace.

National Broadband Taskforce. (2004). *The new national dream: Networking the nation for broadband*. Retrieved June 17, 2006, from http://broadband.gc.ca/pub/program/NBTF/broadband.pdf

National Selection Committee. (2004). S*tronger communities for a stronger Canada: The promise of broadband*. Report of the National Selection Committee: Broadband for rural and northern development pilot program. Ottawa: Industry Canada.

OECD. (1998). *Content as a new growth industry*. Paris: OECD.

Pollack, M. (2003). *Internet2 releases privacy-preserving Web authorizing software*. Retrieved June 17, 2006, from http://archives.Internet2.edu/guest/archives/I2-NEWS/log200307/msg00000.html

Rifkin, J. (2000). *The age of access*. London: Penguin.

Rooney, D. (1997). *Playing second fiddle: A history of technology and organization in the Australian music economy* (1901-1990). Brisbane: Griffith University.

Rooney, D., & Graham, P. (2004). Creative content and sustainable community media organizations: Australian creative resources online. *Australian Studies in Journalism, 13*, 80-93.

Rooney, D., Hearn, G., Mandeville, T., & Joseph, R. (2003). *Public policy in knowledge-based economies: Foundations and frameworks*. Cheltenham: Edward Elgar.

Copyright © 2007, Idea Group Inc. Copying or distributing in print or electronic forms without written permission of Idea Group Inc. is prohibited.

Rooney, D., & Mandeville, T. (1998). The knowing nation: A framework for public policy in a knowledge economy. *Prometheus, 16*(4), 453-467.

Rooney, D., & Schneider, U. (2005). A model of the material, mental, historical and social character of knowledge. In D. Rooney, G. Hearn, & A. Ninan (Eds.), *Handbook on the knowledge economy* (pp. 19-36). Cheltenham: Edward Elgar.

Rushkoff, D. (2002). *Signs of the times.* Retrieved June 17, 2006, from The Guardian, http://media.guardian.co.uk/newmedia/comment/0,7496,763023,00.html

Schiller, D. (1999). *Digital capitalism.* Cambridge, MA: MIT Press.

The Semantic Grid. (2003). *The semantic grid community portal.* Southampton: University of Southampton.

Spedding, V. (2003). *Data preservation: Great data, but will it last?* Retrieved June 17, 2006, from Cambridge Research Information, http://www.researchinformation.info/rispring03data.html

Twitchell, J. (1999). Media and the message. Retrieved June 17, 2006, from *Advertising Age*, http://Web.nwe.ufl.edu/~jgoodwin/f00/enc/twit.html

Warschauer, M. (2003). *Technology and social inclusion: Rethinking the digital divide.* Cambridge: MIT Press.

Wenger, E. (1999). *Communities of practice: Learning, meaning and identity.* Cambridge: Cambridge University Press.

Wenger, E. (2000). *Communities of practice and social learning systems.* Organization, 7(2), 225-246.

Whale, R.F. (1971). *Copyright: Evolution, theory and practice.* London: Longman.

WSIS. (2003). *Declaration of principles.* Geneva: WSIS.

Young, S. (2004). *An evaluation of the regulation of online services in Australia.* Doctoral thesis, University of Queensland.

Endnote

[1]   An example of an open source project addressing these technical issues is MIT's DSpace (DSpace, 2003; Internet2, 2003; The Semantic Grid, 2003).

Copyright © 2007, Idea Group Inc. Copying or distributing in print or electronic forms without written permission of Idea Group Inc. is prohibited.

Chapter IX

Holistic Evaluation of the Roles of ICTs in Regional Development

Chris Keen, University of Tasmania, Australia

Dean Steer, University of Tasmania, Australia

Paul Turner, University of Tasmania, Australia

Abstract

Regional Australia continues to be the recipient of public programs premised on assumptions about the benefits of Information and Communications Technologies (ICTs) related development, at the same time as it is experiencing a reduction in basic services and problems associated with the digital divide. From a research perspective, these circumstances pose challenges on how to evaluate meaningfully the impacts of ICTs on regional development. These challenges are compounded by the considerable confusion that exists over what is meant by regional development, how it can be achieved, and how to measure and evaluate the role ICTs play in reviving and sustaining regional communities. The exploratory research reported in this chapter examines the issues surrounding what is meant by ICT-related development in a regional context. It also explores the usefulness of multiple measures, as opposed to single measures, to describe what in reality is a very complex process. In this context, the chapter outlines the preliminary development of, and the rationale behind, a holistic approach for evaluating the role of ICTs in regional development, based on insights generated from ongoing research in Tasmania.

Copyright © 2007, Idea Group Inc. Copying or distributing in print or electronic forms without written permission of Idea Group Inc. is prohibited.

Introduction

The role of ICT ... in economic growth and social change has received considerable attention in recent years [but] ... reliable and comprehensive indicators are needed to track developments in new information technologies and understand their impacts on our economies and societies. (OECD, 2002, p. 3)

Community informatics researchers are well aware of the huge volume of literature on the impact of ICTs on economic (particularly urban) development. This discourse often relies on a simplistic assumption that "what is good for the economy is good for the community." Too frequently their attempts to assess the impact of technology adoption on the social fabric of communities have been marginalized by the prevalence of this "dominant discourse." While it is clearly problematic to marginalize questions relating to the influence of ICTs on the social framework of communities, particularly in regional areas, it does highlight the challenges that need to be overcome if more effective ICT-related interventions are to be designed, initiated and implemented.

In examining the role of ICTs on regional areas it is easy to be in support of the need for a recalibration from purely economic indicators to an aggregation of indicators encapsulating social and community dimensions. It is however, considerably more difficult to identify those indicators and the mechanisms for their meaningful aggregation. This is the case in regional Australia, where even obtaining an official and consistent definition of "regional" is fraught with difficulties. Indeed, while linking economic, social, and community factors together is an important and worthy step, it has not led to the identification of mechanisms for achieving such a meaningful aggregation (Steer & Turner, 2004).

The exploratory research reported in this chapter aims to contribute to an understanding of the issues surrounding what is meant by ICT-related development in a regional context. It outlines the development of a holistic approach for evaluating the role of ICTs in regional development, based on insights generated from ongoing research into the impact of ICT-based projects in Tasmania.

ICTs and Regional Development

Despite the difficulties of defining "regional" that have been considered elsewhere (Steer & Turner, 2004), it is evident that the overall trends of slower industrial growth, decreasing rural populations, and the emergence of issues associated with the adequacy and/or affordability of telecommunications are very much a part of the everyday experience of the information economy for many Australians in regional areas, outside of the main metro area (DCITA, 2002).

In this context, it is not surprising that there has been considerable support for the deployment of ICTs as a mechanism to revitalise regional Australia. However, while ICTs clearly have the potential to connect regional Australia to the world, their impacts have been far from uniform and not always beneficial. ICTs and in particular e-commerce "raises the possible outcome of increased market share and dominance of large urban based companies in

Copyright © 2007, Idea Group Inc. Copying or distributing in print or electronic forms without written permission of Idea Group Inc. is prohibited.

regional areas rather than the promised expansion of regionally based companies outside their regions" (Coulthard, 2001, p. 420).

The lack of uniformity of benefits is indicative of the fact that the implementation of ICTs are highly differential, depending on existing local regulatory, economic, and social infrastructure context, and that in turn re-emphasizes the importance of an assessment of the unique characteristics and circumstances of individual regional areas (Hearn, Kimber, Linnie & Simpson, 2005). From a different but complementary perspective, Lloyd and Hellwig (2000) have highlighted how socio-demographic factors are also extremely influential in relation to determining the extent to which Australians use ICTs and participate in the information economy. Both perspectives highlight how both regional and individual differences are central to determining the outcomes of the development of ICTs infrastructure.

More broadly, it is interesting to consider the perspective of Hicks and Nivin (2000) who, in examining the huge U.S. investment in ICTs during the 1980s, researched the difficulty of finding consistent evidence of measurable impacts of these investments on overall U.S. economic performance. Hicks and Nivin found that when this ICT investment was assessed in isolation there was "no evidence of IT-induced income gains" (2000, p. 115), rather there was significant evidence to suggest that a "marked geographical concentration of IT investment" underscored the existence of the strong localization effects of ICT impacts. Simpson (2001) also noted that the majority of ICT-related economic growth in the U.S. was centralized in the relatively small locations of Silicon Valley and Seattle (Microsoft's and Amazon.com's headquarters).

The ICT-related investment and the deployment of ICTs has, and is having an impact on regional development. While ICTs can connect a region to the global economy, they also expose the region to global competition and the associated socioeconomic uncertainties of globalisation. What remains unclear is the extent to which this net impact will be positive (Coulthard, 2001; Wilde, Swatman & Castleman, 2000). More seriously, within the current conceptualization of the issues there is no way of meaningfully assessing whether the introduction of ICTs will mitigate, exacerbate, or simply replicate the pre-existing urban/regional divide (Steer & Turner, 2004).

Efforts and Insights to Date

In recent years the provision of telecommunications, and especially broadband services, to rural and remote Australia has become a hot political topic. Not surprisingly this has resulted in a large number of ICT-related policies, projects and schemes aimed at issues such as maintaining equity of access to ICT services, bridging the digital divide, providing regional economic growth, and empowering local communities. It has also given rise to an increasing number of theories and models on best practice. Unfortunately, what is often missing from these endeavors is a clear articulation of the specific goals of the projects in relation to how their impact will be measured, what outcomes are anticipated, and over what time frame.

Copyright © 2007, Idea Group Inc. Copying or distributing in print or electronic forms without written permission of Idea Group Inc. is prohibited.

At the Australian national level this can be seen in the HealthConnect project, estimated to cost $AU300 million (Dearne, 2005), which is the Australian National, State and Territories Governments' planned nationwide electronic health record system "to improve the flow of information across the healthcare system through the electronic collection, storage and exchange of consumer health information" (Productivity Commission, 2005, p. 260).

A report by the Australian Government's Productivity Commission notes, "Overall, the approach taken in assessing the costs and benefits of HealthConnect has been disjointed" and that "the fact that so many unresolved issues remain after seven years of research and development suggests that there have been gaps in the planning and evaluation of the project and/or how these have been acted upon" (Productivity Commission, 2005, p. 260).

In Tasmania, expectations were high for significant change in economic and social terms, based on the promises of several multi-million dollar ICT-based development projects. One of these projects, the AU$30 million Telstra Broadband-eLab, setup in the State's north, is a test and development site for broadband and multimedia applications (Mitchell, 2003). However, according to industry groups in Tasmania the Telstra Broadband-eLab had "not delivered on its promises to either Launceston or the Tasmanian IT industry" (Mitchell, 2006, p. 33).

At the broadest level, this highlights the problem that if the goals of ICT-related regional development are vague, it remains very difficult to be able to assess whether they have been achieved. Indeed, without clarity any project is open to interpretation of success and/or failure depending on an evaluator's perspective and priorities.

This is more than just of academic interest; there can be serious consequences if effective evaluations of such projects are not conducted. If the impact of ICTs is identified overall as positive when in fact it has been negative, this may lead to either a continuation of the same policies that are in reality having a negative effect, or the scaling down or the withdrawal of the initiatives due to the perception that they have accomplished their aim. Conversely, if the impact of ICTs is identified overall as negative when in fact it has been positive again this may lead to undesirable policy changes where successful programmes are reduced or stopped to the detriment of the region (Chester, 2003).

Meaningless Measurement

It is easy to argue that single measures seldom present a meaningful indicator of the state and focus of any individual project, community, or regional economy. For example, the Federal Government's advisory body on broadband development in Australia, the Broadband Advisory Group (BAG) recently called on the Federal Government to "encourage the OECD to introduce mechanisms that measure the effective use of broadband and not merely take-up" (NOIE, 2003, p. 4), without offering any substantial suggestions as to how this would be achieved and how it would be used.

By using multiple, disparate measures the complexity of interpretation of any situation is dramatically increased. This is particularly the case, if there is no consensus amongst researchers on what multiple measures to use or how best to integrate/aggregate the results (Henderson-Montero, Julian, & Yen, 2003). Of course, the accuracy of the measures themselves is also an essential element and relies on tailoring them to the specific situation

Copyright © 2007, Idea Group Inc. Copying or distributing in print or electronic forms without written permission of Idea Group Inc. is prohibited.

under examination.

Moreover, despite the vast amount of data collected, Papadakis (2001) implies that in the main, most of the measures used to date have missed the point – the true significance of ICTs is not in the technology itself, but rather in its use and the consequences of its use.

Similarly, Sorensen (2000) questions the use of a "single picture" representation of regional Australia, insisting that this flawed depiction masks a diverse and complex range of economic and social conditions which are multifaceted, complex, interrelated and dynamic. Further, Sorensen (2000, p. 17) concludes that there is a "need to understand better how Australia's regional economies operate and are evolving," and that "the measurement and analysis of regional economic and social well-being in Australia requires in-depth clarification, focusing especially on the more intangible lifestyle, wealth, taxation, demographic and cost of living aspects."

It can be seen in the literature that scholars have been debating for almost 20 years about the return on investment from large scale ICT projects, without coming to a consensus as to whether the economy as a whole has benefited for this expenditure (Peslak, 2003). A study of data by Peslak (2003) that related to the ten year period from 1989 through to 1999, using both financial and market based productivity measures in the U.S. at the firm level, rather than at the industry or national level, concluded that despite popular rhetoric "the overall results do not show clear consistent positive results for the relationship between information technology spending and firm level productivity" (Peslak, 2003, p. 80).

These discussions reveal the difficulty in developing and utilizing individual measures and aggregating multiple measures. The dependent variables have not been identified, let alone characterisation of the independent variables in the evaluation of these programs. They also point to the difficulty of being able to accurately compare results across regions.

The more geographically specific and sophisticated the tailoring of measurements is to a specific ICT or region, the more difficult it becomes to compare it with other regions. More than this, the outcomes of any regional development initiatives can carry different values in different regions, for example, creating 10 new jobs in a large regional city is always welcomed, but those same jobs created in smaller, struggling regional centers may have a much greater significant impact on the local economy and community.

New Alternatives

From an international perspective, recent work in the United Nations (UN) provides some insights that might assist in refining tools and techniques for measuring the impact of ICTs on regional Australia. The United Nations Development Program's Human Development Index (HDI) and the Genuine Progress Indicator (GPI) are two emerging major alternative measurement processes that are gaining some international support and credibility (ABS, 2002).

The Human Development Index (HDI) "was created to re-emphasize that people and their lives should be the ultimate criteria for assessing the development of a country, not economic growth" (UNDP, 2003). The HDI summarises three basic dimensions of human development: "living a long and healthy life, being educated and having a decent standard of living" (UNDP, 2003, p. 2). This is achieved by combining measures of life expectancy, school

Copyright © 2007, Idea Group Inc. Copying or distributing in print or electronic forms without written permission of Idea Group Inc. is prohibited.

enrolments, adult literacy rates, and per-capita income rates. However, the United Nations Development Program (UNDP) acknowledges that the HDI is only a "useful starting point" as it "omits several vital aspects of human development, notably the ability to participate in the decisions that affect one's life" (UNDP, 2003, p. 60). Further, the UNDP recognizes that more complete pictures of human development require the analysis of "other human development indicators and information" (UNDP, 2003, p. 60).

According to Colman (2001, p. 70), growth in Gross Domestic Product (GDP) "is simply a quantitative increase in the physical scale of the economy, and tells us nothing about our actual well-being." Colman's solution is to use an alternative measuring system, the Genuine Progress Indicator (GPI), which was developed by redefining progress to measure "the real state of our economy, our environment, and social justice" and to "indicate genuine progress in people's quality of life" (RP, 2000, p. 1). The GPI builds upon the personal consumption component of the GDP, and includes capital investment, government spending, and net exports. However it also includes quality of life measures that are not typically measured in monetary terms; for example, the contributions of volunteer work in the community, crime, and family breakdown (Colman, 2001; RP, 2000). When GDP and GPI are compared for the period 1950 to 2002 in the U.S., the distinction is marked. During this period the GDP rose at a relatively steadily rate, while at the same time the GPI, after a peak in the late 1970s, has remained relatively flat (Figure 1).

Yet another model for aggregating multiple measures is the Wealth of Nations Triangle Index for emerging economies, developed by the Money Matters Institute, Inc. This model uses economic environment, social environment, and information exchange variables to comprise legs of an equilateral triangle, and is built on the premise that sustainable growth is dependent on balance between these three areas (Sullivan, 2002). "Each leg contains 21 variables, chosen for both their relevancy and consistency over the years. Each variable is

Figure 1. Gross production vs. genuine progress for USA, 1950 to 2002 (Adapted from RP, 2004)

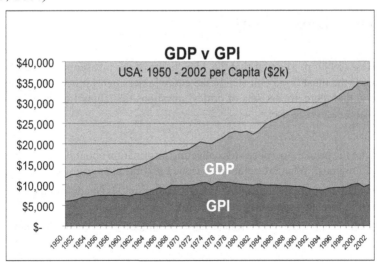

Copyright © 2007, Idea Group Inc. Copying or distributing in print or electronic forms without written permission of Idea Group Inc. is prohibited.

given equal weighting, based on a desire for simplicity, transparency, and balance among the three legs" (Sullivan, 2002, p. 4). The Index includes 70 nations that are considered to be "emerging economies" by the international investment community, and "measures the sustainable economic and social development potential of a nation and related risks, against those of other nations" (Sullivan, 2002, p. 4).

The Australian Bureau of Statistics also recognises that "public interest in the interrelationships between economic, social and environmental aspects of life" is growing (ABS, 2004, p. v), and that their statistical publications have tended to treat these issues as discontinuous. In recognising the current debate, the ABS is periodically publishing a series of discussion chapters called "Australia Now: Measures of Australia's Progress."

It is evident, even from this brief overview of just a few of the many attempts to capture and aggregate multiple measures of development of social progress that accurately measuring the impact and role of ICTs in regional development is likely to be fraught with difficulty. Nonetheless, it is also clear that if meaningful interventions have to be shaped by using ICTs in regional areas, meaningful measures must be obtained that present a more holistic picture of what is occurring.

Developing a Holistic Approach

While numerous measures for economic, social, and community dimensions exist, it is a very difficult in any individual measure to clearly isolate the role of ICTs from other factors that may be at play and to develop a meaningful aggregation of these different measures. This is due to the fact that they often rely on different conceptual and methodological bases. However, despite these difficulties, the development of sophisticated holistic measures is not just of research significance but critical in accurately evaluating ICT-related regional development.

Purposeful Measurement

Ryan and Hess (1999, p. 3) assert that the "the choice of the measurement instruments to be employed is the most important step in the entire [assessment] process." Winter (2001, p. 7) suggests that there are six sets of critical questions that should be considered when deciding what measures to use:

- What are the primary purposes for collecting information about ICT-related development in regions? What information is needed to fulfil the purposes?

- How will the information be used? What decisions will be made based on the assessment of ICT-related regional development?

- Do the measures adequately reflect the breadth and depth of ICT-related regional development? Do they provide information at each potential area of impact? That is,

Copyright © 2007, Idea Group Inc. Copying or distributing in print or electronic forms without written permission of Idea Group Inc. is prohibited.

do they align with expectations?

- Do the measures provide reliable information about the ICT-related regional development process?
- Are there differences between the information needed from the key regional policy stakeholders and what the measures provide?
- Do the various measures, as a whole, serve their intended purpose? (Adapted from Winter, 2001, p. 7)

Winter also suggests that "some of the questions can be answered during the development or selection of the measures." However, "some can be answered only by trying out various techniques for combining data and analysing the characteristics of the measures and how they contribute" to the assessment process (Winter, 2001, p. 7).

Chester (2003) cautions that multiple measures do not necessarily provide a clearer understanding of the underlying issues, but rather it is the reasoning behind the choosing and combining of the measures that determine their accuracy and appropriateness. Further, he states that the way multiple measures are combined is as "important as the measures themselves" (Chester, 2003, p. 9).

Disparate Measurement

However, from ongoing research in Launceston, a regional city in Tasmania, Australia, it is possible to outline the beginnings of an approach to accommodate a diverse range of measures. Launceston, with a population of around 70,000 people, is 200 km north of the State's capital city of Hobart (with a population of 200,000), and is the second largest city in Tasmania.

In his work, which in part assessed the use and implications of ICTs in the household sector, Papadakis' (2001) uses three areas of assessment: the socio-demographics of access and adoption, patterns of IT use, and research on impacts. A preliminary structured approach to evaluate the different measures based on Papadakis' work has been developed. This preliminary structured approach will allow the development of a holistic picture to emerge of the impact of ICT-based projects on regional development in Launceston.

So far within this preliminary structured framework two major types of data are being collected: quantitative data from multiple statistical sources, such as the Australian Bureau of Statistics and the Tasmanian Department of Economic Development (see Table 1); and qualitative data obtained using a combination of semi-structured interviews and surveys of approximately 40 key regional policy stakeholders. The aim of the qualitative data collection is to interpret the assumptions, attitudes, and understandings of issues with regard to ICT-related regional development and associated economic sustainability (see Table 2).

Multiple Measurement

As has been discussed above, the principal difficulty in using diverse measures is how to

Copyright © 2007, Idea Group Inc. Copying or distributing in print or electronic forms without written permission of Idea Group Inc. is prohibited.

Table 1. Quantitative data

Sources:	Data sought: (current and changes over past 5 years)
<ul><li>Australian Bureau of Statistics (ABS)</li><li>Major Australian banks</li><li>Tasmanian Department of Economic Development.</li><li>Tasmanian Department of Education.</li><li>Tasmanian Chamber of Commerce and Industry</li><li>Launceston City Council</li><li>Service Tasmania (A Tasmanian Government agency)</li><li>Tasmania Business Online</li><li>Tasmanian Communities Online</li><li>Tasmanian Electronic Commerce Centre</li></ul>	Home PC ownership / Internet connection and use • Number of people with home PCs • Hours of home PC / Internet use per user • Primary areas of use? • Hours connected to the Internet per user • Type of connection (Dialup, ISDN, ADSL) Business PC ownership / Internet connection and use • Number of Businesses connected • Type of connection (Dialup, ISDN, ADSL) • Primary areas of use • Percent / value of business using ICTs Educational PC access and Internet use • Number of Students per computer in Schools • Number of Students per Internet enabled computer in Schools Online Government Services • Number and percentage of Local, State, and Federal Government services online • Number and percentage of people using online Government services

aggregate these data. The approach being developed in this research program draws on the work of Henderson-Montero, Julian, and Yen (2003, p. 9), who list four possible approaches for meaningfully combining multiple and diverse measures: conjunctive, compensatory, mixed conjunctive-compensatory, and confirmatory:

- Conjunctive approach requires the demonstration of a minimum level of performance across all measures;

- Compensatory approach allows for the poor performance in one or more measures to be counterbalanced by higher performance in another measure;

- Mixed conjunctive-compensatory approach requires a minimum level of performance across the different measures; however, poorer performances measures can be counterbalanced by better performing measures;

- Confirmatory approach uses information from one measure to confirm or evaluate information from another independent measure. (Henderson-Montero, Julian & Yen, 2003, p. 9)

Preliminary research to date indicates that the mixed conjunctive-compensatory approach is providing the best holistic assessment in the Launceston region. However, mixed conjunctive-compensatory is not new and has been used for many years and in many different settings. What is new is its adaptation to the area of assessing ICT-related regional development.

Copyright © 2007, Idea Group Inc. Copying or distributing in print or electronic forms without written permission of Idea Group Inc. is prohibited.

Table 2. Qualitative information: Semi-structured interviews

Sources:	Information sought:
<ul><li>General Businesses – local, state wide, national and international</li><li>ICT-related businesses</li><li>Recipients of ICT-related development funding</li><li>Community Groups</li><li>Schools – Teachers, students, and parents</li><li>Home PC and Internet users and non-users</li><li>Online Access Centre staff and users</li><li>Politicians and Community leaders</li><li>Telecommunications providers</li><li>IT Industry representative groups</li></ul>	Businesses <ul><li>How have ICTs impacted on the business?</li><li>What are the barriers to the adoption or further utilisation of ICTs?</li></ul> Educational Institutions <ul><li>How are ICTs used in education?</li><li>What are the barriers to the adoption or further utilisation of ICTs in the education process?</li></ul> Politicians and Community leaders <ul><li>Have the actual impacts matched original goals?</li></ul> Home PC and Internet users and non-users <ul><li>What are (would be) the benefits of home PC / Internet use?</li><li>Who is (would) using the PC / Internet?</li><li>How did (would) you do previously spend your time now spent using the PC / Internet?</li><li>What are the barriers to the adoption / further adoption of ICTs?</li></ul>

Mixed conjunctive-compensatory techniques have been applied in diverse areas, such as marketing, teamwork evaluation and surveys of community cohesion. A potential application of this technique in the area of ICT adoption may be the development of a longitudinal analysis of the uptake of broadband communication technology. A survey of distinct technologies, such as high bandwidth cable connection, low to medium ADSL connections, and a variety of satellite connections can employ compensatory techniques to accommodate the differential uptake, degree of uptake, and extent of satisfaction with such a range of technologies. The conjunctive element of the analysis arises through the combination of data on different providers, technologies and pricing strategies, both geographically and over time, so that the combination of several factors, including speed of access, price of service provision, download limits, and availability of distinct technologies can be accommodated in the one study.

Analysis and Findings

Return on investment has been identified as the dependent variable for ICT development in regional areas, where this return encompasses both economic outcomes and social outcomes. A complete triple bottom line approach was not considered appropriate since the projects

Copyright © 2007, Idea Group Inc. Copying or distributing in print or electronic forms without written permission of Idea Group Inc. is prohibited.

under consideration had negligible relationship to environmental outcomes. Preliminary analysis of the data collected, using the mixed conjunctive-compensatory approach, has identified the following independent variables as being relevant to the determination of the return on investment in large scale ICT development for the region of Tasmania under consideration:

- Clarity of formulation of project objectives.

- Extent of effective communication of these project objectives to stakeholders and participants.

- Extent of alignment with declared project objectives that is evident in the decision making by the project management team during the project planning and administration phases.

- Extent of communication of project outcomes to stakeholders, especially key interested parties in local government and the community, during and after the project.

- Extent of linkage of these project outcomes with other regional activities, projects and infrastructure.

In comparison with ICT projects, other infrastructure works, such as the construction of new roads and highways, have clearly defined and communicable objectives of providing transport linkages between two or more points. The decision making during such a project is focused on civil construction and engineering. The key interested parties can relatively comprehend the outcomes that will eventuate when the road or highway is completed, and the linkages with economic and social development, and with other regional activities, projects and infrastructure become readily apparent once the road or highway is completed. Despite the widespread adoption of the metaphor of the information superhighway, ICT projects lack transparency of objectives and outcomes, and are far more difficult to comprehend. In particular, the strategic outcomes of a large scale ICT project are very difficult for many communities to envisage and to realize.

The determination of the dependent variable that characterises success in ICT projects has been identified as problematic (Milis, Meulders, & Mercken, 2003). The lack of comparable and statistically consistent data over a long time periods is also exacerbated by the rate of change of the underlying technologies and factors influencing its adoption, such as government polices and competitive pricing structures. Much more research in this field in needed to develop reliable, generalisable statistical frameworks to strengthen and support future investigation.

Copyright © 2007, Idea Group Inc. Copying or distributing in print or electronic forms without written permission of Idea Group Inc. is prohibited.

Conclusion

Evaluating the impact of ICTs on regional development is a complex process. It has been seen from the above discussion that much has been promised of ICT-focused developments, in terms of delivering benefits to regional areas including economic sustainability and connectivity to the global community. Clearly, if community informatics researchers are to assist in ensuring that the ICTs do impact positively on regional areas it is essential that more adequate measures are introduced so that a better picture of the diverse range of impacts (positive and negative) are considered in shaping future interventions.

This chapter has promoted a more holistic view of ICT-related development that includes assessments specifically designed to capture the value of ICTs for social and community development as well as economic, and has outlined an initial approach to doing this based on insights generated from ongoing research in Tasmania.

References

ABS. (2002). *Measuring Australia's progress*. Catalogue No. 1370.0_2002. Retrieved June 25, 2006 from http://www.ausstats.abs.gov.au/ausstats/1370-0_2002.pdf.

ABS. (2004). *Measures of Australia's progress*. Catalgue No. 1370.0_2004. Canberra: Australian Bureau of Statistics.

Chester, M.D. (2003). Multiple measures and high-stakes decisions: A framework for combining measures. *Educational Measurement: Issues and Practice, 22*(2), 32-41.

Colman, R. (2001). Measuring real progress. *Journal of Innovative Management, 7*(1), 69-77.

Coulthard, D. (2001). eCommerce and the region: Not necessarily an unequivocal good. In *Proceedings of the Fourteenth Bled Electronic Commerce Conference* (pp. 419-443), University of Maribor, Bled, Slovenia.

DCITA. (2002). *Connecting regional Australia: The report of the Regional Telecommunications Inquiry, Commonwealth Department of Communications, Information Technology and the Arts*. Retrieved June 25, 2006, from http://www.telinquiry.gov.au/rti-report/rti report text f-a 18.pdf

Dearne, K. (2005, October 27). E-health ailing, says watchdog. *The Australian*, p. 31.

Hearn, G., Kimber, M., Lennie, J., & Simpson, L. (2005). A way forward: Sustainable ICTs and regional sustainability. *The Journal of Community Informatics, 1*(2),18-31.

Henderson-Montero, D., Julian, M.W., & Yen, W.M. (2003). Multiple measures: Alternative design and analysis models. *Educational Measurement: Issues and Practice, 22*(2), 7-12.

Hicks, D.A., & Nivin, S.R. (2000). Beyond globalization: Localized returns to IT infrastructure investments. *Regional Studies, 34*(2), 115-127.

Copyright © 2007, Idea Group Inc. Copying or distributing in print or electronic forms without written permission of Idea Group Inc. is prohibited.

Lloyd, R., & Hellwig, O. (2000). *Barriers to take-up of new technology*. Disscussion Paper No. 53. Canberra: National Centre for Social and Economic Modelling (NATSEM).

Milis, K., Meulders, M., & Mercken, R. (2003). A quasi-experimental approach to determining success criteria for ICT projects. In *Proceedings of the 36th Hawaii International Conference on System Sciences* (p. 260.1), Hawaii.

Mitchell, S. (2003, May 13). Harradine deal a dud: Industry. *The Australian*, (p. 33).

NOIE (2003). *Australia's broadband connectivity: The Broadband Advisory Group's Report to Government*. Retrieved June 25, 2006, from National Office for the Information Economy, http://www.noie.gov.au/publications/NOIE/BAG/report/ 326_BAG_report_setting_2.pdf

OECD. (2002). *Measuring the information economy*. Retrieved June 25, 2006, from http:// www.oecd.org/dataoecd/16/14/1835738.pdf

Papadakis, M.C. (2001). *The application and implications of information technologies in the home: Where are the data and what do they say?* Arlington: National Science Foundation.

Peslak, A.R. (2003). A firm level study of information technology productivity using financial and market based measures. *The Journal of Computer Information Systems*, *43*(4),72-80.

Productivity Commission. (2005). *Impacts of advances in medical technology in Australia* (Research Report). Melbourne.

RP. (2000). *Blazing sun overhead and clouds on the horizon: The genuine progress report for 1999*. Retrieved June 25, 2006, from http://www.rprogress.org/ projects/gpi/gpi1999. pdf

RP. (2004). *The genuine progress indicator 1950-2002* (2004 Update). Retrieved June 25, 2006, from http://www.rprogress.org/newpubs/2004/gpi_march 2004update.pdf

Ryan, J.M., & Hess, R.K. (1999). Issues, strategies, and procedures for combining data from multiple measures. Paper presented at the annual meeting of the American Educational Research Association, Montreal, Canada. In P.C. Winter (2001). *Combining information from multiple measures of student achievement for school-level decision-making*. Council of chief state school officers. Washington, DC. Retrieved June 25, 2006, from http://www.ccsso.org/ Publications/Download.cfm?Filename=CASWinter.pdf

Sorensen, T. (2000). *Regional development: Some issues for policy makers*. Reseach paper: 26 1999_2000. Retrieved June 25, 2006, from http://www.aph.gov.au/library/pubs/ rp/1999-2000/2000rp26.htm

Simpson, R. (2001). *The Internet and regional Australia: How rural communities can address the impact of the Internet*. Report for Rural Industries Research and Development Corporation (RIRDC). Publication No. 01/087. Retrieved June 25, 2006, from http://www.rirdc.gov.au/reports/HCC/01-087.pdf

Steer, D.R., & Turner, P.A. (2004). The role of place: Tasmanian insights on ICT and regional development. In S. Marshall, W. Taylor, & X. Yu (Eds.), *Using community informatics to transform regions* (pp. 67-81). Hershey, PA: Idea Group Publishing.

Copyright © 2007, Idea Group Inc. Copying or distributing in print or electronic forms without written permission of Idea Group Inc. is prohibited.

Sullivan, N.P. (Ed.). (2002). *Wealth of nations triangle index: Statistical GPS to emerging economies*. Retrieved June 25, 2006, from Money Matters Institute, http://www.moneymattersinstitute.org/wni.pdf

UNDP. (2003). *Human development report 2003*. United Nations Development Programme. Retrieved June 25, 2006, from http://www.undp.org/hdr2003/

Wilde, W.D., Swatman, P.A., & Castleman, T. (2000). Investigating the impact of IT&T on rural, regional and remote Australia. In *Proceedings of CollECTeR (USA)*2000, Colorado. Retrieved June 25, 2006, from http://www.collecter.org/collUSA/Wilde.pdf

Winter, P.C. (2001). *Combining information from multiple measures of student achievement for school-level decision-making*.Washington, DC: Council of Chief State School Officers. Retrieved June 25, 2006, from http://www.ccsso.org/Publications/Download.cfm?Filename=CASWinter.pdf

Copyright © 2007, Idea Group Inc. Copying or distributing in print or electronic forms without written permission of Idea Group Inc. is prohibited.

Chapter X

Role of ICTs in Socioeconomic Development and Poverty Reduction

Hakikur Rahman, SDNP, Bangladesh

Abstract

Information and Communication Technologies (ICTs) are often promoted as central to reviving and sustaining regional communities. Apart from these, the revolutionary feature of modern ICTs—mainly the Internet and mobile telephony—facilitate low cost and speedy interaction among network participants. In this context, knowledge and information are fundamental for facilitating rural development and bringing about social and economic escalation. Nowadays, ICTs are universally acknowledged as powerful tools for development. At the same time, ICTs are seemingly essential to social development and economic growth. In recent years, the process of ICTs has been influencing the socioeconomic context in many countries. Despite that, in many countries a significant proportion of the population does not have access to clean water, sanitation, basic health services and proper education; ICTs provide novel opportunities for information interchange and technology transfer. This chapter looks into critical aspects of ICTs in raising socioeconomic development in underdeveloped countries and tries to illustrate success cases in developed countries that can be replicated in developing countries to reduce poverty. Emphasis has been given to analyze the role of ICTs in poverty reduction processes upholding regional developments. Enactment of ICTs has been elaborately discussed for the uplift of community and it has

Copyright © 2007, Idea Group Inc. Copying or distributing in print or electronic forms without written permission of Idea Group Inc. is prohibited.

been observed that solving common causes for common citizens needs strategic implementation of policies at the central core and pragmatic implementation of actions at the grass roots. Simultaneously, this chapter discusses various critical aspects of the development processes to achieve good governance that is vital for sustainable development. However, as ingredients for uplift through ICTs, institutional approaches in various forms have been found to be extremely effective for socioeconomic development and at the same time for regional developments.

Harnessing ICTs for Development

Information and Communication Technologies (ICTs) are frequently promoted as central to reviving and sustaining regional communities (Simpson & Hunter, 2001). In this context, knowledge and information are fundamental for facilitating rural development and bringing about social and economic escalation. The position that ICTs have a role in enhancing sustainability in regional communities has various threads and can be seen from the three spheres; community, government, and business (Kasigwa, Williams & Baryamureeba, 2005).

Many pre-Marchallian classical economists and their immediate post World War II followers like Lewis, Rodan and others viewed "economic development as a growth process that requires the systematic reallocation of factors of production from a low-productivity, traditional technology, decreasing returns, and mostly primary sector to a high-productivity, modern technology, increasing returns, and mostly industrial sector" (Adelman, 1999, p. 1).

In recent years, the process of ICTs has been influencing the socioeconomic environment in many countries. While ICTs provide novel opportunities for information exchange and technology transfer, they have increased deprivation for those nations that have not been able to update with these neoteric adjustments. In many countries, a significant proportion of the population does not have access to clean water, sanitation, basic health services and proper education (Ghaus-Pasha, 2005). To overcome these, ICT procedures can be utilized in bridging the digital divide and harnessing the potential of ICTs as a development tool (European Commission, 2005). Each country needs to find the proper determinants on the use of ICTs for development in the context of acculturation processes of socioeconomic development and poverty reduction (Graham, 2005).

The connection of economic development to ICTs is based both on the communication and the information elements. Communication includes both affective and cognitive analysis, while the information element includes only the cognitive portion (Pigg & Crank, 2004). However, the information function is rather complex due to its variety of features within the network along the Internet-based information transfer. Hence, the information transfer can be treated as *active* (interactive information interchange), or *passive* (repositories or knowledge management features), and can be transmitted in many forms.

The content side of ICTs has often been neglected when dealing with ICTs and development. The creation and strengthening of a content repository in different countries represent significant advantages on the usage of ICTs and their development aspect. First, socially it provides contents for society by operators in close contact with it, its needs, expectations and demands. Second, culturally it helps to keep local cultures alive and allows them to be

Copyright © 2007, Idea Group Inc. Copying or distributing in print or electronic forms without written permission of Idea Group Inc. is prohibited.

presented to the rest of the world, thus safeguarding and enriching cultural diversity. Third, economically it generates local employment based on its own sustainable resources, and even constitutes a source of income when exported (European Commission, 2005).

The revolutionary feature of modern ICTs—mainly the Internet and mobile telephony—is their ability to facilitate low cost and speedy interaction among network participants (Proenza, 2002). It makes the economic aspects of people's lives more efficient, as they keep in touch with personal networks, learn about markets, refine production techniques, eliminate time spent on travel to meet people to get information (Hudson, 1984), and able to take knowledgeable decisions. It also helps to build social capital (Woolcock & Narayan, 2000).

Connectivity to the Internet can help overcome some of the most significant obstacles undermining the development of remote rural areas. It can enable low-cost access to governmental services, agricultural product and market information, local investment opportunities, financial services, distance education, online health services, and job vacancies to uplift community development processes (Proenza, 2002).

The vast majority of donors recognize the potential of ICTs as a catalyst for socioeconomic development but not all of them have reached the same consensus in using ICTs to assist development activities. While some are planning to develop new ICT strategies, others have already used ICTs for years and have drawn lessons from their success stories. In all cases, donors put ICTs to the service of the achievement of their broader strategic objectives in a number of development sectors (health, education, e-commerce, e-government, etc.). However, the overall focus is on meeting specific objectives, not on technology, per se.

Achieving the Millennium Development Goals (MDGs), particularly poverty reduction, is a frequently cited objective reinforcing most donor ICT strategies. These strategies aim at creating an inclusive information society with special attention paid to underserved regions, that is, the least developed countries (LDCs) and marginal communities. In this endeavor most of the donors prefer to build ICTs for development strategy on a partnership basis involving a number of actors from other bilateral and multilateral agencies, ministries, civil society, the private sector, universities and research institutions in both developed and developing countries (OECD, 2003). This has created reinforcement of institutional development approach for socio-economic development in many regions, and in reality immensely increased credibility of institutional partnership at grass roots.

It has been found that regional policies increasingly derive their parameters from a global horizon of different development paths, technological options, product life cycles, and so forth, and must also do justice to regional policy objectives such as employment, income, taxation, and welfare development (Braczyk & Heidenreich, 1996). Thus, global development logics, dynamism (Harvey, 1989), and creation of fluidity vs. regionality (Laepple, 1999) deserves immense dialogues at each and every stakeholders' stake conforming its proper implementation through information networking and upgrading technological knowledge.

Technological knowledge is not only organized in large-scale technical systems (Hughes, 1987), in branches or in professions but frequently also in regional economic areas. And this knowledge incorporated in regional production clusters, cooperative relations, institutions and policy patterns does not usually develop in great leaps and bounds, but incrementally, step by step. Regional economies can be understood from the accumulation of collective technological learning (Braczyk & Heidenreich, 1996). Technological knowledge

Copyright © 2007, Idea Group Inc. Copying or distributing in print or electronic forms without written permission of Idea Group Inc. is prohibited.

and technological learning are, therefore, bound to context, community and region; and "technological capabilities reflect local, regional and national contexts and environments" (Storper, 1995, p. 897).

"Despite the growing importance, civil society organizations in the developing world remain only partially understood" (Ghaus-Pasha, 2005, p. 2), they are the important contributors in raising awareness, creating enable environment and promoting ICTs for potential development of the society. At the same time, the government has a critical role to play in promoting technological dynamism, policy, and in increasing productivity in related sectors, including industry and agriculture. Technological dynamism was the essence of the Industrial Revolution (Adelman, 1999), but, nowadays information dynamism is the core of all development perspectives.

However, rapid technological change and global connectivity has generated an information and knowledge gap between countries, the so-called "digital divide." About half of the world's population has never made a phone call, or Africa has only 2% of the world's telephone mainlines (World Bank, 2000). Only 2.4% of the world populations are users of the Internet (internetworldstats.com, 2005a) and almost all of whom are concentrated in the Organization for Economic Cooperation and Development (OECD) countries. Roughly, 90% of Internet host computers are located in high-income countries that account for only 16% of world population (Global Reach, 2005; World Bank, 2000). Overcoming this dynamically changing digital divide is going to be a potential challenge for many developing countries in the coming years.

This chapter looks into critical aspects of ICTs in raising socioeconomic development in underdeveloped countries and will try to illustrate success cases in developed countries that can be replicated in developing countries to reduce poverty. Furthermore, emphasis has been given to analyze the role of ICTs in poverty reduction processes upholding regional development.

Background

ICTs are universally acknowledged as powerful tools for development. ICTs are seemingly essential to social development and economic growth. Simultaneously, they are critical to the development of good governance, can be effective vehicles for the maintenance of security, and are vital for sustainable development (Pacific Plan, 2005). As discussed earlier, enactment of ICTs in the uplift of community and common causes for common citizens needs strategic implementation policies at the central core and pragmatic implementation at the grass roots. However, as ingredients for uplift through ICTs, institutional approaches in various forms have been found to be extremely effective for socioeconomic development and at the same time for regional development.

Before starting with the arguments on the context of socioeconomical development and relating it to the reduction of poverty utilizing ICTs, the author feels it is important to elaborate on definitions of a few related terms. The first term is development. Development refers to improvement of the economic and social conditions of poorer countries,[1] and can be treated as the process of improving the quality of all people living in a country.[2] Then comes poverty. Poverty can be seen as the state of being deprived of basic essentials

Copyright © 2007, Idea Group Inc. Copying or distributing in print or electronic forms without written permission of Idea Group Inc. is prohibited.

of well-being such as food, shelter, income, employment, access to social services, and social status.[3] Naturally, another question arises. What has been understood by ICTs in this chapter? Generally, it is the acronym for Information and Communication Technologies and used to handle information and assist communication.[4] ICTs are the fusion of computers and telecommunications.[5] But ICTs incorporate innovative ways to provide their users with global access to information, learning, and support.[6] Information technology comprises the knowledge, skills and understanding needed to use ICTs appropriately and effectively[7] to process, transmit, and store data and information[8] for appropriate use.

These background definitions of ICTs can lead the researchers to think ICTs as a catalytic agent of development. Now comes the reasoning. What is social development, what is meant by economic development, and how can institutional development be defined?

Social development encompasses a commitment to individual well-being and the opportunity for citizens to determine their own needs, and to influence decisions that affect them. It incorporates public concerns in developing social policy and economic initiatives.[9]

Economic development can be related to the institutional changes made to promote economic betterment. It is the social organizational changes made to promote growth in an economy.[10] Economic development strengthens an area's economy and employment base[11] with sustained increase in the economic standard of living of a country's population by increasing its stocks of physical and human capital through improved technology.[12] Economic development is the process of improving the quality of human life through increasing per capita income, reducing poverty, and enhancing individual economic opportunities, including better education, improved health and nutrition, conservation of natural resources, a cleaner environment, and a richer cultural life.[13] In other words, economic development is a sustainable wealth creation process that works within the framework of community parameters to maximize the efficient and effective utilization of community resources for economic gain for the local community.[14]

Regional development refers to the improvement in the capability of regions to conduct development programs such as agriculture, education, skill development, research, health, and other public issues, including physical infrastructure, information infrastructure, and institutional infrastructure but primarily aimed to the development of human capital.[15] Regional development is the process of enabling and facilitating a region to develop and increase its capacities and capabilities to meet its desired objectives.[16]

The synthesis above has tried to define all parameters related to ICTs and regional development. Before proceeding towards the main thrust of the chapter, it is important to emphasize on a few intimate contexts of ICTs in poverty reduction phenomenon through several implicit manifestations.

ICTs are cross-cutting technologies with a fundamental impact on the various sectors of society, culture, and the economy. A decade ago, ICTs were considered marginal to the issues of economic growth and poverty reduction. Since then, skepticism has given way to more open cognizant and attitudes. ICTs are now seen as powerful enablers of development goals. In many developing countries, policy attention has begun to turn towards the convergence of industrial policies that emphasize manufacturing capabilities and science, technology. At the same time, innovative policies are increasingly seen as important tools for development because of their power to generate and utilize knowledge (UN, 2005).

Copyright © 2007, Idea Group Inc. Copying or distributing in print or electronic forms without written permission of Idea Group Inc. is prohibited.

More precisely, ICTs are increasingly being seen by global analysts, the governments of many countries (especially developing ones), and development agencies as stimulating catalysts of collective learning. They enhance social development; improve individual people's lives by allowing them to acquire the knowledge and skills that empower them to be productive in innovative ways; and strengthen overall economic growth and income by raising productivity. Policies designed to enhance the role of ICTs in development have created new avenues for reducing poverty, especially through the beneficial effects they have on mainstream development objectives like, health, education, capacity-building, knowledge management and improving overall living conditions (UN, 2005).

Relationships of ICTS with Regional Development

For having clear understanding of relationship between methods of ICTs and factors of socioeconomic development (SED) and poverty reduction (PR) in effect regional development (RD), as depicted in *Figure 1*, a mathematical model was established in this research that was formulated as shown in *Formula 1*. In a broader context, ICTs can be directly related to

Figure 1. Changes in ICTs influencing poverty reduction through regional development

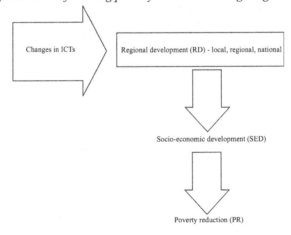

Formula 1. Relationships among factors of socio-economic development and poverty reduction for regional development

$$\int (\text{factors of SED} \pm \text{factors of PR}) \Big|_{\text{ICTs}} \infty\ RD$$

Copyright © 2007, Idea Group Inc. Copying or distributing in print or electronic forms without written permission of Idea Group Inc. is prohibited.

Figure 2. Broad aspect of ICTs for regional development

Figure 3. Changes in ICTs influencing regional development affecting socio-economic development and poverty reduction

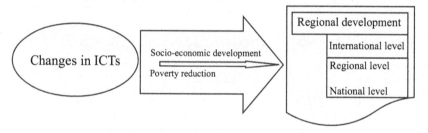

Figure 4. Direct implication of ICTs for regional development through socio-economic development

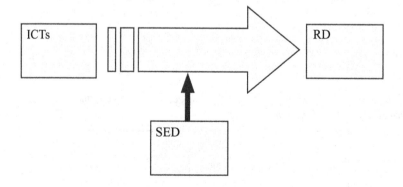

Copyright © 2007, Idea Group Inc. Copying or distributing in print or electronic forms without written permission of Idea Group Inc. is prohibited.

Figure 5. Direct implication of ICTs for regional development through poverty reduction

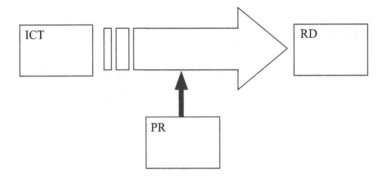

Table 1. Five tiers of regional development

Regional development incorporating aspects of development at	Global Level
	Regional Level
	National Level
	Divisional/Zonal level
	Local level

RD (see *Figure 2*), or in a more specific context (see *Figure 3*), a three tier RDperspective can be portrayed. However, for realistic propagation of ICT effects, a five tier RDcan be more effective as shown in Table 1. Furthermore, a direct relationship between ICTs and RDen effect SED (see Figure 4) and between ICTs and RDen effect PR (see Figure 5) can be transformed into another mathematical model as formulated in Formula 2.

Factors$_1$ of Formula 2 are related to socioeconomic development, but encompass ICT methods in their implementation. Similarly, factors$_2$ are related to poverty reduction processes. With clear understanding of the factors related to SED and PR, and adequate nourishment at each stake during the formulation, formation, and implementation phases can eventually lead to incremental institutional development. Moreover, for having better strategic implementation, a transparent understanding of the input and out determinants specified in Table 2 and 3 would be helpful.

To implement ICT based proponents in consolidating socioeconomic development and poverty reduction processes and make ICTs more meaningful to those who need information and knowledge the most (Adam, 2005), various approaches have been discussed in this section. However, before that, a few objectives have been described that seem essential for strategic planning. An ICT-based system for SED and PR, should:

Copyright © 2007, Idea Group Inc. Copying or distributing in print or electronic forms without written permission of Idea Group Inc. is prohibited.

Formula 2. A mathematical model for regional development [a]

$$\text{RD} \quad \infty \int_{\text{SED}} \text{ICTs} \quad + \quad \int_{\text{PR}} \text{ICTs}$$

$$\approx \sum_{i=0}^{n} \text{factors}_1 \quad + \quad \sum_{k=0}^{p} \text{factors2} ,$$

$$\text{factors}_1 \quad = \quad \frac{\text{factors of SED}}{\text{ICTs}} , \text{ and}$$

$$\text{factors}_2 \quad = \quad \frac{\text{factors of PR}}{\text{ICTs}}$$

factors_1

- science education, [a]
- research and development (R&D), [a]
- coordination and cooperation, [a]
- information dissemination, [a]
- natural resources, [a]
- information technology (education, training, human resource development), [a]
- capital investment (e-commerce), [a]
- higher education, public research system, [a]
- human capital, [a]
- demographic indicators, [a]
- adequate/ reasonable policy, [a]
- networking, [a]

factors_2

- assessing best practices and sharing valuable knowledge, [b]
- governance (top, mid, grass roots), [b]
- partnership (multi-sectoral), [b]
- performance management (monitoring), [b]
- updating information (policy, planning), [b]
- education (basic literacy), [b]
- social protection system, [b]
- information infrastructure, [b]
- technological development, [b]
- regional cooperation, [b]

[a]   *WCS, 1999; Bekkulova, 2004; UNDP, 2003c; Mali, 2002; Ortner, 1999; Joseph, 2003; Government of Ukraine, 2003; World Bank, 2002.*

[b]   *Romanenko, 2003; Government resolution, 2004; Hutagaol & Sugino, 2005; PRSP Report, 2005; NAO, 2002; WCL, 2005; China's Human Rights, 2005, World Bank Group, 2005.*

Copyright © 2007, Idea Group Inc. Copying or distributing in print or electronic forms without written permission of Idea Group Inc. is prohibited.

Table 2. Input determinants for institutional development [c]

Regional development through utilization of information and communication technologies	Input Determinants [c]
	Networking
	Acceptability
	Social norms/behavior
	Economic condition
	Poverty level
	Knowledge services
	Shared vision
	Adaptability
	Local content
	Leadership at grassroots
	Policy initiations at various levels
	Form of content storage
	Resource optimization
	Skill at grass roots
	Content management
	Training schemes
	Investment at local level
	Role of transnational companies
	IP addresses
	Domain name system
	Root server system

[c]   *Amin & Thrift, 1994; Flora, 1998; Lallana, 2004; Onyx Bullen, 2000; Putman, 1993; Roure, Jennings & Shadbolt, 2002; Wall, Ferazzi & Schryer, 1998; UNDP, 2003c, 2004; Woolcock & Narayan, 2000, Giddens, 1990*

- Clearly focus on identifying role of ICTs in generating opportunities that have more of a pro-poor focus.
- Find ways to link e-government, public sector and institutes reform and enhance public service delivery.
- Create opportunities to involve a variety of partners, including local business and telecom operators by linking the development of ICT infrastructure and access the development uses and strategies (UNDP, 2004).

At the same time, the strategies should have:

Copyright © 2007, Idea Group Inc. Copying or distributing in print or electronic forms without written permission of Idea Group Inc. is prohibited.

Table 3. Output determinants of institutional development

Regional development through utilization of information and communication technologies	Output Determinants [d]
	Knowledge base society
	Improved decision support
	Transparency in system
	Industrial districts and their distinctiveness
	Organizational flexibility
	Regional economic planning
	Human capital formation
	Technology parks
	University expansions
	Access to market prices
	Access to information for improved decision-making, technology options and improved family links
	Improved policy environment to attract Foreign Direct Investment
	Equitable universal service policies and provisions
	Establish financial mechanisms to promote cost effective access and connectivity
	Governance (at all levels of the decision making processes)
	Poverty diagnostics, monitoring and evaluation
	Institutional arrangements
	Development of ICT infrastructure
	Creation of a secured cyberspace environment
	Creation and management of local content
	Establishment of effective regulatory policies and agencies
	Launching of education policies that utilize and encourage the expansion of ICT capacities
	Improving economic governance
	Developing human resources, including education and health
	Developing infrastructure, with particular attention paid to ICTs
	Improving market access and trade
	Improving financial flows and managing debt
	Management of IP
	Community networking
	Content repositories
	Availability
	Affordability

[d] *Roure, Jennings & Shadbolt, 2002; Putman, 1993; Flora, 1998; Onyx Bullen, 2000; Wall, Ferazzi & Schryer, 1998; Woolcock & Narayan, 2000; Lallana, 2004; UNDP, 2004; UNDP, 2003c; Amin & Thrift, 1994; Demeksa, 2001, Worldbank, 2004; Marshall & Taylor, 2005; Salvadore & Sherry, 2004*

- a more strategic regional focus and an agreed economic development directive;
- improved knowledge of a region's strengths and advantages that the future projects can be attuned along the success cases;
- extended economic development networks with increased partnership approaches;

Copyright © 2007, Idea Group Inc. Copying or distributing in print or electronic forms without written permission of Idea Group Inc. is prohibited.

- Improved cooperation and trust among groups with better understanding of other stakeholders' goals and processes.

- Better cooperation and alignment between central and local government resources (Government of New Zealand, 2004a).

- A better working environment conducive to improved partnership among various local development agents and stakeholders (representing government, private sector and civil society) (Demeksa, 2001).

Furthermore, to implement these strategies, the institutions should be:

- Decentralized and team-based with strong lateral communication and coordination that crosses functional boundaries within and among organizations.

- Acting to empower stakeholders and facilitate cooperation among them.

- Able to analyze regional development structures and strategies needed to justify the aims, objectives and effectiveness.

- Able to supplant more conventional institutional features of governance (Ansell, 2000).

Formulating a Mathematical Model Leading to ICT Development Matrix

Tichy and Fombrum (1979) and Shrader, Lincoln, and Hoffman (1989) argued that the organic form of organization can be reinterpreted in the terms of mathematical network theory. They also argued that Burns and Stalker's (1994) mechanistic organization corresponds to "sparse" internal networks, low degrees of connectivity, and the predominance of asymmetrical relationships, while organic organizations have "dense" networks, high degrees of connectivity, and a predominance of symmetrical relationships. Structurally, the network organization can be characterized as heterarchical rather than hierarchical (Ansell, 2000). On the other hand, for a N-Form Organization (a symmetrical network) Hedlund argued that in a heterarchy "several strategic apexes emerge, that these shift over time" (Hedlund, 1994, p. 87). What distinguishes a heterarchy from a hierarchy is the capacity of lower-level units to have relationships with multiple higher-level centers as well as lateral links with units at the same organizational level. Figure 6 shows a possible formation of global information backbone through institutional build up (Rahman, 2004a), while Figure 7 illustrates the various network relationships.

Kontopoulos (1993) suggests that while hierarchy entails a "many-to-one" form of structural aggregation, heterarchy entails a "many-to-many" relationship between different nodes in a social structure. The parallel to the mathematical network language is clear: many-to-many relations imply dense networks and high degrees of connectivity (Ansell, 2000). However, an exchange of information is characterized by the ability to be easily transferred, care-

Copyright © 2007, Idea Group Inc. Copying or distributing in print or electronic forms without written permission of Idea Group Inc. is prohibited.

Figure 6. Global Information backbone hierarchy

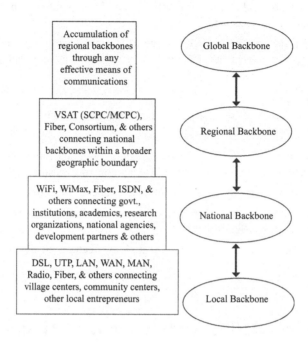

Figure 7. "One-to-one," "one-to-many," and "many-to-many" network relations

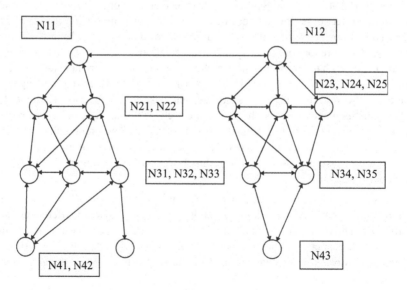

Copyright © 2007, Idea Group Inc. Copying or distributing in print or electronic forms without written permission of Idea Group Inc. is prohibited.

Figure 8. Networking hierarchy within a country (Adapted from Rahman, 2004b)

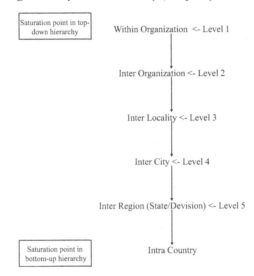

fully measured and can be specified as valuable content, and at the same time it has to be reciprocally exchanged to become a value-added product. Figure 7 represents one-to-one, one-to-many, and many-to-many connectivity relationships within network hierarchies. N11 and N12 designate level 1 (national backbone); N21, N22, N23, N24, N25 designate level 2 (state/division/local region); N31, N32, N33, N34, N35 designate level 3 (city/town/district backbone); and N41, N42, N43 designate level 4 (village centre/call centre/local centre/telecentre/knowledge centre) junctions/terminations.

The degree of a network gives an indication of how many entities a user interacts with. The average degree is calculated by.

Research works indicate that degree of around unity in a typically medium network is acceptable, while degree of around 1.5 can be taken as medium interaction, and greater than 1.5 can be referred as heavy interactions. Figure 8 illustrates acceptable information infrastructure hierarchies and it can be saturated by both hierarchies (top-down, or bottom-up). However, the author proposes establishment of bottom-up networking hierarchy in

Formula 3. Degree of connectivity of a network

$$\bar{d} = \frac{\sum_{i=1}^{n} d(n_i)}{n}$$

where $d(n_i)$ = number of edges incident on node i
         i = node as depicted in figure 8 (Rahman, 2004b).

Copyright © 2007, Idea Group Inc. Copying or distributing in print or electronic forms without written permission of Idea Group Inc. is prohibited.

Figure 9. Person a is virtually linked to persons b, c, d, and e (Adapted from Rahman, 2004b)

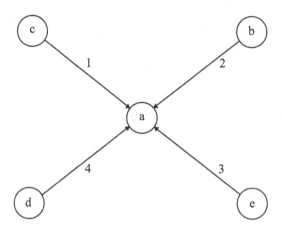

weaker economies. This way network establishment may be made more easily adaptable to the society and may be made more versatile by using indigenous methods. Afterwards, by aggregating in dynamic fashion these hierarchical networks as shown in Figure 8 may be integrated with the next upper layer of aggregation.

Another indicator about the relationship among the member of a network can be derived, if the edges of the network (Figure 9) can be set in a symmetrical matrix, as in Matrix 1.

while in Figure 9, a knows b, c, d and e. But, the relationship between b, c, d and e may not be known (Rahman, 2004b). These relationships will establish the ICT matrix and with point-to-point relationships among the network entities, the ideal relationship value may be given to unity. The ICT development matrix evolves from this unity relationship. Even if the network entity may follow point-to-multipoint, or multipoint-to-point paths, for a development matrix it must be upgraded to provide unity relationship value (either a zero communication, or unity communication). However, alternate to ICT development matrix, a global knowledge pyramid (see Figure 10) may be formed following illustrated hierarchies.

Matrix 1. ICT Development matrix for uniform network distribution

a	|	-	1	1	1	1	|
b	|	1	-	0	0	0	|
c	|	1	0	-	0	0	|
d	|	1	0	0	-	0	|
e	|	1	0	0	0	-	|

Copyright © 2007, Idea Group Inc. Copying or distributing in print or electronic forms without written permission of Idea Group Inc. is prohibited.

Figure 10. Global knowledge pyramid

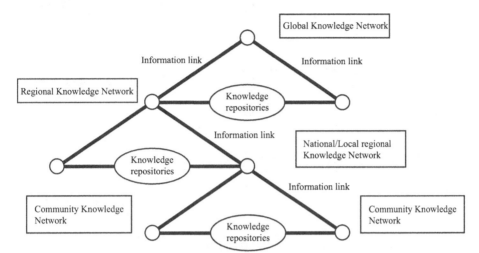

In Figure 10, establishment of a global knowledge pyramid has been shown incorporating community, national, and regional networks.

Approaches to Strengthen Socioeconomic Development

Approaches in different forms that have been taken varying from Keynesian to neo-liberal approaches on economic and regional developments are being indicated in Table 4. However, the author proposes an approach that may be enacted in distributed network driven system to make it sustainable.

As indicated in columns two and three of Table 4, the approaches have been described as "imperative" by Hausner (1995) and referred to be modest in terms of stimulating sustained improvements in the economic competitiveness of the Least Focussed Regions (LFRs). Though Keynesian approaches have assisted in increased employment and income in the LFRs, they have failed in securing increased productivity compared to those in more prosperous regions, and importantly, also failed to achieve sustaining growth in terms of mobilizing resources and becoming less dependent on externally driven growth factors. The market therapy has revealed a far more threatening outcome that by removing barriers on financial and income transferring processes (though vital for social survival), have exposed lower spectrum LFRs to become more deprived of basic social elements, creating by far more divide (digital, economic, social, and others).

Recent global trend has enlarged the free market zones and seemingly failed to balance the flow of relevant input-output parameters. It may be improved through an incentive-based, open-economy approach for quite a few years more, until regional specialization attains at an appropriate state. Each of the LFR governing entities must act through a common achiev-

Copyright © 2007, Idea Group Inc. Copying or distributing in print or electronic forms without written permission of Idea Group Inc. is prohibited.

Table 4. Different approaches for socio-economic development

Level of intervention	Keynesian Approach (Amin, 1998)	Neo-Liberal Approach (Amin, 1998; Hausner, 1995)	Proposed Approach
Financial	Income Redistribution	Market Mechanism	Clustered through distributed networks (uniform distribution)
National Policy	Welfare Policy	Firm Policies	Emphasize SMEs, CBOs, CSOs
Regional Level	Focus Less Favored Regions	Market Deregulation	Integration into a common platform
Local Level	Direct/indirect incentives	Free Market	Transform towards sustainability (long term transparent policy)
All Approaches	Top-Down	Top-Down	Bottom-Up

Table 5. Transformation of approaches for socio-economic development

Conventional approaches	Transformed approaches
Firm centered	Demand driven
Incentive-based	Incentive-based, but with focus on sustainability
State-driven	State-entrepreneurs partnership
Standardized	Dynamically adjusted
Top-down	Bottom-up
National-specific	Region-specific (more meaningful if, local specific)
Short and medium-term	Short, Medium and Longer-term
Single-sectored	Multi-sectored

able platform (MDGs, WSIS[17], WSSD[18], etc. are a few). ICTs, a plethora here can assist in migrating from older to newer approaches.

The local supply side infrastructure (the author prefers information infrastructure) need to be upgraded eventually to accommodate this transformation processes and ultimately compete with the upcoming, seemingly unknown (may be more uneven), distribution of resources. Resources may be propagated from concentrated supply to thinner supply depending on the acceptability, capability, and transformation successes (never be trapped within any nontransparent consequences). For achievable transformation process, a proper information infrastructure is a must.

Copyright © 2007, Idea Group Inc. Copying or distributing in print or electronic forms without written permission of Idea Group Inc. is prohibited.

Figure 11. Workflow on transformation of approaches

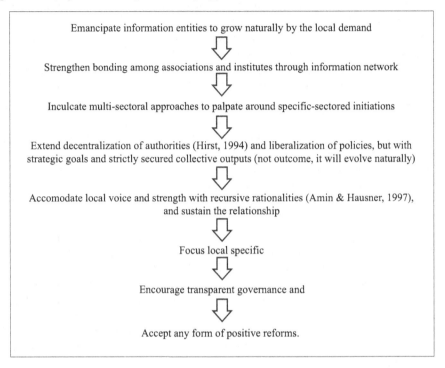

A bottom-up, local-specific, longer-term and multisectored approach has to be initiated at the early stage within all the developing economies. The author has tried to compile the transformation of approaches in Table 5.

The author describes a workflow on approaches to transform a conventional economy towards networked information driven economy as shown in Figure 11.

Many of the so called learning regions (Morgan, 1997) such as Silicon Valley in the U.S., Baden Wurttemberg in Denmark, Indian IT Parks, and the Italian industrial districts have gained comparative advantages over others along these years in forming information networks with specialization (Amin, 1998) have found to adopt similar transformation in their approaches.

Effort has been made here to incorporate the determinants related to the institutional development on effect of ICTs with a few successful approaches. Firstly, the author would like to relate the potential of community enhancement that leads to institutional development.

Community Development Approach

Community informatics represents an emerging subset informatics that addresses the community-based institutional dimensions (Gurstein, 2001; Loader, Hague & Eagle, 2000).

Copyright © 2007, Idea Group Inc. Copying or distributing in print or electronic forms without written permission of Idea Group Inc. is prohibited.

Sometimes, community informatics tends to concentrate on communities of place rather than communities of interest. Hence, this field has to focus on social capital as well as studies related to community development (Doheny-Farina, 1996; Kavanaugh & Patterson, 2001; Pigg, 2001), rural economic development (Pigg & Crank, 2004), health care, and education. This approach and its work plan should address issues on sustainability of technology development, community networking, digital divide factors (Civille, Gurstein & Pigg, 2001), design issues, and effective usage (Gurstein, 2004; Pigg & Crank, 2004) of ICTs.

Rhetoric abounds regarding the importance of social capital in considerations of community sustainability. Considerable rhetoric also exists regarding the potential of modern ICTs to affect the development of social capital in positive ways (Pigg & Crank, 2004). Furthermore, integrating low income or hard-to-employ workers and targeting disadvantaged groups are also important cornerstones of poverty alleviation strategies at the grass roots (Ghaus-Pasha, 2005). ICTs in this context can act as the facilitator of local content and information interchange and can enhance the process of development and create bonds of relationship among the stakeholders.

Social content is a second dimension of exchange relationships. Communication among parties and their respective knowledge of one another can complete the exchange. Common normative commitments are unimportant, and the value of the relationship is limited to the value of the exchange. They share common normative commitments and these relationships produce value-added products at the end. Together these two independent but often closely correlated dimensions—discreetness and social content—allow in drawing a relative (but not absolute) distinction between demands, markets, and networks (Ansell, 2000). ICTs can transform this discreetness towards togetherness and thus leading to empowerment of the community.

So, empowerment of societal actors and the creation of networks among them is an essential characteristic of the networked society for reasons identified both by work on the embeddedness of states in society (local demand) and work on constitutional order (state demand) (Ansell, 2000; Sabel, 1989, 1994). It is not difficult to imagine a community-based system that would act primarily on information function and then support the networking component of social capital building. Following Kretzman and McKnight's (1993) "asset model" of community building, the development of a searchable database that contains a brief description of community members' interests and skills (assets) could be useful in creating new networks among community members based on those interests or on skill building (Pigg & Crank, 2004).

However, economic behavior is embedded in networks of interpersonal relations, and therefore, crucially influenced by aspects such as mutuality, trust, and cooperation (Amin, 1998; Ingham, 1996; Smelser & Swedberg, 1994) and economy is shaped by enduring these forces collectively (Amin, 1998; Hodgson, 1994; Samuels, 1995), especially their role in disseminating information, knowledge, and learning for economic adaptability (Amin, 1998). These call for collective approaches through networked institutes of similar nature or of associations linking markets and states in participatory form. Institutional building in various natures has been evolved in many countries that have contributed positively in their development processes. Establishment of various civil societies across the globe can be cited here.

Copyright © 2007, Idea Group Inc. Copying or distributing in print or electronic forms without written permission of Idea Group Inc. is prohibited.

Civil Society Approach

Civil society is comprised of autonomous associations to develop a dense, diverse and pluralistic network. As it extends, civil society may consist of a range of local groups, specialized organizations and linkages among them to amplify the corrective voices of civil society as a partner in governance and in economy (Connor, 1999). Civil society should not be commensurate to non-government organizations (NGOs). NGOs are a part of civil society though they play an important and sometimes leading role in activating citizen participation in socioeconomic development and in shaping or influencing policy. Civil society is a broader concept, encompassing all organizations and associations that exist at the outer periphery of the state and the economy (Ghaus-Pasha, 2005).

"Civil society" is a relatively loose concept. Customarily used in reference to civil society organizations (CSOs), civil society includes a wide spectrum of community-based organizations (CBOs), trade unions, local communities, advocacy groups, policy research institutions, private entrepreneurs, and social movements (Gabriel, 2003).

Through the free flow of information, which is clear and accessible, civil society groups with a vibrant media, can serve as a monitoring mechanism to ensure that government policies are carried out in a manner intended and thereby significantly contribute to good governance. Social mobilization (organizational strengthening) of CBOs at grassroot/sectoral levels is another major contribution of CSOs. It has been found that many civil society groups are constituted around specific issues of social concern such as the environment, labor rights, gender equity, and public health (Ghaus-Pasha, 2005). Encouraging new technologies including policy advice, technical support, information sharing, and resource optimization to establish their own businesses in the form of entrepreneurship, partnership, cooperative, or community enterprises in various agricultural, trade, or consumer commodities can promote RD. Simultaneously, integrating low income or hard-to-employ workers and targeting the marginal communities can form an important cornerstone of poverty alleviation strategies at local level.

Telecenter Approach

The deployment of ICTs in developing countries has become a key tactics of the international development community to support poverty reduction strategies. In this context, telecenters are seen as a tool to bring the benefits and potential of ICTs to locations that have so far been suffering from their remoteness and lacking connectivity to the world's information alliance. Very often telecenters are established to target communities in their entirety, providing Internet access, e-mail services, telephone services, educational services, and also library services or even postal services to large parts of the community. Consequently, these "Multipurpose Community Telecenters (MCT)" take an approach to improve the access to ICTs on a broad range, in order to narrow the "digital divide" (UNIDO, 2003). Globally, telecenters is not a new concept anymore. However, Murray and Comford (1998) found that more than 60% of them in the UK and Ireland have been operating on a sustainable basis, though they may or may not be profitable.

Copyright © 2007, Idea Group Inc. Copying or distributing in print or electronic forms without written permission of Idea Group Inc. is prohibited.

UNIDO has clear finding on the success of MCT in Sri Lanka and Uganda which contribute to their national economic development. The Uganda Business Information Network (UBIN) in its capital, Kampala, is acting as an "infomediary," a One-Stop-Shop (OSS) in the form of a physical location operated by a private entrepreneurship that provides information services, ICT support services, and enterprise Internet solutions to SMEs on a commercial and demand driven basis (UNIDO, 2003).

Inclusion in PRSPs

At this moment, Poverty Reduction Strategy articles (PRSPs) are being treated as the driving force behind the overall development strategy of many developing countries. It is, therefore, essential to consider the role of information infrastructure in poverty reduction process (Murooka, 2004). In this context, private sector development comprising support for Small- and Medium-scale Enterprises (SMEs) also forms one of the contemporary strategies in PRSPs that may lead to socioeconomic development.

Like other developing countries of this region, in 2004 the Government of Lao PDR completed its National Growth and Poverty Eradication Strategy (NGPES) as the country's poverty reduction strategy article (PRSP). The NGPES identifies agriculture, education, health, and transport as priorities for public investments, and sets the country's medium-term development objectives. As an instrument to implement the NGPES, the Government has launched preparation of its Five-Year Socioeconomic Development Plan (SEDP) for 2006-2010, and is keen to incorporate the management for development results (MfDR) approach in its formulation that undoubtedly involves ICT applications (Government of Lao PDR, 2005). However, countries of similar context must launch even longer-term initiatives to stabilize the economy and social sustainability.

They can establish programs enhancing the three-tier effect of ICTs:

- By enhancing access to information and creating and sharing of knowledge.
- By effectively speeding up the production processes and facilitating financial transactions throughout the economy with reduced costing.
- By connecting individuals, groups, enterprises, communities, and governments faster and more cost-effectively. (Lallana, 2004)

Arguments

Pervasive poverty and inequality are the major threat to prosperity, stability, and peace at the dawn of the 21st century. Notwithstanding extensive anecdotes about the digital divide, most ICT initiatives start by encouraging nations to become e-ready: to boost economic growth and increase e-commerce. These initiatives may assist countries to grow and contribute to

Copyright © 2007, Idea Group Inc. Copying or distributing in print or electronic forms without written permission of Idea Group Inc. is prohibited.

poverty alleviation. However, globalization and ICT development tend to increase the inequality. Countries that seek widespread prosperity and sustainability may focus on e-ForAll; that is, on making the opportunities of ICTs open up for individual and social improvement accessible to all its citizens; and on applying ICTs to empower common folk and engage their participation in national and local development initiatives (Proenza, 2002).

There has been much experimentation, and much discussion, in recent years on the contributions that ICTs can make in combating poverty and promoting broad-based economic and social development. Yet, there is still much needed to know about the actual impact of ICTs relative to other tools and resources; about the most effective strategies for mainstreaming ICTs as strategic tools of development and poverty reduction; about the necessary enabling factors for assuring maximum effective access to and sustained impact of ICTs in poor communities; and about how developing countries can use ICTs for growth and competitiveness in a global economy (infoDev, 2005). The question that always remains is how to effectively mainstream ICTs as tools of development and poverty reduction. Poverty reduction should be considered the entry point and not ICTs per se (UNDP, 2004).

By its very nature, ICT development tends to increase income inequality within the country for several reasons: (1) it requires relatively good education and special skills to make full use of ICTs for socioeconomic gains, (2) ICT infrastructure is more profitable and therefore easier to develop in urban areas, thus further broadening the gap between urban and rural access to ICTs, (3) those who developed widely used ICT applications are mainly from urban areas who could reap benefits from being first in tapping the ICT market in the country. However, despite the inequality bias, ICTs have the potential to improve the livelihoods of low-income earners by enhancing delivery of socioeconomic services, offering them opportunities to increase income and empowering them through participation in decision making processes.

Case Studies

This section puts forward several case studies from different countries ranging from developed to developing with varying nature of ICT implementations, but mainly related to regional development through socioeconomic development and poverty reduction. Many of them are successful cases in their own localities, countries, and regions, and may be replicated elsewhere, while a few had some difficulties that have been discussed here. Activities of a few organizations with tangible output have also been noted in this section.

Despite the poor growth of the overwhelming majority of developing countries, that of East Asian and some South Asian countries, in which governments continued to play an active role, had been remarkably good in managing ICT for development (Adelman, 1999). The use of ICTs in non-formal education programs to foster participation of marginal community in literacy, basic education, and continuing education activities in Indonesia, Lao PDR, Sri Lanka, Thailand, and Uzbekistan has launched with funds from Japan as UNESCO's Asia-Pacific Program of Education for All (APPEAL) (UNESCO, 2004). Table 6 shows the program that has been started in those countries. This program mainly aims at PR through ICTs, which ultimately improves SED.

Copyright © 2007, Idea Group Inc. Copying or distributing in print or electronic forms without written permission of Idea Group Inc. is prohibited.

Table 6. Countries and programs under APPEAL

Country	Program(s)
Lao PDR	Non Formal Education (NFE) to strengthen Community Learning Centres (CLCs)
Sri Lanka	Sarvodaya
Thailand	NFE with inter-village connectivity
Uzbekistan	Community empowerment
Indonesia	NFE through CLCs

In 2002-2003, New Zealand's Ministry of Economic Development (MED) undertook a review of the Regional Partnership Program (RPP). That review included an assessment of regional development policy in building local economic development capability and governance, development of partnerships and networks, and building of institutional linkages (Government of New Zealand, 2004a).

The review reveals that the RPP was performing against policy objectives, and the indicators of success that were selected to measure impact on outcomes. The indicators were mainly focused on changed economic development partnership behaviors (Government of New Zealand, 2004b). After the review, two sets of changes were recommended, including those associated with the program itself, a few changes in the RPP, and changes in policies. Among many, one is "building better information into the next stage of strategy development (where there are regional data and information needs and gaps), to strengthen existing strategies, and in particular, identified regional specializations" (Government of New Zealand, 2003, p. 4).

In 1992, Estonia had just lost its major trading partner and was experiencing hyperinflation and a 15% fall in GDP (Darling, 2001). The country was turned around with sound economic policies and a thrust to modernization in which equitable ICT development played a key role. In similar context, building on a traditional policy of equitable growth, South Korea's informatization program has raised the number of Internet users from 2% in 1995 (Park, 2001) to 55% in 2001 (ITU, 2003) to 63% in 2004 (Internetworldstats.com, 2005b). Primarily both countries have a substantial educational base that developed through sustained effort over the years. Furthermore, their action programs include cost-effective comprehensive measures to ensure that all citizens have access to and partake in the benefits of ICT development (Proenza, 2002).

In the U.K., Scotland and Wales have been adopting a "network strategy" for creating regional interfirm networks. In Belgium, creation of smaller "impulse regions" has encouraged the formation of a social network and network among municipal bodies to provide comprehensive ways of thinking about the region (Ansell, 2000; Scottish Enterprise Network Strategy, 2005). This process of "regional networking and comprehensive thinking can be considered an important innovation in regional development practice" (Houthaeve, 1998, p. 172).

In 1973, Ireland's membership in the EEC enhanced its economic development. From 1973 to 1981, foreign direct investment increased by more than 27% per year. However, at the same time, traditional businesses were impacted by severe competition and from 1973 to 1988, 75% of domestic textile and apparel firms and 50% of domestic metal and engineer-

Copyright © 2007, Idea Group Inc. Copying or distributing in print or electronic forms without written permission of Idea Group Inc. is prohibited.

ing organizations collapsed. By 1987, Ireland took some measures through the Program for National Recovery and these actions helped restore confidence in the management of the public finances, break a cycle of inflationary wage expectations, improve relationships with the commercial sector, and establish an ongoing focus on economic development reform through partnership. During the 1990s, Ireland was ranked high for growth and development among many "rapid technological advances in industries" and "competitive telecoms and e-commerce infrastructure" (Dravis Group, 2004, p. 4) that could encourage foreign direct investments.

Malaysia, a high middle-income country is leading among many Asian counterparts in terms of telephone (fixed and mobile) and Internet penetration. Malaysia is also well known for its Multimedia Super Corridor (MSC) initiative. The Philippines is emerging as one of the key players in ICT enabled services like call centers and Business Process Outsourcing (BPO). Similarly, Sri Lanka has boldly declared that by 2007 it will be better known as the "e-SriLankan Miracle," a model achieving global recognition in the deployment of ICTs towards the achievement of Social and Economic Development (Lallana, 2004).

On March 29, 2001, the "e-Japan Priority Policy Program" was adopted to realize the e-Japan Strategy and taken all measures that the government should rapidly implement it by 2006. The roles of the private and public sectors are detailed in the program with the private sector playing the leading role in the area of IT. The Program also identifies five areas for action:

1. Formation of the world's most advanced information and telecommunications networks.
2. Promotion of education and learning as well as development of human resources;
3. Facilitation of electronic commerce.
4. Digitization of the administration and application of IT in other public areas.
5. Ensure security and reliability of advanced information and telecommunications networks. Further to this, in July 2003, "e-Japan strategy II" was launched aiming to create a "vibrant, safe, impressive and convenient" society with the active use of IT (Lallana, 2004, p. 5).

The South Korean government unveiled its fourth ICT master plan in December 2003, named "Broadband IT Korea Vision 2007." This new master plan focuses on improving national productivity and individual quality of life through informatization (Lallana, 2004). Among its objectives, "e-Korea Vision 2006" aimed to facilitate continued economic growth by promoting the IT industry and advancing the information infrastructure.

By far the biggest contribution to Vietnam's development process and poverty reduction over the past fifteen years has come from the *doi moi* reform process aimed at transforming the economy towards being more market oriented. ODA and UNDP have key roles in providing research based policy advice and analysis to facilitate the reform process (UNDP, 1999). Among four of the socioeconomic development strategies 2001-2010, "science and technology for modernization" with practical implications in education and information technology has accelerated the increasingly knowledge-based economy in Vietnam. The

Copyright © 2007, Idea Group Inc. Copying or distributing in print or electronic forms without written permission of Idea Group Inc. is prohibited.

Socioeconomic Development Strategy (2001-2010) aims to accelerate economic growth and poverty reduction through macroeconomic and structural policies designed to protect macroeconomic stability. It has been observed that, in the absence of a long-term strategic framework to guide and coordinate microfinance activities, the response to emergency challenges would be ad hoc. At the same time, the technical assistance program financed by the Japan special fund has emphasized enhancing the institutional capacity of various organizations within the economy. In this program, a microfinance library including a Web site and data center has been targeted (ADB, 2001) for ICT facilitation.

In accordance with the International Monetary Fund (IMF) and World Bank framework, the Royal Government of Cambodia (RGC) prepared an interim Poverty Reduction Strategy Article (IPRSP) in October 2000 based on a broad consultative process launched with active participation from inter-ministerial setup, development partners, and NGOs. The RGC has identified a number of priority public actions to reduce poverty. Among many, agriculture, rural development, trade, infrastructure, education, and health validates the potential areas where ICTs can be utilized for strategic implementation (Royal Government of Cambodia, 2001).

The Jamaican national poverty eradication program may have contributed, tangentially, towards the reduction of absolute poverty levels over the last half-decade, as claimed by the government, but a close examination of program management revealed deep-seated problems. These included a weak political analysis, poor coordination at the national and local levels (weak information backbone), and a lack of adequate institutional support (Osei, 2001).

The Government of Guyana and UNDP have agreed that the main thrust of UNDP's assistance to Guyana should be directed towards supporting policies and programs for the eradication of poverty in the country. It was consistent with the strategies laid out in the two key Government policy documents, namely the National Development Strategy (NDS) and the Interim Poverty reduction Strategy chapter (IPRSP). Both of these documents recognize that no individual factor can be singled out as the cause of poverty in Guyana (IPRSP Guyana, 2000). However, a project support document (UNDP, 2005) suggests the involvement of ICTs by creating a modern and cost-effective management information system to facilitate aid coordination and management, including strengthening institutional capacity within central government agencies and increased ability to interface with donors and line ministries.

On June 7, 2004 the Government of Albania publicly presented its second Annual Progress Report (APR-2) of the National Strategy for Socioeconomic Development (NSSED). Among several recommendations, strengthening the monitoring and evaluation functions within key line ministries and monitoring indicators for each line ministry were emphasized. In addition, a department of the NSSED (DoNESSED) has been established for coordination of all NSSED-related activities (IMF, 2004). These entail articulation of ICT applications within the Government systems. UNDP Albania has been supporting projects fostering capacity building and deployment of ICTs or the facilitation of their use within other development activities for many years. In 2001, the Country Office, with assistance of the regional SURF/BDP, formulated an ICTs for Development Framework document designed to focus ICTs for Development (ICTD) activities to have maximum impact and effectively mainstream ICTD tools within all UNDP programme areas. In June 2003, the document was updated to reflect the efforts of UNDP to support national efforts on the MDGs and create a comprehensive MDG Umbrella Support Program (UNDP, 2003a).

Copyright © 2007, Idea Group Inc. Copying or distributing in print or electronic forms without written permission of Idea Group Inc. is prohibited.

Over the years, the Government of Malawi has taken a number of steps within specific socioeconomic development frameworks and programs to address some of the social and economic challenges facing the country. The Vision 2020 recognized the important role that ICTs can play in national development. Malawi has acknowledged the need to emphasize on ICT usage to solve its multifarious socioeconomic problems that include widespread poverty, rising urban unemployment and rural under-employment, deteriorating terms of trade and balance of payments, low growth in output, and environmental degradation (SDNP Malawi, 2003).

Philanthropy Australia is a peak national body in Australia in the philanthropic sector, representing individuals, families, communities, and corporate grant making trusts and foundations. Since 2001, Philanthropy Australia's ICT environment has improved significantly. The successful redevelopment of its ICT base has contributed to the development of more positive attitudes to the use of ICTs in the philanthropy sector and created more operational transparency (Government of Australia, 2005a). Barnardos Australia, another leading children's charity organization in Australia has developed an innovative ICT application, the Looking After Children Electronic System (LACES) to create a streamlined case management system and ultimately assists in improving children's community in Australia (Government of Australia, 2005b).

Between two of the very small organizations, SIDSNet (http://www.sidsnet.org) the Small Island Developing States Network, is a communication medium to discuss and share information on biodiversity, climate change, coastal and marine management, energy sources and trade. It promotes sharing experiences and developing a global SIDS agenda through information networking (World Bank, 2002). The other one, Fantsuam Foundation of Nigeria uses Microfinance and ICTs as complementary tools for poverty alleviation. The ICT program started with only two rooms provided by the community. One of the rooms was the Community Library and the second was the IT training room (Comfort, Goje & Funmilola, 2003).

The New partnership for Africa's Development (NEPAD) strongly advocates private sector development for increased trade and investment as a key component to Africa's growth for poverty reduction (DBSA, 2003). However, Africa is already too dependent on the rest of the world. Sub-Saharan Africa's trade in goods with the rest of the world accounted for 56% of GDP in 2001 while the same ratio for North America was only 13.2%, 12.8% for Western Europe, 23.7% for Latin America, and 15.2% for Asia (World Bank, 2003). This does not translate into more effective poverty reduction processes. Increased trade could guarantee foreign debt service capacity but will not guarantee progress towards poverty reduction targets. Partnerships across social sectors and spheres of governance and policy development are, therefore, emphasized. These demand more effective civil society formation with better communication strategies (Gabriel, 2003).

On the other hand, recognizing the role of science and technology in socioeconomic development, many countries of Sub-Saharan Africa established science and technology policy-making bodies and research and development institutions. The United Nations Education and Scientific and Cultural Organization (UNESCO) acted as a catalyst by organizing the CASTAFRICA conferences for African ministers responsible for science in 1974 and 1987. The 1979 Vienna global conference on science and technology for development organized by the United Nations further sensitized and spurred African countries towards action. Along this path, Science and Technology policy making bodies and research and develop-

Copyright © 2007, Idea Group Inc. Copying or distributing in print or electronic forms without written permission of Idea Group Inc. is prohibited.

ment institutions that were formed during the decade of independence are the National Council for Scientific Research (NCSR) in Zambia, the Council for Scientific and Industrial Research (CSIR) in Ghana, the National Council for Science and Technology (NCST) in Kenya, and the Commission for Science and Technology (COSTECH) together with its many other research institutes and centers in Tanzania. The recognition of the role of ICTs in development by governments continues till today by putting in place national policies on science and technology, by the enactment of science and technology legislation and by the establishment of ministries of science and technology (Siamwiza, 2002).

The Organization for Economic Cooperation and Development (OECD) defines an international non-governmental organization (INGO) as "an organization established and governed by a group of private citizens for a stated philanthropic purpose, and supported by voluntary individual contributions" (Wheeler, 1988, p. 2). Throughout the 1980s, INGOs from around the world had been learning to use a computer network for socio-economic development. In 1984, a few INGOs agreed to establish a computer network, Interdoc, with member institutions from four continents. Interdoc formalized its mandate with an international accord called the Valletri Agreement, and aimed to manage the system from a social perspective. Mainly, the network was used to inform and empower organizations, and disseminate information on sustainable development. Later on, Interdoc and its members assisted in forming the Association for Progressive Communications (APC). APC is one of the world's largest computer networking institution at this moment, and serving NGOs dedicated to human rights, social, economic, and environmental aspects (Murphy, 2005).

ICTs was one of the major subjects that were discussed at G8 Kyushu-Okinawa Summit in July 2000, which adopted the "Okinawa Charter on Global Information Society." In the Charter, ICTs were defined as one of the most potent forces in shaping the twenty-first century as well as an important means for communities to fulfill their potential demand. The Charter urged all stakeholders concerned, including the private sector, to participate in constructing a global information society in which everyone, no matter where they live, can benefit from ICTs (JICA, 2001).

UNESCO recognizes the importance of using ICTs to achieve broad development goals. It has also given importance in the learning processes in understanding how ICTs can play an effective role in economic development, social transformation, political empowerment, and cultural enrichment.

The Global Village Energy Partnership (GVEP) was launched at the World Summit on Sustainable Development (WSSD) in Johannesburg in 2002. As a "partnership of partnerships," it brings together a wide variety and number of partners. By accelerating the pace and scope of energy activities in a more coordinated fashion to reach the target of improving access to energy services for an additional 300 million people, mainly living in rural areas, by 2015. GVEP mainly rely on a multi-sectoral partnership approach (UNDP, 2003b).

InfoDev is an international consortium of official bilateral and multilateral development agencies and other key partners, facilitated by an expert Secretariat housed at the World Bank. Its mission is to assist developing countries and their partners in the international community to use ICTs effectively and strategically as tools to combat poverty, promote sustainable economic growth, and empower individuals and communities to participate more effectively and creatively in their societies and economies. It is an ongoing effort to develop innovative forms of partnership for knowledge-sharing and joint action bring-

Copyright © 2007, Idea Group Inc. Copying or distributing in print or electronic forms without written permission of Idea Group Inc. is prohibited.

ing together government, the private sector and civil society in developing countries with the international donor community, the international private sector and other key partners (InfoDev, 2005).

There is a growing stake in using ICTs to support poverty reduction efforts and strategies to achieve the Millennium Development Goals (MDGs). However, many development initiatives are increasingly incorporating an "ICT component" in their activities, but mostly as mere projects without a focus on policy variables that could enhance longer term impact and sustainability. UNDP is supporting this initiative in many countries by integrating ICTs appropriately into poverty reduction processes and other development strategies with linkages between ICT development strategies and policies, with a view to identifying opportunities, constraints, and priority areas of focus (UNDP, 2004).

Future of ICTs in the Context of Socioeconomic Development

ICTs, as enabling technologies are being used in almost all sectors of economy and facets of human life. However, how they impact on the development of the ICT sector remains always critical. Subsequently, it is equally important to assess the wider ramifications of ICTs on society at large. Delving more deeply, there is consensus in many researches that ICTs will shape the future of the world through growing reliance on the technology itself, in all aspects of life and in all sectors—at work, at home, in medicine, in communications, in transport, and so forth The Internet is seen as the lynchpin, ushering in a world that is more "connected" than ever before. Nevertheless, concerns are raised in some studies that access may become increasingly restricted to those who can afford the technology by creating the information rich and information poor. There has been a paradigm shift in innovation of ICTs with convergence between ubiquitous computing, ubiquitous communication, near-zero telecommunications costs and intelligent user interfaces providing seamless interoperability of devices across networks (EMCC, 2003a, 2003b).

ICTs can play a variety of roles in sustainable development in many countries, acting as monitoring tools, assisting improved production techniques, enhancing resource optimization, assisting environmental management, improving lifelong learning, and so forth. At the same time, ICTs should not be allowed to create negative impact through channeling any obsolete technology (EMCC, 2003a). The technology gap may grow (DotCom, 2005). However, ICTs should not just be treated as tools for development; rather, they should be treated as tools for empowerment.

At the end of 2000, the U.S. had about 135 million Internet users. Between 1990 and 1995, the compound annual growth rate of U.S. Internet users was over 73%, and from 2000 to 2007, the growth rate is expected to be less than 8% per year, while, the Asia Pacific region became the largest with 178 million Internet users in 2001 and it is expected to grow to over 615 million in 2007. At the same time, the wireless Internet users are expected to grow at a very rapid pace. Wireless Internet users in 2001 were about 102 million, and it is expected that in 2007 it will be more than 800 million (about 41% rise per year). Thus, the wireless

Copyright © 2007, Idea Group Inc. Copying or distributing in print or electronic forms without written permission of Idea Group Inc. is prohibited.

Internet will take off rapidly as an always on service, readily available and a useful content provider with small displayable wireless devices (eTForecasts, 2005).

Enterprise development at the marginal end requires adoption of ICTs by SMEs. Duncombe and Heeks (2001) conducted a study for DFID and found that the most direct benefit (employment, growth and local capacity) within the ICT sector itself goes to the institutes that are working at the grass roots. Raising local ICT sector capacity was identified as a key enabler for other sectors—government, private, and NGOs—particularly those concerned with implementing ICTs within wider poverty alleviation programs—in health, education, environment, and governance (ICT4D Social Enterprise Toolkit, 2005).

Many policies, initiatives and measures concerning ICTs exist, impacting at the national, regional, as well as at global level. In the global context, there are international agreements, treaties (concerning international trades, protection of intellectual property, Internet domain name system coordination, telecommunication standards, etc.) enhancing parameters of development at all levels. Activities of the World Trade Organization, the World Intellectual Property Organization, the Internet Corporation for Assigned Names and Numbers, and the International Telecommunication Union are there to name a few (EMCC, 2003c).

Despite all the massive obstacles that stand between small and medium sized enterprises (SMEs) in developing countries and state-of-the-art entrepreneurs in developed countries, there are opportunities to create demand, provided that the establishment has something of quality to offer and deliver it reliably (Southwood, 2004). ICTs can assist there to bridge the gap and able to make them easily achieve the target. Ranging from controlling internal cash flow, to zero-time-delayed order placing via Internet, to secured financial transaction, to management of entire operation can be effectively controlled by ICT applications.

ICTs allow a reduction in transaction costs, improved communications with different marketing interfaces, and improved information about new opportunities. They can remove the constraints in obtaining and communicating information through empowerment of Micro and SMEs. Evidence suggests that service based enterprises (business, financial, technical) and value-added entrepreneurs (tourist sector, manufacturing—ready made garments, and so forth—utility, call centers, offshore software houses, etc.) will reap most benefit from ICTs and will be in a better position to transmit benefits to the wider community (ITDG approaches, n.d.).

Emphasizing on increased engagement of community groups and development NGOs in the design of regulatory frameworks for public-private-partnership-based ICT access in remote areas might result in more balance in the competitive bidding of operators between achieving least cost (and/or subsidy) and livelihood-driven performance. The design parameters of partnership projects should be formulated for ICT entrepreneurs to test the financial viability of marketing or products/service development targeted to low-income consumers. And, successful partnership business models should be replicated into low-income consumer market in developing countries (UNICT Task Force Report, 2004a).

However, to take full advantage of these relative strengths demands vision and leadership in different segments of the society with a clear and renewed definition of roles and responsibilities among government, business, civil society, academia and international organizations. Active leadership is needed in regulatory support for the breakthrough of wireless solutions and delicensing of frequency spectrum. Sustained funding for digital divide research and development projects and pilots is another prerequisite. Leadership is also essential in areas

Copyright © 2007, Idea Group Inc. Copying or distributing in print or electronic forms without written permission of Idea Group Inc. is prohibited.

that can employ ICTs by reengineering the public sector such as e-government (UNICT Task Force Report, 2004a draft).

For business, leadership is needed for the allocation of investment in financial, human and organizational resources in ICTs. For civil society, leadership is needed for leveraging the process of transforming ICT technology into tools for transparency emphasizing the benefits of the poor. For multilateral institutions and international agencies, leadership in the form of funding is needed for continued and renewed support in mobilizing resources for roll-out of ICT infrastructure, and continued support for applications of ICTs in all sectors (UNICT Task Force Report, 2004a draft).

Strategic alliances amid government, business, civil society and international organizations are a growing feature of both developed and emerging economies. Such multi-stakeholder partnerships (MSPs) are essential because it is evidently clear that no other sector in society can deliver the complexities of sustainable human development alone. MSPs are alliances of parties drawn from government, business, civil society, and international organizations that strategically aggregate the resources and competencies of each to resolve the key challenges of ICTs as enablers of empowerment that are founded on principles of shared risk, cost, and mutual benefit (UNICT Task Force Report, 2004b).

Conclusion

Despite the huge potential of ICTs in assisting communities to increase their overall well-being through community development, there are relatively a few examples of sustained community networks built around ICTs when compared to commercial applications, even in the developed countries where the technologies have been increasingly available for more than 20 years (Marshal and Taylor, 2005). Koanantakool (2002) stated that though the burgeoning use of ICTs is widely acknowledged and discussed today in the global economy, it remains largely undefined and unrecognized in official ICT statistics. This is mainly because various data on ICTs are not readily available or differ widely or varied in nature, depending on the definition and methodology used by each entity collecting them. Therefore, the ICT measurement is becoming a universal issue in many countries and international organizations, comprised of agreed definitions, methodologies, and guidelines.

It demands combined and complementary efforts by international agencies, national governments, local authorities, private sector, and civil society organizations (CSOs). In this aspect, civil society can make a larger contribution both directly and indirectly to the process of poverty reduction and attainment of other MDG targets (Ghaus-Pasha, 2005). The question remains how to effectively mainstream ICTs as tools of socioeconomic development and poverty reduction (InfoDev, 2005). Given the ability to accept and control the situation at local level, the local infrastructure is not always a barrier to use but skill, resources, and funds remain always susceptible to sustained operation.

It is important to distinguish between the incidence of poverty as a percentage of the total population and the absolute number of the poor. The share of the population in poverty has declined for many developing countries as a whole (28.3% in 1987 to 24% in 1998 based on $1/day and from 61% in 1987 to 56% in 1998 based on $2/day), and in all developing

Copyright © 2007, Idea Group Inc. Copying or distributing in print or electronic forms without written permission of Idea Group Inc. is prohibited.

regions except Sub-Saharan Africa and Eastern Europe and Central Asia. Declines have been pronounced and sustained over a longer period for the most populous developing countries (World Bank, 2000).

When choosing the appropriate technology for any poverty intervention project, particular attention should be paid to infrastructure requirements, local availability, training requirements, and technical challenges. Innovative technology solutions can be used to take advantage in development projects when they respond to user requirements at the grassroots. Existing technologies, particularly the telephone, radio, and television, can often convey information at less expense, in local languages, and to larger numbers of people than can newer technologies. In some cases, the former can enhance the capacity of the latter (InfoDev, 2003). However, financial sustainability remains as the most important challenge for ICTD initiatives.

The impact of ICTs in rural areas and particularly on rural poverty is very limited despite its penetration into every corner of society. Although, experiences abound demonstrating that ICTs can make a significant contribution to reduce poverty, the list of failed initiatives appears even longer. One of the major reasons for this mixed performance in rural areas is that its adaptation to the local needs was left either to the private sector or to non-governmental organizations. These organizations seldom operate without an official framework of policies and guidelines and a clear definition of tasks and responsibilities for the different "players."

Development of national ICT strategies for poverty alleviation is a relatively complex matter. There is no single solution or best ICT project to fit all situations, but a variety of approaches would be needed, particularly in the early stage of ICT insemination. Understanding how ICTs can service specific development goals requires both knowledge of appropriate technologies and how these technologies could be operationalized to address socioeconomic goals. Key policymakers need to make informed decisions to enact "enabling" policy frameworks appropriate for their contexts and demands (Expert Group Meeting, 2003). It has to be understood that:

- ICTs alone are insufficient for making significant benefits to emerge in a near future.

- ICTs will not transform bad development into good development in a nightfall but can make good development better in a few years.

- Effective applications of ICTs comprise both a technological infrastructure and an information infrastructure.

- In rural settings in developing countries (where the vast majority of poor people live), it is always a challenge to install the technological infrastructure, but the task is relatively simple in establishing the information infrastructure.

- The application of ICTs in the absence of a national development strategy will inevitably result in sub-optimal outcomes.

- Though ICTs provide opportunities for development, desirable outcomes always arise from the actions of people at large (Lallana, 2004).

There is no clear-cut measurement for the value and significance of institutional consistency or their partnerships in regional context. Firstly, the resource functions are associated with

Copyright © 2007, Idea Group Inc. Copying or distributing in print or electronic forms without written permission of Idea Group Inc. is prohibited.

the limitation to trusted and tried development paths, the concentration on certain contents, the exclusions of other possibilities—up to institutional lock-ins (Grabher, 1993). Secondly, regions are neither autonomous nor sovereign in the relations to the national state or supranational organizations (Braczyk & Heidenreich, 1996). Thirdly, regional innovation capacity depends mostly on the individual elements of local order (Friedberg, 1995) and their inherent governance elements (Braczyk & Heidenreich, 1996). Finally, attention should be paid to the process of how poverty is perceived and defined vis-à-vis ICTs at both ends of the pipeline.

If all agreed that poverty is the sum of all hungers then ICTs can play a definite role as tools to provide information. Furthermore, links to other seemingly unrelated areas such as energy provision services, disaster prevention and management, and education and learning should become more self-reliant (UNDP, 2005). For optimal partnership effectiveness among development actors, there is a need to patronize coordination and cross sectoral fertilization within and among the regions (World Bank, 2003b).

References

Adam, L. (2005, January). *Financing ICT's for development with focus on poverty*. Montevideo, Uruguay: Instituto del Tercer Mundo (ITeM).

ADB. (2001, October). *Technical assistance to the Socialist Republic of Vietnam for preparing the framework for microfinance development*. Asian Development Bank, TAR: VIE 34368.

Adelman, I. (1999, May). *The role of government in economic development* (Working Paper No. 890). University of California at Berkley: CA Agriculture Experiment Station.

Amin, A. (1998, July 3). *An institutionalist perspective on regional economic development*. Paper presented at the Economic Geography Research Group Seminar, Institutions and Governance, London.

Amin, A., & Hausner, J. (1997). *Beyond market and hierarchy: Interactive governance and social complexity*. Edward Elgar: Aldershot.

Amin, A., & Thrift, N. (Eds.). (1994). *Globalization, institutions, and regional development in Europe*. Oxford University Press.

Ansell, C. (2000, July). The networked polity: Regional development in western Europe. *Governance: An International Journal of Policy and Administrative, 13*(3), 303-333.

Bekkulova, J.E. (2004). *Transboundary water resources management issues*. Tashkent: UNDP Uzbekistan.

Braczyk, H.-J., & Heidenreich, M. (1996). Regional governance structures in a globalized world. In H.-J. Braczyk & M. Heidenreich (Eds.), *Regional innovation systems* (pp. 414-440). London: UCL Press.

Burns, T., & Stalker, G.M. (1994). *The management of innovation*. Oxford: Oxford University Press.

Copyright © 2007, Idea Group Inc. Copying or distributing in print or electronic forms without written permission of Idea Group Inc. is prohibited.

China's Human Rights. (2005). *Backgrounder: The global conference on scaling up poverty reduction.* Retrieved June 27, 2006, from China Society For Human Right Studies http://www.humanrights.cn/news/

Civille, R., Gurstein, M., & Pigg, K. (2001). *Access to what? First mile issues for rural broadband* (Report prepared for the Computer Science and Tele. Board, Broadband Last Mile Technology Project). Washington, DC: National Research Council.

Comfort, K., Goje, L., & Funmilola, K. (2003, August/September). *Relevance and priorities of ICT for women in rural communities: A case study from Nigeria.* Bulletin of the American Society for Information Science and Technology, pp. 24-25.

Connor, D.M. (1999, December). Public participation and civil society. *Constructive Citizen Participation, 27*(3). Connor Development Services Ltd.

Darling, P. (2001). *From communism to dot com.* Retrieved June 27, 2006, from EuroViews 2001, http://manila.djhdk/estonia/stories/storyReader$4

DBSA. (2003). *The development report.* The Development Bank of Southern Africa (DBSA).

Demeksa, K. (2001, July 23-24). The new Africa initiative: A view from the Economic Commission for Africa. In *Proceedings of the Peace, Human Security and Conflict Prevention in Africa*, UNESCO-ISS Expert Meeting, Pretoria, South Africa.

Doheny-Farina, S. (1996). *The wired community.* New Haven, CT: Yale University Press.

DotCom. (2005, October 22). *DOT-COM TAG shares thoughts on future of ICT and development.* Paper presented at the First Annual Technical Advisory Group (TAG) Meeting. Retrieved June 27, 2006, from http://www.dot-com-alliance.org/newsletter/

Dravis Group. (2004, October). *Ireland: Their ICT success story.* The Dravis Group LLC, San Francisco, CA.

Duncombe, R., & Heeks, R. (2001). *Enterprise development and communication technologies in developing countries: Supporting "ICT-Flyers."* UK: Institute for Development Policy and Management, DFID.

EMCC. (2003a). *Sector futures: Shaping the future of ICT.* Dublin: European Monitoring Centre on Change.

EMCC. (2003b). *Sector futures: The future of IT—now it's getting personal.* Dublin: European Monitoring Centre on Change.

EMCC. (2003c). *Sector futures: Policies, issues and the future of ICT.* Dublin: European Monitoring Centre on Change.

ETForecasts. (2005). Retrieved June 27, 2006, from http://etforecasts.com/products/ES_intusersv2.htm

European Commission. (2005). *Towards a global partnership in the information society: The contribution of the European Union to the second phase of the World Summit on the Information Society*, a communication from the commission to the Council, the European Parliament, the European Economic and Social Committee and the Committee of the Regions, Brussels, 02.6.2005, COM(2205) 234 Final.

Flora, J. (1998). Social capital and communities of place. *Rural Sociology, 63*(4), 481-506.

Copyright © 2007, Idea Group Inc. Copying or distributing in print or electronic forms without written permission of Idea Group Inc. is prohibited.

Friedberg, E. (1995). *Ordnung und Macht. Dynamiken organizierten Handelns, EuropSisches Zentrum Wien [Order and Power: Dynamiken organizierten acting, EuropeScience Center Vienna]*, Frankfurt: Campus.

Gabriel, N. (2003, July 2-4). *The millennium development goals: Towards a civil society perspective on reframing poverty reduction strategies in southern Africa.* Paper presented at the Southern Africa MDGs Forum, Johannesburg, South Africa.

Ghaus-Pasha, A. (2005, May 24-27). *Role of civil society organizations in governance. In Proceedings of 6th Global Forum on Reinventing Government Towards Participatory and Transparent Governance*, Seoul, Republic of Korea. Retrieved November 14, 2006 from http://unpan1.un.org/intradoc/groups/public/documents/un/unpan019594.pdf

Giddens, A. (1990). *The consequences of modernity.* Stanford, CA: Stanford University Press.

Global Reach. (2005). Online documents. Retrieved June 27, 2006, from http://www.glreach.com

Government of Australia. (2005a, January). *Philanthropy Australia, In case study: Enhancing operational efficiency and capability, information technology and the arts.* Author. ISBN: 0 642 75268 0.

Government of Australia. (2005b, January). *Barnardos Australia, In case study: Enhancing operational efficiency and capability, information technology and the arts.* Author. ISBN: 0 642 75232 X.

Government of Finland (2004). Government Resolution 5.2.2004. *Development Policy*, Ministry for Foreign Affairs of Finland. Helsinki, Finland.

Government of Lao PDR. (2005). *Concept paper: Capacity development for monitoring development results of the National Growth and Poverty Eradication Strategy.* Vientiane: Author.

Government of New Zealand. (2003, June 18). *Regional Partnerships Programme review.* (Final report). Ministry of Economic Dev. (MED), Government of New Zealand.

Government of New Zealand. (2004a). *Regional Partnership Programme review. Ministry of Economic Development.* Retrieved June 28, 2006, from http://www.med.gov.nz

Government of New Zealand. (2004b). *Regional Development and Regional Partnerships Programme review: A report from the office of the Minister*, Ministry of Industry and Regional Development to the Chair, Cabinet Economic Development Committee. Author.

Government of Ukraine. (2003). *Mykola Azarov: Under the economy growing of Ukraine is powerful base.* Ministry of Finance, Ukraine.

Grabher, G. (1993). The weakness of strong ties. The lock-in of regional development in the Ruhr area. In G. Grabher (Ed.), *The embedded firm. On the socioeconomics of industrial networks* (pp. 255-277). London: Routledge.

Graham, G. (2005). Community networking as radical practice. *The Journal of Community Informatics, 1*(3), 4-12.

Gurstein, M. (Ed.). (2000). *Community informatics: Enabling communities with information and communications technologies* (pp. 596: 1-30). Hershey, PA: Idea Group Publishing.

Copyright © 2007, Idea Group Inc. Copying or distributing in print or electronic forms without written permission of Idea Group Inc. is prohibited.

Gurstein, M. (2004, December). Effective use: A community informatics strategy beyond the digital divide. *First Monday*.

Harrington, J.W. (2001). *Readings in regional economic development*. Seattle: University of Washington.

Harvey, D. (1989). *The condition of postmodernity*. Cambridge, MA: Blackwell Publishers.

Hausner, J. (1995). Imperative vs. interactive strategy of systematic change in Central and Eastern Europe. *Review of International Political Economy*, *91*, 481-510.

Hedlund, G. (1994). A model of knowledge management and the N-form corporation. *Strategic Management Journal*, *15*, 73-90.

Hirst, P. (1994). *Associated democracy*. Cambridge: Polity.

Hodgson, G.M. (1994). The return of institutional economics. In N. Smelser & R. Swedberg (Eds.), *The handbook of economic sociology* (pp. 86-106). Princeton, NJ: Princeton University Press.

Houthaeve, R. (1998). Changing aspects of the role of regional development agencies in Flanders (Belgium): The case of West Flanders. In H. Halkier, M. Danson, & C. Damborg, (Eds.), *Regional development in Europe (pp. 21-45)*. London: Jessica Kinsley.

Hudson, H. (1984). *When telephones reach the village*. Paris: Ables Publications.

Hughes, T.P. (1987). The evolution of large technical systems. In W.E. Bijker (Ed.), *The social construction of technological systems* (pp. 51-82). Cambridge: MIT Press.

Hutagaol, P., & Sugino, T. (2005). *Policy framework for poverty reduction by realizing sustainable diversified agriculture through the development of secondary crops*. Retrieved June 28, 2006, from the Palawija News, The UNESCAP-CAPSA Newsletter, http://www.cgprt.org/palawija_detail.asp?VJournalKey=105

ICT4D Social Enterprise Toolkit. (2005). *Empowering disadvantaged communities in developing countries*. Retrieved June 28, 2006, from http://www.un.org.kh/undp/ict-4dToolkit/ICT4D.htm

IMF. (2004, July). *Albania: Joint staff assessment of the Poverty Reduction Strategy paper: Annual progress report* (IMF Country Rep. No. 04/205).

infoDev. (2003). *ICT for development: Contributing to the millennium development goals: Lessons learned from seventeen infoDev projects*. The World Bank.

infoDev. (2005). *Mainstreaming ICTs: Mainstreaming ICT as tools of development and poverty reduction*. Retrieved June 28, 2006, from http://www.infodev.org/section/programs/mainstreaming_icts

Ingham, G. (1996). Some recent changes in the relationship between economics and sociology. *Cambridge Journal of Economics*, *20*, 243-275.

Internetworldstats.com. (2005a). Retrieved June 28, 2006, from http://www.Internetworldstats.com/

Internetworldstats.com. (2005b). Retrieved June 28, 2006, from http://www.Internetworldstats.com/stats3.htm

IPRSP Guyana. (2000, October). *Interim Poverty Reduction Strategy paper* (Prepared by the Guyanese Authorities).

Copyright © 2007, Idea Group Inc. Copying or distributing in print or electronic forms without written permission of Idea Group Inc. is prohibited.

ITDG approaches (n.d.). *ITDG approaches, enterprise development and ICTs*. Retrieved June 28, 2006, from http://livelihoodtechnology.org/home.asp?id=ict2Intro1

ITU. (2003, March). *Broadband Korea: Internet case study*. Geneva: Author.

JICA. (2001, June). *The information revolution in development assistance*. Tokyo: Institute for International Cooperation, Japan International Cooperation Agency.

Joseph, K.J. (2003, September 18-19). *Development of enabling policies for trade and investment in the sector of the Greater Mekong Subregion*. Paper presented at the National Workshop on Development of Enabling Policies for Trade and Investment in the IT Sector of the Greater Mekong Subregion, Hanoi, Vietnam.

Kavanaugh, A.L., & Patterson, S. (2001). The impact of community computer networks on social capital and community involvement. *American Behavioral Scientist, 45*(3), 494-509.

Kasigwa, J., Williams, D., & Baryamureeba. V. (2005). *A critical analysis on the role of ICTs and its sustainability in developing countries*. Retrieved June 28, 2006, from http://cit.ac.ug/events/srec/PapersSubmitted/Justine_SAREC_paper_Aug_2005.pdf

Koanantakool, T. (2002, September 19-20). Forward of the executive summary. In *Proceedings of the ASEAN Workshop on Measurement of Digital Economy,* (p. 3). Bangkok, Thailand.

Kontopoulos, K. (1993). *The logic of social structure*. New York: Cambridge University Press.

Kretzman, J.P., & McKnight, J.L. (1993). *Building communities from the inside out*. Evanston, IL: Center for Urban Affairs and Policy Research, North Western University.

Laepple, D. (1999, July 8-11). Ambiguities of globalization: The urban economy as a nexus of disembedding and reembedding processes: The case of the City of Hamburg. In *Proceedings of the 11th International Meeting on Socio Economics*, Madison, Wisconsin. Retrieved November 14, 2006 from http://www.sase.org/conf1999/papers/dieter_laepple.pdf

Lallana, E.C. (2004). *An overview of ICT policies and e-strategies of select asian economies*. New Delhi, Elsevier. ISBN: 81-8147-753-7. Retrieved June 28, 2006, from http://www.adbi.org/book/2004/11/05/725.implementing.egovernment.book/2.summary.of.country.reports/

Loader, B.D., Hague, B., & Eagle, D. (2000). Embedding the Net: Community empowerment in the Age of Information. In M. Gurstein (Ed.), *Community informatics: Enabling communities with information and communications technologies* (pp. 81-103). Hershey, PA: Idea Group Publishing.

Mali, F. (2002). *Is it possible to come to balance of different functions in academic research systems of small transitional countries of Central and Eastern Europe? The case of Slovenia*. Retrieved June 28, 2006, from the Sociology of Science and Technology NETwork, http://sstnet.iscte.pt/

Marshall, S., & Taylor, W. (2005, March 26). Facilitating the use of ICT for community development through collaborative partnerships between universities, governments and communities. *International Journal of Education and Development using ICT, 1*(1). Retrieved June 28, 2006, from http://ijedict.dec.uwi.edu/viewarticle.php?id=24

Copyright © 2007, Idea Group Inc. Copying or distributing in print or electronic forms without written permission of Idea Group Inc. is prohibited.

Morgan, K. (1997). *The learning region: Institutions, innovation and regional renewal* (paper from Planning Research 157). Cardiff: Department of City and Regional Planning, University of Wales.

Murphy, B.M. (2005, May). Interdoc: The first international non-governmental computer network. *First Monday, 10*(5). Retrieved June 28, 2006, from http://firstmonday. org/issues/issue10_5/murphy/index.html

Murooka, N. (2004, October 27-29). *Role of infrastructure in economic growth and poverty reduction: Lessons learned from PRSPs of 33 countries.* Paper presented at the POVNET Infrastructure for Poverty Reduction (InfraPoor) Task Team Workshop, Berlin, Germany.

Murray, B., & Comford, D. (1998). *Universal access: Telecottage and Telecentre Survey 1998.* Small World Connections, International Telecommunication Union (ITU).

NAO. (2002). *Performance management: Helping to reduce world poverty.* London: National Audit Office, Department of International Development, The Stationery Office.

OECD. (2003, December). *Donor ICT strategies matrix.* Development Assistance Committee.

Onyx, J., & Bullen, P. (2000). Measuring social capital in five communities. *Journal of Applied Behavioral Science, 36*(1), 23-42.

Ortner, G.E. (1999). *Socioeconomics of virtual universities.* Hagen Germany: Fern University.

Osei, P.D. (2001, September 10-12). *A critical asessment of Jamaica's national poverty eradication policy and programme.* Paper presented at the Development Studies Association Conference, Manchester, England.

Pacific Plan. (2005). *Pacific Plan for strengthening regional cooperation and integration: Regional digital strategy.* Retrieved June 28, 2006, from http://www.pacificplan. org/tiki-page.php?pageName=Digital+Strategy

Park, H.W. (2001, November). *Digital divide in Korea: Closing and widening the divide in the 1990s.* Paper presented at the Symposium on the Digital Divide, Austin, TX.

Pigg, K. (2001). Applications for community informatics for building community and enhancing civic society. *Information, Communication, & Society, 4*(4), 507-527.

Pigg, K.E., & Crank, L.D. (2004). Building community social capital: The potential and promise of information and communications technologies. *The Journal of Community Informatics, 1*(1), 58-73.

Proenza, F.J. (2002). *e-ForAll: A poverty reduction strategy for the Information Age.* Retrieved June 28, 2006, from http://communication.utexas.edu/college/digital_divide_symposium/papers/index.html

PRSP Report. (2005). *Poverty Reduction Strategy paper: Progress report: August 2003-December 2004.* Yerevan: Republic of Armenia.

Putnam, R.D. (1993). *Making democracy work: Civic traditions in modern Italy.* Princeton, NJ: Princeton University Press.

Rahman, H. (2004a). Social impact of virtual networking. In S. Dasgupta (Ed.), *Encyclopedia of virtual communities and technologies* (417-423). Hershey, PA: Idea Group.

Copyright © 2007, Idea Group Inc. Copying or distributing in print or electronic forms without written permission of Idea Group Inc. is prohibited.

Rahman, H. (2004b, December 15-17). Information dynamics in developing countries. Paper presented at the *5th International Conference on IT in Regional Areas*, Caloundra, Queensland, Australia.

Romanenko, N. (2003). *Assessment of NGO activity in Rovenskaya, Sumskaya and Khersonskaya Oblasts of Ukraine* (Short-term Mission Report: NGO Needs Assessment), Donetsk, Ukraine.

Roure, D.D., Jennings, N.R., & Shadbolt, N.R. (2002, December). *The semantic grid: A future e-science infrastructure* (Tech. Rep. No. UKeS-2002-02). National e-Science Centre.

Royal Government of Cambodia. (2001, December). *PRSP: Preparation status report*. Ministry of Planning.

Sabel, C. (1989). Flexible specialization and the re-emergence of regional economies. In P. Hirst & J. Zeitlin (Eds.), *Reversing industrial decline? Industrial structure and policy in Britain and her competitors* (pp. 23-49). Oxford: Berg.

Sabel, C. (1994). Learning by monitoring: The institutions of economic development. In N. Smelser & R. Swedberg (Eds.), *The handbook of economic sociology* (pp. 137-165). Princeton, NJ: Princeton University Press.

Salvadore, T., & Sherry, J. (2004). Local learnings: An essay on designing to facilitate effective use of ICTs. *The Journal of Community Informatics, 1*(1), 76-83.

Samuels, W. (1995). The present state of institutional economics. *Cambridge Journal of Economics, 19*, 569-590.

Scottish Enterprise Network Strategy. (2005). Retrieved June 28, 2006, from http://www.scotent.co.uk/netstrat.html

SDNP Malawi. (2003). *Malawi ICT policy framework 2002*. Retrieved June 28, 2006, from http://www.sdnp.org.mw/ict/framework-2002/

Shrader, C.B., Lincoln, J.R., & Hoffman, A.N. (1989). The network structures of organizations: Effects of task contingencies and distributional form. *Human Relations, 42*(1), 43-66.

Siamwiza, M.N. (2002). *The impact of globalization on science and technology in sub-Saharan African countries* (Series No. 3). Kenya: African Technology Policy Studies Network. ISBN: 9966-916-63-6/9966916636.

Simpson, R., & Hunter, A. (2001). *The Internet and regional Australia: How rural communities can address the impact of the Internet*. Canberra: Rural Industries Research and Development Corporation.

Smelser, N., & Swedberg, R. (Eds.). (1994). *The handbook of economic sociology*. Princeton, NJ: Princeton University Press.

Southwood, R. (2004, March). *ICT and small enterprise: A motor of economic development in Africa* (Brief No. 9). The Hague: IICD Research.

Storper, M. (1995). Regional technology coalitions: An essential dimension of national technology policy. *Research Policy, 24*, 895-911.

Tichy, N.M., & Fobrun, C. (1979). Social network analysis for organizations. *Academy of Management Review 4*, 507-559.

Copyright © 2007, Idea Group Inc. Copying or distributing in print or electronic forms without written permission of Idea Group Inc. is prohibited.

UN. (2005, July 27-29). *Note by the Secretary-General*, Third annual report of the ICT Task Force, Substantive session of 2005. New York: Author.

UNDP. (1999). *Research and policy advice* (UNDP Vietnam Annual Report).

UNDP. (2003a). *ICT for development program framework: Achieving the millennium development goals through the use of information and communication technologies* (ICT) (UNDP Albania ICTD Framework, Revised Document) Albania: Author.

UNDP. (2003b, November). *SURF-WA Newsletter, 1*(2).

UNDP. (2003c). *National ICT strategy paves the road for a new generation of "e-citizens."* Hanoi, Vietnam: Author.

UNDP. (2004, November 2-3). *Report: Workshop on Policy Tools to Support ICT Use for Poverty Reduction and the Achievement of the MDGs.* Dakar SURF: Author.

UNDP. (2005). *Programme support document, Strengthening capacity for the reduction of poverty in Guyana*, Programme of the Government of Guyana. Author.

UNESCO. (2004). *Five Asian countries start using ICT for community empowerment.* Retrieved June 28, 2006, from http://portal.unseco.org

UNICT Task Force Report. (2004a, November 18-20). *Mainstreaming information and communication technologies for the achievement of the millennium development goals* (draft). Berlin, Germany.

UNICT Task Force Report. (2004b, November 18-20). *Mainstreaming information and communication technologies for the achievement of the millennium development goals* (final). Berlin, Germany.

UNIDO. (2003, December). *Review of telecenter sustainability criteria for the establishment of sustainable rural business resource centers for SMEs in developing countries* (prepared by C. Jauernig for the Small and Medium Enterprises Branch). Vienna, Austria.

UNESCAP (2003, January 28-29). *Expert Group Meeting on ICT for rural poverty reduction: Developing national policies.* UNESCAP, Bangkok, Thailand.

Wall, E., Ferazzi, G., & Schryer, F. (1998). Getting the googs on social capital. R*ural Networks, 18*(3), 347-354.

WCL. (2005). *Millennium goals, time for striking a first balance!* Brussels: WCL Press Department. Retrieved June 28, 2006, from http://www.cmt-wcl.org/cmt/

WCS. (1999, March 1-3). Basic sciences for development of Eastern and South Africa. In *Proceedings of the World Conference on Science*, Arusha, Tanzania.

Wheeler, J.C. (1988). *Voluntary aid for development: The role of non-governmental organizations.* Paris: Organization for Economic Cooperation and Development.

Woolcock, M., & Narayan, D. (2000). Implications for development theory, research and policy. *The World Bank Research Observer, 15*(2).

World Bank. (2000, October). *Poverty in an Age of Globalization.* retrieved November 14, 2006 from http://www1.worldbank.org/economicpolicy/globalization/documents/povertyglobalization.pdf.

World Bank. (2002). *Small island developing states network*, Retrieved June 30, 2006 from http://wbln0018.worldbank.org/html/smallstates.nsf

Copyright © 2007, Idea Group Inc. Copying or distributing in print or electronic forms without written permission of Idea Group Inc. is prohibited.

World Bank. (2003a). *World development indicators 2003*.

World Bank. (2003b, February). *Culture and the corporative priorities of the World Bank* (Report on progress from April 1999 to December 2002). Retrieved November 14, 2006 from http://siteresources.worldbank.org/INTCHD/Resources/report-progress-april99-december02.pdf

World Bank. (2005). *ICT and environmental sustainability: Selected World Bank Group funded projects*. The World Bank Groups, Washington DC

Endnotes

[1]   www.interenvironment.org/wd1intro/glossary.htm

[2]   www.bized.ac.uk/virtual/dc/resource/glos2.htm

[3]   www.undp.org/rbec/nhdr/1996/georgia/glossary.htm

[4]   www.defra.giv.uk/corporate/ebus/maffrole/annexe.htm

[5]   www.fraw.org.uk/library/005/gn-irt/glossary.html

[6]   http://asp2.wlv.ac/its/Website/everyone/its_jargon.htm

[7]   www.ictadvice.org.uk/index.php

[8]   www.mckinnonsc.vic.edu.au/la/it/ipmnotes/misc/glossary.htm

[9]   http://envision.ca/templates/profile.asp

[10]   http://oregonstate.edu/instruct/anth370/gloss.html

[11]   www.mbaa.org/consumer/mterms.cfm

[12]   www.personal.umich.edu/~alandear/glossary/e.html

[13]   www.agtrade.org/glossary_search.cfm

[14]   www.delawarecountybrc.com/glossaryterms.htm

[15]   http://pdacrsp.oregonstate.edu/pubs/admin/admin_12/admin12.appA/admin12.ap-pAhtml

[16]   www.undp.org/rbec/nhdr/1996/georgia/glossary.htm

[17]   World Summit on Information Society (WSIS) held in 2003 and 2005

[18]   World Summit on Sustainable Development held in 2002

Copyright © 2007, Idea Group Inc. Copying or distributing in print or electronic forms without written permission of Idea Group Inc. is prohibited.

Section IV

Success Stories/Case Studies

Chapter XI

A Dissemination Strategy for the Management of Knowledge in Rural Communities

Ken Stevens, Memorial University of Newfoundland, Canada

Abstract

Schools in rural communities of the Canadian province of Newfoundland and Labrador have been reorganized in the last decade. Because of rural to urban migration and the consequent challenge to the continued existence of many small schools, new academically and administratively open structures have been established within an Internet-based environment. Accordingly, traditional closed, autonomous schools in this province have increasingly become open sites within Internet-linked teaching and learning environments. What began as a research project linking eight schools in a single Digital Intranet has been extended to include schools across the province managed by a recently established branch of the Department of Education of Newfoundland and Labrador—the Centre for Distance Learning and Innovation. This chapter provides an outline of how information and communication technologies have been used to reshape education in a predominantly rural Canadian province, thereby preparing people for participation in the emerging knowledge-based economy.

Copyright © 2007, Idea Group Inc. Copying or distributing in print or electronic forms without written permission of Idea Group Inc. is prohibited.

Introduction

A decade ago tele-learning (e-learning) was described as the future of distance learning (Collis, 1996). In spite of this, e-learning remains, for many people, an unfamiliar term in the educational lexicon, the implications of which for teaching, learning, the management of schools, and educational policy are unclear. At the present time, many schools are in transition between traditional and virtual ways of organizing teaching and learning as they seek to integrate information and communication technologies in classrooms. This chapter outlines the transition from traditional (face to face) to virtual teaching and learning environments in a small network of rural Canadian high schools. It is argued, on the basis of research in science classes in this network in Newfoundland and Labrador, that the introduction of e-learning in schools involves a shift from a closed to an open model of teaching and learning. The shift from closed to open teaching and learning has implications beyond the school for regional development.

In most states of the United States and provinces of Canada there are communities that live beyond major centers of population. Although most North Americans live in urban centers, many Americans and Canadians live in small communities in rural and sometimes remote parts of the continent, in Alaska, Wyoming, and Montana, for example in the United States, and the in the Canadian prairie provinces of Saskatchewan and Manitoba as well as in Atlantic Canada. The development of natural resources such as lumber and fishing and the extraction of oil and gas that are important to the economies of both countries, often takes place in locations far from major centers of population. In the resource-based Canadian economy rural schools are, therefore, integral to the economic infrastructure. A decline in the viability of rural education has implications for provincial, and, indirectly, national economic infrastructures. However, it is sometimes difficult for professional people to justify enrolling their sons and daughters in small schools in rural communities if they provide fewer curriculum options than urban institutions.

Information and communication technologies (ICTs) are central to the development of the knowledge economy whose significance for rural schools was recognized in the mid-1990s (Barker, 1994; Stevens, 1994). Almost a decade ago the Canadian government set out two documents (1995, 1997) to prepare the country for the digital world. Small schools in rural communities have been particularly active in Canada (Cey, 2001; Healey and Stevens, 2002; Stevens, 2000, 2001) in using new technologies to promote educational opportunities for students and more efficient ways of organizing and managing knowledge in connected (Ertl & Plante, 2004), collaborative, electronic structures. The rapid growth and educational application of the Internet has led to a challenge to traditional ways of teaching and learning at a distance (Ben-Jacob, Levin & Ben-Jacob, 2000) that were based on paper and the postal system. The introduction of e-learning in schools in Atlantic Canada has been particularly noticeable in rural communities and has been influenced by declining enrollments because of rural to urban migration (Brown, Sheppard & Stevens, 2000). While the population of rural Atlantic Canadian communities has declined, the management of schools has been changed so that actual and virtual classes have, to some extent, been integrated. One of the Atlantic Canadian provinces—Newfoundland and Labrador—provides an example of rural population decline, a challenge to the continued existence of many small schools and a loss of local educational and economic opportunities. These changes have been countered by the

Copyright © 2007, Idea Group Inc. Copying or distributing in print or electronic forms without written permission of Idea Group Inc. is prohibited.

development of a dissemination strategy for the management of knowledge in small communities in this province that provides a possible model for other parts of North America.

Rural Education in Atlantic Canada: Newfoundland and Labrador

Atlantic Canada consists of four provinces: New Brunswick, Prince Edward Island, Nova Scotia, and Newfoundland and Labrador. Newfoundland and Labrador covers by far the largest area of Atlantic Canada and, particularly in Labrador, there is very sparse population settlement. Newfoundland and Labrador's small population of approximately 550,000 residents in a large geographic area (156,185 square miles) presents challenges for the delivery of education, particularly at the senior high school level. Newfoundland and Labrador has many small coastal communities a predominantly rural lifestyle in most of the province and a distinctive history and culture.

31% of educational institutions in the Canadian province of Newfoundland and Labrador are designated "small rural schools" (N = 122) and 75 of these have fewer than 100 students. 70 of the small rural schools in this province are classified as "all-grade" (K–12) which means that they must offer a senior high school program. The search for appropriate new educational structures for the delivery of education to students in rural Newfoundland and Labrador led to the development of School District Digital Intranets, within which virtual classes, based on e-learning, have been organized. The large proportion of small schools located in rural communities, required special consideration in the development of these new, electronic educational structures.

In the last decade there has been considerable reorganization of the school system in Newfoundland and Labrador, largely because of rural to urban migration together with a net outflow of people from the province. Small schools are not only getting smaller; many of them have been closed permanently. In 1996, 10 Anglophone school district boards were created in the province together with one province-wide Francophone board, a reduction from 26 school boards. In this reorganization of school boards, the Vista School District was created. With continued reduction in school size in most rural Newfoundland and Labrador communities, the provincial administration of schools was further reorganized in 2003 to create four Anglophone and one Francophone school board. This study was conducted before the most recent reorganization, when there were ten school boards, one of them serving the Vista district.

The Vista School District contained 18 schools ranging in student enrollment from 650 down to 40, including Eastern High School (not its real name). The region in which the Vista School District is located extends from Bonavista in the north, (the place where John Cabot landed in North America in 1497) to the Burin Peninsula in the South. It is a large geographic area covering about 7,000 square kilometers. The region had a population of about 35,000 people and an economy supported by a diverse infrastructure including fishing, forestry, farming, mining, aquaculture, and tourism. There were 5,165 students enrolled in 18 schools in the district, taught by 366 teachers. The Vista School District was approximately two hours by

Copyright © 2007, Idea Group Inc. Copying or distributing in print or electronic forms without written permission of Idea Group Inc. is prohibited.

road from the capital city, St Johns. Eastern High School, (not its real name) with a student enrollment of 480, was initially chosen for intensive study.

The path from a closed model of the school in rural Newfoundland and Labrador to the beginnings of an open model began in selected science classes of Eastern High School. At the time of the study, computers and the Internet were fairly new in schools and many teachers were not aware of the nature and potential extent of their applications for teaching and learning. Five phases can be identified in the ways these technologies were organized in what became a move from closed to open teaching and learning in the Vista School District.

Five Phases in the Move from Closed to Open Classes

The introduction of computers and the Internet to schools in Newfoundland and Labrador took place gradually, in closed teaching and learning environments which gradually became more open. At the beginning of the study, Eastern High School was at phase four.

Phase One: The Introduction of Computers in Schools

In the late 1980s and early 1990s computer technology was introduced to classes with little of no formal training of the teachers who used it. Teachers frequently learnt how computers worked though their own study of them with little help from outside sources. In this phase of e-learning, computers were a subject of study. Some teachers studied computers to find out how they worked and how they could be programmed while, to most of the profession, this technology was not considered to be directly relevant to classroom life. There was little thought given to the integration of computers to teaching and learning.

Phase Two: Computers and Course Redevelopment

In the early 1990s increasing numbers of teachers began to realize the potential of computers for both teaching and student learning. Local Area Networks (LANs) were introduced in Newfoundland and Labrador. While there was awareness of the Internet, it was not used in Newfoundland and Labrador schools at this time. However, computers were used to capture data for science experiments using Vernier hardware and software. Students were shown how to use word processing, spreadsheets, and graphing software in completing their assignments and some entire courses were re-developed around such uses of computer technology.

Phase Three: Internet Access

In 1993 the introduction of Internet access to selected teachers in Newfoundland and Labrador led to the formation of STEM~Net, the provincial arm of the federal program SchoolNet which was established to encourage computer and Internet use in Canadian classrooms. STEM~Net was based at Memorial University of Newfoundland, the only university in the province. Within a two-year period more than 5,000 teachers were provided with access to

Copyright © 2007, Idea Group Inc. Copying or distributing in print or electronic forms without written permission of Idea Group Inc. is prohibited.

the Internet through STEM~Net. Training sessions were provided in the use of e-mail and the development of Web pages using HTML.

Phase Four: Integrating Technologies

By 1996-97 Newfoundland and Labrador schools had a high level of connectivity, per capita. The development of Web pages by students in schools was accompanied by the introduction of other areas of school life to the Web such as homework exercises, answers to questions, school policies, and schedules of events. Early attempts to bring information technologies into teaching and learning were in the form of text on line and links to other sites (mostly universities). Internet resources and CD-ROMs became increasingly available to both teachers and learners, facilitating interaction between dispersed sites.

Phase Five: The Vista School District Digital Intranet

The Vista School District Digital Intranet project that began in 1998 was an attempt to determine how to deliver real-time instruction across dispersed sites, all of which were located in rural Newfoundland. Lead teachers in biology, chemistry, mathematics, and physics piloted the delivery of Advanced Placement (AP) courses in these subjects. Advanced Placement courses are available to students in both Canada and the United States. As the name suggests, these courses are designed for students who wish to prepare for university by undertaking studies over and above their final-year high school program. Universities throughout North America determine the level of credit towards first-year courses they will award students who pass AP subjects. Students who pass AP courses, therefore, often enter North American universities with a small part of their degrees already completed. Success in AP examinations (all of which are moderated in Baltimore, Maryland) gives students confidence that they can succeed in university-level courses and provide a useful bridge between high school and university-level studies. AP credits are of considerable value to high school leavers in gaining entry to the college or university of their choice.

The Closed Model of Teaching Science Using Information Technologies: Biology at Eastern High School

Biology was chosen for study at Eastern High School because of the breadth it provided for research. Physics and chemistry were not considered to be as appropriate because of the much narrower and more academic stream of students who enrolled in these courses. Biology attracted a wider range of students within the school than either chemistry or physics. All the biology courses in this school were taught by one teacher who had advanced computer skills.

Copyright © 2007, Idea Group Inc. Copying or distributing in print or electronic forms without written permission of Idea Group Inc. is prohibited.

Students taking the course Biology 2201 were involved in a study to evaluate the use of Internet resources to enhance their education in this subject. Three Biology 2201 classes were selected to take part in the study. The study involved three topics taken from Unit IV—Homeostasis. Each of the three classes was taught using three different methods of instruction defined as:

1.   **Traditional** (lectures and assignments). In the traditional group, students were taught face to face by the teacher from the textbook. This was the way in which students were used to being taught so this created no change for either teacher or students. The students in this group did not experience any changes in their mode of instruction.

2.   **Cooperative** (students being much more responsible for their own learning and sharing what they learn with their peers). In the cooperative group, students were able to work together on learning biology, using text sources as well as a Web site that enabled them to visit appropriate areas of the Internet that were selected by their teacher. These students worked with a lot less direct teaching from their biology teacher.

3.   **Internet** (students gathering information from Internet resources to complete the intended learning outcomes). In this group, students were to work individually and to use Internet sources to complete their biology units of study. Internet students were able to work with more freedom than those being taught face to face and were, therefore, dependent to some extent on personal discipline as well as facility in using information technologies.

Each topic of study involved 9 periods (57 minutes) of instructional time and one period for evaluation (pre-test and post-test) over a 14 day school cycle. Upon completing each cycle of instruction in a given methodology, each study group began the next topic using a different instructional practice. By the end of the study each class group would be exposed to all three instructional methodologies. The topics chosen were considered by the instructor to be of equal difficulty. Pre-test and post-test data was collected so that a quantitative comparison could be made. Upon completion of the study, students completed a qualitative evaluation which asked them to provide information about their preferences for each instructional method. All students had the same prescribed text, Biology: The Study of Life (Schraer & Stoltze, 1995). The tables below indicate the pre-test and post-test class averages and standard deviations. Each pre-test and post-test (Tables 2, 3, and 4) contained 25 multiple choice questions, and each question had 4 possible answers. Data in the tables are raw scores and are not corrected for guessing.

Table 1 compares the three Biology 2201 classes that took part in the study. The letters "B," "C," and "D" only refer to the slot within the school timetable and have no other significance. The Eastern High School timetable ran over a period of 14 school days. Each 14 day cycle had 10 periods (57 min. each) of biology instruction. "Number" refers to the number of students in each of the Biology 2201 classes. "Class Average Prior to Study" refers to the class average mark based on all work prior to the start of the study. This mark represents the average of 27 pieces of evaluation in each of the three classes. Each quiz, lab report, and assignment was the same for all students and all three classes and was collected throughout the year of instruction prior to the study period. "Class Average Unit Examination" refers to the class average on the unit examination completed at the end of the study. "Standard

Copyright © 2007, Idea Group Inc. Copying or distributing in print or electronic forms without written permission of Idea Group Inc. is prohibited.

Table 1. General information for comparison

Class	Number of Students	Class Average Prior to Study	Class Average Unit examination	Standard Deviation Unit Examination
B	21	61.7	46.8	12.7
C	33	68.5	60.6	17.5
D	29	68.4	58.2	14.4

Table 2. Chapter 14

Class	Method of Instruction	Pretest Average Mark	Pretest Standard Deviation	Posttest Average Mark	Posttest Standard Deviation
B	Traditional	25.0	8.2	54.9	14.6
C	Cooperative	30.6	9.5	59.9	23.3
D	Computer	25.9	10.0	59.4	21.8

Table 3. Chapter 15

Class	Method of Instruction	Pretest Average Mark	Pretest Standard Deviation	Posttest Average Mark	Posttest Standard Deviation
B	Computer	N/A	N/A	41.6	21.3
C	Traditional	N/A	N/A	63.6	22.8
D	Cooperative	N/A	N/A	64.9	18.6

Deviation Unit Exam" is the standard deviation for each class on the unit examination. The unit examination covered five (5) sections (Chapters 12-16) of work. Only three sections (Chapters 14-6) were part of the study.

Table 2 shows the results of the first round in the study. This was a study of the nervous system (Chapter 14). Each class was taught using a different teaching strategy as indicated in the table. Students received 9 periods of instruction during a 14 day cycle. Period 10 of the cycle was used for evaluation.

Table 3 indicates the results of the second round (Chapter 15). The classes remained the same in terms of the students but the teaching strategy was changed as indicated under "Method of Instruction." Again, students received 9 periods of exposure to the teaching strategy in the 14 day cycle. The 10th period was used for evaluation.

Copyright © 2007, Idea Group Inc. Copying or distributing in print or electronic forms without written permission of Idea Group Inc. is prohibited.

Table 4. Chapter 16

Class	Method of Instruction	Pretest Average Mark	Pretest Standard Deviation	Posttest Average Mark	Posttest Standard Deviation
B	Cooperative	27.5	11.0	67.4	8.2
C	Computer	31.8	7.7	66.4	19.9
D	Traditional	29.0	13.2	71.7	11.1

Table 4 indicates the results of the third round in the study (Chapter 16). Again the students remained the same but the teaching strategy was shifted. Students of Class B and D received 9 hours of instruction and 1 hour for evaluation. Class C (33 students) received six periods using computer, three periods using traditional instruction, and one period for evaluation. With 33 students in the Class C, it became necessary to abandon the study after six periods (rather than the intended nine periods). This was due to several factors including: students complaining about overcrowded conditions, the room being too hot and uncomfortable, no printer, and only 11 computers were in service.

On completion of the study students completed a qualitative evaluation survey intended to gather data regarding their experience with each teaching method. Each student was asked to explain in their own words, what "traditional," "cooperative," and "computer" teaching strategies meant to them. The student also wrote a brief description of what they believed represented the best teaching method—how they would like to be taught in future.

Traditional:

> *"The teacher told us what we needed to know and gave us notes."*

> *"The teacher stands in front of the class writing out notes ... it's basically boring."*

> *"I feel this type of learning was good, but it is the most boring."*

Cooperative:

> *"I think this is a very effective way of learning"*

> *"Students look for information themselves and help each other. The teacher is just there for guidance."*

> *"The teacher gives us a concept or question—we form into groups and do the research."*

Copyright © 2007, Idea Group Inc. Copying or distributing in print or electronic forms without written permission of Idea Group Inc. is prohibited.

Internet:

> *"Very hard to use but if used right it can help a great deal."*
>
> *"This was the greatest method but people got off the topic."*
>
> *"Most students spend their time on topics completely unrelated to the subject and the teacher doesn't know."*

The feedback indicated that students preferred to be taught using a combination of strategies. All three groups indicated that reliance on a single instructional strategy was not to their benefit. It was suggested that students first receive training in the use of the technology (to become familiar with the software and hardware) before they could make efficient use of Internet resources. Most students reported some degree of frustration, mostly associated with their lack of computer skills and their inability to focus on the task assigned.

It was found, from this experiment, to be necessary to provide time for students to learn how to make efficient use of the technology before engaging in the study of science. It appeared, however, that use of Internet resources had some potential to enhance student learning in biology. The possibility of using computers in other subjects was raised in an end of year meeting during which the above work in biology was outlined. Other schools in the district were interested in the possibilities that computers offered for teaching and learning.

The closed model of the teaching of science in a single high school, using computers, was the basis for the creation of the open model that followed. In the closed model, the school teachers and students engage with one another within a single, autonomous institution to which teachers are exclusively appointed and students enrolled. From this traditional model of schooling a new possibility emerged based on earlier work in New Zealand (Stevens, 1995a, b) and Iceland (Stefansdottir, 1993) in which selected classes in some schools within a district were linked so that teachers and learners could collaborate. This became known as the open model within which schools began to open to one another both academically and administratively. Teachers appointed to a particular institution also taught selected classes in other schools by linking them electronically from the school to which they were appointed. In Newfoundland and Labrador the open model had its beginnings in the Vista school district digital Intranet.

The Open Model of Teaching Science: The Development of a School District Digital Intranet

The electronic linking of nine rural schools across dispersed sites within the Vista School district to collaborate in the teaching of Advanced Placement biology, chemistry, mathematics, and physics created a series of virtual classes in Newfoundland. Classes began in September 1998 and several reports were completed (Stevens, 1998, 1999; Stevens, Piper & Power,

Copyright © 2007, Idea Group Inc. Copying or distributing in print or electronic forms without written permission of Idea Group Inc. is prohibited.

1998; Stevens, Power & Barry, 1999). The introduction of the Vista School District Digital Intranet represented two dimensions of change: in the relationship between curriculum and technology and the reorganization of classes within an Intranet.

The Integration of Information Technologies into the Science Curriculum

The development of Advanced Placement Web-based courses in biology, chemistry, mathematics, and physics took place within a development team in each subject area. A lead science teacher in each discipline was paired with a recent graduate in Biology, Chemistry, Mathematics and Physics respectively who possessed advanced computer skills including Web page design, Java and HTML. The lead teacher and the graduate student were, ideally, to have been assisted by a Faculty of Education specialist in each curriculum area together with a scientist from the Faculty of Science at Memorial University of Newfoundland. The extent to which each Web-based course was developed by a team of four people varied. Most of the development was through interaction between the lead teacher and the recent graduate with reference, as appropriate, to two professors (of science education and science). This model provided a measure of interaction between schools, graduate students, and the Faculties of Education and Science of Memorial University of Newfoundland. To provide a connection between the high school and Memorial University, faculty members were asked to take part in providing resources, quality control evaluation, and suggestions for improvement. Although at times professors had different opinions as to the most appropriate way to design the courses, this approach enabled each of the four subjects to be developed over the summer vacation in time for the new school year. Many software packages were evaluated and finally WebCT was selected. This package enabled the instructor to track student progress, it contained online testing and evaluation, private e-mail, a calendar feature, public bulletin board for use by both instructor and student, a link to lessons and chat rooms for communication between teacher and student. For real time instruction, Meeting Point and Microsoft NetMeeting were selected. This combination of software enabled a teacher to present real-time interactive instruction to multiple sites. An orientation session was provided for students in June of the year prior to implementation. Visits by instructors were made to participating schools from time to time and students learnt how to communicate with each other and with their instructor using these new technologies.

The Reorganization of Classes in a School District Digital Intranet

The question how students would work in a largely independent learning environment was prominent in the minds of researchers from the outset of each AP course. There was no AP teacher present on site for these courses. Students were not used to being alone and largely

Copyright © 2007, Idea Group Inc. Copying or distributing in print or electronic forms without written permission of Idea Group Inc. is prohibited.

unsupervised for much of the time even though most of the initial AP students were considered by their schools to be "independent learners."

It was recognized that a common schedule had to be adopted throughout the Vista school district to allow students to interact in real time with their instructors at selected times during the week. The initial plan was to allow for five online sessions and five offline sessions. This schedule was not followed in all schools. Online sessions were scheduled in the mornings when network traffic was at its lowest point. Offline sessions were scheduled for afternoons. Some schools chose not to be coordinated with the AP schedule for various valid reasons. As a result the instructor might be teaching another subject when the AP student would be in a traditional face to face class. Students in different schools throughout the Vista district, therefore, had differing access to their AP Instructors.

Five Phases in the Development of a Dissemination Strategy for the Management of Knowledge

The move from closed to open classes in Newfoundland and Labrador, based on the introduction of computers and the Internet and the creation of school district digital Intranets, provided a basis for the dissemination of knowledge among the participant schools. There were five phases in this process.

Phase One: The Introduction of a Digital Intranet

The creation of the School District Digital Intranet within which AP biology, chemistry, mathematics, and physics were taught, was an attempt to use information and communication technologies to provide geographically-isolated students with extended educational and, indirectly, vocational opportunities, that would otherwise not be locally available. This was part of a broader pan-Canadian initiative since 1997 to prepare people in Canada for the Information Age (Information Highway Advisory Council, 1997). The significance of the first digital Intranet within a single school district was in moving the management of knowledge from closed, autonomous schools to an open teaching and learning structure for selected students. Adjustments had to be made administratively and academically in each participating site so that AP classes could be taught within the fledgling open learning structure.

This development was a milestone in the organization of education in Newfoundland and Labrador for two reasons. First, while AP courses are a well-established feature of senior secondary education in the United States and Canada, it was unusual for students to be able to enroll for instruction at this level in small schools in remote communities. The organizers of the project could find no other rural sites in North America in which AP subjects were available. Second, the provision of AP subjects within the Vista school district digital Intranet was, as far as could be established, the first time this curriculum had been offered online, anywhere.

Copyright © 2007, Idea Group Inc. Copying or distributing in print or electronic forms without written permission of Idea Group Inc. is prohibited.

Phase Two: The Development of Online Courses

In the process of developing e-teaching and e-learning within digital Intranets in rural Newfoundland and Labrador, teachers, learners and administrators had to adapt to a new, electronic educational structure. In the open teaching and learning environment of a school district digital Intranet, participating institutions academically and administratively interface for that part of the school day during which classes are being taught. This is a different educational structure from the traditional and, by comparison, closed educational environment of the autonomous school with its own teachers and its own students. There is a potential conflict between a school as an autonomous educational institution serving a designated district and schools which become, in effect, sites within electronic teaching and learning networks. Principals and teachers appointed to the closed, autonomous learning environments of traditional schools frequently discovered that the administration of knowledge required the development of open structures within which they were increasingly expected to collaborate with their peers located on a range of distant sites. Some principals found that the positions to which they were appointed in traditional (closed) schools had become, in effect, collaborative roles within the new open electronic environment.

Students in the initial digital Intranet were frequently subject to scrutiny by their peers as they responded through chat rooms, audio, video, and with their AP online teacher. The digital Intranet provided students with access to multiple sites simultaneously, as well as the opportunity to work independently of a teacher for part of the day. The need to prepare for classes before going online became increasingly apparent to both teachers and students if the open, synchronous, science classes were to succeed. The advent of the Vista School District Digital Intranet had implications for students who began to interact with teachers and their peers in a variety of new ways. Many students experienced difficulty in expressing themselves and, in particular, asking questions in open electronic classes when they did not know their peers from other small communities. The organization of social occasions for students learning science in open classes in the first Intranet in the province helped overcome these problems. As students became more comfortable with one another after meeting in person, inhibitions such as asking questions online were overcome.

Phase Three: Increased Access to Online Courses

The Vista School District Digital Intranet provided new pathways for senior students to higher education through the initial AP subjects. By linking traditional schools to create open teaching and learning environments expertise was shared and new learning spaces for students were created. Since this pioneering venture in rural Newfoundland, other AP subjects have been added, as well as subjects from the regular school curriculum. The Internet-enhanced learning environments that have succeeded the initial Intranet have been extended province wide, including schools in Labrador, by a branch of the provincial Department of Education. The Centre for Distance Learning and Innovation (CDLI) has extended learning opportunities for students in the province's schools to all school districts and across the curriculum (http://www.cdli.ca/). Henceforth, online education is no longer the preserve of AP students in the senior school.

Copyright © 2007, Idea Group Inc. Copying or distributing in print or electronic forms without written permission of Idea Group Inc. is prohibited.

Although the Vista School District Digital Intranet opened new possibilities for teaching and for learning, particularly for senior students, many adults in rural Newfoundland and Labrador remain unemployed or underemployed in their rural communities. This is an outcome of the demise of the traditional source of employment in this province—the cod fishery. While an increasing number of schools in Newfoundland and Labrador have become high-technology beacons that connect with one another to add a virtual dimension to traditional face to face instruction, many adult learners have not been able to take advantage of the new, open learning environment. Therefore, exploration of the adult-learning potential of the high-technology hubs that many small schools throughout rural Newfoundland and Labrador have become remains an untapped aspect of regional economic development.

Phase Four: The Integration of On-Site and Online Teaching and Learning

The advent of digital Intranets across all school districts of Newfoundland and Labrador has led to a prominent role for the Centre for Distance Learning and Innovation in the organization of the province's schools. Distance learning, in the form of e-learning, is increasingly integrated with traditional face to face instruction. Students in many of the province's rural schools now receive part of their education on-site in traditional classrooms through face to face instruction. E-teaching has developed from the initial four teachers in the Vista School District Digital Intranet to become an established part of the profession today. New professional positions have been established to support e-teaching: m-teachers and a range of technical support staff. M-teachers (mediating teachers) support e-teachers within schools that receive e-learning for students on-site (Barbour & Mulcahy, 2005). Usually, m-teachers have traditional classroom roles but also have responsibilities to support e-learners by mediating between problems they present on site, with e-teachers who provide instruction from other places. Recently the concept of m-teams, outlined below, has been considered to replace m-teachers that include technical and administrative support as well as the on-site mentoring of e-students.

Phase Five: A Dissemination Strategy for the Management of Knowledge

The introduction of inter-school electronic networks added a new dimension to education in Newfoundland and Labrador and continues to bring new challenges for teachers and learners (Stevens & Stewart, 2005; Van Manen, 2002), and administrators. The linking of schools within an interactive electronic structure was a direct use of ICT for rural development that had three immediate outcomes for regional development. First, rural to urban student migration was considerably reduced as senior students could access an extended range of subjects within the School District Digital Intranet. Second, new Internet-based pathways from schools to homes became possible with implications for adult learners, although there is much work still to be undertaken in this sector of Newfoundland and Labrador society, and thirdly, access to information became transparent, facilitating engagement between schools and local as well as non-local expertise.

Copyright © 2007, Idea Group Inc. Copying or distributing in print or electronic forms without written permission of Idea Group Inc. is prohibited.

The Coffin Model of M-Teaching to Integrate On-Site and Online Education

In the development of small schools in rural Canadian communities as centres of information and communications technologies for teaching and learning, a more central role for all staff, particularly those at the senior high school level, is needed. In a concept paper that compared m-teachers and m-teams, Coffin (2002) pointed out that:

The benefits of a technology-enabled school will not be realized unless the human resources in those schools also possess the knowledge and skills needed to function effectively in those technologies. Technologically advanced schools need to prepare and organize their human resources so as to support an alternative delivery method which operates not as a competitor to traditional face to face (teaching and learning), but as a complement to it. Assigning one individual as a school's only resource to mediate between e-teachers and e-learners is far from sufficient to realize that vision. (p. 2)

Coffin (2002) argued against the practice of appointing m-teachers to support e-teachers and e-learners by creating a team approach. He suggested that m-teams be established, with specific responsibilities to replace m-teachers in rural schools in Newfoundland and Labrador:

The report Supporting Learning (Government of Newfoundland and Labrador, 2000) envisioned a teaching role to provide school-based support for students who were instructed by an off-site e-teacher. Initially conceived of as a singular role, that is, one performed by a single teacher, evolving research … suggests that a team concept is perhaps better suited to fulfilling CDLI's vision of small schools as "beacons of technological innovation" with respect to distance learning. Conceptually, then, e-learning needs the support of a team of people providing four sets of skills: technical, coaching, administrative and resource advisor. We can attach an order of priority to those tasks as well, based on research. We have noted that students in e-learning courses have a high dependence on the technology used to deliver the courses. The higher the dependency, the greater the requirement that the technology be reliable. This feature is so important that it deserves the highest ranking among tasks performed by m-teams. Using students' assessments of the role of m-teachers, the coaching function is the next most helpful role, followed by administrative and, then, that of the resource teacher. Teams may be real or virtual or a combination of both.

By that we mean the expertise can reside on-site in the form of a teacher or staff person or it can exist apart from the school, for example, a content-area Web-site maintained by a teacher in another school or province. So the idea of a team doesn't have to imply people getting together periodically to plan strategy or solve problems. The team represents more of a bank of resources easily accessible to on-line students which can be used to facilitate their learning. (p. 1)

An m-teaching scenario, outlined by Coffin (2002) in a moderate-size rural high school with 100-250 students may have:

Copyright © 2007, Idea Group Inc. Copying or distributing in print or electronic forms without written permission of Idea Group Inc. is prohibited.

- At least six teachers teaching high school courses.
- A resource center with at least a part-time resource teacher.
- Some secretarial time assigned to the school.
- Technical expertise located in the school (or community) and additional expertise available within two hours drive of the school.
- A toll-free help-line for technical advice.
- There is no on-site subject area expertise that can be made available to online students.
- The technology teacher and coach would have some time in their schedules for discharging their responsibilities to online students.

The m-team could consist of a technology teacher, a technician, help line desk, advanced computer studies student(s), a coach (another teacher with an interest in distance learning), the school secretary, the resource teacher, and an administrator. Each person on the team would be responsible for specific support services. The technology teacher, the technician and the help-line desk and students will handle technical problems according to an agreed set of protocols. The coach will provide the nurturing, encouragement and advice that students need to persist in their studies. The technology teacher could also be the coach. The coach will also be the school-based contact for the e-teacher when that is necessary. These two professionals together will handle most of the pedagogical functions associated with online learning. Coaches should be assigned to students, rather than courses because the services they need to provide are client-oriented rather than content-oriented. The school secretary will take responsibility for conveying hard-copy correspondence between the e-teacher and students and other clerical functions.

The resource teacher will provide services similar to those provided for classroom instructed students. This person could also catalog, store and control the distribution of the learning resources for the online courses. The administrator would provide the administrative support services that ensure the smooth and efficient operation of online learning (including supervision of instruction).

In the Coffin model, the m-team may be the whole staff, consisting of teachers, support staff, and administration. The configuration of small schools varies considerably, so it is not appropriate to consider a single model for m-teams in all schools. This approach to supporting e-learning in rural schools has recently been adopted in Newfoundland and Labrador by the Centre for Distance Learning and Innovation and m-teams are replacing m-teachers.

Future Research

There have been major changes in the management and dissemination of knowledge in rural communities in the last decade and this has been particularly noticeable in the Canadian province of Newfoundland and Labrador. With the introduction of new organizational structures such as digital Intranets and the Centre for Distance Learning and Innovation together

Copyright © 2007, Idea Group Inc. Copying or distributing in print or electronic forms without written permission of Idea Group Inc. is prohibited.

with internet-based instruction, there are several possibilities for research in the immediate future. The term "digital divide" is often heard in relation to those who are technologically literate and those who are not. Nowhere is this more evident than in rural communities. With the introduction of an increasing range of online courses, young people who live in rural communities in Newfoundland and Labrador have been provided with electronic educational pathways to other institutions while their parents are often left behind both figuratively and actually. They are left behind because the new technologies that have transformed small rural schools into regional high-technology hubs for accessing educational facilities and, thereby, job opportunities, have not yet been able to influence the lives of unemployed local people who have little formal education. Future research could very useful in finding ways of strengthening regional economic development by linking adult learners in local (and non-local) homes with the technologically enhanced rural schools that have emerged in the last decade in Atlantic Canada.

A second area of future research is the implications of mobile technologies for rural schools and regional economic development. Computers have become increasingly mobile in the ubiquity of laptops (Lowther, Ross & Morrison, 2003; Rockman, 2003; Russell, Bebell & Higgins, 2004), an expanding range of hand-held devices (Norris & Solloway, 2004), and wireless technology. The possibilities of using mobile technologies for linking homes and, if appropriate, workplaces, in rural communities with technologically enhanced local schools has not been considered.

Finally, there is the possibility of making much stronger teaching and learning connections between small schools in rural communities and large urban schools, particularly in specialized areas of the senior curriculum. The developments outlined above in Newfoundland and Labrador provide a possible template for sharing educational resources, particularly teachers, and enabling students to engage in enlarged peer groups. There is now a need for policy research into the significance of geography and school size (as determined by students who physically attend on a daily basis), into the equitable distribution of educational resources.

Conclusion

The claim a decade ago that e-learning was the future of distance learning (Collis, 1996) has proved to be the case in the Canadian province of Newfoundland and Labrador and in other places with many rural schools (Griffin & Sherrod, 2005; Hawkes & Halverson, 2002). New electronic structures in the form of school district digital Intranets to support e-learning have developed that have changed the nature of schools, encouraging them to become increasingly open to one another. Within the electronic structures that have become part of the education system in this province new processes have also emerged. As electronic structures have been developed to complement traditional schools, particularly in rural communities, the possibility of new pedagogy has emerged (Cavanaugh, 2001) and with it, new expectations for teaching (Mathiasen, 2004). The term "cybercell" (Stevens & Stewart, 2005) has recently been coined to describe the integration of actual and virtual classes. A cybercell is a face to face group whose members extend their discussions to include virtual visitors.

Copyright © 2007, Idea Group Inc. Copying or distributing in print or electronic forms without written permission of Idea Group Inc. is prohibited.

As students and teachers across Newfoundland and Labrador further integrate actual and virtual teaching and learning, cybercells are likely to develop.

Schools in rural Newfoundland and Labrador have been reorganized in the last decade. Traditional (closed, autonomous) schools have increasingly become open sites within Internet-linked teaching and learning environments. What began as a research project linking eight schools in the Vista School District Digital Intranet has been extended to include schools across the province managed by a recently established branch of the Department of Education of Newfoundland and Labrador—the Centre for Distance Learning and Innovation. Perhaps the most significant development that has taken place is one that is not readily seen—the challenge to the notion of the school as an autonomous institution with its own teachers and its own students. Because of rural to urban migration and the consequent challenge to the continued existence of many small schools, new administratively and academically open structures were created. The next challenge is to develop pedagogy that will take advantage of the extended learning environments across Newfoundland and Labrador. Cybercells—within which actual and virtual teaching and learning take place simultaneously—may become the next step in the management of knowledge in rural communities.

The establishment of electronic educational structures and processes linking small, dispersed communities in Newfoundland and Labrador has provided a model for economic development in the knowledge society that Canada has become. Through the dissemination of these methodologies and the effective utilization of ICT in other parts of the world, competitive knowledge based communities can be created. Knowledge based communities are likely to yield knowledge products that could act as catalytic agents for regional development.

References

Barbour, M., & Mulcahy, D. (2005, September). The role of mediating teachers in New-foundland's new model of distance education. *The Morning Watch. 32*, 1-2. http://www.mun.ca/educ/faculty/mwatch/fall04.htm

Barker, B.A. (1994). Distance education in rural schools: Technologies and practice. *Journal of Research in Rural Education, 10*(2), 126-128.

Ben-Jacob, M.G., Levin, D.S., & Ben-Jacob, T.K. (2000). The learning environment of the 21st century. *Educational Technology Review, 13*, 8-12.

Brown, J., Sheppard, D., & Stevens, K. (2000) *Effective schooling in a tele-learning environment*. Newfoundland: St. John's, NL, Centre for Tele-Learning and Rural Education, Faculty of Education, Memorial University of Newfoundland.

Cavanaugh, C. (2001). The effectiveness of interactive distance education technologies in K-12 learning: A meta-analysis. *International Journal of Educational Telecommunications, 7*(1), 73-88.

Cey, R. (2001). *Technology use in rural Saskatchewan: Opportunities and challenges* (unpublished manuscript). Saskatchewan, Canada: University of Saskatchewan, Saskatchewan, Canada. Retrieved June 26, 2006, from http://www.usask.ca/education/coursework/802papers/ceyr/ceyr.pdf

Copyright © 2007, Idea Group Inc. Copying or distributing in print or electronic forms without written permission of Idea Group Inc. is prohibited.

Coffin, G. (2002). *Mediating e-learning: M-teacher or m-team?* Newfoundland: Centre for Distance Learning and Innovation, Department of Education of Newfoundland and Labrador, St John's.

Collis, B. (1996). *Telelearning in a digital world: The future of distance learning.* London: Thompson Computer Press.

Ertl, H., & Plante, J. (2004). *Connectivity and learning in Canada's schools.* Ottawa: Statistics Canada, Government of Canada. Retrieved June 26, 2006, from http://www.statcan.ca/english/research/56F0004MIE/56F0004MIE2004011.pdf

Government of Newfoundland and Labrador. (2000). *Supporting learning: Report on the ministerial panel on educational delivery in the classroom.* St John's, NL, Department of Education.

Griffin, D., & Sherrod, B. (2005). *Technology use in rural high schools improves opportunity for student achievement.* Southern Regional Education Board, Atlanta, GA. Retrieved June 26, 2006, from http://www.sreb.org/programs/EdTech/pubs/PDF/05T01-TechnologyUseinRuralHS/pdf

Hawkes, M., & Halverson, P. (2002) Technology facilitation in the rural school: An analysis of options. *Journal of Research in Rural Education, 17*(3), 162-170.

Healey, D., & Stevens, K. (2002). Student access to information technology and perceptions of future opportunities in two small labrador communities. *Canadian Journal of Learning and Technology/La Revue Canadienne de l'Apprentissage et de la Technologie, 28*(1), 7-18.

Information Highway Advisory Council. (1995). *The challenge of the information highway.* Ottawa: Industry Canada.

Information Highway Advisory Council. (1997). *Preparing Canada for a digital world.* Ottawa: Industry Canada.

Lowther, D., Ross, S., & Morrison, G. (2003). When each has one: The influences on teaching strategies and student achievement of using laptops in the classroom. *Educational Technology Research and Development, 51*(3), 23-44.

Mathiasen, H. (2004). Expectations of technology: When the intensive application of IT in teaching becomes a possibility. *Journal of Research on Technology in Education, 36*(3), 273-294.

Norris, C., & Solloway, E. (2004). Envisioning the handheld-centric classroom. *Journal of Educational Computing Research, 30*(4), 281-294.

Rockman, S. (2003). Learning from laptops. *Threshold, 1*(1), 24-28.

Russell, M., Bebell, D., & Higgins, J. (2004). Laptop learning: A comparison of teaching and learning in upper elementary classrooms equipped with shared carts of laptops and permanent 1:1 laptops. *Journal of Educational Computing Research, 30*(4), 313-330.

Schraer, W.D., & Stoltze, H.J. (1995). *Biology: The study of life.* Englewood Cliffs, NJ: Prentice Hall.

Copyright © 2007, Idea Group Inc. Copying or distributing in print or electronic forms without written permission of Idea Group Inc. is prohibited.

Stefansdottir, L. (1993). The Icelandic educational network—Ismennt. In G. Davies & B. Samways (Eds.), *Teleteaching—Proceedings of the IFIP TC3 Third Teleteaching Conference* (pp. 829-835). Amsterdam: Elsevier Science Publishers.

Stevens, K.J. (1994). Australian developments in distance education and their implications for rural schools. *Journal of Research in Rural Education, 10*(1), 78–83.

Stevens, K.J. (1995a). Geographic isolation and technological change: A new vision of teaching and learning in rural schools in New Zealand. *The Journal of Distance Learning, 1*(1) 32-38.

Stevens, K.J. (1995b). The technological challenge to the notion of rurality in New Zealand Education—Repositioning the small school. In I. Livingstone (Ed.), *New Zealand Annual Review of Education, 5*, 93-102.

Stevens, K. (1998). *The Vista Digital Intranet: Initial observations on the teaching of Advanced Placement biology, chemistry, mathematics and physics* (Report 1 to the Vista School District Intranet Advisory Committee, p. 10).

Stevens, K. (1999). *The Vista Digital Intranet—A model for the organization of virtual classes* (Final Report on the Vista Digital Intranet). Presented to the Information Highways Applications Branch, Industry Canada, Ottawa.

Stevens, K. (2000). Télé-enseignement et éducation en milieu rural en Nouvelle Zélande et à Terre Neuve. (Telelearning and the education of rural students in New Foundland and New Zealand). *Géocarrefour -Revue de Geographie de Lyon -Espaces Ruraux et Technologies de L'Information, 75*(1), 87-92.

Stevens, K. (2001). The development of digital Intranets for the enhancement of education in rural communities. *Journal of Interactive Instruction Development, 13*(3), 19-24.

Stevens, K., Piper, T., & Power, D. (1998). *From closed to open classes—TeleLearning and the management of isolation in Newfoundland and Labrador.* Presented to the TeleLearning Network of Centres of Excellence (TL.NCE) Vancouver, British Columbia, Canada.

Stevens, K., Power, D., & Barry, M. (1999). *State of the art in K-12: Research advances in teaching and learning science in rural Newfoundland schools.* Presented to the TeleLearning Network of Centres of Excellence (TL.NCE), Montreal, Quebec.

Stevens, K.J., & Stewart, D. (2005). *Cybercells—Learning in actual and virtual groups.* Melbourne: Thompson-Dunmore.

Van Manen, M. (2002). The pedagogical task of teaching. *Teaching and Teacher Education,18*(2), 135-138.

Copyright © 2007, Idea Group Inc. Copying or distributing in print or electronic forms without written permission of Idea Group Inc. is prohibited.

Chapter XII

Role of ICT in Development Process:
A Review of Issues and Prospects in South Asia

Dilip Dutta, University of Sydney, Australia

Abstract

Empirical studies that focus on impact of ICT for development usually make a distinction between ICT as a production sector and ICT as an enabler of socioeconomic development. Although the developed countries are reaping very high benefits from the ICT, its diffusion in developing countries has been limited. It is often argued that for developing countries benefits from ICTs are more likely to accrue from consumption rather than production. In the context of the selected five South Asian countries, the ICT penetration is relatively very low, although there have been some success stories in software production sector and IT-enabled service sector in the region. Generally speaking, the author argues that the developing countries need to integrate ICT policies more closely into economic strategies, which can be done by strengthening the links between development and technology agencies via the organizational structure of policy-making bodies.

Copyright © 2007, Idea Group Inc. Copying or distributing in print or electronic forms without written permission of Idea Group Inc. is prohibited.

Introduction

Capacity to use conventional technologies varies from country to country and often tends to be location or industry specific. This limitation has been more prominent in developing countries due to a number of reasons. First, imported technologies may not always be appropriate to their endowments of labor or technical skills, or to their scales of operation. Second, limited scope for diffusion of knowledge and imperfect market competition restrict assimilation of these technologies in these countries. Third, inability to upgrade the technologies they utilize into new technologies to suit in new conditions. Finally, many other circumstantial situations play important role in hindering the transition that may or may not be visible. Technological capabilities (technical, managerial, and institutional) in the industrial sector, therefore, become more often enterprise specific accumulated skills with a tendency for their technical efficiency to lag behind world technological frontiers. As a result, many developing countries may have stayed at, what Lall (1993, p. 20) calls, "low value added end of the industrial spectrum, falling behind world technological frontiers as others forge ahead."

Over the past two decades or so, the application of new technologies especially, information and communication technology(ICT),[1] has been credited for its positive role in economic growth and development. Although the developed countries are reaping very high benefits from the ICT, its diffusion in developing counties is still very limited. The role of ICT as a means for accelerating development in underdeveloped and developing societies has been lately questioned especially in terms of their social capacity to process and use the growing volume of information for the society as a whole. While assessing the potential development impacts of ICT many pertinent issues are often raised that include (Morales-Gomez & Melesse, 1998, p. 2):

- who benefits and who loses from the introduction of these technologies;
- how can ICT be made useful and meaningful to the developing countries' poor majority who are struggling to meet their basic needs;
- what are the social and cultural opportunities and risks they present;
- how can developing countries meaningfully adopt these technologies while lessening their undesirable social and cultural consequences?

ICT and Economic Globalization: Emerging Trends

The new technologies such as information and communication technology (ICT), biotechnology, nanotechnology, and so forth, have been contributing to the rapid transformation particularly of the developed societies. The ICT is, however, singled out as the most pervasive technical innovation of the post Second World War era in the sense that it gives rise to a wide range of new products and services, its applications affect almost all sectors of an economy, it generates strong industrial interest as a means for profitability and competitive advantage,

Copyright © 2007, Idea Group Inc. Copying or distributing in print or electronic forms without written permission of Idea Group Inc. is prohibited.

and it gains widespread social acceptance (Avgerou, 1998). ICT is classified as a "general purpose technology" and, therefore, it is a form of drastic technological innovation that can be applied to a wide range of sectors with dramatic change in their existing modes of operations (Helpman, 1998). As Prakash (2002) further elaborates, ICT has wide applicability in various manufacturing and services sectors. It has strong spread effects and extensive linkages with the rest of the economy. However, its potential forward linkages extend to custom made configuration while its backward linkages extend to material sciences.

ICT includes a heterogeneous series of products and services including semiconductors, voice telephony technologies, and technologies supporting high speed data and audio visual systems, as well as computers and packaged and customized software (Mansell, 1999). Starting from the birth of the Internet in the late 1960s, advents of e-mail in the late 1970s, domain name system in the 1980s, the World Wide Web in the 1990s, and repository/portal concepts in the 2000s are the popular applications of ICT, which have emerged as powerful tools for business and development. Afterwards, ICT has integrated computing, communications, and graphics through digitalization. It has thrived on Web sites with the use of broadband optical-fiber lines and made headway into wireless mode. It is becoming more and more personalized with greater use of personal digital aids (PDAs) (Prakash, 2002).

Although there are differences in the definitions of ICT, there is general consensus that the main ICT components (already in existence and expected to be added in the near future) such as sensors and detectors, control and display systems, and so forth, are all interconnected with computers and knowledge-based systems, and do function interdependently and, thereby, form an intelligent communication network. This network becomes the main force behind a national information infrastructure and is linked to its global counterpart. Along with globalizing forces of the world economy, today's progress in ICT has been creating a new paradigm of network age with clear advantage over the industrial age. The implication of this historic shift, as has been summarized in *Human Development Report* (2001), is as follows:

Structures of production and other activities have been reorganized into networks that span the world. In the industrial age—with its high costs of information access, communications and transportation—businesses and organizations were vertically integrated. In the network age, with the costs of communications and information down to almost zero, horizontal networks make sense. Production is increasingly organized among separate players—subcontractors, suppliers, laboratories, management consultants, education and research institutes, marketing research firms, distributors. Their complex interactions, with each playing a niche role, create the value chains that drive the technology-based global economy. (p. 31)

Since the early 1980s, there have been two major trends visible in the globalizing world:

- A strong interaction between market & technology related factors.
- Shifting of the determining factors of competitiveness towards social and economic institutional characteristics of a country.

Copyright © 2007, Idea Group Inc. Copying or distributing in print or electronic forms without written permission of Idea Group Inc. is prohibited.

Technology related factors, such as componentization of production, facilitated by advancement in both manufacturing technologies and ICT have led to lowering costs and making geographical distances irrelevant (ESCAP, 1999). Market related factors such as increased competition for resources in the production of the same products, greater engagement in international trade, enhanced effort to attract foreign direct investments, etc., have been greatly influenced by technological as well as information-related innovations. Along this process, the multi-national corporations (MNCs) in both production and service sectors have been exerting competitive pressures on domestic firms and, thereby, leading to some pattern of technological specialization in their favor. For instance, the multi-national retail giants such as Wal-Mart, Metro, Target, and Tesco have recently issued directives to the Indian suppliers to replace bar codes with radio frequency identification (RFID) technology. To the retail giants, RFID is fast emerging as the best option for keeping costs low. Embedded in plastic product tags, RFID chips can track goods, signal the need for restocking, and thus boost supply efficiency. This has caused domestic companies' sleepless nights simply because the cost of RFID labels will squeeze their profit margins. In fact, the cost of one RFID tag results in a loss of about 30 U.S. cents (Jayeswal & Verma, 2005).

Regarding other major trends in the globalizing world, the physical infrastructure, the rules and regulations (applied to business and individuals), the degree of transparency, perception of fairness (or lack of corruption), the investment climate and functioning of the legal system, and so forth, have lately become important elements for inducing investments in the production of goods and services. Technology and skilled labor can move easily as usual, but ability of a country to be competitive in the contemporary globalizing world depends more and more on the above infrastructural, as well as social, legal and various institutional factors.

ICT and its impact on Economic Growth

OECD (1989) and ESCAP (1999) reiterate at least four dimensions of the positive contribution of ICT to economic growth in the globalizing world:

- **ICT allows process innovation (new ways of doing old things)**. Smaller, faster, and cheaper ICT helps to reduce the cost-to-performance (output) ratio of its application and, thereby increases productivity level. Use of ICT could also promote more efficient utilization of inputs such as raw materials, energy and land. Some new applications of ICT may not only make products economical, but also help to customize them. Drawing closer attention to customer's tastes and preferences with the help of ICT, producers could increase the value added (usefulness and appeal) to their products and, thereby improve their quality. The adoption and dissemination of ICT could also contribute to the formation of networks which, in turn, likely to lead to innovation.

- **ICT helps to generate innovative economic activities (new ways of doing new things).** Various new applications of ICT do now allow some small scale production and service activities to be carried out efficiently both within a country and across borders. These have assisted the creation of new opportunities for regional and global subcontracting, and the decentralization and globalization forces have greatly enhanced

Copyright © 2007, Idea Group Inc. Copying or distributing in print or electronic forms without written permission of Idea Group Inc. is prohibited.

the speed of this process. Through organizational changes made possible by ICT, developing countries may plan for better spatial distribution of economic activities, especially those industrial and service operations centralized in large cities.

- **ICT can lead to economic restructuring through being a new factor of production (in addition to the conventional factors of land, labor and capital).** With the help of new and varied applications of ICT, a rapid integration of markets across countries has been taking place through the transmission of market signals and consumer/producer responses. As a result, market horizons are becoming broader, with more information available on the nature of various markets, retail outlets, electronic linkages to clients and distributors, and so forth. More and more producers with computer-assisted design are now capable of responding to market signals with greater flexibility and speed. Their capability to provide consumers with tailor-made products and services and to create market niches has, therefore, been increasing. Built-in software and "intelligence" in many products, automatic diagnosis of malfunctions, and electronically assisted after-sales service help to increase their adaptability and substitutability, which, in turn, increases competition. The resulting competition and the pressures of market integration in the globalizing world have compelled most large-scale manufacturers to go global in terms of sources of inputs, markets and competitors.

- **ICT adds a new means of organizing various activities through its synergies with other technologies.** ICT has revolutionized the marketing systems for commodities on international markets due to producers' instantaneous access to the prices of their products on a real time basis through mobile phones, the Internet, facsimile machine, and so on. The nature and structure of the services sector have also undergone drastic changes as a result of various ICT enabled improvements made in the speed, reliability and cost of processing vast quantities of information related to financial, inventory and sales. Generally speaking, flexible automation technologies and organizational innovations are being combined into new best practice manufacturing systems and service providers. All the above potential contributions of ICT could directly increase a nation's economic growth and indirectly influence (through multiplier effect) its price and income structures.

ICT as a Tool for Socioeconomic Development of the Developing Countries

Several studies including reports by the United Nations Development Program (*Human Development Report*, 2001), the United Nations Educational, Scientific and Cultural Organisation (UNESCO, 2004), the World Bank (*World Development Report, 1998/99*), the Organisation for Economic Cooperation and Development (OECD, 2004) have identified specific socioeconomic areas within developing countries where ICT can have potential impact. Among these, poverty alleviation, empowerment of socially and economically disadvantaged, agricultural and rural development, population and human resource development, and infrastructural development are important. Lopez and Vilaseca (1996) and Mansell (1999), among others, have listed several sector specific impact of ICT application in developing countries:

Copyright © 2007, Idea Group Inc. Copying or distributing in print or electronic forms without written permission of Idea Group Inc. is prohibited.

- **Industrial sector:** Creation of new industries (in the form of microelectronics and software-based products) or the integration of IT with other technologies (biotechnology) has enabled some developing countries to modernize traditionally "low tech" and labor intensive industries by taking significant steps towards closing the technology gap. Many Asian and Pacific developing economies have been successful in this direction in the areas of ICT industry's hardware production, particularly personal computer (PC), as well as software development and services. The success of South Korea and Taiwan lies in their supply of ICT products and components to the world market, while that of Hong Kong and Singapore is in ICT related trading and manufacturing. Subsequently, Malaysia, Thailand and recently China have all followed suit in ICT related manufacturing and packaging. India has emerged as a world leader in software development since the mid 1990s.

- **Service sector:** Adoption of technologies and changes in service sector technologies has major implications for developing countries. This is due to their impact on fundamental process and organizational changes in different areas including product distribution, financial services, engineering, insurance, marketing, transports, and so forth. This impact is, however, not restricted only on economies, it has certainly spillover effects on education, consumer behavior, and quality of life. Many developing countries which have relatively large pool of skilled or semiskilled labour force with some knowledge of English language are found to excel in the IT enabled service activities. These activities include various types of services such as handling of large volumes of marketing and post sale service related telephone communications with existing or potential customers (call centers); data entry, transcription or digitalization, insurance claim processing, compilation of abstracts, and typesetting for publishing companies, design and maintenance of Web sites (business process centers); preparation and collation of research materials (technical support centers), and so forth.

- **Public sector:** Because this sector is highly information dependent, ICT has a very far reaching impact on it. ICT is being increasingly applied to different processes used by governments in developing countries. These processes include policy making, planning and budgeting, debt management, macroeconomic analysis, community participation, monitoring the quality of provided services, implementing new services, and overall, financial accountability and control. "Given the developmental potential of ICTs, there is," as Morales-Gomez and Melesse (1998, p. 2) argue, "a growing trend among industrialized countries, governments, large transnational corporations, donor agencies, and international organizations to see these technologies as a panacea to underdevelopment."

Avgerou (1998) warned that, the developing countries may face several problems in introducing ICTs in different sectors with the adoption of economic and organizational forms that have been transferred from the industrialized countries. There is no unique proven "best practice" or best policy that could be locally effective for achieving socioeconomic benefits from ICT diffusion. Here comes the notion of "appropriate technology" that is also relevant in this context.[2] Among many of its comparative advantages, availability of local managerial and technical skills, cultural proximity of producers to intended customers, existence of institutionalized user producer networks, and accumulated tacit knowledge are notable. However, adoption of economic mechanisms and organizational practices from the "postin-

Copyright © 2007, Idea Group Inc. Copying or distributing in print or electronic forms without written permission of Idea Group Inc. is prohibited.

dustrial" world may connect organizations of developing countries to the global business, but it may not guarantee them a competitive position in the global economy.

In the following section on impact of ICT in South Asia, the author will draw some attention to how the policy makers are making efforts to ensure the co-ordination of ICT policies could maximize the spillover effects across the society.

ICT Related Policy Initiatives and their Developmental Impact in South Asia

Empirical studies that focus on impact of ICT for development usually make a distinction between ICT as a *production sector* and ICT as an *enabler of socioeconomic development*. ICT as a production element (including ICT enabled production services) for commercial use requires huge capital (physical and human) investments in information infrastructures (including telecommunications), hardware and software. At the same time, ICT as an *enabler of socioeconomic development* requires increased ICT consumption (public and private). However, as preconditions private consumption in developing countries depends largely on public investment in ICT infrastructure, and type of ICT strategy adopted for harnessing wider development objectives. For these reasons, Pigato (2001) argued that "for developing countries benefits from ICTs are more likely to accrue from consumption rather than production" (p. 4).

This section focuses on ICT policy initiatives in the developing nations. To make it more realistic and reach out the largest base of low-income communities, the region of South Asia has been selected. Though in terms of ICT development, a few Asian countries emerge as giants, but South Asia is yet to remain as one of the two poorest regions (with very high incidence of absolute poverty) of the world, the other one being Sub-Saharan Africa. To compare the ICT development in South Asian region, several indicators have been chosen. As shown in Table 1 below, this region has very low intensity of ICT consumption per 1000 inhabitants. Sri Lanka leads ahead in its overall ICT consumption intensity among the five selected South Asian countries, although recently India and Pakistan tend to move ahead of others in Internet users per 1,000 inhabitants and Internet hosts per 1,000 inhabitants, respectively.

On the production front of the information technology (IT) industry,[3] India has early success in software sector since the mid 1990s, and then in IT enabled service sector since the beginning of the new millennium. Some of the other South Asian countries have either made similar attempt or have been following the transition. However, before analyzing India's success story, a brief information on recent ICT profile for each of the other four selected South Asian countries (Bangladesh, Nepal, Pakistan, and Sri Lanka) will be given first.

Copyright © 2007, Idea Group Inc. Copying or distributing in print or electronic forms without written permission of Idea Group Inc. is prohibited.

Table 1. ICT at a glance in selected South Asian countries

	Bangladesh			India			Nepal			Pakistan			Sri Lanka		
	1997	2001	2004	1997	2001	2004	1997	2001	2004	1997	2001	2004	1997	2001	2004
Telephone main lines (per 1,000 inhabitants)	3.0	4.3	5.5	19.0	37.5	40.7	8.0	13.1	15.6	19.0	22.8	31.0	17.0	44.2	51.4
Telephone subscribers (per 1,000 inhabitants)	n.a.	8.3	34.4	n.a.	43.8	84.4	n.a.	13.9	22.5	n.a.	28.5	62.7	n.a.	79.8	166.2
Cellular mobile subscribers (per 1,000 inhabitants)	0	4.0	28.9	1	6.3	43.7	0	0.8	7	1	5.7	31.9	6	35.6	114.7
Personal computers (per 1,000 inhabitants)	n.a.	1.9	11	2.1	5.8	12.1	n.a.	3.5	4.6	n.a.	4.2	n.a.	4.1	9.3	27.5
Internet hosts* (per 1,000 inhabitants)	n.a.	n.a.	n.a.	0.013†	0.081	0.13	0.00†	0.067	0.11	0.023†	0.079	0.165	0.029†	0.122	0.107
Internet users (per 1,000 inhabitants)	n.a.	1.42	2	n.a.	6.82	32.4	n.a.	2.64	6.8	n.a.	3.51	13.2	n.a.	8.01	14.5

Source: International Telecommunication Union (www.itu.int/ITU-D/ict/statistics); World Development Report 1999/2000, World Bank, Table 19 (for 1997 figures).

Notes: * "Internet hosts" are computers connected directly to the world wide network and are not necessarily physically located in the country; many computer users can access the Internet through a single host; † Figures correspond to January 1999 earliest available from Table 19 of WDR, 1999/2000.

Copyright © 2007, Idea Group Inc. Copying or distributing in print or electronic forms without written permission of Idea Group Inc. is prohibited.

Bangladesh

Although sales of ICT related consumer products such as mobile phones, desktop computers, modems, networking equipment, and so forth, have been increasing fast, the use of ICT has remained confined mainly to entertainment, voice communication, and basic Internet access for browsing and e-mail. The Bangladesh Telecommunications Regulatory Commission (BTRC) has reported that there were 150 registered Internet Service Provider (ISP) licence holders (not necessarily operational) at the end of 2003. Among these lincensees, 14 were registered as "nationwide service providers." Apart from ISPs, four registered Very Small Aperture Terminal (VSAT) hub operators had planned to provide satellite terminal and gateway services in December 2003, but a year later only one of them was open for business providing services to financial institutions (Haque, 2005/2006).

As Islam (2005) writes, Bangladesh seems to be waiting for a take off in ICT. Bangladesh's skilled labor force with expertise in ICT is growing. Training centers, computer institutes, and both private and public universities are all increasingly contributing to this pool of technical labor force. The present government had approved the National ICT policy in October 2002 with the objective of building an ICT driven knowledge based society. An ICT Task Force with the Prime Minister as its chairperson has also been created for making policy decisions related to various ICT activities. It is expected that the recently established Incubation Center at Kawranbazar in the capital, Dhaka, with data transmission facility and uninterrupted electric supply, will attract companies involved in software and IT enabled services. Establishment of a planned high-tech park with all modern infrastructural facilities at Kaliakair near Dhaka will certainly boost ICT industry and ICT related developmental impacts in Bangladesh.

There seems to have a general feeling that the overall growth of the ICT industry in Bangladesh had been hampered during 2003-2004 due to lack of coordination and cooperation between private and public sector agencies (Haque, 2005/2006). However a recent Springboard Research study[4] on the Bangladesh IT market finds that its domestic IT spending amounted to US$235 million, an increase of 9% over the previous year, despite various obstacles such as natural disasters, economic setbacks, political instability, and social unrest. The IT market in Bangladesh is largely dependent on hardware, which represents more than 75% of total IT spending. The software market is stifled by the early state of market development and prevalent piracy, which exceeds 90% in the consumer market. The government sector accounts for over 40% of total spending, and the investment by non governmental organizations (NGOs) such as World Bank, Asian Development Bank, and so forth, is a major driver for market expansion. Apart from these two key market segments, the finance and telecommunications industries also play vital role. These four segments together represent over 70% of total ICT spending in the country.

Nepal

After the launching of IT Policy 2000, Nepal's progress in its implementation has been slow. "However, some of the key national initiatives to develop the ICT infrastructure, such as the construction of the first IT park and the information superhighway, are," as Pandey and

Copyright © 2007, Idea Group Inc. Copying or distributing in print or electronic forms without written permission of Idea Group Inc. is prohibited.

Shrestha (2005/2006, p. 1) note, "on the verge of completion." Among the recent efforts taken by the government include establishment of telecenters, licensing of private rural telecommunications operators, liberalization of the telecommunications market, enactment of the long-awaited Electronic Transactions Act in 2004, and so forth. One of the important initiatives taken by the Ministry of Science and Technology in line with the IT Policy 2000 was on human resource development (HRD). Accordingly, the ministry was determined to make sure that sufficient number of people trained at the semiskilled, skilled, and advanced levels could be made available for employment in ICT sector. A long term ambitious program with the slogan "Computer education to all by 2010 A.D." has also been formulated. Five Nepalese universities are offering IT related courses. The total number of private firms engaged in IT sector exceeds 1,000. The majority of these firms are concentrated in Kathmandu Valley and more than half provide various types of training in ICTs. There are about 15 software development companies. Five or six of these companies are export oriented, while the rest cater to the limited demand of the local market (APDIP, 2005).

The number of Internet users has increased sharply in the recent years (see Table 1), due to the private sector's leading role in introducing Internet services. The private sector first connected Nepal to the Internet in 1995. Since then, 12 ISPs have begun their operations in the country, 5 of them are VSAT providers. Although all of the 12 municipalities in Nepal are served by ISPs, but most of the subscribers and users are concentrated in capital Kathmandu. The state owned Nepal Telecommunications Corporation had been attempting to set up 1,000 VSAT connections for rural telephony with the aim of providing at least two telephones to each Village Development Committee by 2004. The United Nations Development Program (UNDP) and the Nepalese government have recently signed an agreement to run a US$625,000 two-year pilot project in ICTs (APDIP, 2005).

Pakistan

As a continuation of the IT Policy 2000, the new government of Pakistan which took office in November 2002 has taken a number of initiatives for ICT development. Masood (2005/2006) notes that the current government has been supporting ICT development with a two-pronged strategy. The first part of the strategy aims at generating work for the local ICT industry which is still reeling from the 2001-2002 economic downturn. The second part is designed to assist the small and medium enterprises (SMEs) so that they can embrace ICT to enhance their performance and competitiveness. The Telecom Deregulation Policy approved in 2003 has been taking effect in recent years in terms of the opening up of the telecommunication sector to major investors. Two new cellular licenses have been awarded in April 2004 resulting in an accelerating growth of cellular networks (Table 1).

Pakistan Telecommunication Company Limited (PTCL), the exclusive provider of telecommunication services, is the major Internet backbone in the country. National Telecommunication Corporation (NTC) is the organization entrusted with the responsibility of providing telecommunication services to government agencies and designated users. NTC is deploying a countrywide automatic teller machine (ATM) based multiservices data network capable of carrying voice, video, and multimedia traffic. In addition to public sector operators, there are 80 private sector ISPs and nationwide data communication network operators who provide Internet access in all major cities of Pakistan. Already, more than 1,800 cities and towns

Copyright © 2007, Idea Group Inc. Copying or distributing in print or electronic forms without written permission of Idea Group Inc. is prohibited.

have been connected to the Internet and plans to expand this service are progressing. The use of broadband services has also started to grow in households and offices mainly located in major cities (APDIP, 2005).

Following Masood (2005/2006), an overall state of Pakistan's ICT development and related issues in the recent past has been summarized here. As he mentioned, the ICT sector appeared to have shrunk during the first half of 2004 when a number of ICT companies had closed their operation. This seemed to be partly due to the spillover effect of the global dotcom crash and partly due to geopolitical insecurity. Also, the *e-commerce* and *e-government* initiatives, which were the core of the ICT industry development strategy during 2000-2001, could not achieve much success apparently due to low inertia in government's own system. Meanwhile, the human resource development (HRD) initiative has achieved mixed results. Universities and other educational institutions have been upgraded, and a critical mass of people has been trained in various facets of ICT. However, the pilot programs adopted in these critical areas started to act as agents of change during the second half of 2004 and saw some revival of the ICT industry, especially the outsourcing segment. The companies that survived the downturn during 2001-2002 have emerged to be more focused in terms of their strategies. New firms have also sprouted to capitalize the new opportunities of outsourcing. A number of companies have set up call center operations to provide back office services to foreign-based companies. It is expected that this segment of the ICT services market will grow in the years to come because of favorable business climate.

Sri Lanka

As could be seen from Table 1, Sri Lanka has the highest tele-density (both land line and mobile) and ownership of personal computers in the region. About 70% of the country's communication infrastructure is, however, concentrated in the Western Province where the country's capital, Colombo, is located. ICT proliferation outside Greater Colombo is still limited. In the case of Internet density, India seems to have overtaken Sri Lanka in 2004 (Table 1). Sri Lanka, which ranks first in South Asia on the Human Development Index (HDI), has a large pool of skilled labor force, as well as an open business culture to global partners and investors. Low cost offshore data entry operations have thrived in Sri Lanka since the early 1980s. The Sri Lankan Government has actively encouraged the spread of computer literacy by providing custom duty concessions on hardware imports and introducing appropriate data transmission systems. Also, in many cases, a large Sri Lankan Diaspora has brought in their knowledge, contacts, and capital back to help integrate companies into the global market of software and tele-services (SLICTA, 2004).

Seven universities in Sri Lanka produce graduates in engineering, electronics, and computer science. In addition, four institutes provide training in electronics. Sri Lanka has recently gained recognition as a competitive choice for top quality ICT outsourcing and call centers in the region of South Asia. Currently, Sri Lanka's ICT industry has an estimated export earning of U.S. $100 million and has a potential for growth in both ICT and ICT-enabled service industry. About 80 software development companies are in operation. Most of them started their operation since 1996, when the Board of Investment (BOI) offered special incentives in the form of tax holidays and duty free imports for software exporters. Sri Lanka also acts as an offshore development center for companies in USA, UK, Ireland, Australia,

Copyright © 2007, Idea Group Inc. Copying or distributing in print or electronic forms without written permission of Idea Group Inc. is prohibited.

and so forth, and joint venture development center for those in Sweden, Norway, USA, Japan, and so forth.

As noted in MAIT (2005), "Open Source" software[5] presents an opportunity to revolutionize the ICT industry of Sri-Lanka. Among the 800 committed participators involved in open source projects worldwide, 30 are based in Sri Lanka. The Lanka Software Foundation, a nonprofit organization, has been formed to assist Sri Lanka utilize the opportunities offered by the open source projects. These participators currently operate open source related development laboratories at the Universities of Colombo and Moratuwa, and the Sri Lanka Institute of Information Technology. Among the other significant ICT related initiatives taken in Sri Lanka is the Government's launching of an ICT program in 2003 for the societywide development widely known as *e-Sri Lanka*. Its principal objectives are to foster the local ICT industry, transform the way Government works, improve the quality of life and create opportunities for all Sri Lankans. The first phase of the program focuses on rural connectivity and re-engineering the government. The priority projects for the latter include e-Monitoring, e-Pensions, e-HRM (Human Resource Management), and e-Foreign Employment (MAIT, 2005). As Sri Lanka seems to be gradually recovering from a prolonged civil war, the strategic use of ICT can play a key role to rebuild the country.

India

Significant progress in electronics and computer technology and, therefore, the growth of IT industry has been a major success story in India's economy since the mid 1990s.[6] From 1996-1997 to 2001-2002 the industry's production grew substantially from Rs. 26,640 crore (US$7,504 million) to Rs. 80,884 crore (US$17,324 million).[7] While the share of hardware products and nonsoftware services (such as system integration including packaged application implementation and custom application development) in the IT sector has declined in the recent past, the share of software services in electronics and IT sector has gone up from 38.7% in 1998-99 to 61.8% in 2003-04. Recently, however, there has been some acceleration in the growth of hardware sector. Output of computers in value terms has, for example, increased by 36.0%, 19.7%, and 57.6% in 2000-2001, 2002-2003, and 2003-2004, respectively (Economic Survey 2004-2005, p. 147).

During 1990s, the software sector of India's information technology services (ITS) industry has developed as one of the fastest growing sectors in its economy at the compound annual growth rate (CAGR) of 50%, although India's share in the global IT software and services markets was only 2.4% during 2003-2004. A unique feature of India's IT software industry has been its export orientation. Exports of computer software and IT enabled services[8] have become important sources of India's export earnings in the recent period. The value of India's IT software and services export is estimated to have increased by 30% to US$12.5 billion in 2003-04 (Economic Survey 2004-2005, pp. 147-148). The general thrusts behind the success of the ICT industry have been highly competitive private sector, public investment in human capital, government's support in IT policies in general, and recent telecommunication policy in particular.

Since the beginning of 2001, India's traditional ITS companies have been focusing more on the IT enabled services (ITeS) including business process outsourcing (BPO) components.

Copyright © 2007, Idea Group Inc. Copying or distributing in print or electronic forms without written permission of Idea Group Inc. is prohibited.

The ITeS segment provides people-intensive services that are delivered over telecom networks or Internet to a range of business works and verticals. Services included in this segment are telemarketing, help-desk support, medical transcription, back-office accounting, payroll management, legal database maintenance, insurance claim, and credit card processing. ITeS businesses are operating in India under two categories: *outlocation* services and *outsourcing* services. While the former services are for captive use mainly by foreign companies, the latter ones are through a third-party service provider (*Dataquest*, 2002). Multinational companies such as *General Electric* (GE) that invested in remote services as captive facilities for worldwide group operations have adopted a primarily outlocation focus. But Wipro's *Spectramind*, for example, operates as a pure outsourcing service provider, which is funded by banks and venture capital finance, and operates as a niche of contact centre services for Fortune 200 companies. In fact, the ITeS-BPO segment has quickly emerged as a key source of export growth for India's ITS industry.

Following Karnik (2004), major specific factors (external and internal), responsible for high growth rate of India's ITeS-BPO market can be summarized as follows:

External

- Worldwide advancement in technology and infrastructure maturity, which has allowed more complex processes to be off-shored.

- Rapidly improving communications infrastructure for data and voice has enabled this trend to gain pace.

- Competitive pressures faced by global organizations which have been forced to cut costs by outsourcing their non-critical processes.

- Success stories of the BPO route have encouraged other global organizations to opt for the same.

Internal

- Efficiency and productivity improvements achieved by the major Indian outsourcing companies have helped them speed up operations and provide 24x7 customer services.

- Indian IT companies' access to skilled manpower with specific domain knowledge including English-language ability at relatively lower costs is also another advantage.

- Indian IT industry's accelerated pace of consolidation and service convergence has helped stabilize the ITeS-BPO market.

- Success stories of Indian IT companies that have been able to focus on their core business and optimize existing processes by taking the BPO route have been an inspiration to other Indian organizations to follow suit as well.

However, at the same time, the success of the Indian ITeS-BPO sector due to above factors is also creating challenges in order to maintain its current momentum. Again, following Karnik (2004), some of the major challenges can be noted as follows:

Copyright © 2007, Idea Group Inc. Copying or distributing in print or electronic forms without written permission of Idea Group Inc. is prohibited.

- Because of inadequate ICT infrastructure support, a number of small and medium sized BPO companies have not yet achieved the world class status in terms of communication and other physical infrastructure, which could create shortfalls in this sector's overall service level.

- Performance gap between the top-of-the-line and mediocre suppliers needs to be closely looked into, especially when the lower-rung vendors are also achieving scales, quality levels and portfolio of services by matching to those of the more reputed providers.

- A significant challenge facing Indian BPO vendors today is to cope and successfully combat the backlash against outsourcing, which is creating a negative sentiment for the activity, particularly in the U.S.

- Human resource issues are arising especially in the case of high attrition level, lack of relevant manpower availability and also maintaining the satisfactory level of work environment.

- The Indian ITeS-BPO sector's profit margin seems to be shrinking due to the emergence of competitors especially from China, the Philippines, Vietnam, Ghana, Czechoslovakia, Poland, Romania, Bulgaria, Slovakia, and others.

The increasing importance and growth of ITeS-BPO activities in India have led to specific policy initiatives for this particular segment. These include measures, to name a few, for adjusting the regulatory and legal framework, rationalizing tax provisions, and improving communication infrastructure. The government is also actively involved in a proper settlement of the backlash against outsourcing through General Agreement of Trade in Services (GATS) negotiations at the World Trade Organization (WTO) level.

In order to meet the challenge of zero custom duty regime in 2005 under the Information Technology Agreement (ITA-1), a number of initiatives have recently been taken by the Indian government. Tariffs on raw materials, parts, other inputs and capital goods have been rationalized to make domestic hardware manufacturing viable and competitive. For example, customs duty on computer parts, static converters for automatic data processing machines and parts thereof has been fully exempted during 2004-2005. Also, computers have been exempted from excise duty (Economic Survey: 2004-2005, pp. 148-49).

Regarding initiatives on ICT as an *enabler* of socioeconomic development, the Department of Information Technology has taken up the following steps:

- An ambitious program of PC and Internet penetration to the rural and underserved urban areas has been launched.

- A program to establish State Wide Area Network (SWAN) up to the block level to provide connectivity for e-governance has been announced.

- Community Information Centers (CICs) have been set up in hilly, far-flung areas of the North-East and Jammu and Kashmir to facilitate the spread of ICT related benefits.

- setting up of CICs in other hilly, far-flung areas of Uttaranchal, Andaman, and Nicobar and Lakshadweep has also been proposed (Indian Economic Survey: 2004-2005, pp. 148-49).

Copyright © 2007, Idea Group Inc. Copying or distributing in print or electronic forms without written permission of Idea Group Inc. is prohibited.

Role of Networking Process[9]

Like most of the developed countries, the developing countries need to integrate ICT policies more closely into societal development strategies. This can be done by strengthening the links between, for example, economic development and technology agencies via the organizational structure of policy-making bodies. Here comes the importance of appropriate networking process at national, regional, and international levels. In the context of South Asia, the countries belonging to the *South Asian Association for Regional Cooperation* (SAARC), a regional institution called the SAARC Agricultural Information Centre (SAIC), has been functioning in Dhaka since January 1989. Because the problems and prospects of agriculture and ecology of the SAARC countries are more or less the same, its main objective is sharing information mutually for the advancement of agriculture, livestock, fisheries, forestry, and allied disciplines. Recently, the SAARC Governing Board has prioritized a program called "SAICNet" with its following specific objectives (SAIC, 2004):

1.   Develop Web-based information network that will bring in the synergy of the potential collaborators of SAIC.

2.   Establish a gateway mechanism to improve access to agricultural information, which is relevant for researchers, extensionists, policy makers, educationists, students and agribusiness entrepreneurs and through them to the end user, the farmers in the SAARC region.

3.   Capture, organize, and disseminate information, wherever it is available, that is relevant for agricultural development in SAARC region.

4.   Design and introduce value added services that are based on the ever-changing information needs of the users.

5.   Improve use-friendly access to SAIC's information services on the Web site that will lead to increased relevance and use of information.

6.   Expose and train SAIC staff on the tools and technologies related to Web development and networking.

7.   Enhance network activities with the participation of collaborative institutions in sharing information and knowledge resources.

Effectiveness of similar objectives as the above also depends on appropriate networking process among various country specific governmental and non-governmental institutions on the one hand, and the national and regional ICT networks on the other hand. Many non-governmental institutions which have been engaged in introducing ICT for the benefit of rural/urban masses include, among others, *Sustainable Development Networking Program* (SDNP) in Bangladesh, *M.S. Swaminathan Research Foundation* in India, *International Centre for Integrated Mountain Development* (ICIMOD) in Nepal, *All Pakistan Women Association* (APWA) in Pakistan and *Sarvodaya Shramadana Movement* in Sri Lanka. Similarly, various national/regional ICT network agencies have helped different institutions in the South Asian countries to adopt ICT as a means to address their developmental

Copyright © 2007, Idea Group Inc. Copying or distributing in print or electronic forms without written permission of Idea Group Inc. is prohibited.

activities. The national ICT networks in the South Asian region include *Bangladesh Advanced Education Research & Information Network* (BAERIN), *Bangladesh Research and Educational Network* (BERNET), *ERNET-India*—India's education and research network, *Pakistan Educational Research Network* (PERN), *Lanka Educational And Research Network* (LEARN) of Sri Lanka. Among the regional ICT network agencies, important ones are *South Asian Network Operators Group* (SANOG)—a regional forum, *Pan Asia Networking* (PAN)—a program initiative of the International Development Research Center of Canada, *Asia-Pacific Advanced Networks* (APAN)—a non-profit high-performance network for research and development on advanced next generation applications and services, *Asia Pacific Network Information Centre* (APNIC)—responsible for addressing the challenges of Internet resource distribution in the Asia Pacific region.

Because of a variety of country specific socioeconomic needs and challenges, namely in the areas of health, education, livelihoods, and governance of the South Asian countries in particular or developing countries in general, it is very crucial that the economic development and technological policy making agencies must not only make sure to select the most appropriate ICT available (of course subject to financial constraint), but also try to gather information on the recent technological changes, especially in the area of ICT networks.

Conclusion

Developing countries have different levels of socioeconomic development depending on the structural, institutional and infrastructural constraints at their economic, political, and social levels. In fact, efforts undertaken in a coordinated way with systemic approach seem to have a greater chance for faster socioeconomic development than otherwise. In most cases, level of socioeconomic development has a direct bearing on a country's level of technological development. The recently published UNCTAD's *Information Economy* Report 2005 illustrates that many developing countries are undertaking vigorous efforts to catch up with their more developed partners in the dissemination and use of ICT; it also shows that the gaps are still far too wide and the catching-up far too uneven.

It is true that the ICT as a *production sector* or as an *enabler of socio-economic development* has potential for economic growth and development. Because of the availability of surplus skilled labor force in many developing countries including those in South Asia, there is some prospect for them to participate in the production of the IT services related to ITeS-BPO segment. However, unless the fundamentals as required by the globalizing world are made favorable for this segment, there is little hope for this to happen. Similarly, to take advantage of the ICT as an *enabler of socio-economic development*, the country's strategies and actions must make sure that its marginalized social and economic groups are not left out, otherwise the *digital divide* within the country will choke its overall socio-economic development.

The ICT penetration in five countries selected from the poverty stricken South Asian region can easily be seen to be very low in comparison to the newly industrializing countries (NICs) in other part of Asia. This low ICT penetration also indicates the existence of *digital divide* within each of these countries. What is needed to combat with digital divide that exits

Copyright © 2007, Idea Group Inc. Copying or distributing in print or electronic forms without written permission of Idea Group Inc. is prohibited.

both across various developing regions and within developing countries is "the sustained engagement of national governments, the business sector, and civil society, and the tangible solidarity of the international community" (UNCTAD, 2005, p. xv).

References

APDIP. (2005). *Asia-Pacific development information program*. UNDP. Retrieved June 26, 2006, from http://www.apdip.net

Avgerou, C. (1998). How can IT enable economic growth in developing countries? *Information Technology for Development, 8*(1), 15-28.

Chakraborty, C., & Dutta, D. (2003). Indian software industry: Growth patterns, constraints and government initiatives. In R. Jha (Ed.), *Indian Economic Reforms* (pp. 317-333). New York: Palgrave Macmillan.

Dataquest. (2002, July 29). *IT-enabled services: Indian IT's lone crusader*.

Dutta, D. (2005). Role of science & technology in development process: A review of major historical perspectives and issues. *Ritsumeikan Journal of Asia Pacific Studies, 15*, 11-24.

Dutta, D., & Sekhar, A. (2005). Major Indian ICT firms and their approaches towards achieving quality. In R. Jha (Ed.), *Economic growth, economic performance and welfare in South Asia* (pp. 225-248). New York: Palgrave-Macmillan.

Economic Survey. (2002-2003). New Delhi: Government of India.

Economic Survey. (2004-2005). New Delhi: Government of India.

ESCAP. (1999). *Economic and social survey of Asia and the Pacific 1999*. Economic and Social Commission for Asia and the Pacific, United Nations.

Haque, S.E. (2005/2006). *Digital review of Asia Pacific*. Retrieved June 26, 2006, from http://www.digital-review.org/05_Bangladesh.htm

Helpman, E. (Ed.). (1998). *Introduction: General purpose technologies and economic growth*. Cambridge, MA: MIT Press.

Human Development Report. (2001). *Today's technological transformations—creating the network age* (Ch. 2). UNDP.

International Telecommunication Union. Retrieved June 26, 2006, from http://www.itu.int/ITU-D/ict/statistics

Islam, M.A. (2005, February 15). ICT in Bangladesh: Waiting for a take-off? *The Daily Star*.

Jayaswal, R., & Verma, P. (2005, May 21). Local retailers hit hard by big bros' demand for RFID code. *The Economic Times*.

Karnik, K. (2004, February). *Editorial. BPO Newsline*. National Association of Software and Services Companies (NASSCOM).

Copyright © 2007, Idea Group Inc. Copying or distributing in print or electronic forms without written permission of Idea Group Inc. is prohibited.

Lall, S. (1993). *Understanding technology development. Development and Change*, 24, (pp. 719-753).

Lopez, E., & Vilaseca, M. (1996). IT as a global economic development tool. In E.M. Roche & M.J. Blaine (Eds.), *Information technology, development and policy*. (99. 57-75). England: Avebury.

Manufacturers' Association for Information Technology (MAIT). (2005, July). Sri Lankan ICT Industry. *Country Intelligence, 49*.

Mansell, R. (1999). Information and communication technologies for development: Assessing the potential and the risks. *Telecommunications Policy, 23*, 35-50.

Masood, J. (2005/2006). *Digital review of Asia Pacific*. Retrieved June 26, 2006, from http://www.digital-review.org/05_Pakistan.htm

Morales-Gomez, D., & Melesse, M. (1998). Utilising information and communication technologies for development: *The social dimensions. Information Technology for Development, 8*(1), 3-14.

OECD. (1989). *Information technology and new growth opportunities*. Paris: Author.

OECD. (2004). *Information technology outlook 2004*. Paris: Author.

Pandey, S., & Shrestha, B. (2005/2006). *Digital review of Asia Pacific*. Retrieved June 26, 2006, from http://www.digital-review.org/05_Nepal.htm

Pigato, M. (2001). *Information and communication technology, poverty, and development in sub-Saharan Africa and South Asia*. Africa Region: World Bank.

Prakash, B. (2002). *Information and communication technology in developing countries of Asia. Technology and poverty reduction in Asia and the Pacific*. Manila: Asian Development Bank.

SAIC. (2004). *SAICNet project*. Retrieved June 26, 2006, from http://www.saic-dhaka.org/AnnualReport2004.htm

SLICTA. (2004). *Sri Lanka IT industry. World Information Technology and Services Alliance*. Retrieved June 26, 2006, from http://www.witsa.org/profiles/slicta.htm

UNCTAD. (2005). Information economy report 2005. *United Nations Conference on Trade and Development*, Geneva.

UNESCO. (2004). *ICT innovations for poverty reduction*. United Nations Educational, Scientific and Cultural Organisation.

World Development Report. (1998/1999). *Knowledge for development*. World Bank/Oxford University Press.

World Development Report. (1999/2000). *Entering the 21st century*. World Bank/Oxford University Press.

Copyright © 2007, Idea Group Inc. Copying or distributing in print or electronic forms without written permission of Idea Group Inc. is prohibited.

Endnotes

[1]   Following OECD (2004, p. 63), the term "information and communication technology" (ICT) is broadly used to refer the family of related technologies that process, store, and transmit information by electronic means. The term "information technology" (IT) is narrower and is used to denote computer, software, and related technologies not including communications and network technologies. The boundary between the two is, however, getting increasingly blurred.

[2]   The author (Dutta, 2005, pp. 15-16) has recently summarized the "appropriate technology" movement in the context of earlier industrial technology.

[3]   The term "information technology (IT) industry" generally covers development, production, and services related to IT products. Hence, it contains three basic sub sectors: hardware, software, and services. IT services include those services which result from the use of any IT software over a system of IT products for realizing value addition. There are three broad categories of the entire IT services (ITS) industry: (1) system integration, which includes packaged application implementation, custom application development and integration; (2) application outsourcing, which includes support and maintenance services; and (3) IT consulting, which includes strategic consulting, business process consulting and change management (Retrieved June 26, 2006, from www.expressindia.com/fullstory.php?newsid= 29232&spf-true).

[4]   http://economictimes.indiatimes.com/articleshow/1214281.cms (Retrieved June 26, 2006)

[5]   "Open Source" software is a method of software creation, distribution, and licensing, which permits accessibility of its source code. In contrast, for the proprietary companies such as Microsoft, IBM, Oracle, and so forth, the source code is a closely guarded secret.

[6]   Some detailed analysis of India's software industry and major Indian ICT firms' quality achievement process can be found, respectively, in Chakraborty and Dutta (2003), and Dutta and Sekhar (2005).

[7]   Note that 1 crore = 10 million. The rupee figures are from Economic Survey: 2002-2003, p. 143. Exchange rates used are: US$1.00 = Rs 35.50 in 1996-1997 and US$1.00 = Rs. 46.69 in 2001-2002.

[8]   The IT enabled service industry in India began to evolve in the early 1990s, when companies such as American Express, British Airways, General Electric and Swissair set up their offshore operations in India. A large number of foreign affiliates now operate IT-enabled services in India (Ibid., p. 148).

[9]   The author is grateful to Dr. H. Rahman who has provided the names of most of the national and regional ICT networks included in this section.

Copyright © 2007, Idea Group Inc. Copying or distributing in print or electronic forms without written permission of Idea Group Inc. is prohibited.

Chapter XIII

Potential Challenges of ICT Implementations in Sri Lanka

Kennedy D. Gunawardana, University of Sri Jayewardenepura, Sri Lanka

Abstract

This chapter offers a state-of-the-art review of the implementation of ICTs strategies in a developing country with special reference to Sri Lanka as a case study. This chapter is based on primary and secondary sources (books, articles, Web sites, white papers, and grey literature). It also brings in a small number of empirical studies that serve to illustrate the practical use of the ICT to support arguments. Traditionally, access to ICTs and information has not been viewed as basic a need. However, if needs are interpreted as being dynamic and changing over time and culture (Max-Neef, 1986), access to information and knowledge could be treated as a basic need. Information and knowledge have become increasingly important in the contemporary globalized economy, as advancement in ICTs has enabled larger amounts of information to circulate at a much higher speed and at lower cost. This is partly due to the balance between knowledge and natural resources, but with regard to being the most important factor in determining the standard of living in a country, it is said to have shifted in favor of knowledge. This has led many authors to claim that the people are now living in an information society or a knowledge-based economy (Drucker, 1993). Nowadays, it is a country's ability to assimilate, use, and diffuse knowledge that will essentially determine its chances of uplift in the new economy.

Copyright © 2007, Idea Group Inc. Copying or distributing in print or electronic forms without written permission of Idea Group Inc. is prohibited.

Emerging ICT Issues in Sri Lanka

Sri Lanka's ICT industry is thriving but faces significant problems, such as lack of transparency in government acquisitions (the largest prospective client); lack of moderately priced international bandwidth; lack of trained ICT professionals and classes knowledgeable about ICT; and a tax structure that does not reward local sales. In recent years, USAID has funded a number of projects aimed at increasing the competitiveness of various industries in Sri Lanka, and ICT is one of their prime foci. Their ICT sector studies have been well-performed, and their recommendations, if followed, will help guide the industry. However there is some danger that they may widen their scope to include the application of ICT in peripheral areas and, as a result, dilute their resources to no longer focus on their original crucial targets.

In general, the use of ICT in the commercial sector is irregular. Often, computers only seem to be found in managers' offices; they are rarely integrated throughout all levels of an organization. Some financial institutions have invested heavily in ICT, and as a result they are country leaders in the use of technology. Other sectors are far behind and their use of ICT is not visible. Even those companies that have invested in ICT often do so in restricted ways that are poorly integrated into their businesses. The same is true in case of the use of the Internet. In part, this is a small percentage (less than 10% of their total revenue) of Sri Lankan's access to the Internet, but the prime reason is, no doubt, the low level of managerial knowledge about the ICT capabilities in their business area.

At all levels of aggregation, statistics about any aspect of ICT in Sri Lanka are highly misleading and can be deceptive when used for policy purposes. Virtually all ICT activity is centered in Colombo, with small pockets in the Galle and Kandy areas (100 kilometers away from Colombo city). There is clearly a desire to spread ICT development over a wider geographic area than just in Colombo, but it appears that it is not going to be an easy task.

The regions outside the urban areas are particularly poorly served with respect to electricity and telecommunications. Total consumption of the western province is 3,699 Gwh in 2003, compared to the rural sector's consumption with an average of 340 gwh. Moreover, the rural areas do not provide the level of comforts and conveniences often expected by people with the high-end technical and managerial skills needed to drive this sector. Lastly, the supply of lower level technical skills is substantially lower in these regions.

The telecenter movement is in its infancy in Sri Lanka. In many countries, telecenters have become the focal point for introducing technology into rural areas, and in fact to disadvantaged groups in urban settings. The concept shows up in many reports and plans, but despite this, there are a very few active telecenters. Of more concern is that the groups that are developing telecentre plans are doing this in isolation from each other, and from the worldwide community that has a rich knowledge on what works and what does not.

Underlying most issues in Sri Lanka is the 19-year civil unrest and conflict between the Government of Sri Lanka and the Liberation Tigers of Tamil Eelam (LTTE), which has controlled territories in the northern and eastern parts of the island and been the source of disruptions in the south. There are 362,000 (both Tamils and non-Tamils displaced due to Tamil conflict) who have been killed by the war.

Copyright © 2007, Idea Group Inc. Copying or distributing in print or electronic forms without written permission of Idea Group Inc. is prohibited.

When it comes to socioeconomic development and the uses of technology, Sri Lanka is a country of achievements and contrasts. It has achieved high levels of life expectancy, education, and health at par with countries having a Gross Domestic Product (GDP) per capita more than twice than Sri Lanka. Sri Lanka's per capita income was US$1,000 in 2005.

Albeit all these constraints, the country has achieved a United Nations Development Program Human Development Index that is impressive relative to its GDP per capita. Its healthcare system includes the latest technologies: open-heart surgery, CT, and MRI scans (although access to some of these in public hospitals is limited). The southwest and the Colombo area in particular, have fiberoptic networks running along roads where carts are pulled by bullocks. Universities teach not only advanced computer science programs, but also the entire administration of the university, including students' academic records that was based on paper and manual operations, is being computerized.

Background

The speed of global technological and economic transformation demands urgent action to turn the present digital divide into digital opportunities for all. A discussion about the allocation of resources is imminent if looked at the connectivity of the Internet in developing countries. One way to measure the digital divide is to monitor the penetration of telephone subscribers and Internet users, as well as literacy rates in developing countries. Poor access to the Internet in Sri Lanka is widely acknowledged.

A few of the ICT parameters have been discussed here to illustrate the current scenario of ICT in Sri Lanka.

Telecommunications

Over the years, with the advances in the telecommunications field, Sri Lanka Telecom Corporation (SLT) has taken steps to upgrade and strengthen the telecommunications infrastructure in the country. Strategies such as expanding the optical fiber network and applying new digital technologies have contributed to greater reliability and efficiency. According to 2003 data, there were 822,992 telephones in Sri Lanka. It had 85,500 Internet customers by 2003. The services provided include PSTN dial-up at 56 kbps, ISDN dial-up at 64 kbps and 128 kbps, Internet Leased Line services at 64 kbps, 128 kbps, 256 kbps, 512 kbps, and 2Mbps, client mail server installations and Web hosting.

Other than SLT, there are a number of private telecommunications service providers, cellular mobile telephones, pay phones, trunk telecommunications networks, radio paging service, and trunk radio networks. Mobile cellular phone services, which started in 1989 (a first among South Asian countries), continue to grow very rapidly. The number of cellular connections, which stood at 1,800 in 1991, increased to 2.5 million in 2005. Phone charges per minute are comparatively high. The price $0.25 per minute for local calls and $0.40 for International. Domestic phone rates continually increase, and vary from zone to zone, while IDD rates have decreased slightly in recent years. Cellular phone rates are also high,

Copyright © 2007, Idea Group Inc. Copying or distributing in print or electronic forms without written permission of Idea Group Inc. is prohibited.

but have declined gradually due to intense competition. Restructuring of telecom services started in 1995, and since then steps have been taken to privatize SLT in stages, opening for foreign investment and with the intention of making the services more efficient.

Internet and Computer Networks

Lanka Internet Services initiated commercial operations in 1995 and SLT started its Internet service facility in 1996. At present there are over 20 Internet Service Providers (ISPs), including SLT and private companies. The services of ISPs cover a wide geographical area, and Internet connectivity and e-mail software are readily available. Despite this fact, the cost is high and it costs around $0.45 per hour. Currently, most of the Internet usage is in the commercial sector.

In 2003, there were 85,500 Internet users in Sri Lanka. According to the Telecommunications Regulatory Commission of Sri Lanka (TRCSL), the total number of Internet accounts was 121,532 (0.02% of total population of Sri Lanka) in 2005.

Although government initiatives have attempted to provide Internet facilities and access in schools and other educational institutions such as the National Colleges of Education, its use is minimal due to prohibitive cost. The Lanka Educational Academic and Research Network (LEARN) is a facility that interconnects educational and research and development institutions throughout the country. Initiated in 1990 as a project by the Department of Computer Science and Engineering (CSE) at the University of Moratuwa, it provided LEARN mail, the first e-mail service in Sri Lanka. Now administered by the Institute of Computer Technology at the University of Colombo, with technical operations being carried out by the CSE at the University of Moratuwa, it provides e-mail, dial-up, and dedicated Internet connections to its members.

IT in Primary and Secondary Education

Since 1983, the Ministry of Education and Higher Education has taken steps to familiarize and encourage school children in the use of IT. Computers were provided to some schools in 1984. In 1994, Computer Resource Centers (CRCs) were set up in a number of schools with the assistance of the Asian Development Bank. The main objective of setting up CRCs was to provide basic computer literacy to students during their vacations or after they had left school. In 1999 and 2002, a small number of computers were supplied to selected schools in all provinces. This was done with the intention of implementing the "activity room" concept, where students of junior secondary level (Grades 6-9) were to be familiarized with computer use. Despite all these attempts, IT was not integrated into the formal school curriculum. The major emphasis seemed to be on hardware supply for schools rather than on IT education.

Realizing this shortcoming, the IT unit of the Ministry of Education and Higher Education initiated a National Policy on Information Technology in School Education (NAPITSE). It has implemented a number of strategies to improve the situation. This policy includes a six-year strategic plan from 2002 to 2007, which is divided into three stages. Focusing on

Copyright © 2007, Idea Group Inc. Copying or distributing in print or electronic forms without written permission of Idea Group Inc. is prohibited.

two main aspects—use of IT in education (learning and teaching) and use of IT in management of the education system—the strategic plan is being implemented under four major themes: curriculum development, human resource development, physical/infrastructure development, and support initiatives development. As a result of NAPITSE, syllabi on General Information Technology (GIT) and Computer Assisted Learning (CAL) courses for GCE A-Level and GCE O-Level classes have been developed, and GIT for GCE A-Level has already been implemented. About 700 A-Level teachers have been trained up to now and 5,000 teachers will be trained next.

IT in Higher Education

The National Policy on IT made several recommendations to enhance IT in university education. These included providing IT awareness to all undergraduates, establishing campus-wide networks in all 14 universities, providing Internet access to all, and introducing computer science courses. Open University of Sri Lanka (OUSL) offers six programs of study including IT courses, ranging from certificate level to master's degrees. All registered students at OUSL are provided with the opportunity to undergo a basic computer awareness course, and to use the computer facilities available at the elementary computer laboratories at the Colombo Regional Centre and other regional centers. Internet facility is also provided to students free of charge at these labs and in the main library. The campuswide computer network integrates resources such as the library and IT division.

Initiatives to integrate e-learning with the existing courses are currently being implemented. The staff development center of OUSL conducts multimedia training sessions for its staff, as well as staff from other universities. The IT division also conducts IT training sessions for staff. The Institute of Computer Technology, an independent institution established within the University of Colombo, with modern facilities, is well-recognized by the University grant commission in Sri Lanka.

Providing IT training for students at universities, it is also involved in software development and research in IT (ICT, 2001).The Sri Lanka Institute of Information Technology (SLIIT) was also recently established by the Government of Sri Lanka to train IT professionals. At this institution, courses are offered in IT, development of software, and research and development in IT. The SLIIT conducts a program of study leading to a Bachelor of Science degree in Information Technology (SLIIT, 2004).

The Sri Lankan educational environment is undergoing a phase of rapid transformation with adoption of information technology at various levels. Teacher training on various educational media such as online resources has been identified as one of the key approaches to integrating ICT in the classroom. At the same time, efforts to develop learning materials indigenously are ongoing at various educational institutions.

Before proceeding to the next section, author would like to detail out a comprehensive ICT based educational plan of the Sri Lankan government for national capacity development that will assist to face the challenges of the ICT implementations.

The National Policy on Information Technology in School Education (NAPITSE) affirms the commitment of the government towards providing the state of the art knowledge in IT to Sri Lanka's younger generation, preparing them to face the challenges in the 21st century.

Copyright © 2007, Idea Group Inc. Copying or distributing in print or electronic forms without written permission of Idea Group Inc. is prohibited.

This policy will provide a clear vision and direction in making this a reality, followed by an action plan as a six-year strategic plan from 2002 to 2007. This six year project period is divided into three stages:

- Stage 1: 2002-2003
- Stage 2: 2004-2005
- Stage 3: 2006-2007

The NAPITSE will be implemented via an action plan titled, "National Policy on Information Technology in School Education, Action Plan, and Operational Strategies." It will be in the form of a rolling plan, undergoing periodic changes with necessary academic and professional inputs being incorporated as and when necessary.

The action plan will focus on:

- Use of IT in education (Learning and Teaching)
- Use of IT in management of the education system

Vision:

- A new generation of Sri Lankans empowered with Information and Communication Technology
- To facilitate the planning, implementation, and sustenance of Information Technology education in schools to enhance student's learning and quality of teaching

Goals

The NAPITSE will have the following overarching goals:

- Envisage and foresee the future global challenges in IT education and lay the foundation for appropriate human resource development to meet such challenges
- Create conditions enabling the effective use of IT as a tool in learning and teaching at all levels in the general school education
- Provide "information literacy" for all school leavers
- Create conditions for effective involvement of school system in lifelong education
- Create an information literate population of teachers/educators

Copyright © 2007, Idea Group Inc. Copying or distributing in print or electronic forms without written permission of Idea Group Inc. is prohibited.

Objectives and Strategic Themes

In order to reach the goals, the following objectives would be achieved under four major strategic themes:

- **Curriculum Development**
  - o To introduce, sustain, and enhance IT involvement into general education in schools and create opportunities for IT based learning and teaching
  - o To introduce IT into pre-service and in-service teacher development and training programs, and create opportunities for system-wide professional development of teachers

- **Human Resource Development**
  - o To provide necessary education and training to all teachers in government schools and making them competent in using IT for teaching purposes
  - o To upgrade officers in the education system to handle IT related activities competently and with ease
  - o To create opportunities for out of school population to utilize resources in school based IT resource centers, thus creating an environment for community learning

- **Physical/Infrastructure Development**
  - o To allocate and distribute optimal resources in an equitable manner to meet the learning needs of students and learning/teaching requirements of teachers
  - o To set up an Information Technology Education Resource Center (ITERC) at the national level, provincial level and zonal level ITERCs for teacher training/ development
  - o To establish an IT education laboratory at the National Institute of Education (NIE) to improve curriculum development
  - o To establish an ITERC at the Center for Professional Development of Management of Education
  - o To dedicate a National College of Education (NCOE) for development of IT teachers under pre-service teacher training
  - o To provide innovative means of training through activities, such as mobile training laboratories
  - o To set up a Multimedia Education Software and Web Development Center

- **Support Initiatives Development**
  - o To establish IT school clubs
  - o To encourage preparation of Web sites for schools
  - o To encourage teachers to own personal computers
  - o To design, develop, and maintain a Web site for the Ministry of Education and Higher Education to assist the school system in e-learning and information management

Copyright © 2007, Idea Group Inc. Copying or distributing in print or electronic forms without written permission of Idea Group Inc. is prohibited.

o   To convene appropriately time-framed IT education research and development conferences/colloquia

o   To facilitate the setting up of a professional body for those who are involved in IT education in schools

o   To establish a fund to support innovative approaches and creative initiatives for school IT education development

o   To initiate an award scheme to encourage educators for promoting innovative IT in education

o   To forge strategic partnerships with other government institutions, Sri Lankan Missions abroad, foreign missions in Sri Lanka and national and international NGOs and the private sector to extend the coverage of IT education, promote, and enhance the quality of IT education in the school system

In the new millennium, nations are judged by the well-being of their citizens; level of education is one of the major determinants. Computer literacy of a nation in the future will be a yardstick to measure the level of education. Sri Lanka's success in achieving high levels of basic literacy and numeracy can be capitalized on by pursuing a well thought-out strategy on achieving high quality IT education in the general school system.

Under various foreign-funded projects, the Ministry of Education is currently taking several measures to enhance IT facilities in schools. For instance, under the World Bank funded General Education Project II, planning is underway to provide 400 schools island-wide with ICT centers, equipped with 10 computers each and other accessories, as well as Internet facilities. The pilot project, in which ICT centers were established in 80 schools, was implemented in 2001 and was evaluated in 2003. The initiative was found to be providing the opportunity for students and teachers to develop basic competencies in the use of IT in education; and, despite various constraints, all schools are attempting to make the best possible use of the centers (Karunanayaka, Kularatne, & Udugama, 2003). The Secondary Education Modernization Project currently being implemented with the support of the Asian Development Bank intends to develop computer literacy and narrow the digital divide. During 2001-2006, about 2,300 schools will receive 10-20 computers; and the project envisages improving access for an additional 5,000 poor students annually, by upgrading 1,000 existing schools (Reddi & Sinha, 2003).

The Challenges

A few parameters will be discussed here that may be treated as potential challenges for ICT implementations in Sri Lanka.

Copyright © 2007, Idea Group Inc. Copying or distributing in print or electronic forms without written permission of Idea Group Inc. is prohibited.

Lack of Skilled ICT Professionals

The lack of sufficient, trained ICT professionals has been a recurring focus in ICT studies and reports in Sri Lanka. There seems to be four main drivers for this shortage:

- Sri Lanka produces only a small number of ICT-trained university graduates (albeit high quality) each year. The number of positions in the state-funded universities is severely limited. This is part of a bigger problem. Sri Lanka has a good record for primary and secondary education but admits to university only about 6% of successful secondary school leaves (16,000 out of 200,000).

- Sri Lanka has about 30 state-supported, commercial and quasi-private technical training institutes. However, the quality of training at these institutes is highly variable.

- Sri Lanka loses many ICT graduates soon after graduating. Their ICT skills demand far higher salaries abroad. An IT-qualified graduate earns per month US$800 to $1,000 locally.

- Sri Lanka faces a serious shortage of experienced ICT professionals. Senior people with 6-10 years experience are lacking in software design, project management, and network design and management. This shortage is felt both in industry and education. Sri Lanka has only 10 IT graduates out of 500 graduates.

The problem of insufficient ICT graduates has several dimensions, some of which are addressed below:

- All 14 state-funded universities provide some form of ICT education. However, in the majority of them, it is just computer science or information management courses within a general BS degree.

- Several fee-levying institutes (arms of foreign universities) offer computer science programs, but the prices tend to be above what most of the population can afford. It costs around US$10,000 for a 3-year program and normally recruits 120 students per batch.

- Though in state-funded universities ICT training is being increased (a recent example being the new Faculty of Information Technology at the University of Moratuwa), this effort is tightly constrained by the lack of senior instructors.

- The University of Colombo has recently begun an innovative 3-year program called the External Degree of Bachelor of Information Technology (BIT). Under this program, the university sets the curriculum and the exams. Student can prepare for examinations through self-study, or they can go to one of about 40 fee-for-service institutes that provide training and/or tutoring. To promote the quality of such sources of training, the university will publish on its Web site student success rates by institution attended. The BIT program is designed to allow students to stop with a Certificate of Information Technology after year one, an Advanced Certificate of Information Technology after year two, or a full Degree Certificate after completion of year three and other degree requirements. This strategy produces three levels of ICT skills.

Copyright © 2007, Idea Group Inc. Copying or distributing in print or electronic forms without written permission of Idea Group Inc. is prohibited.

For the application of ICT across the non-ICT sectors of Sri Lanka (government, health, primary/secondary education, small and medium enterprise (SME), and the rural sector) more people will need to be computer literate and computer trained. There are many user training programs in place, but as in the case of more technical training, the quality of the training programs remains uneven and erratic. The institution providing the Computer Driver's License may be effective in helping to manage and measure the growth in computer literacy, and offer employers a measure of confidence in hiring staff.

Two skills retention strategies that seem to be underdeveloped in Sri Lanka are the virtual repatriation of the skills of expatriates, and the retention of ICT professionals by linking them online to education, research, and work abroad. Some Latin American countries, for example, resort to the Internet to repatriate the skills of overseas nationals, for use in education, research and development, industry, and for civil society activities. Such efforts are low cost and in many cases the expatriates themselves organize them. Other countries, Ghana for example, have used the Internet to retain local skills, by linking local medical researchers to overseas research networks.

Basic ICT Skill Development

The twin problems of how to increase both the supply and the quality of training, across a number of skill areas and skill levels, should be addressed in collaboration across the relevant stakeholders, including the training institutes. Sri Lanka is not in a position to simply institute various levels of formal certification of ICT training facilities. There can be schemes such as the University of Colombo external BIT plan that certify skills.

Furthermore, publishing students' performance by training institute will allow students, and their families, to identify quality, and influence training quality. Publishing statistics on how many graduates obtain employment utilizing their new skills will also provide a measure of success, but one must be careful that these statistics are honestly presented.

There are discussions going on at a number of levels to institute formal certification of ICT professionals. Certification not only labels the prospective employee, but the type of certification will provide guidance to employers who do not themselves have the skills to identify good employees. The relevant stakeholders, including the training institutes, should consider a mix of *guard dog* and *guide dog* strategies to improve ICT skills and the performance of ICT training institutes. The objective is to expand the supply of quality ICT skills, not to restrict supply just to those that currently produce quality ICT skills.

Weak Strategies for Retaining ICT Professionals

There remains a serious obstacle to a rapid ramp up of ICT activity in the software sector, and the large-scale application of ICT to organizations. While it is possible to quickly expand the supply of entry-level ICT personnel, it is not possible to immediately produce high-level professionals, especially when that includes 6-10 years of proven experience in software design, project/implementation management, and network management. Some of

Copyright © 2007, Idea Group Inc. Copying or distributing in print or electronic forms without written permission of Idea Group Inc. is prohibited.

this demand could be met by the virtual repatriation of the senior skills of expatriate Sri Lankans abroad. Again, an end to the civil unrest will also help, both in the potential for full-time repatriation of ICT skills, and for the short term return work stints of expatriates whose ICT skills are being repatriated online the rest of the time. It remains to be seen as to who might organize such efforts.

One interesting and successful way to circumvent this problem is to subcontract high-end tasks to the Computing Services Center (CSC), a group within the Institute of Computer Technology (ICT) of the University of Colombo. ICT is one of the few really concentrated centers of technological expertise in the country, and the CSC has been involved in many successful projects. These have included feasibility studies, project specification and design, tender evaluation, network design and implementation, as well as overall system development. This group has been involved in some of the most strategic projects involving both government and private enterprise. As a side-benefit, this also serves to give staff members an additional source of income, partially alleviating the low academic salaries. The salary of the university senior professor is around US$600 per month.

Overcoming the Challenges

The author proposes a few strategies to overcome the challenges and uplift the human capacity of Sri Lanka.

Computer Literacy in the General Population

As information and communication technologies (ICTs) become a part of everyday life, it will be increasingly necessary for all citizens to have some basic familiarity with computers. Technology revolutions are complete when such skills are taken for granted and the technology seems to have disappeared into the background. It is necessary to (a) be clear as to what the actual goals are, (b) have an evidence-supported strategy for getting there, and (c) engage in a planning process in which both stakeholders and champions are brought on same side. It is essential to convert strategy into resources, or Sri Lanka will run the risk of reproducing the shortcomings of similar efforts elsewhere.

The main shortcoming is the tendency to substitute the provision of technology with implementation strategy. It is better to deploy one-half, or one-quarter of it, rather than engaging in a technology-intense strategy. One such strategy is helping donor agencies understand the issues, in terms of providing computers in the school and computers in the community.

A method that has been successful elsewhere is to provide technology to a school if there is a local champion and the school management is commited to the success of the project. A champion could be a staff member at the school, or a local company that will provide help and guidance. The essential characteristic of champions is that they passionately care for the computers' better use, and will do whatever is necessary to ensure that outcome. A success in a school with a local champion tends to spread to nearby schools with a ripple effect.

Copyright © 2007, Idea Group Inc. Copying or distributing in print or electronic forms without written permission of Idea Group Inc. is prohibited.

It is also noteworthy that, to date, the technology has not been used in support of other educational goals, specifically those related to English and other language training. It has been found that exposure to the still largely English-dominated computer and Internet world does wonders to increase functional English language skills. And the poor quality of English language education, particularly in rural areas, was highlighted as a major problem by several interviewees. There are 196,597 teachers in 2003 and English teachers who can teach English as a subject in schools are only 10% out of this number.

Improved Internet Access

There are six ISPs in Sri Lanka, with Sri Lanka Telecom (SLT) being the largest. Most of these players are quite small. SLT has 50,000 subscribers out of 19 million of the total population. SLT provides simple dial-up, dedicated to broadband Internet services through its Internet Service Provider (ISP) SLTNet. SLT has points-of-presence (POPs) across the country and this allows its subscribers to access the Internet for the cost of a local call through a single number (150) using SLT's unmatched superior quality backbone bandwidth of 90 Mbps.

SLT currently offers Internet-leased lines at 64 kbps, 512 kbps, and 2 Mbps, mail server services, Web and Domain Name Server (DNS) hosting are other value added products for business customers. SLT also provides Internet services to most of the other ISPs. All ISPs (or their downstream supplier) interconnect at the Sri Lanka Domestic Interchange, so that, intra-country traffic will never go offshore. SLT provides domestic leased circuits under the name of SLT Data. It offers data circuits of capacities ranging from 64 kbps up to 2 Mbps and in multiples of 2 Mbps. Our services include domestic and International Private Leased Circuits (IPLCs), Frame Relay (FR) circuits, Internet Leased Lines (ILLs), Direct Inward Dialling (DID) and Direct Outward Dialling (DOD) connections.

The cost of Internet ISP access is comparable to similar services elsewhere in the world. Many non-SLT providers only offer 28.8/33.6 kbps dial service, and access from many non-SLT local loops is limited to 28.8 (presumably due to the use of compressed 32kb voice services). A typical cost (from SLT) is US$11 per month for 150 hours. But, the actual per minute cost of dialup Internet access is normally high because of the additional per-minute cost of voice service. The base cost of a telephone line is low (about US$3-4 per month). However, the cost per minute, particularly during weekday daylight hours, is abnormally high (for SLT it is US$1.80 per hour after the first 8 hours).

Incorporate New Technologies

Virtual Private Networks (VPNs) have emerged as a modern solution for meeting the challenge of integrating data, voice and video traffic in an easily manageable, scalable, and flexible network. VPNs provide economical, efficient, and secure solutions for modern businesses.

SLT has launched its IP-VPN service in 2003 and built a Managed Private Leased Circuit (MPLC) based IP-VPN network covering almost all commercial locations in the Western Province (including Katunayake and Kandy). SLT now offers IP-VPN services to virtually

Copyright © 2007, Idea Group Inc. Copying or distributing in print or electronic forms without written permission of Idea Group Inc. is prohibited.

any location within Sri Lanka by providing access through leased lines, frame relay or Digital Subscriber Lines (DSL).

The Managed Private Leased Circuit (MPLC) protocol has emerged as the preferred protocol. It combines the security and performance of Frame Relay Services with the flexibility and cost-effectiveness of IP.

Deregulation of ICT Policies

The telecommunications sector in Sri Lanka was at first a state-owned department. The department was converted to a corporation and regulation was introduced in 1991. The Sri Lanka Telecommunications Authority (SLTA) was created by an Act of Parliament in 1991. It was converted to a commission in 1996. The dominant operator Sri Lanka Telecom (SLT) was privatized in 1997 with the government of Sri Lanka disposing of 35% of the share to the NTT Corporation of Japan. Licenses were issued to two operators for fixed access telephone services using WLL technology to compete with SLT. At present there are also four cellular operators, six facility based international data transmission providers, twenty-two licensed ISPs and two licensed pay phone operators. To show the current status of ICT, a few parameters are given in Table 1 below.

The new National Telecom Policy recommends the support for the establishment and promotion of the Sri Lanka information infrastructure and includes focus on new ICTs such as the Internet and e-commerce. In order to develop information technology, the Council for Information Technology (CINTEC) was established under an act of parliament. CINTEC has been involved in the development of e-commerce in Sri Lanka. It has several subcommittees and one of them is on law and computers.

This institution came under the purview of the Ministry of Telecommunications and Information Technology in October 2001. The growth of the telecommunications sector has given the foundation for developing the e-commerce industry in Sri Lanka. Within this improvement, e-commerce has received the attention of consumers, business persons, journalists, private and government organizations during the last few years. It brings a new trend in the policy agenda of Sri Lanka. With the development of technology and Internet applications, the e-commerce operations are becoming very fast, cheap, and simple.

Table 1. A few ICT parameters of Sri Lanka

Item	2000	2001	2002	2003	2004
Wireless local loop telephones	11,4267	12,1082	11,4488	11,6021	N/A
Cellular mobile telephones	430,202	667,662	931,580	1,393,403	2,211,000
Radio paging	7,009	6,535	5,516	2,851	3,679
Public payphones	8,222	7,281	6,681	6,440	N/A

Source: Sri Lanka Telecom LTD 2004 (NA-Not available)

Copyright © 2007, Idea Group Inc. Copying or distributing in print or electronic forms without written permission of Idea Group Inc. is prohibited.

Better Utilization of the Internet

As mentioned above, various industries in Sri Lanka are making use of e-mail and the Web. However, it is notable that virtually none of them have truly integrated them into their business. It was difficult to find examples where the use of either e-mail or the web was a crucial link to business success.

The attitude of communities is changing with the introduction of Internet at all levels. It is now used extensively in schools, universities, private and government organizations, banks, journalists, and business organizations. This is a very important aspect for the development of e-commerce in Sri Lanka. The business community of the country started to gradually experience applications such as online merchandising, stock trading, and banking and information database. These applications promote the e-business culture locally. A limited number of the organizations are using e-commerce for their international business activities.

Sri Lanka is also in the process of establishing an Electronic Data Interchange Network, which would link up all key public organizations. This development will help to the penetration of an e-business environment in Sri Lanka.

The SMEs use the Internet extensively for trade research. As in any other country, Sri Lankans use the maximum potential of the Internet to absorb the technical know-how from the outside world. Almost 100% of the SMEs who used the Internet at the time of our survey reported that they were using the Net for at least one of the following:

- Free downloading of devise drivers from the OEMs
- Free evaluation software downloads
- Obtaining technical documentation/research papers
- User manuals and sales catalogues
- Getting competitor information
- Getting trade know-how and new ideas

Sampath Bank (one of the leading IT introduced local banks from inception) and HSBC Bank are the main bankers used by the Sri Lankan SMEs for Internet banking. The reasons for using them were convenience, proven security, fewer conflicts (words from a respondent), economical operation, and so forth. The normal Internet banking operations were balance verification, requesting statements, transferring funds between accounts, paying bills, requesting check books, and so forth. The length of period of use averaged to about one year. Almost all respondents agreed that Internet banking once implemented with proper security precautions would benefit the customer providing state-of-the-art technology at a touch of a button. The major advantage being the rapid response and dynamic operation without having to waste time in the traffic jams.

Copyright © 2007, Idea Group Inc. Copying or distributing in print or electronic forms without written permission of Idea Group Inc. is prohibited.

Wireless Application Protocol (WAP) Implementations

The mobile phone companies have been promoting WAP applications for quite sometime now. The available applications include exchange rates, cricket scores, horoscopes, stock market, flight information, and so forth.

However, the business volumes on WAP implementations are low due to the lack of proper equipment, lack of customer awareness, and attitude, and so forth. At the same time, the phone companies see that high promotional and operational costs are main barriers to enhance this service.

Improved Policy Initiations

The rapid developments of ICTs in Sri Lanka have significantly affected the current legal system. Many privacy experts in Sri Lanka have shown that there is a need for new laws to adequately regulate new technologies.

The absence of a data protection law and a data protection authority in Sri Lanka is a real threat to the recently introduced e-Sri Lanka program. The e-Sri Lanka program aims at computerizing all governmental departments in the country and facilitating electronic documentary service, as opposed to the traditional government service that still processes everything manually.

In 2003, the Parliament passed the ICT Act No. 27 for the establishment of a national policy on information and communication technology and for the preparation of an action plan. Under this Act, the Information and Communication Technology Agency (ICTA) has given the responsibility to implement the national policy in both the public and the private sectors. The agency functions as the single highest body involved in ICT policy in the nation. It also assumes the role of implementing the e-Sri Lanka initiative.

The Computer Crime Bill of 2003 has also been approved by the Cabinet of Ministers and established by the Parliament. This act aims at combating computer crime in Sri Lanka. The Electronic Transaction bill Act has been established for providing the legal recognition of electronic transaction and other transactions carried out by means of electronic communications commonly referred to as "electronic commerce." This act is based on the UNCITRAL Model Law on E-Commerce 1996 and the 2001 UNCITRAL Model law on Electronic signatures.

Enhanced Governance

The e-government index of Sri Lanka is 0.92 which is below the global mean e-government index of 1.62 and it indicates that present e-government capacity of Sri Lanka is poor. A research on the Web survey of government institutes revealed that 30% of ministries in the country do not have Web sites or may not be access able since they are inactive. 38 of the ministries are still in the early stage and information available in Web pages in terms of content is not rich. Only about 17% of ministries offer interactive Web content, where

Copyright © 2007, Idea Group Inc. Copying or distributing in print or electronic forms without written permission of Idea Group Inc. is prohibited.

users have access to regularly updated information and can communicate through e-mail and download government documents through the Internet. 15% of the ministries provide some online services to the citizens. In same study a sample e-mail was sent and the time taken to reply was recorded. It was found that 99% of e-mails were not responded to by the Web masters (E-government survey, 2004).

The State Accounts Department (part of the Ministry of Finance) is leading a government-wide effort to progressively adopt International Public Sector Accounting Standards (IPSAS) for the reporting of government accounts (revenue and expenditure). The financial statements (i.e., accounts) for 2002 were prepared for the first time in accordance with the IPSAS cash accounting formats and have received a clean audit opinion from the Auditor General (except for a historical reconciliation issue). The previous 198-page dense financial report has been drastically reduced to just nine pages of well laid-out information (a one-page consolidated statement of cash receipts and payments with eight pages of supporting notes) designed to be read and understood by non-accountants.

The technical assistance project funded by the Asian Development Bank has provided the international good practice functional expertise to guide the adoption of the IPSAS cash accounting format. This assistance was grant funded at no cost to the Government of Sri Lanka. The cost of developing the overall information systems that underlie this project has been significant—recent costs for consultancy inputs, training, and overall Web site construction alone (excluding hardware costs and earlier construction of information systems) totals around US$150,000. However, construction cost of the financial statements and directly-related Web outputs has been reduced to a few thousands of U.S. dollars.

The improved quality and accessibility of accounts have a positive knock-on for transparency and accountability. Expected gains in this regard include but are not limited to informed parliamentary debate, media coverage based on financial facts, and increased reliance on government financial reports by international investors. Such non-quantifiable benefits will take some time to accrue and perhaps the greatest benefit in quantifiable terms might be the willingness of the international financing institutions to commit additional aid funds on the basis of increased transparency and accountability in government financial management.

Support Outsourcing in Software

Sri Lanka has a small emerging software development industry concentrating on exports, which ran at about $50 million in 2000 with a high percentage on a subcontract basis. Most of the industry consists of small firms founded by computer professionals, some returning from the U.S. to start their own companies. The industry faces constrains from shortage of skilled professionals, lack of venture capital, and narrow telecommunication bandwidth. Sri Lanka has not been able to take advantage of its high literacy rate to promote the IT industry. Local IT entrepreneurs, however, remain guardedly optimistic that Sri Lanka can carve a niche for itself in the high value-added software product development rather than the low value-added IT services which gravitate to India because of its large English-literate population and low wages.

The recent expansion of the software development industry has resulted largely from outsourcing for American, Middle Eastern, and European clients in Internet-based software develop-

Copyright © 2007, Idea Group Inc. Copying or distributing in print or electronic forms without written permission of Idea Group Inc. is prohibited.

ment and business applications. Only a handful of companies are engaged in internationally recognized product development. In offshore services sector, local programmers produce software for overseas clients based on their designs and specifications. Some companies providing outsourcing services have dedicated support service centers abroad as well. John Keells Computer Services (JKCS), a subsidiary of Sri Lanka's leading conglomerate John Keells Holdings (JKH) and one of the leaders in software services in Sri Lanka, employs nearly 2,000 programmers in 2003, and after they recruit every year, 50 qualified people go to their companies. Another major player in software outsourcing is eRunway. eRunway, headquartered in Boston, has an Internet software development center in Colombo employing over 300 software engineers.

Millennium Information Technologies (MIT), founded by a local computer professional, is the most successful company in product development. Valued at over $100 million, MIT hopes to list on NASDAQ. MIT has built an international reputation for capital market and telecommunication industry software. Its state of the art stock exchange suites are used in stock exchanges in Malaysia (MESDAQ), Croatia, Mauritius, and Sri Lanka. The Colombo Stock Exchange (CSE) is one of the world's most technologically advanced stock exchanges. The catalyst for this change was a systems integration contract from the Colombo Stock Exchange, which was reinterpreted as an opportunity to design and install a straight-through processing system which actually worked. The CSE solution became the basis for Millennium IT's suite of capital markets software products.

Various programs are underway to develop the software development industry in Sri Lanka. The government has recently created a separate Ministry for Information Technology and Higher Education. Despite government's precarious fiscal position leaves little room for investment in related infrastructure, the government believes that due to the high literary rate, Sri Lanka can be converted to an information technology savvy nation by 2010. Bureaucratic barriers have prevented setting up of a regional Java Training Center in Sri Lanka by SunMicro systems. The software industry, according to industry leaders, will continue to develop more on individual company efforts. For instance, some software developers have set up their own training institutes to meet the human resources shortage.

Elevated E-Readiness

Sri Lanka is ranked 54th out of 82 developed and developing countries in the Networked Readiness Index published in the Global Information Technology Report (2002/2003). The report, the collaborative effort of leading academics worldwide, seeks to benchmark and monitor the progress of nations in different dimensions in the field of ICT.

The report highlights the networked readiness of the three major stakeholder's viz. individuals, businesses and governments within a country's economic and political context. The variables used to measure the Networked Readiness Index are grouped into three broad categories, particularly environment, networked readiness, and network usage. Each component index is composed of three subindexes with the computation of the final Networked Readiness Index being based on the 64 variables included in 9 subindexes.

The final index captures the critical factors relating to the environment, readiness, and usage of ICT by the three stakeholders. The rankings relating to both the component index

Copyright © 2007, Idea Group Inc. Copying or distributing in print or electronic forms without written permission of Idea Group Inc. is prohibited.

Table 2. Human development indices of Sri Lanka and other regions

Country or Group	HDI Value
Countries with high human development	0.908
Sri Lanka	0.730
World (Average)	0.722
Countries with medium human development	0.691
Developing Countries	0.655
South Asia	0.582

Source: UNDP (2003) Human Development Report

and subindex, help in identifying the relative strengths and weaknesses in specific areas of competence. The Index therefore provides a useful measure of benchmarking the progress in networked readiness across a wide spectrum of nations worldwide.

Sri Lanka, with a score of 4.66 in the subcategory government readiness, is ranked 25th a high rank in comparison to its overall position of 54. This is a firm indication of the top priority and the thrust provided by the government to ICT in Sri Lanka.

Workforce Strengths

The key to any successful development initiative is the development of its stakeholders. Sri Lanka's labor is reputed for its precision, quality of its work, and productivity. English is widely spoken and understood throughout the island. The World Bank reports have indicated that Sri Lanka has one of the highest literacy rates (92%) among designated low-income countries; a population of 19.2 million has a workforce of approximately 6.7 million. There is a steady pool of manpower resources for both existing and new industries. The government provides free education from kindergarten to university. Sri Lanka is also ranked high on the Human Development Index and compares well with developed countries. Table 2 shows the Human Development Indices of Sri Lanka in comparison to the global or regional context.

Future Issues

Sri Lanka has the highest literacy rate in the South Asian region and has a large pool of educated persons with skills in computer programming. At the higher end of the skill spectrum, qualified software engineers offer levels of supervisory skill that is among the best in the world. The country's IT leaders believe that software development, outsourcing, systems integration, and a vast range of IT related services are the passport to the future.

Copyright © 2007, Idea Group Inc. Copying or distributing in print or electronic forms without written permission of Idea Group Inc. is prohibited.

The Sri Lankan Government has actively encouraged the spread of computer literacy by providing duty concessions on hardware imports. This environment is further enhanced by modern data transmission systems and complementary hardware. Low cost offshore data entry operations have also thrived in Sri Lanka since the early 1980s. Sri Lanka already serves as the headquarters of one of the largest software development houses in South East Asia.

It has to be remembered that in Sri Lanka, data communication facilities are limited within Colombo and its peripheries, the western province and the major provincial towns such as Kandy, Galle, Batticaloa, Ratnapura (about 100KM from Colombo main Capital city), and so forth. Individual usage and, to a great extent, access in the workplace is tied heavily to social class and income. Internet access remains unaffordable for the majority of the people, and cyber cafes, though increasingly spreading, are still limited to urban areas. However, there are a few pilot projects currently being implemented to achieve island-wide coverage through VSAT technology.

In recent years, the growth in ICTs in Sri Lanka has been rapidly increased. At present, the number of websites that cater to the Sri Lankan diasporas as well as to the Sri Lankan public is on the rise with an emphasis on Sri Lankan content either in Sinhalese, Tamil, or English (main languages used by Sri Lankan citizens).

E-mail and Internet reached Sri Lanka at the end of the 1980s making it one of the first countries in Asia to use the Internet, though the potential of the Internet for conflict transformation and resolution remains largely untapped in Sri Lanka, with a few notable exceptions. Sri Lanka still believes that the mere creation of Web sites engenders the use of the Internet, and does not place an onus of educating the masses on how to best use the Internet. However, given these limitations, some NGOs are taking the lead in the creation of interactive Web site that provoke and stimulate online discussion and sharing of viewpoints as an underpinning of classic conflict transformation.

The importance of ICT cannot be ignored by government, civil society, and NGOs in Sri Lanka. ICT by itself is an impotent tool. What animates it is a culture in which stakeholders use ICT to buttress and build confidence between communities, engender discussion, and help in the dissemination of information regarding state-of-the-art conflict resolution techniques and events. Though there are no easy solutions for the peaceful settlement of protracted ethnic, a realization of the power of ICT can help efforts on the ground to bring a negotiated and justified solution to war in Sri Lanka.

Conclusion

Sri Lanka's greatest weakness is the poor telecommunication infrastructure. Complete lack of telephone connections to some areas of the country is evidence of this. While Internet connections and e-mail software is now readily available, the pricing puts them beyond the reach of a greater majority of the population. In 2004, the telecommunication sector, in terms of subscriber network, expanded by 36 percent. The external gateway operation, which was the monopoly of Sri Lanka Telecom (SLT), was opened for competition in 2003 with 32 licenses being granted by the end of 2005.

Copyright © 2007, Idea Group Inc. Copying or distributing in print or electronic forms without written permission of Idea Group Inc. is prohibited.

The Government of Sri Lanka has initiated the e Sri Lanka plan which, aims to electronically connect and service the entire country. The labor force is being enhanced with education, skills training and a focus on productivity. Hoping to use trade to spur growth, Sri Lanka is emphasizing its central position in the region and key shipping lanes, Free Trade Agreements with its neighbors and its relatively friendly business climate to grow into a regional hub for manufacturing, commerce, and transport. The private sector also has responded to the peaceful environment with increased business activity and investment. Sri Lanka's economy expanded by 5.6% in 2005, and further progress was made on macroeconomic stabilization.

The government has committed itself to reduce corruption, but problems remain. Tender procedures are opaque, decision making is slow, enforcement of intellectual property right s (IPRs) is uneven, and bureaucracy, caused by a large public sector, hinders efficiency. However, the progress largely depends on the continuation of the peace process, policy adjustments, private sector development and structural reforms. Though still faced with substantial economic, social, and political challenges, Sri Lanka accomplished much in 2005, a fact recognized by the international community.

On 26 December 2004, an undersea earth quick registering 9.3 on the richter scale struck in the Indian Ocean, off the Western coast of Northern Sumatra, Indonesia. Sri Lanka was seriously affected by the tsunamis. They caused extensive damage along more than two thirds of over 1,000 km of the coastline extending from the northern coast, through the eastern and southern coasts to the western coast. The total damage is estimated to be around US$1 billion (4.9% of the GDP) and the reconstruction, which is likely to spread over a period of about three years, is estimated to cost around US$1.8 billion (8.9% of the GDP). It is expected that this will create new coping strategies and a natural disasters plan, in addition to developing new IT culture in the country.

References

Adams, C.W. (1992). *Implementing computer-based communication services in Sri Lanka.* Paper presented at the 12th National Computer Conference (Vol. 1), University of Colombo.

Akpan, P. (2000, May). Africa and the new ICTs: Implications for development. In *Proceedings of International Federation for Information Processing Conference*, Cape Town, South Africa.

Alfonso, M. (2003). The digital divide: The need for a global e-inclusion movement. *Technology Analysis and Strategic Management, 15*(1), 137-151.

Avgerou, C. (1998). How can IT enable economic growth in developing countries? *Information Technology for Development, 8*(1), 15-29.

Baro, R.J. (1997). *The determinants of economic growth.* Cambridge, MA: MIT Press.

Bera, M. (2003) Information communications technology and local development. *Telematics and Informatics, 20*(3), 215-234.

Copyright © 2007, Idea Group Inc. Copying or distributing in print or electronic forms without written permission of Idea Group Inc. is prohibited.

Bolou, F. (2005) *Ten years of technical progress in telecommunications in the Ivory Coast: An analysis of total factor productivity in Ivorian ICT Sector 1993-2002.* (IRTMOL Working Paper 2005-8-164).

Bolou, F. (2006). ICT infrastructure expansion in Sub-Saharan Africa: An analysis of six West African countries from 1995-2002. *Communications and Strategies: The Economic Journal on Telecom, IT and Media, 59,* 1.

Broadcast in Sri Lanka: Potential and performance. Centre for Media and Policy Studies,

Braga, C.A., Kenny, C., Qiang, C., Crisafuli, D., Di Martino, D., Eskinazi, R., Schware R., & Ker-Smith, W. (2000). *The Networking revolution: Opportunities and challenges for developing countries.* Washington, DC: World Bank Group.

Central Bank of Sri Lanka. (2002). *Annual report for 2001.* Sri Lanka Council for Information Technology (CINTEC) (1998).

Chen, Y., & Zhu, J. (2004). Measuring information technology's indirect impact on firm performance. *Information Technology & Management Journal, 5*(1-2), 9-22.

Crafts, N. (2003). *Quantifying the contribution of technological change to economic growth in different eras: A review of the evidence.* London: The London School of Economics, Department of Economic History.

Davison, R.M., Vogel, D.R., Haris, R.W., & Jones, N. (2000) Technological leapfrogging in developing countries: An inevitable luxury? *Electronic Journal of Information Systems in Developing Countries, 1*(5), 1-10.

Deliktas., E., & Kok, R. (2003). *Efficiency convergence in transition economies: 1991-2002. A non parametric frontier approach.* Ege University, Department of Economics.

Depotis, D. (2005). Measuring human development via data envelopment analysis: The case of Asia and the Pacific. *Omega: International Journal of Management Science, 33*(5), 385-390.

Desai, M. (1991) Human development: Concepts and measurement. *European Economical Review, 35*(2-3), 350-357.

Dey, A. (2002). *A brief note on ICT and economic development.* University of California Berkley.

Drucker, P.F. (1993). *Post-Capitalist Society.* Harper Business, Inc.

Eggleston, K., Jensem, R., & Zeckhauser, R. (2002). *Information and communication technologies, markets and economic development* (Discussion Papers Series). Department of Economics, Tufts University 0203.

Fielding, D. (2002). Health and wealth: A structural model of social and economic Development. *Review of Development Economics, 6,* 393-414.

Gholami, R., Lee, S., & Yong, T.Y. (2005). Time series analysis in the assessment of ICT impact at the aggregate level—lessons and implications for the new economy. *Information & Management, 42*(7), 1009-1022.

Gilhooly, D., & Ocampo, J. (2005). *Creating an enabling environment: Toward the millennium development goals.* New York: The United Nations Information and Communication Technologies Task Force.

Copyright © 2007, Idea Group Inc. Copying or distributing in print or electronic forms without written permission of Idea Group Inc. is prohibited.

Government of Sri Lanka. Department of Census and Statistics. (2002). The government of Sri Lanka national policy on information technology in school education. In *ICT Policy and Strategy: Sri Lanka*. Colombo: Government Printing Office.

Gylfason, T. (2001). Natural resources, education and economic development. *European Economic Review, 45*(4-6), 847-859.

Hardy, A. (1980). The role of the telephone in economic development. *Telecommunications Policy, 4*(4), 278-286.

Hicks, N., & Streeten, P. (1979). Indicators of development: The search for a basic needs yardstick. *World Development, 7*(6), 567-580.

Hoekman, B.M., Maskus, K.E., & Saggi, K. (2005). Transfer of technology to developing countries: Unilateral and multilateral policy options. *World Development, 33*(10), 1587-1602.

Isurupaya, B.(2004). *Education Publications Department,*(pp. 1–7).

ITU. (2003). *World summit on the information society: Declaration of principles*. Geneva: International Telecommunications Union and United Nations. Retrieved June 26, 2006, from http:/www.itu.int/wsis/docs/geneva/oficial/dop.html

ITU. (2003). *World telecommunication development report 2003: Access indicators for the information society*. International Telecommunications Union. Retrieved June 26, 2006, from http:/www.itu.int/ITU-D/ict/publications/wtdr_03/index.html

Iyigun, M., & Owen, A.L. (forthcoming). Experiencing change and the evolution of adaptive skills: Implications for economic growth. *European Economic Review*.

Jalavaa, J., & Pohjolab, M. (2002). Economic growth in the new economy: Evidence from advanced economies. *Information Economics and Policy, 14*(2), 189-210.

Joseph, K. (2002). *Growth of ICT and ICT for development: Realities of the myths of the Indian experience* (Discussion Paper No. 2002/78). United Nations University.WIDER, Helsinki. Retrieved June 26, 2006, from http://www.unu.wider.edu

Karunanayaka, S.P., Kularatne, N.G., & Udugama, L.S.K. (2003). *Process evaluation of the ICT centres established under the General Education Project II* (Report of an evaluation commissioned by the Sri Lanka Ministry of Human Resource Development, Education and Cultural Affairs). Colombo: National Education Commission.

Kenny, C. (1995). The missing link: Information. *Information Technology for Development, 6*(1), 33-38.

Kenny, C. (2000). Expanding internet access to the rural poor in Africa. *Information Technology for Development, 9*(1), 25-31.

Mahlberg, B., & Obersteiner, M. (2001). *Remeasuring the HDI by data envelopment analysis* (IASA Interim Report IR-01-069). Luxemburg.

Max-Neef, M. (1986). Human scale economics: The challenges ahead. In P. Ekins (Ed.), *The living economy* (pp. 198-206). MCB UP Ltd.

Mbarika, V.W.A., Okoli, C., Byrd, T., & Data, P.(2005). The neglected continent of IS research: A research agenda for Sub-Saharan Africa. *Journal of the Association for Information Systems, 6*(5), 130-170.

Copyright © 2007, Idea Group Inc. Copying or distributing in print or electronic forms without written permission of Idea Group Inc. is prohibited.

Molina, A. (2003). The digital divide: The need for a global e-inclusion movement. *Technology Analysis and Strategic Management, 15*(1), 137-151.

Mwesige, P.G. (2004). Cyber elites: A survey of Internet café users in Uganda. *Telematics and Informatics, 21*(1), 83-101.

National Policy on Information Technology (NAPITSE). (2001). The Council for Information Technology, Sri Lanka. Government of Sri Lanka.

Neumayer, E. (2001) The human development index: A constructive proposal. *Ecological Economics, 39*(1), 101-114.

Ngwenyama, O., Bolou, F., & Morawczynski, O. (2006, forthcoming). A DEA investigation of the contribution of ICT to development in five African countries. In *Operations research in Africa*. United Nation University Press.

Noorbakhsh, F. A modified human development index. *World Development, 26*(3), 517-528.

Noris, P. (2000). *The worldwide digital divide: Information poverty, the Internet and development*. John F. Kennedy School of Management, Harvard University.

Open University of Sri Lanka (OUSL). (2003). Retrieved June 26, 2006, from http://www.ou.ac.lk

Pohjola, M. (2001). *Information technology, productivity, and economic growth: International evidence and implications for economic development*. Oxford University Press.

Reddi, Dharni P. Sinha (2003). *Utilization of scarce resources: An analysis of government health*. Ashok Kumar and Hari Haran. Viva Books.

Reddi, U.V., & Sinha, V. (2003). *Sri Lanka: ICT use in education*.

Reforms in General Education—Sri Lanka. Government Publications, Colombo. National Education Commission (1999). Reforms in Primary Education—Sri Lanka. Government Publications, Colombo.

Presidential Task Force on General Education. (2000). The general education reforms and primary education. In A. Little (Ed.), *Primary education reforms in Sri Lanka*.

Sri Lanka Institute of Information Technology (SLIIT). (2001). Retrieved June 26, 2006, from http://www.sliit.lk

Sri Lanka Telecom (SLT). (2001). *Annual report*. Retrieved June 26, 2006, from http://www.slt.lk/inpages/aboutus_pages/slt_annual2001/slt_full_report.pdf

Telecom Act of Sri Lanka. (1996). Retrieved June 26, 2006, from http://www.trc.gov.lk/telecom1.html

Copyright © 2007, Idea Group Inc. Copying or distributing in print or electronic forms without written permission of Idea Group Inc. is prohibited.

Chapter XIV

E-Government Practices
in Regional Context:
Turkish Case

Derya Altunbas, Canakkale Onsekiz Mart University, Turkey

Elif Karakurt Tosun, Uludag University, Turkey

Abstract

This chapter introduces the importance of the Information and Communication Technologies on the regional development in Turkey. Socioeconomic transformation can be done with the efficient service opportunities in regions that have different growth rates. Specially, some regions have migration problems for economic and emplyoment reasons in Turkey. Growth poles are a typical development style for Turkey. Therefore, less developed regions should should have more advantage from national economic programs. In this chapter, included in Regional development programs of Turkey in the context of Information and Communication Technologies. The objective of this chapter is to point out importance of improvements of Information and Communication Technologies and e-governmnent programs in Turkey. At this time, it is defined the role of e-government programs on social, economic and political structures of the regions in Turkey.

Copyright © 2007, Idea Group Inc. Copying or distributing in print or electronic forms without written permission of Idea Group Inc. is prohibited.

Introduction

Network economies which arise with the development of Information and Communication Technologies (ICTs) have caused unavoidable transformation of the paradigm in the social dimension. This is the transformation that has harmonized the information revolution and Information Society. This socioeconomic transformation effects directly the shape of the administration, the working mechanisms of the state, the level of economic development, and the relationships of the citizen.

The transformation of ICTs offers different alternatives to countries that are efficient and produces service opportunities for their citizens on social, economic, political, and cultural platforms. Specially with this transformation, underdeveloped countries and developing countries could find opportunities of supply by using their resources efficiently, similar to the developed countries.

Beside the potential of minimization of differentiations at development among the countries, regional differentiations are also removed in a country which is another function of ICTs. At the same time, it has given opportunities that are distributed equally among the citizens of a country. In this study, the basic hypothesis is depending on the idea that ICTs can act as instruments for governments to remove the differentiations of development either among different countries or within each country. However, efficient use of this instrument depend directly on the current socioeconomic conditions of the country. This study examined a few cases on efficent use of the e-government system in Turkey. In this framework; first of all, government decisions are analyzed that were used in the regional policy, including development planning decisions about underdeveloped areas or the regions with priority of development. Secondly, it has tried to assess the level of ICTs in Turkey. Finally, it analyzed the effects of ICTs on the socioeconomic life in the regions that have priority for development.

Regional Development: Definition and Terminology

Differentiations of development can be based on differentiations of capital and skilled labor investment in certain regions that accumulate imbalances apart from the different geographical conditions in a country (Ozturk, 2001). So, regional planning must include social and economic needs of the citizens when making settlements for inhabitants. Therefore, the aim of the regional planning should be to increase the social and economic welfare of people and at the same time improve the condition of physical living place or working place.

It has been observed that the interregional balanced development in industrialized countries is decreasing the income inequalities, source spending, and harmful effects of the industrialization in more developed regions. But, underdeveloped or developing countries are mostly determining which strategical point is suitable as the starting point of development and deciding whether strategical public investments will make it possible or not (Gurbuz, 2001).

There are two functions to perform in regional planning. First, regional planning must be efficient to increase the country's economic development. In this view, when the settlement

Copyright © 2007, Idea Group Inc. Copying or distributing in print or electronic forms without written permission of Idea Group Inc. is prohibited.

system is establishing and decision of infrastructure is taking place, each decision must be efficient enough for betterment of the economy or at least able to create additional positive effects. Second, the function of regional planning is a tool for preventing regional differentiations. In this context, regional planning seems like a mechanism of use to reverse the unequal development in the country (Tekeli, 1981). The aims of the regional development should ensure that (Gurbuz, 2001):

- Regional imbalance is decreased.
- Each source and economic activity must be compatible in delivering within the geographical regions.
- Source of the region must be properly evaluated.
- Regional development must be dispersed in the country.
- Healthy growth in the region must be promoted.
- Interregional distribution of the industry must be balanced.
- Less developed regions should have more advantage from the national economic development programs.

Furthermore, there are three principles in development policies. They are social revenues, growth poles, and citizen participation. Each of them complement each other (Akder, 2003; Gurbuz, 2001; Kurt, 2003; Tavgac, 2001). The social revenue principle is a short term process and is not economical, but at the same time long term application gives economic benefit to underdeveloped regions. This type of investment must be made by governments (Dinler, 1998). The Growth Poles principle is applicable to the industries that have motor effects in the regions in one or more points of the country. With this investment in the region, the importance of the region is increased and differentiation emerges. This type of development has poles effect on the country's economy. The principle of citizen participation in development policies suggests that if a region's inhabitants have effective participation in policy making, the country will experience success in regional economic and social development.

Regional Development Programs in Turkey

For regional development programs in Turkey this study has covered two periods of time: before planning and after planning periods. From 1923-1963 is the "before planning" time period. In this period there were not many systematical programs for regional development because the country's overall regions had underdeveloped characteristics. After 1960, the State Planning Organization (SPO) was estabished for preparing regional planning making (Regional Development Specialization Commission Report, 2002). There are Eight National Development Plans and each of them was prepared to each five years until today. In the regional context, there are some chosen pilot regions for development at the beginning of the first National Development Planning period. Several different development plans were completed during these periods, such as Eastern Marmara Planning Project, Zonguldak

Copyright © 2007, Idea Group Inc. Copying or distributing in print or electronic forms without written permission of Idea Group Inc. is prohibited.

Project, Antalya Project and Çukurova Projects. At the begining of seventh National Development Plan, some larger regional scale projects were planned in Turkey. They are Eastern Anatolian Project, South-Eastern Anatolian Project, Eastern Black Sea Regional Growth Planning, Zonguldak Bartın Karabük Regional Growth Project and Yeşilırmak Sphere Growth Project. The aim of Regional Development Projects in Turkey is to minimize the regional differentiation, to encourage private sector, to develop infrastructure of the transportation, to increase the facilities of health and education, to increase productivity of agriculture, and to increase employment rate. During this period, there were no recommendations about the development of information and knowledge technologies that relate to the regional context. The reason is that they were taken before the 7th Five Years Development Plan. Most of the regional development projects were in a preparatory stage from 1996-2000. In fact, since October 4, 2001, the E-Turkey Action Plan was integrated with the Europe+ Action Plan. However, in Turkey, programs on the knowledge and Information Technologies develop faster than adoptation of regional development application. Thereby, is has been realized that, development rate of knowledge and Information Technologies must be in sequence to the development rate of the investments for these technologies to reach each region in Turkey. A few of the cases are discussed here.

Eastern Anatolian Project (State Planning Organization, 2000)

This project includes 16 cities in the east region of Turkey, covering 158.972 km.2 The population of the region is 6,147,603 as per the 2000 census. The regional area is 20.4% of the total area of Turkey and the population is 11.03% of the total of Turkey. The 16 cities that fall in this region are ranked in comparison to Turkey's 81 cities (see Table 1), according to socioeconomic factors.

South Eastern Anatolian Project (http://www.dpt.gov.tr/bgyu/bkp/gap.html)

This project has components comprising the development of agricultural infrastructure, industrialization, education, health, and other sectors. Beside the transportation opportunities, in this project dams were built on the Dicle and Firat rivers, and hydroelectric power plants were installed, including some irrigation facilities. In this context it can be seen as a multi dimensional project. Table 2 shows its ranking.

Eastern Black Sea Regional Growth Planning

This project is third of the regional development projects. This region's people have the least portion of income in Turkey. Because of low income and fewer employment opportunities there was a migration problem in this region. Cities in the region and their socioeconomic ranking can be seen in Table 3.

Copyright © 2007, Idea Group Inc. Copying or distributing in print or electronic forms without written permission of Idea Group Inc. is prohibited.

Table 1. Cities of Eastern Anatolian Regional Project

Cities	Population	Annual population increase rate (%)	Gross Domestic Product per person (Dollar)	Socio-economic Development of cities (81 inside in Turkey)	Socioeconomic Development Index
AĞRI	528 744	19.03	568	80	-1.28116
ARDAHAN	133 756	-20.22	842	74	-1.07318
BİNGÖL	255 395	2.51	795	76	-1.12469
BİTLİS	388 678	16.33	646	79	-1.15736
ELAZIĞ	572 933	13.97	1074	36	-0.10131
ERZİNCAN	315 806	5.38	1158	58	-0.49288
ERZURUM	942 340	10.52	1061	60	-0.53286
HAKKARİ	235 841	31.28	836	77	-1.13956
IĞDIR	168 634	38.43	855	69	-0.89089
KARS	327 056	-8.43	886	67	-0.81944
MALATYA	853 658	19.22	1417	41	-0.22627
MUŞ	453 654	18.63	578	81	-1.43956
TUNCELİ	93 584	-35.58	1584	52	-0.40003
VAN	877 524	31.96	859	75	-1.09297

Source: State Planning Organization, 2006; State Statistical Institute, 2003; Dağ, 2002

Table 2. Cities of South Eastern Anatolian Project

Cities	Population	Annual population increase rate (%)	Gross Domestic Product Per Person (Dollar)	Socio-economic Development of Cities (81 inside in Turkey)	Socio-economic Development Index
ADIYAMAN	623,811	19.98	918	65	-0.77647
BATMAN	446,719	26.09	1,216	70	0.90456
DİYARBAKIR	1,364,209	21.84	1,313	63	-0.66993
GAZİANTEP	1,293,849	24.72	1,593	20	0.46175
KİLİS	114,724	-12.65	1,817	54	-0.41175
MARDİN	705,098	23.34	983	72	-0.98944
SİİRT	264,778	8.40	1,111	73	-1.00644
ŞANLIURFA	1,436,956	36.10	1,008	68	-0.83158
ŞIRNAK	354,061	30.10	638	78	-1.13979

Source: State Planning Organization, 2006; State Statistical Institute, 2003

Copyright © 2007, Idea Group Inc. Copying or distributing in print or electronic forms without written permission of Idea Group Inc. is prohibited.

Table 3. Eastern Black Sea cities included in the regional growth planning

Cities	Population	Annual population increase rate (%)	Gross Domestic Product per person (Dollar)	Socio-economic development of cities (81inside in Turkey)	Socio-economic Develoment Index
ARTVİN	191,934	-10.33	2,137	43	-0.26018
BAYBURT	97,358	-9.75	1,017	66	-0.80176
GİRESUN	524,010	4.7	1,443	50	-0.36696
GÜMÜŞHANE	186,953	10.18	1,075	71	-0.92501
ORDU	887,765	7.10	1,064	62	-0.64489
RİZE	365,938	4.8	1,897	37	-0.17840
TRABZON	979,295	20.74	1,506	38	-0.18582

Source: State Planning Organization, 2006; State Statistical Institute, 2003

Table 4. Cities of Zonguldak Bartın Karabük of the Regional Growth Project

Cities	Population	Annual population increase rate(%)	Gross Domestic Product per person (Dollar)	Socioeconomic development of cities (81 inside in Turkey)	Socioeconomic Development Index
ZONGULDAK	615,599	-6.01	2,969	21	0.44906
BARTIN	184,178	-11.11	1,061	55	-0.41550
KARABÜK	225,102	-8.13	1,587	27	0.21332

Source: State Planning Organization, 2006; State Statistical Institute, 2003

Table 5. Cities of Yeşilırmak Sphere Development Project

Cities	Population	Annual population increase rate (%)	Gross Domestic Product per person (Dollar)	Socioeconomic development of cities (81 inside in Turkey)	Socioeconomic Development Index
AMASYA	365,231	1.65	1,439	39	-0.18591
ÇORUM	597,065	-1.92	1,654	46	-0.32761
SAMSUN	1,203,681	3.59	1,680	32	0.08791
TOKAT	828,027	14.15	1,370	61	-0.59010

Source: State Planning Organization, 2006; State Statistical Institute, 2003.

Copyright © 2007, Idea Group Inc. Copying or distributing in print or electronic forms without written permission of Idea Group Inc. is prohibited.

Zonguldak Bartın Karabük Regional Growth Project

The economy is especially dependent on agriculture and the coal mining establishment in this region. Population was 1.024879 million in 2000 and the population was 0.015 % of Turkey's population. The annual increase rate of this region's population is -8.416 % (2.17 % is for all of Turkey). This region has annual migration of 1.7% in comparison to other parts of the Turkey. Table 4 shows this region's socioeconomic ranking.

Yeşilırmak Sphere Growth Project
(http://www.dpt.gov.tr/bgyu/bkp/yesilirmak.html)

In the Sphere River, there is erosion and environmental pollution. Some problems were there due to the overflowing and water pollution, too. With the project of Yeşilırmak Sphere Growth Project the most suitable land use and economic benefits were searched. Ecological equlibrium is the base issue in this project, and by making economic land use planning management of the natural resources and following the nature accurately it has tried to decrease the differentiation of development within the other regions. This project has contributed to the country's economy, and the population's welfare has improved in the region (see Table 5 for ranking).

E-Government Conceptual Evaluation

In the 21st century, the transformation of Information Technologies plays an important role for the transformation of relationships between government and society. The public managment process runs more efficiently through effective participation of citizens using Information Technologies. Within this context it has emerged as the e-government model at the management level. In this model, citizens are able to express their opinions about the administration to public clearly and easily to impact the local or national administration processes in their country. Electronic government can be defined as the government services and duties that belong to the government and must be made available without cutting; and they should be carried out with the mutual participation of citizens in a safe atmosphere within the electronic Information Technologies (State Planning Organization, 2005c). At the same time, it is important to perform the services, rather than technologies. The government should not only perform electronic shape of services to citizens, but also prepare to use them (Yıldırır & Karakurt, 2004). In another view, e-government system is used to process the public institutions, support the public services, and develop the capacity of citizens. However, some academicians reject the definition of the easiest way to reach to deliver services because it seems too narrow and simple. As a matter of fact, the use of ICTs is not only limited within the Internet or Web sites, but at the same time there are geographical knowledge systems, the tools that are used institutional efficiency and helps public decision makers (Yıldız, 2003; Uckan, 2003).

Copyright © 2007, Idea Group Inc. Copying or distributing in print or electronic forms without written permission of Idea Group Inc. is prohibited.

E-Government Objectives and Practice Areas

In e-government processes, all the services and duties to citizens given by the government must be equal, fast, safe, and efficient. In this process not only does technological renewal happen, but at the same time renewal of the government structure for citizens occurs. Public institutions, local administrations, and other institutions in the public sector, private institutions, and citizens benefit from this opportunity (State Planning Organization, 2005c). Targets of the e-government practices are:

- Visual clarity in the state.
- Fastest process for citizens and government relationship.
- More participation at each level of public administration.
- Citizens lives must be easier when the government gives public sevices to them.
- More effective working atmosphere in the units of public services.
- Information entirety must be provided and prevented to abuse it.
- Data and work repetition must be prevented and knowledge flow must be provided among the institutions.
- Bureaucracy must be decreased.
- Citizens must have the opportunities by benefiting from public services in all day.
- Public services must be accessible and widespread.
- In public service production and the consumption process, participating citizens must be supported, and their desires or tendencies must be evaluated efficiently.
- Instutitions of the state must work to be productive and rational.

The Role of E-Government on Social, Economic, and Political Development

Renewal of the social, economic, and political platforms by utilizing the development of ICTs is most important for developing countries like Turkey. The development process will be faster and easier at each economic platform and, therefore, economic productivity will increases and costs of processes will decrease. However, it is more important to decrease the costs and increase the productivity in the context of the global economy to protect countries' competition power. Specially, if a country has scarce sources as developing countries, thereby using the existing sources more efficiently, the production sector can find more important place in global competitive conditions. Using the ICTs intensively, acceleration will also be created in the social platform. It can be possible with these technologies to increase the quality of life of each person's isochronal throughout the country. However, to achieve this aim, the education program needs to be reframed, at first. Thus, social development should be considered initially, so that underdeveloped regions and people living in those regions are able to find opportunities for establishing a higher level of standard in their work. By using ICTs the political arena can benefit, too. In this way, perception of the government

Copyright © 2007, Idea Group Inc. Copying or distributing in print or electronic forms without written permission of Idea Group Inc. is prohibited.

and citizenship is changed, and participation of the citizens to administration process acts efficiently. Thus, democracy is also realized. Therefore, reliance of the government and citizen is constructed (Turkey Information Foundation Association of Turkey Information Industrialists and Businessmen, 2004). A few of the benefits of the information and communication technologies in the social structure are given below:

- Behavior of public services is changed.
- Brings transformation in perceptiveness about administration.
- Bureaucracy is decreased.
- Cost of management is decreased due to the decreased use of files.
- Productivity increases.
- Effective and efficient services are given.
- E-democracy moves into the country.
- Tax revenues are increased.
- Accessibility to the information will be easier for people.
- Each person will be responsive to the world and participate in the country's development processes.
- Administrative participation process for citizens increases.
- Shorter time is needed to reach information at grass roots.
- Service costs will be minimized at all level for the citizens.
- Quality of education will be increased.
- Employment possibilities will increase.
- E-commerce will create new tools for innovative projects with least cost and fast dissemination.
- Connectivity among the establishments and business houses will be renewed.

E-Government Programs in Turkey

Objectives

After realizing that Europe needs benefit from the opportunities of the new economy, and especially what the Internet brings, the European Council prepared an Action Plan that was decided to be supported and developed by the European Commission in December 1999, not only to decrease the distance between Europe and the U.S., but also to decrease the imbalance among regions of Europe (European Commission,1998, 2000). Within the European Union, the Middle and East European Countries' high level Committee on Information Society was given responsibility to compose an Action Plan similar to E-Europe, at the Information Society European Ministers International Conference organized in Varshova during in May 2000. This enterprise was primarily called an "E-Europe-like Action Plan" and afterward named "E-Europe+." Later on, the European Council assembled in Lizbon in March 2000

Copyright © 2007, Idea Group Inc. Copying or distributing in print or electronic forms without written permission of Idea Group Inc. is prohibited.

and determined an objective to make Europe the most competitive and dynamic information based economy of the world (Cayhan, 2002). Main objectives of these initiatives are to:

- Provide faster, cheaper, and secured Internet infrastructure
- Cheaper and faster Internet for everybody
- Faster Internet for students and researchers
- Secured nets and intelligent cards
- Increased investment for people and their capacity development
- Prepare European youth for digital age
- Labour power for information economy
- Participation of everybody in the information economy

Encourage the use of Internet to speed up:

- E-Trade
- E-Government: Communication for public services
- Online health
- European digital contents for global nets
- Intelligent transportation system

After achieving the objectives determined by the 2002 Action Plan for E-Europe, European Union Countries determined long term objectives for themselves and prepared the continuation of the previous "E-Europe 2005 Action Plan." The aim of this new plan is to provide contemporary public service for private investigators, to increase productivity, to create suitable conditions for new jobs, and to give the opportunity for everyone to participate in the global Information Society. Furthermore, the goals of E-Europe 2005 (Communication From The Commission To The Council of The European Parliamanet, 2002) are to provide contemporary online public services, such as:

- E-Government
- E-Knowledge
- E-Health

However, it has been found that, dynamic e-work conditions provide the following benefits, such as:

- Competitive price
- Secured information infrastructure

Copyright © 2007, Idea Group Inc. Copying or distributing in print or electronic forms without written permission of Idea Group Inc. is prohibited.

While using E-Europe 2002 Action Plan for themselves, EU countries prepared E-Europe+ Action Plan for nominees in order to provide them an opportunity to achieve the same social transformation. It has been planned for the candidate countries to achieve these objectives till the end of the year 2003. By the E-Europe+ Action Plan, it is aimed for candidate contries to speed up their economic renewal, to support their institutional development, to develop their power for general competition and prepare plans for those deserving special conditions. According to this plan, the candidate countries agreed on political determination for four main objectives until the end of 2003.These four objectives are:

- To speed up the formation of the basis of information.
- To provide cheaper, faster, and a more-secured Internet.
- To provide investment for human research.
- To inspire Internet usage.

Before proceeding to discuss an e-government practice in Turkey, authors would like to focus on Turkey's transformation processes, which are structurally illustrated in Table 6.

E-Turkey Transformation Process

Turkey as a candidate country of the European Union, after agreement with the E-Europe+ Action plan, started working towards formation of an e-Turkey Action Plan parallel to the E-Europe+ Action Plan under the coordinaton of the Prime Ministry Counselorship since October 2001. For this purpose, 13 different working groups have been assembled comprised of private and civil social establishment representatives. At the end of an 18 month study of these groups, an Action Plan has been prepared and presented to the European Union with a situation determining First Midreport in May 2002. Furthermore, it has been decided that the preliminary conditions determined as the objectives of Turkish e-transformation programs have to be achieved. This preliminary determination is to speed up the main procedures of the Information Society:

- To provide appropriate priced communication services for everybody.
- To attract European Union about the Information Society.

At this level the agreement dates for adaptation criteria will be given to the European Union that have been determined by meetings under the Turkish Scientific Research Institute (TU-BITAK) secretaryship and in coordination with the European Union General Secretaryship and Ministry of Foreign Affairs (TUBITAK, 2002). According to the determined outline, Turkey has to meet all these criteria in 2006. Depending on this date of agreement, the European Mediterranean Partnership (MEDA) projects will end in 2006 (Cetin, Aydogan & Ertugrul, 2002).

Copyright © 2007, Idea Group Inc. Copying or distributing in print or electronic forms without written permission of Idea Group Inc. is prohibited.

Table 6. Work phases that Turkey performed

Related Institutions	Work	Year
ULAKBIM	Research net will be priority: National research nets will be developed in order to provide appropriate data for researchers and students in candidate countries by using MED foundations over more powerful nets.	Till the end of 2002
MEB, YOK, DTM, TUBITAK, TSE, private sector	General security of online processes will be increased: Cooperation among public/private sector on information basis and dependence to each other will be formed, partners will be educated about technological criminology and security, basic specifications for intelligent cards to be developed and security will be established. Common strategies for expanding the usage of intelligent cards will be developed and put into practise.	
UBAK, TELECOMMUNICATION INSTITUTION (TK), RTUK	Telecommunication sector will be liberated: Internet service will be appropriate for everybody, and arrangements will be completed.	Till the end of 2003
DPT, GAP Management, National treasury, Private sector, TK	Increasing support will be given on development of projects and Information Society; primarily in less developed regions.	
DTM, ETKK, Nongovernmental Organizations KOSGEB	Usage and recognition of electronic signature and studies for basis of e-trade will be accelerated.	
Ministry of Health, TT, Private sector	European Public health nets and databases will be established, infrastructure for health tematic will be developed.	
MEB, YOK, TBD	Expanded usage of a European certificate about basic Information Technologies will be promoted	Till the end of 2004
Ministry of Justice, DTM, ETKK, organizations of consumers, private sector, nongovernmental organizations	Reliance for e-trade among consumer groups and industry cooperation will be increased Appropriate attempts will be formed and efficient codes will be supported.	
UBAK, Ministry of Public Works, KGM, TT, TK	Development Plans, especially for highway infrastructure and intelligent transportation services, will be prepared.	
MEB, UBAK, TK, TT, TISSAD	Every school, student, and teacher will be able to use Internet: Support services and educational sources will be established. Educational curriculum and methods of teaching will be made dependent on ICTs.	Till the end of 2006
Ministry of Working and Social Security, working institution, Chambers of occupation, Nongovernmental Organizations	Appropriate education for finding jobs for people unemployed for a long time will be given	
Ministry of Working and Social Security, UBAK, TK, Management of the defectives, YOK, Private sector	Design of standards for the handicapped ones will be improved for access of Information Technologies. For excellence on this issue, national centers nets will be formed.	
Prime Ministry	Online data will be provided about legal, cultural, environmental, and traffic information. Online access to basic public services, easy online administrative procedure for commercial sector e-signature among public will be supported, and e-market for bids for the public contracts will be formed.	

Copyright © 2007, Idea Group Inc. Copying or distributing in print or electronic forms without written permission of Idea Group Inc. is prohibited.

To enhance the processes further, the Turkish Telecommunication Company has been given responsibility to develop the e-government portal in coordination with the State Planning Organization under guidance of the Council of Ministers on January 25, 2005 (State Planning Organization, 2005b). Previous to this, the State Planning Organization Counselorship was responsible for coordination, observation, evaluation, and direction of the E-Transformation Turkey Project as the Chairmanship of Information Society.

The goals, institutional structure, and application principles of the E-Transformation Turkey Project were delivered by a printed notice on February 27, 2003 (State Planning Organisation, 2005b). The Emergency Action Plan, E-Transformation Turkey Project is being held in three phases. These are (Ilter, 2000; State Planning Organisation Information Society Department, 2004):

- Phase one is comprised of preparation and review of the existing situation, especially for e-Turkey; and similar efforts will be evaluated. In this phase, report on recommendations based on applications of good examples in Turkey will be prepared.
- E-Transformation National Action Plan will be prepared in the second phase.
- In the third phase, the Action Plan will be put into practise. Report on observation of applications of the plan will be delivered to State Planning Organization Counselorship (State Planning Organization, 2002; Ulusoy & Karakurt, 2003).

As per the project under Turkish National Information Main Plan (TUENA), the cost price for the infrastructure is calculated to be $35 billion and under this project each of the citizen could reach national information infrastructure by 2010. It is foreseen that 14 billion of this amount will be spent for infrastructure, and $21 billion for output units like computers, Web, TV, and so forth.

It has been observed that among macroeconomic policies, e-government investments have a priority as far as the E-Transformation Turkey Project is concerned. However, it is stated that among the projects in practice, the ones which can be adopted to the E-Transformation Turkey Project will have priority parallel to sectoral and regional priorities (State Planning Organization, 2005c). Moreover, about e-government studies, it is stated that e-government services will be established holistically instead of individual institutional approaches. In this manner, it is mentioned that bureaucracy and other problems emerging from recessive connection among institutions will be decreased.

E-Government Practices in Turkey

With the Primeministry circular on December 4, 2003 (State Planning Organisation, 2005b), the application of the E-Transformation Turkey Project Short Term Action Plan had started an organizational struture. The Ministries of Industry and Commerce, Transportation, Education, Health, Justice and State Planning Organization, Institute of Turkey Standartization, Association of Turkey Information and Communication worked together in coordination for the Short Term Action Plan during 2003-2004. From a legal perspective, "Having Knowl-

Copyright © 2007, Idea Group Inc. Copying or distributing in print or electronic forms without written permission of Idea Group Inc. is prohibited.

edge Law" on 24th April 24, 2004 and "Electronic Signature Law" on July 23, 2004 came into effect and rules and regulations on electronic signatures were in operation beginning January 6, 2005 (State Planning Organisation, 2005b).

In addition to these, there is an important tool for transformation of Information Society working in Turkey, that is, "The Project of E-Transformation in Turkey." Targets of this project are development of social welfare, efficient use of investments, effective use of information to decrease the cost of services, and increased international competition. In this context, policies and strategies are being taken. Technical infrastructure and safety of information, education, human resource, legal infrastructure, standardization, e-management, e-health, and e-commerce are taken as a base for the process of transformation. The Board of Directors of "E-Transformation of Turkey" has prepared the Document of Transformation Policy for Information Society. In that document, it is recommended that public institutions and civil society institutions should work together. Furthermore, in the document the most important thing which has been raised is e-government. In this context, studies have already started and important steps have been achieved by the state. For example, literacy rates and Internet use have increased. In this framework, the Ministry of Education and Turkish Telecommunication Company has developed a protocol. According to the protocol, 42,534 schools throughout the country could have Asymmetric Digital Subscriber Lines by the end of 2005. At the same time, 58,900 schools are to have computers and Internet connections. By this time, 578,800 teachers were educated by using the computer as an educational tool. Another project has been launched in the e-government context that aims to increase numerical illiterate people that exist in the public institution.

In the framework of the E-Transformation Turkey Project, the tendency of investment in public institution for ICTs has increased. In 2002, under the National Investment Program, 203 projects were taken with 286,013 billion TL (158.8 million US$); in 2003 for 204 projects 369,321 billion TL (208.6 million US$) were allocated; in 2004 for 211 project 451,181 billion TL (281.3 million US$) budget was given; and in 2005 for 200 projects 626, 253 YTL (388.4 million US$) was disbursed. It has been observed that, in this area investment for public services increased by 16.6% from 2002 to 2003, by 8.4% from 2003 to 2004 and in 2005 special investment was made in education. At the Investment Program about ICTs cost of the project investments was 2,088,708,000 YTL (1,295,725 US$) in 2005. The rates of it inside the total public ivestment is 2.9% in 2002; 3.0% in 2003; 3.8% in 2004; and 3.9% in 2005 (Odabas, 2005; State Planning Organization, 2005a).

In August 25, 2005, there were 6,722 Internet hosts in Turkey that belonged to institutions providing public services. Distribution of them, especially belong to the central administration. These are 3,029 for central administration (gov.tr), 1,001 for local administration (bel.tr), 2,372 for primary and secondary schools (k12.tr), 186 for university or institute (edu.tr), 8 for military service (mil.tr), and 126 for security (pol.tr) (State Planning Organization, 2003; TUBITAK, 2002). Figure 1 shows the distribution of subdomains of .tr and it can be observed that .com remains at the top with 48,136 hosts.

Usually, land phone, mobile phone and Internet penetration are being accepted as the basic indicators of ICT. Surprisingly, it was found that in Turkey, only in 2002, 10,000 people had new subscriptions for phones, but it was decreased in 2003. Mobile phone subscription growth was fast especially in recent years, that is, looking at the period of 1994 until today. In 2003, it had reached to approximately 27.9 million subscribers in Turkey. In this rank-

Copyright © 2007, Idea Group Inc. Copying or distributing in print or electronic forms without written permission of Idea Group Inc. is prohibited.

Figure 1. Distribution of the name servers according to the subdomain names

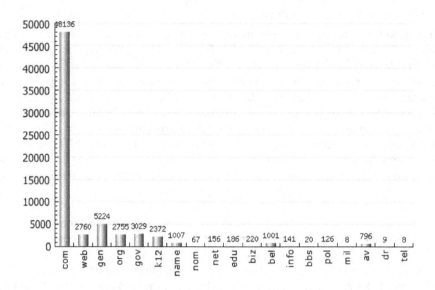

Table 7. Infrastructure of information technologies in different countries of the world

COUNTRIES	PC/100	İnternet PC/10000	Online population %	Phone/ 100	Mobile/ 100	TV/1000
USA	59	2,928	62	70	37	847
Australia	47	844	53	53	45	639
New Zealand	36	901	46	50	40	501
Singapore	48	438	50	49	68	348
Norway	49	1,009	54	73	70	579
Canada	39	769	47	68	29	715
England	34	281	55	57	67	645
Holland	40	1,017	54	61	67	543
Denmark	43	627	55	75	61	585
Germany	34	248	35	60	59	580
Sweden	51	671	70	68	71	531
Finland	40	1,023	48	55	73	64
İsrael	25	288	17	1	70	318
Brazil	4	52	7	18	14	316
İtaly	21	178	33	48	74	486
Arab Emirates	13	176	33	42	59	294
İrland	37	296	33	43	67	456
Kuwait	12	18	8	24	25	491
Argentina	5	73	11	21	16	289
Lebanon	5	23	9.0	20	19	352
TURKEY	4	11	6	28	25	286

Source: U.N. (2002)

Copyright © 2007, Idea Group Inc. Copying or distributing in print or electronic forms without written permission of Idea Group Inc. is prohibited.

ing, Turkey has ranked as sixth among the European Union member countries. Internet use is also increasing year by year in Turkey. In 2003, the Internet users in Turkey increased by 5.8% in comparison to 31.1% in the European Union; in 2002, Internet users increased to 7.1% in Turkey, while there was a 35.7% increase in the European Union; and in 2003 Turkey's Internet user growth rate was 8.48%, while the European Union rate was 38.50% (Oruc & Arslan, 2002). Table 7 shows a few ICT indicators and they have been compared with other countries.

Furthermore, in the report on "Global Information Technology," prepared by the World Economic Forum, there are ranked countries related to transformation of information tech-

Table 8. Basic indicators related to the ICTs in Turkey

	2003	2004	2005
Capacity phone switchboard (thousand people)	21.163	21.006	21.106
Phone subscribers (thousand people)	18.917	19.125	19.000
Concentration of phone subscriber (%)	26.8	26.7	26.2
Mobile subscribers (thousand people)	27.925	34.708	43.000
Concentration of mobile subscriber (%)	39.5	48.5	59.3
Internet users (thousand people)	6.000	10.000	15.000
Concentration of internet users (%)	8.5	14.0	20.7
Wide band users (thousand people)	100	500	1.500
Cable TV Subscribers(thousand people)	1.044	1.127	1.250
Market length (in billions/dollars)	10.3	11.9	13.8

Source: State Planning Organization, 2005.

Table 9. E-Readiness preparation to information society in different countries

2002-2003			2003-2004		
RANK	COUNTRIES	POINT	RANK	COUNTRIES	POINT
1	Finland	5.92	1	USA	5.50
2	USA	5.79	2	Singapore	5.40
3	Singapore	5.74	3	Finland	5.23
4	Sweden	5.58	4	Sweden	5.20
5	Iceland	5.51	5	Denmark	5.19
6	Canada	5.44	6	Canada	5.07
7	England	5.35	7	Switzerland	5.06
8	Denmark	5.33	8	Norway	5.03
9	Taiwan	5.31	9	Australia	4.88
10	Germany	5.29	10	İceland	4.88
...	...	...	...	...	...
50	TURKEY	3.57	56	TURKEY	3.2
Total 82 countries			Total 102 countries		

Source: State Planning Organisation, 2005b; World Economic Forum, 2005

Copyright © 2007, Idea Group Inc. Copying or distributing in print or electronic forms without written permission of Idea Group Inc. is prohibited.

Table 10. Computer ownership in Turkey

YEAR	1994	1995	1996	1997	1998	1999	2000	2001	2002	TARGET 2015
Computer Ownership	790	920	1100	1300	1700	2200	2500	2700	3000	14100
Computer ownership for each 100	1.3	1.49	1.1	2.31	5.16	11.6	22.2	26.6	33.5	17.2

Source: State Planning Organisation & United Nations Mukim Coordinatorship, 2005

Table 11. Internet users in Turkey

YEAR	1999	2000	2001	2002	2003	2004	TARGET2015
Internet users for each 100	900	1,500	2,500	4,000	6,000	10,000	22,000
Internet using for each 100 %	1.35	2.22	3.65	5.76	8.52	14.01	27.0

Source: Turkish Telecommunication Company, 2005

nology. In this ranking, technical infrastructure remains an important indicator as compared to service performance and development. Technical production ability and legal regulations criteria are also taken into account. Turkey's placement in this ranking within the countries is given in Table 8. Table 9 provides an e-readiness comparison, Table 10 gives an overview on computer ownership since 1994 with a target indicator in 2015, and Table 11 gives an overview on Internet users from 1999 with a target of 20,000 in 2005.

E-Government Application Studies in the Context of Regional Development in Turkey

The searching of following a definite policy in the field of science and technology and the formation of this matter started with a planned period and TUBITAK was founded in 1963 during the first Five Year Development Plan (1963-67); the Second Five Years Plan (1968-1973); the Third Five Years Plan (1973-1977); and the Fourth Five Years Plan (1979-1983) were successfully implemented. Thus, Five Five Year of Development Plans were prepared and the technological improvements and the technology transfer regions were included in this plan. The fourth Five Year Development process dealt with the policies of technology, and it was foreseen that the policies of technology should be considered as a whole stucture with employment and investment policies. The same subjects are also mentioned in the latest, the eighth Five Year Development Plan in 2004 (State Planning Organization, 2002).

Copyright © 2007, Idea Group Inc. Copying or distributing in print or electronic forms without written permission of Idea Group Inc. is prohibited.

In the context of the European Union Adaptation process, the studies about Turkey's communication and information fields are also increased. On October 4, 2001, the studies on formation of E-Turkey Action Plan were started in coordination with the E-Europe Action Plan under the Prime Ministry's Councillor. By January 25, 2005, the responsibility was given to the Turkish Telecommunication Company e-government portal under the coordination of the State Planning Organization. In this way, the projects of information and communication of Turkey have been carried out rapidly. These projects are carried out in such a way that entails the whole country. In other words, none of the existing projects could avoid the digital division in socioeconomically less developed regions (Cetin, Aydogan & Ertugrul, 2002).

However, in accordance with the aims of regional development, no special work regarding the communication and information was confirmed in the projects which were started during the period of the Seventh Five Year Development Plan. These projects are Eastern Anatolian Project, South-Eastern Anatolian Project, Eastern Black Sea Regional Development Project, Zonguldak Bartın Karabük Regional Growth Project, and Yeşilırmak Sphere Growth Project; and they are working with the following objectives to:

- Increase the income and the employment per person.
- Reform the income distribusion inside the regional areas.
- Widen the activities which will speed up the developments.
- Acquire the long term continuing development by protecting the natural resouces and the capacity of the region.
- Provide the continuation of development.
- Improve (develop) the subregional centers as industrial and service centers.
- Improve the private sector.
- Increase the opportunities of employment.
- Increase the agricultural productivity.
- Develop the manufacturing sector related with agriculture.
- Increase the indicators of health and education up to the level of country's average.
- Increase the inside-region and outside-region connectivity.
- Prepare the practice devoted to human improvement.
- Form a filter against the East-West immigration.

In Turkey, related to ICTs projects, it is seen that the required infrastructure projects are being planned by choosing pilot regions which are developed socioeconomically throughout the country, instead of preparing special projects for undeveloped or underdeveloped regions. The reason for this is, when compared to various countries worldwide, the infrastructure of data processing in Turkey is quite insufficient. And what is more the Turkey prefers; by applying all these projects initially in order to use those experiences in socioeconomically developed regions. After realization for these regions then transmit them to the underdeveloped regions of the country. By using this method, implementation will be less expensive

Copyright © 2007, Idea Group Inc. Copying or distributing in print or electronic forms without written permission of Idea Group Inc. is prohibited.

and, at the same time, the results will be reached in a short period in terms of ICTs. However, these may be applicable for government run initiatives.

In Turkey, the relationship between information and knowledge technologies and regional development was weak until 2000. After the E-Turkey Action Plan that is related to the E-Europe+ Action Plan to constitute e-transformation, Turkey has been trying to complete faster organizational, legislation and infrastructure works. In this period of time Turkey has moved forward working about knowledge society importantly, in order to decrease the knowledge disparities within the society. The primary target of Turkey is to transform to an Information Society in the next five years (San, 2005).

In the Preliminary National Development Plan (2004-2006), long term knowledge society strategies have been included that will be completed by 2023 (State Planning Organization, 2003). Turkey will also update the programs of the institutions according to the 2006-2008 program that included regional, national, and international improvements and demands. Besides this, it is implied that the development of the information in the areas of trans-portation, education, health, agriculture, industry, mining, and manufacturer sectors have been taken into account in the framework of knowledge and information technologies, and infrastructures will be developed throughout the country (State Planning Organization, 2005a). According to the report on the e-transformation in Turkey 2006, it is determined that knowledge and information technologies have focused primarily on investment in e-government. These investments will be distributed with balance among the regions. To realize this, apart from the central administration, local administrations, non-governmental organizations, universities, private sector entrepreneurs, and local unions will be included in some projects. This will be done firstly, to realize regional development and secondly, to achieve a high rate of welfare succession on the global platform. However, within the perspective of these targets, it is important to have e-strategy. Turkey has the aim to com-plete the infrastructure in relation to the e-strategy to be included in the first 15th rank on knowledge economy in the world by 2015 (State Planning Organization, 2005c). It is also important to realize governance along with this aim. Nongovernmental organizations, local administrations, and professional institutions will be included to work to achieve this aim. At the same time, to increase qualified people and to widen remote education, programs will be applied in the e-strategy. Specifically, this will create new employment facilities in underdeveloped regions, income levels will be increased, competition power will be strengthened, necessary technical infrastructure systems will be established all over the country, and legislation will be accomplished.

Result and Evaluation

In this document, it is analyzed that Turkey has used the ICTs in the undeveloped areas in order to provide the socioeconomic escalation as summarized as follows:

- According to the Census 2000, Turkey, having the population of 67,844,903, with a rate of 18.34% population increase, and national income of US$4,744 per person

Copyright © 2007, Idea Group Inc. Copying or distributing in print or electronic forms without written permission of Idea Group Inc. is prohibited.

(according to the 2005 data), is included as one of the developing countries. However, there are regions differing from each other in the concept of socioeconomic development.

- In Turkey, various policies have been produced since 1963 (the planned period) in order to develop the socioeconomically backward regions. State Planning Organisation has been responsible for this to provide the coordination and to activate the projects.

- In Turkey, the targets of the regional development policies are to minimize the socioeconomic differences among regions, to improve the private sector, to complete the infrastructure of transportaion, to increase the education and health services, to increase the productivity of agriculture, to increase employment, and to increase the income per person.

- Recently,Turkey has accelerated the programs in the field of ICTs in order to compete with the other countries in the global aspect and to get benefit from the positive values resulting from the differences in the ICTs. As Turkey is a candidate country for the European Union membership and as the European Union is giving importance to the projects on ICTs, it is important for Turkey to carry out similar projects.

- On October 4, 2001, the project on formation of an E-Turkey Action Plan was started in coordination with the E-Europe Action Plan under guidance of the Prime Ministry's Councillor. On January 25, 2005, Turkish Telcommunication Company started implementing the E-government Portal under the coordination of the State Planning Organisation. Similarly, the Information Society Department Presidency was founded in the structure of SPO which is responsible for the coordination, observation, evaluation, and the orientation of the E-Transformation Turkey Project.

- When compared to various other countries of the world the infrastructure of data processing in Turkey is at the bottom levels. It has been found that, one of the most important problems about the usage of ICTs is the digital division. This is due to low income status of each individual in the country.

- The programs regarding the ICTs in the country are applied in the pilot regions where the results of the projects are supplied with a lower cost and in a shorter time.

- In a developing country like Turkey, use of ICTs in socioeconomic and social development is a great opportunity, but regarding the use, in terms of time and funding, it is quite insufficient. Turkey cannot properly take this opportunity as an advantage, unless every kind of project has been practiced in educational, legal, political, economical, and social aspects in order to increase the ability to compete with other countries in the global aspect and to use the ICTs effectively within the country.

Turkey has a young and dynamic population and this is an advantage to e-transformation. If there is an integration between the regional development projects and knowledge and information technologies development, regional migration tendencies will be decreased and the population will be employed in the regions. In conclusion, with knowledge and information technologies, differentiation or polarization of the regions will be prevented and certain socioeconomic levels will be reached in all the regions of Turkey.

Copyright © 2007, Idea Group Inc. Copying or distributing in print or electronic forms without written permission of Idea Group Inc. is prohibited.

References

Akder, H. (2003). *Regional inequality and rural poverty in Turkey: Human development approach*.Ankara, Turkey: State Planning Organization Press. Retrieved June 29, 2006, from http://www.tesev.org.tr/projeler/ yoksulluk_bolgesel_metin_teblig2.php

Cayhan, E. (2002). E-Government in European Union. In *Proceedings of the National Information Economy and Management Conference* (pp. 315-332), University of Sakarya Press.

Cetin, H., Aydogan, O., & Ertugrul, Z. (2002). *E-Turkey condition analysis and solution propsals*.Ankara, Turkey: Telecommunication Institute Publications.

Communication from the commission yo the council the european parliamanet. (2002, August 28). E-Europe 2005: An information society for all action plan to be presented in view of the Sevilla European Commission. The Economic and Social Committe Of Regions.

Dag, R. (2002). *Development of eastern and south eastern regional: Marco politics of regional development.* Ankara, Turkey: State Planning Organization Press.

Dinler, Z. (1998). *Regional Economy.* Bursa, Turkey: Ezgi Publications.

European Commission. (1998). *Public sector information: A key resource for Europe.* Green Paper on Public Sector Information in the Information Society, COM 585.

European Commission. (2000, June 19-20). *E-Europe 2002: An information society for all.* Action Plan Prepared By The Council and the European Commission For Feira European Council.

Gurbuz, B. (2001). *Planning of rural development: Example of brusa administrative province and district keles.* Unpublished doctoral dissertation, University of Uludag, Bursa.

Ilter, G. (2000). *Government and Internet strategies.* Retrieved June 29, 2006, from http://www.edevlet.net/eTurkiye/devletveinternet.pdf

Kurt, M. (2003). *Development of Turkey economy for a model proposal: Foundation of knowledge development.* Retrieved June 29, 2006, from http://www.bilgiyonetimi.org/cm/pages/mkl_gos.php?nt=551

Odabas, C. (2005). Strtegical Adminstration and E-Government. *Periodical of Sayistay, 1*, 83-93

Oruc, E., & Arslan, S. (2002). *Prevent of numerical gap: Stratgical plan.* Ankara,Turkey: Telecommunication Institute Press. Retrieved June 29, 2006, from http://www.tk.gov.tr/Yayin/Raporlar/ pdf/Sayisal_Ucurumun_onlenmesi.pdf

Ozturk, N. (2001). *Regional development in Turkey and south eastern anatolian project.* Unpublished doctoral dissertation, University of Uludag, Bursa.

Regional Development Specialization Commission Report. (2002). *Eighth five year of development plan.* Ankara, Turkey: State Planning Organization Press.

San, M. (2005). *Knowledge management at devlopment planning and instutitional knowledge politic model for state planning organization.* Ankara, Turkey: Management Information Center Department Presidency Press.

Copyright © 2007, Idea Group Inc. Copying or distributing in print or electronic forms without written permission of Idea Group Inc. is prohibited.

State Planning Organization. (2000) *Eastern Anatolian Project*. Ankara, Turkey: State Planning Organisation Press.

State Planning Organization. (2002). *AR-GEAR-GE group work report*, Second Science Council of Turkey. Ankara, Turkey: State Planning Organization Press.

State Planning Organization. (2003). *Turkey Republic Forepart of National Development Plan*. Ankara, Turkey: State Planning Organization Press.

State Planning Organisation Information Society Department. (2004, January). Information economy strategies and politics of information society in Turkey, 22. Working Group: Outline Report of Information Society and Information Economy. In *Proceedings of the Izmir Economy Conference*. Ankara, Turkey: State Planning Organisation Information Society Department Press.

State Planning Organisation & United Nations Mukim Coordinatorship. (2005). *Turkey Millennium Year Development Aims Report*. Ankara,Turkey: State Planning Organisation Press. Retrieved June 29, 2006, from http://www.un.org.tr/undp_tur/docs/mdg/binyil05.pdf

State Planning Organization. (2005a). *Middle term program 2006-2008*. Ankara, Turkey: State Planning Organization Press. Retrieved June 29, 2006, from http://ekutup.dpt.gov.tr/program/2006-2008pdf

State Planning Organisation. (2005b). *E-Transformation Turkey Project 2005 action plan*. Ankara, Turkey: State Planning Organisation Information Society Department Presidency Press. Retrieved June 29, 2006, from http://www.bilgitoplumu.gov.tr/2005EP/2005EylemPlani.pdf

State Planning Organization. (2005c). *E-Transformation Turkey Project with information and communication about technologies subjects in 2006 year programme*. Ankara, Turkey: State Planning Organization Press.

State Planning Organization. (2006a). Retrieved June 29, 2006, from http://www.dpt.gov.tr/bgyu/bkp/gap.html

State Planning Organization. (2006b). Retrieved June 29, 2006, from http://www.dpt.gov.tr/bgyu/bkp/yeşilırmak.html

State Statistical Institute. (2003). Retrieved June 29, 2006, from http://www.die.gov.tr

Tavgac, G. (2001). *Inter regional development policy in Turkish development plans*. Unpublished master's dissertation, University of Uludag, Bursa.

Tekeli, İ. (1981). *Regional politics in period of Four plan and space differentiation of economic growing. Periodical of ODTÜ Gelişme*. Ankara, Turkey.

TUBITAK. (2002). *Turkey information society: Strategic country [TUENA Declaration]*. Retrieved June 29, 2006, from http://www.tuena.tubitak.gov.tr/basin/basin-5-haziran.pdf

Turkey Information Foundation Association of Turkey Information Industrialist and Businessmen. (2004). *E-Transformation Turkey Executive Comittee short term action plan of information society strategic plan preparation*. İstanbul, Turkey: Turkey Information Foundation Association of Turkey Information Industrialist and Businessmen Press.

Copyright © 2007, Idea Group Inc. Copying or distributing in print or electronic forms without written permission of Idea Group Inc. is prohibited.

Turkish Telecommunication Company. (2005). *The statistics of Turkish telecommunication*. Ankara, Turkey: Turkish Telecommunication Company Press.

Uckan, Ö. (2003). *E-Government, E-Democracy and Turkey*. Istanbul, Turkey: Literatür Publications.

Ulusoy, A., & Karakurt, B. (2003). Necessity of transition to e-government in Turkey. In *Proceedings of the National Information Economy and Management Conference*, University of Kocaeli, Turkey.

U.N. (2002). *Benchmarking e-government: A global perspective*. United Nations.

World Economic Forum. (2005). Retrieved June 29, 2006, from http://weforum.org

Yıldırır, H., & Karakurt, E. (2005). E-Government and applications. *Periodical of Isguc*, *6*(1). Retrieved June 29, 2006, from http://www.isguc.org

Yıldız, M. (2003). *Evaluation and general of view of electronic (E)-Government theories and applications*. Contemporary Public Administration I. Istanbul, Turkey: Nobel Publication.

Copyright © 2007, Idea Group Inc. Copying or distributing in print or electronic forms without written permission of Idea Group Inc. is prohibited.

Chapter XV

ICTs as Tools for Poverty Reduction:
The Tanzanian Experience

Zaipuna O. Yonah, Tanzania Telecommunications Company Ltd., Tanzania

Baanda A. Salim, Sokoine University of Agriculture, Tanzania

Abstract

This chapter attempts to enhance the understanding and knowledge of Information and Communication Technologies (ICTs) in relation to the Tanzania National ICT Policy as a case study. The authors extensively explore these pervading technologies as they impact on the education, commerce, social, cultural, and economic life of the poor Tanzanian people. The chapter looks at how Tanzania is coping with the issue of poverty eradication as one of the eight UN Millennium Development Goals (MDGs). It addresses the issue of digital divide and the role that ICTs can play in poverty reduction. Tanzania's efforts in embracing ICTs and the challenges facing the country in its efforts are also addressed. Overall, the chapter demonstrates that ICTs are a set of tools for knowledge sharing, which is a powerful means for poverty reduction. Furthermore, it is advisable to focus on information literacy rather than just focusing on computer literacy.

Copyright © 2007, Idea Group Inc. Copying or distributing in print or electronic forms without written permission of Idea Group Inc. is prohibited.

Introduction

In this chapter, an attempt has been made to enhance the understanding and knowledge of Information and Communication Technologies (ICTs) in relation to the Tanzania National ICT Policy as a case study. The authors extensively explore the evolving frontiers of these pervading technologies as they impact on education, commerce, social, cultural and economic life of the poor Tanzanian people. The chapter also attempts to show case examples of ICT national projects in Tanzania to demonstrate how the government of Tanzania, entrepreneurs, and some of the rural communities are appropriating ICTs to fit into their needs. The chapter reflects on perspectives, trends, and potential of using ICTs to develop innovative approaches and methods for poverty reduction in Tanzania.

The chapter is organized into six sections. The Background section looks at the general issues, putting Tanzania into perspective and how it is coping with the issue of poverty eradication as one of the eight U.N. Millennium Development Goals (MDGs). Targets for achieving poverty eradication are articulated in the National Poverty Eradication Strategy. The Development Vision 2025 aims at guiding Tanzania to achieve five goals by year 2025, namely, (1) high quality livelihood, (2) peace, stability, and unity, (3) good governance, (4) a well educated and learning society, and (5) a strong and competitive economy. This section further puts into perspective Tanzania's position on the role of ICTs in meeting the goals of the Vision 2025 as well as the MDGs. The framework for appropriating these ICTs for national development and poverty reduction is articulated in the National ICT Policy.

The second section attempts to answer the question: what is poverty and what causes it? It is noted that ICTs are now acknowledged to be a set of powerful tools for building the capacity for knowledge management and hence for building the capacity for poverty reduction. It also addresses the issue of digital divide. The third section addresses the role that ICTs can play in poverty reduction. It outlines the desirable characteristics and attributes of the modern ICTs useful for poverty reduction. This section further addresses issues of connectivity, affordability, and capability. The fourth section details efforts that Tanzania has made in embracing ICTs. It narrates on various projects being undertaken in Tanzania such as projects on increasing capacities and opportunities; projects on reducing vulnerabilities; projects on enhancing government capacity, efficiency, and accountability; and projects on participation, empowerment, and the strengthening of civil society.

The fifth section looks at the challenges facing the country in its efforts to embrace ICTs. It also looks at the prospects and try to project the trend of adoption of ICTs in the country in the next five or so years. In the last section of the chapter, some recommendations are drawn on "an entry point" into dissemination of ICTs to the rural areas of Tanzania. In this section, the authors try to lay out priority areas in harnessing the power of ICTs in bringing about development to the rural people of Tanzania.

Background

Tanzania is one of the 191 United Nations member states that have pledged to meet the eight UN Millennium Development Goals (MDGs) by year 2015 (URT, n.d.). These goals

Copyright © 2007, Idea Group Inc. Copying or distributing in print or electronic forms without written permission of Idea Group Inc. is prohibited.

are: (a) Eradicate extreme poverty and hunger, (b) achieve universal primary education, (c) promote gender equality and empower women, (d) reduce child mortality, (e) improve maternal health, (f) combat HIV/AIDs, malaria and other diseases, (g) ensure environmental sustainability and (h) develop a global partnership for development. In response to this pledge, Tanzania restated the UN-MDGs and came out with its own nine (9) development goals, herein to be referred to as TZ-MDGs, namely (URT, n.d.):

a.   **Extreme poverty:** Halve the proportion of people living below the national poverty line by 2015.

b.   **HIV/AIDS:** Halt and reverse the spread by 2015.

c.   **Hunger:** Halve the proportion of underweight, under five year olds by 2015.

d.   **Basic amenities:** Halve the proportion of people without access to safe drinking water by 2015.

e.   **Primary education:** Achieve universal primary education by 2015.

f.   **Gender equity:** Achieve equal access for boys and girls to primary and secondary schooling by 2015.

g.   **Reproductive health:** Reduce maternal mortality ratio by three-quarters by 2015.

h.   **Under-five mortality:** Reduce under five mortality by two-thirds by 2015.

i.   **Environmental sustainability:** Reverse loss of environmental resources by 2015.

The focus of this chapter is on the first TZ-MDG, which is on eradication of extreme poverty. As is in many developing countries, poverty in Tanzania is characterized by low income and expenditure, high mortality and morbidity, poor nutritional status, low educational attainment, vulnerability to external shocks like natural disasters (e.g. drought, pests, diseases and floods), and exclusion from economic, social and political processes. Generally, poverty is particularly widespread in the rural areas, but is not insignificant in urban areas. There are also important regional and district differences in the levels and specific dimensions of poverty. Those most at risk of being trapped to live under poverty are young children and youths, the elderly, women, those in large households and those involved in subsistence agriculture, livestock production and small-scale fishing.

The primary targets for achieving the first TZ-MDG on poverty eradication are articulated in the National Poverty Eradication Strategy (NPES) (URT, 1997). The set timeline for this TZ-MDG, which is more ambitious than the international one (2015), is to halve extreme poverty (measured by income and expenditure) by 2010 and eradicate it by 2025, which corresponds to the articulation of the goals of the Tanzania Development Vision 2025 (URT, n.d.). The Development Vision 2025 aims at guiding Tanzania to achieve five goals by year 2025, namely: (1) high quality livelihood, (2) peace, stability and unity, (3) good governance, (4) a well-educated and learning society, and (5) a strong and competitive economy capable of producing sustainable growth and shared benefits. Overall, the Vision foresees that by the year 2025:

Copyright © 2007, Idea Group Inc. Copying or distributing in print or electronic forms without written permission of Idea Group Inc. is prohibited.

Tanzania should have created a strong, diversified, resilient and competitive economy, which can effectively cope with the challenges of development and, which can also easily and confidently adapt to the changing market and technological conditions in the regional and global economy.

The challenge is, therefore, to mobilize massive resources towards the realization of the Vision 2025 goals.

It is worth noting that the Government of Tanzania has already acknowledged that ICTs can be harnessed to meet the goals of the Vision 2025, as well as that of the TZ-MDG on poverty reduction. In broad terms, ICTs refer to any technique or knowledge used to create, store, manage, and disseminate information. They include simple information centres with notice boards, books, brochures, posters, and newspapers, simple content systems running on cheap (safely disposable) hardware, for example, audio and video cassettes, disconnected mailing systems, to locally browse-able content accessible through a range of electronic technologies such as telephone, fax, television, and radio. Modern ICTs include the Internet, e-mail, computers, mobile phones, digital cameras, online databases and portals.

In a sense, ICTs enable communication, a process that links individuals and communities, governments and citizens, in participation and shared decision making. This is done through use of a variety of ICTs to engage, motivate, and educate citizens of opportunities for development and poverty reduction, in this way promoting changes in peoples attitudes and behaviours and thus increasing their participation in the development or poverty reduction processes (Gillman, 2003).

The framework for appropriating these ICTs for national development and poverty reduction is articulated in the National ICT Policy (United Republic of Tanzania, 2003). In the policy framework, it is clearly shown that ICTs are crosscutting in nature, an attribute well shared with poverty. As such, therefore, ICTs can indeed be appropriated as tools for realizing effective communication processes to achieve, among others, distribution and sharing of knowledge and information for supporting poverty reduction initiatives.

In this chapter, an attempt is made to enhance the understanding and knowledge of ICTs and the evolving frontiers of these pervading technologies are explored as they impact on education, commerce, social, cultural and economic life of the poor Tanzanian people. It also attempts to show case examples of ICT national projects that demonstrate how the government of Tanzania, entrepreneurs, and some of the rural communities are appropriating ICTs as tools to fit into their needs and empower themselves to fight poverty. Further, an attempt is made to stimulate debate to reflect on perspectives, trends, and potential of using ICTs to develop innovative approaches and methods for poverty reduction.

What is Poverty and What Really Causes It?

Widespread and persistent poverty in Tanzania is the main development challenge since the 1990s. Currently, about 40% of the population lives below the basic needs national poverty line (World Bank, 2004), that is, a population surviving on less than US$2 per day.

Copyright © 2007, Idea Group Inc. Copying or distributing in print or electronic forms without written permission of Idea Group Inc. is prohibited.

A debatable issue arises here: *what does poverty really entail?* Poverty is often viewed from an income-based perspective as lack of income and measured in terms of income and expenditure. In recent years, however, the concept has been enlarged. Poverty is now seen as a multidimensional concept that is the opposite of well-being, which includes more than income. Therefore, apart from the inability of poor people to meet basic needs (such as nutrition, clothing, and shelter), poverty also refers to disadvantages in access to land, credit, and services (e.g., health and education), vulnerability to violence, external economic shocks, natural disasters, powerlessness, and social exclusion (Shaffer, 2001; Williams, Sawyer & Hutchinson, 1999).

According to the Government Poverty Reduction Strategy Paper (PSRP) (URT, 2000) and the Poverty Monitoring Master Plan (PMMP) (URT, 2001), people living in poverty in our society are reidentified to include: illiterate people; unskilled labourers; self-employed micro-entrepreneurs; subsistence farmers; women; children; and population living in remote (rural) areas. Those in the group that are extremely vulnerable include children, persons with disabilities, youths, elderly, people living with HIV/AIDS, women, drug addicts, and alcoholics.

Poverty, the simplest indicator of alienation (Allen, 2002), causes a citizen to feel devalued, resentful, frustrated, and angry. Despite the vast advances that are being made in the spheres of science and technology, medicine, capital mobility, and so forth, income disparities are ever widening, both within countries and between nations. This imbalance in equity is characteristic of alienation—alienation between developed and developing nations; alienation between civilizations or cultures; alienations within our nation (regions, districts, etc.) and even alienation within families. Therefore, overcoming poverty, a consequence of alienation, will require the full participation of every member of the Tanzanian society. It is worthwhile to note that ICTs are now acknowledged to be a set of powerful tools for building our capacity to care, knowledge management, and hence for building the capacity for poverty reduction. In the literature, alienation based on modern ICTs is also popularly known as the digital divide (Weigel & Waldburger, 2004).

Poverty Reduction

The poverty reduction challenge is about how to empower the poor with knowledge and skills, thus availing to them new opportunities to improve their livelihood (Weigel & Waldburger, 2004). In terms of income and expenditure this would mean an increase in income, and hence capacity to afford food, health services, and other basic needs.

The strategic approach is to use ICTs in a creative manner to level the playing field in economic, social, cultural, and political terms by reducing the rapidly growing gap caused by a very asymmetric architecture of opportunities between the rich and the poor. As a matter of emphasis, the role of ICTs in poverty reduction is not limited to reducing income poverty, but also includes non-economic dimensions, in particular, empowerment (Gerster & Zimmerman, 2003). This can be accomplished through a variety of strategies ranging from the *sustainable livelihoods approach*—by putting people first; *production-oriented growth strategy*—which focuses on pro-poor corrective measures; a *distribution-oriented*

Copyright © 2007, Idea Group Inc. Copying or distributing in print or electronic forms without written permission of Idea Group Inc. is prohibited.

strategy—which emphasizes the redistribution of wealth within the nation; and a *rights and empowerment strategy*—which promotes knowledge about basic rights and empowerment (Gerster & Zimmerman, 2003;Weigel & Waldburger, 2004).

It was stated earlier that modern ICTs facilitate the creation, storage, management, and dissemination of information by electronic means much more easily, efficiently, and conveniently. Some of the desirable characteristics and attributes of these modern ICTs useful for poverty reduction include:

a. **Interactivity:** ICTs are effective two-way communication technologies, which have drastically changed the way individuals, organizations, and enterprises interact. This is made possible by the fact that modern ICTs embody broad communication and processes of economics, social, political activity, and organization to empower citizens. At the same time ICTs increases transparency within and among societies, fostering empowerment and accountability (Sharma, n.d.; Spence, 2003).

b. **Permanent availability:** The new ICTs are available 24 hours a day, seven days a week. For this reason they can be mainstreamed into our daily activities.

c. **Global reach:** When ICTs are embraced in any socioeconomic activity, geographic distances hardly matter anymore. This has changed the shape of the socioeconomic activities. One of the impacts is in conditioning and changing the structure of markets, hence pushing the world towards globalization. This is true for the case of the Internet, which enables individuals in any country to participate in markets or activities beyond the immigration constraints determined by geographic locations (Sharma, n.d.).

d. **Reduced per unit transaction costs:** Relative costs of communication have shrunk to a fraction of previous values and this effect has impacted on the cost of business transactions. Transaction costs have tended to rise with time, distance, and correlated variables, especially as the global economy has expanded and become more integrated. With modern ICTs, time and distance essentially do not matter. Therefore, the reduction in transaction costs can be larger in absolute and percentage terms than the rising trend. A good example is on long distance or international telephone calls vis voice over IP (VoIP) calls.

e. **Creates increased productivity and wealth or value:** ICTs are value adders and amplifiers in products and services. In addition to lowering transaction costs, modern ICTs can be very liberating by enabling wholly new possibilities of creating wealth/value. For example, by making services previously difficulty to trade or non-traded at all to become easily tradable—within countries and internationally. ICTs also are capable of untrapping the value of human resources or human capital (e.g., with local skills) by marketing such capital globally than just locally, for example, in the case of outsourced jobs and offshore opportunities (Proenza, n.d.; Yonah, 1999).

f. **Multiple sources of information and knowledge:** Modern ICTs embody a lot of knowledge, particularly if such ICTs include electronic networks. These embody and convey knowledge and in this sense provide important intermediate products and services and content in education, human, and social capital formation activities. In this context, it is a fact that the creation of knowledge and access to information is the basis of new prosperity. Access by the poor to high-tech opportunities empowers them

Copyright © 2007, Idea Group Inc. Copying or distributing in print or electronic forms without written permission of Idea Group Inc. is prohibited.

with valuable knowledge and equips them with productivity skills, which is essential in any poverty reduction process. In this respect, poor people do not have a simpler set of living needs and aspirations, as may be assumed (Gates, 1999; Kao, 1996).

Despite these powerful attributes of ICTs, access to information using ICTs is determined by (a) *connectivity*—are the services available? (b) *affordability*—can the targeted poor users afford the access, and (c) *capability*—do the targeted users have skills required to support and utilise profitably the access? The user's skills relate to technical abilities, language, and literacy. Therefore, for ICTs for poverty reduction to succeed they need to be integrated and mainstreamed in the national development priorities and projects.

Showcase Experiences

It is worthwhile to note that ICTs are impacting on all dimensions of life: education, health, quality of family, culture, leisure and arts, scientific and technological world. The way people do business globally is changing beyond imagination. ICTs are helping economies expand at an unprecedented rate and competitiveness has become the motto of the way. However, for ICTs, as tools of empowerment, to contribute to the poverty reduction initiatives, certain conditions have to be met. These relate to ownership, local content, language, culture and appropriate technology enabled by adequate functional basic amenities and connectedness, e.g. roads, electrical power, telephone, water, etc. Access becomes important only once these conditions have been met. Due to this requirement of connectedness most of the ICTs have an urban bias and discriminate against rural areas.

Since the 1990s, years of economic liberalization in Tanzania, there has been a large wave of investment in ICTs for development and some significant part of this has been aimed at poor people—both in terms of bringing ICT access to poor communities, and in using ICTs in many other ways which support poverty reduction. These investments have produced *many* documented successes, lessons learned, and experiences. Most of the documented materials on ICT projects are mostly sector and application specific covering multipurpose community access; access technologies amenable to poverty reduction; gender equality; education and human resource development; science, high-tech, and ICT-sector growth; business and livelihoods development and support; public sector, services, and poverty management; environmental and natural resource management; and transparency, accountability, and empowerment.

The many experiences that are discussed in the subsequent sections offer a lot of insight and value, though it is difficult to consistently maintain focus on poverty, and separate poverty reduction from broader economic development insights. However, it has to be noted that growth and development are necessary but not sufficient for poverty reduction; and also that pro-poor strategies and investments are as important for ICTs and knowledge-economy strategy as for other connected areas of social and economic development. This section uses some of the material from publicly available websites carrying content about Tanzania.

Copyright © 2007, Idea Group Inc. Copying or distributing in print or electronic forms without written permission of Idea Group Inc. is prohibited.

Projects on Increasing Capacities and Opportunities

One of the many deprivations that compound the misery of the poor and prevent them from rising out of poverty is their lack of access to adequate education, training, skills development, broader information, and knowledge resources that could help them improve their lives and livelihoods. One of the show case projects on information sharing is the *Sharing with Other People Network* (SWOPNet) managed by the Tanzania Commission for Science and Technology (COSTECH). It may be found at www.swopnet.or.tz. The SWOPNet portal electronically brings together all owners of ICTs projects under one roof. The site is essentially very useful for publishing outputs from different research and devolopment projects in the field of ICTs conducted within Tanzania.

It has been envisioned that education and knowledge helps the poor to improve their current livelihoods, address impediments and vulnerabilities that prevent them from seeking opportunities to improve their lives, and participate in new sectors of the economy that require advanced skills and, therefore, offer higher incomes. ICTs can help make educational institutions more efficient and responsive, both by improving communication flows within them and between them and their various constituencies; and by increasing their access to global knowledge and good practice in education. One of the most promising areas where ICTs can help improve education quality and outcomes is in teacher training. The Tanzania educational system is, in general, plagued by inadequate resources for teacher training and curriculum development leading to low quality of education. Creative combinations of the Internet (for content access and interactivity) and digitally stored training materials (including CD-ROMs) can dramatically increase both the *reach* and the *yield* per unit cost of teacher training efforts. The government of Tanzania is making efforts to build strategy to integrate ICTs in the Tanzanian secondary schools (Menda, 2005b). There is also a showcase ICT project owned by the Ministry of Education and Vocational Training (MEVT) geared at integrating ICTs in Secondary Education and Teachers Training colleges (TTCs). These are the preferred entry points for integrating ICTs into the secondary education in Tanzania (more at www.pambazuka.org/index.php?id=26807).

Projects on Reducing Vulnerabilities

Poverty and illness go hand in hand and feed upon each other. Poor people are particularly prone to disease and illness.

There are several ways that ICTs can help to address the health challenges facing developing countries. First, the capacity to monitor, respond to, and thus hopefully control disease outbreaks and address their causes, can be significantly enhanced by improving communication flows and the information-management capabilities of health care professionals at community, district, regional, and national levels. In many cases, time is of the essence in responding to disease outbreaks, and faster communication and information gathering can often make a dramatic difference in how well an outbreak is contained. More generally, the ability of health care providers to assemble and share timely information about health trends and needs enables a country's health care system to adapt more quickly and allocate resources more effectively.

Copyright © 2007, Idea Group Inc. Copying or distributing in print or electronic forms without written permission of Idea Group Inc. is prohibited.

The government of Tanzania is ready to adopt ICTs in the provision of health services (International Institute for Communication and Development, 2004; Menda, 2005a), a commitment made recently by the Permanent Secretary in the Ministry of Health and Social Welfare, Hilda Gondwe, when officiating at a national roundtable workshop on the application of ICTs in the country's health sector. The workshop was organized by Christian Social Services Commission (CSSC) and financed by the Catholic Organization for Relief and Development (CORDAID) and International Institute for Communication and Development (IICD) (The Guardian, 2006).

Several show case projects that show how ICTs are being appropriated to realise health information system, to collect health data at village levels, and on child vaccination programs are reported at http://www.swopnet.or.tz/ws_projs.html.

Projects on Enhancing Government Capacity, Efficiency and Accountability

Government officials, and the institutions in which they work, are hampered in many ways by poor information and knowledge flows. They often have weak access to even basic current data about the issues and trends in the country. Information flows poorly within most government departments because of a combination of weak communications infrastructure, hierarchical structures, and rigid bureaucratic cultures.

In addition, government officials have limited information on global good practice, and few opportunities for consultation and collaborative problem solving with colleagues elsewhere. At the same time, citizens, entrepreneurs, and particularly the poor, often have limited information about their rights and the services available to them, about the structure and functioning of government agencies, and about procedures for requesting services.

ICTs can help in a variety of ways to address these problems. ICTs can be used to reorganize and speed up administrative procedures, to increase the volume and speed of information both within government institutions and between them and the larger society, to train government officials in global best practices, and to allow greater collaboration and sharing of experience among government officials both within a country and across borders. The government of Tanzania is exemplarily active in appropriating ICTs to improve its e-readiness and the delivery of public services. The official online gateway of the United Republic of Tanzania is accessible at http://www.tanzania.go.tz. Information accessible from this site includes fully analysed population census data, and most of the government policies and presidential speeches are hosted at this site.

There are several other information gateway projects in the country, for example, the Tanzania Online Information Gateway at www.tzonline.org and the Tanzania Country Gateway project at www.tanzaniagateway.org. Collectively these Internet-based gateways give Tanzania a global presence. The gateways provide links to ideas and good practice, information about development activities and industry trends, funding and commercial opportunities. These portals provide and promote exchange and dissemination of information on development matters.

Another project is the Tanzania National Assembly (Parliament or "Bunge") portal at www. parliament.go.tz. Acts, bills, and useful Bunge documents are readily available from this

Copyright © 2007, Idea Group Inc. Copying or distributing in print or electronic forms without written permission of Idea Group Inc. is prohibited.

site through its Parliamentary Online Information System (POLIS). This Internet-based global presence clearly demonstrates that the Tanzania Parliament is appropriating modern ICTs to transform the Bunge from an old-fashioned institution to a new, modern, paperless electronic parliament. Furthermore, the Tanzania Investment Center website at www.tic. co.tz acts as the official investor's guide to Tanzania.

ICTs can also play an important role in combating corruption and making government institutions more transparent, by reducing the opportunities and incentives for, and increasing the costs of, corruption. The most obvious role for ICTs is to "disintermediate" between the citizen and the services, procedures, and documents by automating and making widely accessible, many of the simpler procedures which have traditionally depended on the involvement of a local government officer. If a citizen can directly access a needed form, acquire required documents, permits and certifications, or register a new small business, using automated procedures, the opportunities for corruption are reduced. ICTs can also empower individual citizens and groups to hold government officials publicly accountable. These efforts are evident from the TIC Web site www.tic.co.tz especially links to the Business Registration and Licensing Agency (BRELA); www.necta.go.tz for the National Examination Council of Tanzania; and www.isd.co.tz for the insurance supervisory department.

Projects on Participation, Empowerment, and the Strengthening of Civil Society

ICTs can play an important role in informing and empowering citizens and strengthening the capacities of a wide range of civil society organizations and institutions. This is important not only in increasing the demand for good governance and strengthening the voice of citizens in government policy, but also for promoting both the stability and responsiveness of the political system and for the economy and society as a whole.

By facilitating new forms of many-to-many communication, collaboration, and information-sharing, both within a given country and among groups with similar interests and concerns across borders, ICTs can add to the vibrancy of civil society institutions and networks as a check on government. They can also act as a source of ideas and innovations, and an outlet for the interests, concerns, and desires for solidarity on the part of individuals and groups. This will reduce the alienation of the poor from feeling isolated, powerless, and neglected. A contrast can be found between a physical rally meeting to the famous eThinkTank user group at www.eThinkTank.org focused on issues concerning ICTs. Another portal is at www. hakikazi.org, a civil society meeting place for sharing ideas promoting the rights of all people to fully participate on social, technical, economic, environmental, and political (STEEP) issues. The portal carries a cartoon-based guide to popularize the PRSP (URT, 2000).

By definition, however, the poor have scarce resources, and the burdens of their daily lives often leave them little discretionary time to engage in activities designed to protect their interests and articulate their needs. Their limited education, and in many cases illiteracy, puts them at a disadvantage when faced with sophisticated ICTs that are not adapted to their most pressing needs, their modes of communication (including a frequent preference for oral communication), their cultural norms, and the social contexts in which they typically interact and pursue joint action. In such cases, community radio and video conferencing

Copyright © 2007, Idea Group Inc. Copying or distributing in print or electronic forms without written permission of Idea Group Inc. is prohibited.

facilities (like that at the Tanzania Global Development Learning Center (TGDLC—www. tgdlc.go.tz) become very appropriate.

Projects/Challenges on Appropriating ICTs for Income Generation

Economic programs implemented by the Tanzania Government have been based on the philosophy that Tanzania is committed to a market economy whereby the private sector will take the lead in creating incomes, employment, and growth. On the other hand, the State will be a producer of public goods, play a regulatory role to level the playing field, and create conducive environment for the private sector to take the lead in driving economic growth. The private sector has started playing an ever increasing role in creating incomes and employment. Small and Medium Enterprises (SMEs) account for a large share of the enterprises active in Tanzania. In fact, SMEs are the emerging private sector and do form the base for private sector led growth (Hakikazi Catalyst, 2001; URT, 2002, 2003a).

According to Drucker, there are eight key areas that constitute any business (Drucker, 2001), namely: *marketing, innovation, human resources, financial resources, physical resources, productivity, social responsibility,* and *profit requirements*. Let us recall Gandhi's test for technology appropriateness: to "*find out how the last man would be affected by it*" (Gates, 1999). The authors, therefore, propose to apply Gandhi's test for the effectiveness of ICTs in each selected income generating activity by examining the impact of mainstreaming ICTs into the eight key business areas.

The Ultimate Challenge: To Focus on Information Literacy and not only on Computer Literacy?

The Tanzania Vision 2025 (URT, n.d.) would like to see Tanzania be a well educated and a learning society. What does this mean in relation to ICTs as tools for poverty reduction? It has been said earlier that ICTs are embedded in networks and services that affect the local and global accumulation and flows of public and private knowledge.

The authors hold the view that the government of Tanzania needs to focus more on information literacy rather than mere computer literacy. Information literacy is the ability to access, evaluate, and use information from multiple formats—books, newspapers, videos, CD-ROMs, or the Web. Information literacy is a set of competencies, skills that will grow with the people as the society evolves towards a knowledge society, even when current computer operating systems, search engines, or computing platforms and devices are obsolete.

To date, however, it has been observed that, in promoting the information society agenda, citizens and the government are still focused on technology. However, they must focus on increasing awareness of the potential applications; on improving the availability of and access to modern digital communications; and on encouraging people and organizations to use technology more efficiently and effectively. It also has to advocate for policies that

Copyright © 2007, Idea Group Inc. Copying or distributing in print or electronic forms without written permission of Idea Group Inc. is prohibited.

encourage and allocate funding towards the development of skills to use technology and improve computer literacy. This focus has been, and is still, invaluable. To really move into the information age and get benefit from the potential of a knowledge based society, it needs a new focus, that is, on the content that flows through the ICTs, a focus on information and knowledge, and focus on how to create it, manage it, and use it. To do this a new focus on information literacy is needed. An information literate person is one who (American Library Association, 2000):

1.   Recognizes the need for information and determines the extent of the information needed;

2.   Identifies potential sources of information, accesses the needed information effectively and efficiently from sources of information including computer-based and other technologies;

3.   Evaluates information and its sources critically and incorporates selected information into his or her knowledge base and value system;

4.   Recognizes that accurate and complete information is the basis for intelligent decision making, develops successful search strategies, then organizes information for practical applications and uses information effectively in critical thinking to accomplish a specific purpose;

5.   Identifies potential sources of information and understands the economic, legal, and social issues surrounding the use of information and accesses and uses information ethically and legally.

Therefore, there is a challenge: how to ensure that the Tanzanian society becomes information-literate? It is the ultimate challenge to the government, public sector, private sector, development partners, and the whole Tanzanian community though all of the society, that especially the poor people are flooded with information options on day-to-day basis.

Conclusion

Tanzania, like other developing countries, is confronted with the challenge of eradicating extreme poverty and hunger. It is acknowledged that the new opportunities which ICTs are opening up can be harnessed in Tanzania's efforts to eradicate poverty. The framework for appropriating ICTs for national development and poverty reduction is articulated in the National ICT Policy.

This chapter has attempted to enhance the understanding and knowledge of ICTs in relation to the National ICT Policy and has extensively explored the evolving frontiers of this pervading technology as it impacts on education, commerce, social, cultural, and economic life of the poor Tanzanian people. The chapter has also presented several show case examples of projects in Tanzania that demonstrate how the government of Tanzania, entrepreneurs, and some of the rural communities are appropriating ICT tools to fit into their needs. Some

Copyright © 2007, Idea Group Inc. Copying or distributing in print or electronic forms without written permission of Idea Group Inc. is prohibited.

challenges have been identified and presented with the aim of stimulating debate to reflect on perspectives, trends, and potential of using ICTs to develop innovative approaches and methods for poverty reduction. It is emphasised that, since these ICTs are not solutions to social problems by themselves, they must be carefully chosen and implemented for each appropriate purpose. Overall, the chapter demonstrates that ICTs are a set of tools for knowledge sharing, which is a powerful means for poverty reduction. Further, it is shown that ICTs could only be tools of empowerment for those who have access to them. And that "I" (Information) and the "C" (Communication) are far more important than the various technologies which are just means to an end. Therefore, ICTs cannot turn bad development into good development; they can make good development better. It all has to do with focusing on information literacy as opposed to just focusing on computer literacy.

References

Allen, I.G. (2002). *Can we eradicate poverty while tolerating alienation?* Retrieved June 29, 2006, from the Christian Mission for the United Nations Community, http://www. Christianmission-un.com

American Library Association. (2000). *American Library Association Presidential Committee on Information Literacy.* Retrieved June 29, 2006, from http://www.ala.org/acrl/nili/ilit1st.html

Drucker, P.F. (2001). *The essential Drucker.* Harvard Business School.

Gates, B. (1999). *Business @ the speed of thought: Using a digital nervous system.* Warner Books.

Gerster, R., & Zimmermann, S. (2003). *ICTs for poverty reduction: Lessons for donors.* Retrieved June 29, 2006, from http://www.commint.com/strategicthinking/st2003/thinking-187.html

Gillman, H. (2003). *Fighting rural poverty—The role of ICTs.* Paper presented at IFAD side event at the WSIS-Geneva. Retrieved June 29, 2006, from http://www.ifad.org/events/wsis/synthesis/index.htm

Gunawardene, N. (n.d.). *ICT for poverty reduction: Think big, act boldly.* Retrieved June 29, 2006, from http://www.teriin.org/terragreen/issue71/essay.html

Hakikazi Catalyst. (2001). *Tanzania without poverty—A plain language guide to Tanzania's poverty reduction strategy paper.* Retrieved June 29, 2006, from http://www.hakikazi.org/eng/

Hakikazi Catalyst. (2003). *Millennium development goals—No more broken promises.* Retrieved June 29, 2006, from http://www.srds.co.uk/mdg/nmbp-draft-04.pdf

IICD. (2004). *Telemedicine hampered by infrastructure and awareness—says Tanzanian health expert during seminar by SWOPNet.* Retrieved June 29, 2006, from International Institute for Communication and Development (IICD), http://www.iicd.org/articles/iicdnews.2004-09-02.7493425067

Copyright © 2007, Idea Group Inc. Copying or distributing in print or electronic forms without written permission of Idea Group Inc. is prohibited.

Kao, J. (1996). *Jamming: The art and discipline of corporate creativity.* Harper Business Publishers.

Mandela, N. (2005, February 3). *Make poverty history* (Speech during The Global Campaign for Action Against Poverty). London's Trafalgar Square.

Menda, A. (2005a). *ICT experts probe methods in Tanzania to train medics outside hospitals.* Retrieved June 29, 2006, from International Institute for Communication and Development (IICD), http://www.iicd.org/articles/iicdnews.2005-07-15.2614286290

Menda, A. (2005b). *Stakeholders build strategy to integrate ICT in the Tanzanian secondary school.* Retrieved June 29, 2006, from International Institute for Communication and Development (IICD), http://www.iicd.org/articles/iicdnews.2005-07-15.3965031729

Proenza, F.J. (n.d.). e-ForALL: *A poverty reduction strategy for the information age.* Retrieved June 29, 2006, from http://communication.utexas.edu/college/digital divide symposium/papers/index.html

Shaffer, P. (2001). *New thinking on poverty dynamics, implications for policy.* Retrieved June 29, 2006, from http://www.un.org/esa/socdev/poverty/paper_shaffer.pdf

Sharma, M. (n.d.) *Information technology for poverty reduction* (Proposal to Asian Development Bank, Manila, Philippines). Retrieved June 29, 2006, from http://topics.developmentgateway.org/ict

Spence, R. (2003). *ICTs, the Internet, development and poverty reduction—Background paper for discussion, research and collaboration.* Retrieved June 29, 2006, from http://www.mimap.org/

The Guarduan, (3rd February, 2006). *Govt ready to adopt ICTs in health services.* By Gardian Reporter. Retrieved from http://www.ipp.co.tz/ipp/guardian/2006/02/03/59218.html

United Republic of Tanzania (URT). (2000). *Poverty reduction strategy paper (PRSP).* Dar es Salaam: Government Printer. Retrieved June 29, 2006, from http://www.tanzania.go.tz

United Republic of Tanzania (URT). (n.d.). *IDT/MDG progress—The United Nations and the International/Millenium Declaration development goals (MDG)—on United Republic of Tanzania.* Retrieved June 29, 2006, from http://www.undp.org/mdg/Tanzania.pdf

URT. (1997). *National poverty eradication strategy.* Dar es Salaam: Government Printer.

URT. (2001). *Poverty monitoring master plan.* Dar es Salaam: Government Printer.

URT. (2002). *Small and medium enterprise development policy.* Dar es Salaam: Government Printers.

URT. (2003). *National information communication technologies policy.* Dar es Salaam: Government Printer.

URT. (2003a). *The Cooperative Societies Act—No. 20 of 2003.* Dar es Salaam: Government Printers. Retrieved June 29, 2006, from http://www.parliament.go.tz

URT. (n.d.a). *The Tanzania development vision 2025.* Retrieved June 29, 2006, from http://www.tanzania.go.tz

Copyright © 2007, Idea Group Inc. Copying or distributing in print or electronic forms without written permission of Idea Group Inc. is prohibited.

Weigel, G., & Waldburger, D. (Eds.). (2004). *ICT4D—Connecting people for a better world—Lessons, innovations and perspectives of information and communication technologies in development.* Swiss Agency for Development and Corporation (SDC) and the Global Knowledge Partnership (GKP).

Williams, B.K., Sawyer, S.C., & Hutchinson, S.E. (1999). *Using information technology—A practical introduction to computers & communications* (3rd ed.). Irwin McGraw-Hill.

World Bank. (2004). *2004 world development indicators.* Retrieved June 29, 2006, from http://www.worldbank.org/data/wdi2004/pdfs/table2-5.pdf

Yonah, Z.O. (1999). Orienting engineers in exploiting applied engineering and information technology in Tanzania: Challenges, opportunities and practical solutions. In *Proceedings of the ERB Press Seminar on Engineers as a Resource for Sustainable National Development* (pp. 64-76). Arusha, Tanzania.

Copyright © 2007, Idea Group Inc. Copying or distributing in print or electronic forms without written permission of Idea Group Inc. is prohibited.

Chapter XVI

Management of New Genetic Knowledge for Economic and Regional Development of Ethnic Minorities in China

Jan-Eerik Leppanen,
International Institute for Asian Studies (IIAS), The Netherlands

Abstract

The banking of genetic appliances and DNA represents an attempt to understand sustainable use and preservation for the benefit of current and future generations. The goal of this chapter is to highlight BioBanking as a tool for accelerating knowledge, understanding, conservation, and sustainable use of biodiversity. Genetic biobanks, collected from indigenous peoples, may pose some ethical risks for the ethnic populations. The new information in the hands of insurance companies, employees or governmental agencies could mean insecurity for ethnic minorities if the use of information violates the fundamental human rights of ethnic people. The new genetic knowledge may alter the relations between the individual (the self) and the community; the individual and the state; and the community and the state. This chapter will explore the technical issues, difficulties and benefits this tool provides when dealing with marginalized ethnic populations in Southwest China.

Copyright © 2007, Idea Group Inc. Copying or distributing in print or electronic forms without written permission of Idea Group Inc. is prohibited.

Introduction

In this chapter, the author has tried to give an overview on genetic sampling[1] of ethnic minorities (*minzu*)[2] in China and to the different claims companies and research ventures have on this industry. It will look at the following question: how the new genetic knowledge—acquired by biobanking activities—could be turned into ethically sustainable, economic, and regional development of ethnic minorities in China.

The banking of genetic appliances and DNA represents an attempt to understand sustainable use and preservation for the benefit of current and future generations. The goal of this chapter is to highlight BioBanking as a tool for accelerating knowledge, understanding, conservation and sustainable use of biodiversity. This chapter will explore the technical issues, difficulties, and benefits this tool provides when dealing with marginalized ethnic populations in Southwest China. This theoretical framework can be applied to the lives and conditions of ethnic people in other parts of East Asia (southwest), Southeast Asia (north, mainland) and in South Asia (far west).

Indigenous people groups in Southwest China and in other parts of northern Southeast Asia (mainland)[3] go through development challenges that are, most of the time, transboundary. Some of the issues concern migration, effects of reforms (P.R.C), and technological knowledge. Genetic biobanks, collected from indigenous peoples, may pose some ethical risks for the ethnic populations. The new information in the hands of insurance companies, employees or governmental agencies could mean insecurity for ethnic minorities if the use of information violates the fundamental human rights of ethnic people. The new genetic knowledge may alter the relations between the individual (the self) and the community; the individual and the state; and the community and the state. This chapter focuses on genetic sampling holistically. This implies that the processes of change alter the social constructions in which minority people live.

However, the banks are also a new potential source of material wealth and health knowledge resources if the new information is applied according to local needs. The issue of information management with genetic knowledge is an ethical one, since businesses are primarily looking for profits, not for the rights of vulnerable people. It is probably impossible to find a perfect solution for biobanking enterprises. However, to avoid the mentioned problems, a model named "Charitable Trust" could be a resourceful framework to apply for the ethnic communities in the Southeast Asian region. This bank, originally proposed by D. and R. Winickoff, is a model for genomic biobanks, which is seen as superior to commercial bio-banking. A biobank organized as a charitable trust is created by a trust agreement between the research subject and the owner of the bank. Since the relationship with the "bank" ma-nager and the research subject is mutual, it will be less easy to mishandle the rights of the sampled population. It would be even more advantageous if the "trust" being community based and owned biobank and resource rights regimes that seek to recognise the essentially community-based nature of much of the knowledge related to biodiversity.

The transformations brought about by the "knowledge economy" or "Information Society" are conventionally thought of in global or national terms. But as globalisation and the out-comes of new information and communications technology (ICT) have influenced people around the globe, they are also reformulating and restructuring the regions, though in multiple routes and often with highly differentiated results. The resources accessed from this article

Copyright © 2007, Idea Group Inc. Copying or distributing in print or electronic forms without written permission of Idea Group Inc. is prohibited.

focus on the use by Asian regions and localities of ICT to support and promote the wealth and welfare of their citizens, businesses, and environments.

Background

Economic and regional development in the context of Chinese minorities is interlinked. Minority dwellers in mountainous regions are, in general terms, worse- off compared to their fellow countrymen. This is because steppe regions means of livelihood are more limited and means of communication and transportation are restricted due to the great financial costs resulting from the demanding geography. In China, the minorities' migration from the plains to the mountains have taken several routes and included a multiple number of historical events. A dominant theory claims,[4] that minorities were pushed, step-by-step, ever higher to the mountains by the majority (Han) people, when the competition of the cultivable land area became more intense. Although this is not the *de facto* situation in the case of many minorities, moving up to the mountains is not all natural phenomenon and the regional development efforts involves both parties, majority people and minorities alike.

Economic-regional development of ethnic minorities suggests that in order to advance the business and profit-making changes of indigenous peoples, the regional and geographic conditions need to be taken into account. The goal of any development plan must be to ensure that communities are strengthened, and rural people are not pressured to abandon their native lands and move to bigger cities and suburbs in the hope of better financial prospects and economic stability.

Economic Development of Ethnic Minorities in China and Asia

Most of China's rural poor live in its hilly and mountainous regions, and in recent years the government has concentrated its "war on poverty" in these areas. Among the poorest of the poor are China's minority peoples, not least because they are outside the dominant culture and language. Unemployment is a huge problem in China, and the Yunnan province is among the country's poorest. Half of the population earns less than $80 a year. Bureuacrats and population planners often see few options for the employment of ethnic minorities. The options are limited to tourism industry, service industry, or to tertiary industry (Yardley, 2004).

The economic importance of migration, and its effect on social change, is also a key factor among the minority peoples in the Southeast Asia region. Ethnic men seek casual unskilled work, often over the border, in Myanmar or Laos. But these laborers seem to be even more vulnerable to exploitation by employers, as their own languages are not spoken on the plains and in the cities. Indeed, each minority group has its own distinct customs, practices and language, which remain a source of pride and definition. Low levels of literacy and limited

Copyright © 2007, Idea Group Inc. Copying or distributing in print or electronic forms without written permission of Idea Group Inc. is prohibited.

access to news and information, plus some residual prejudice against minority peoples, make life even harder.

The ethnic informants talk of enlarged opportunities to earn money since China's economic reforms took hold, and express a preference for the new system of working for oneself rather than communally. Family networks remain a crucial source of support, financial and practical. Health facilities are both limited and too costly for some, especially for reproductive health, and this, combined with women's heavy workload meant many narrators suffered constant ill-health.

There is a strong belief among most narrators that they could raise their living standards significantly if they could get a little more training and investment. Being minority people with different languages, some feel they have not benefited from the same educational opportunities as the majority Han. But poor roads still limit people's ability to market their produce, and several ethnic subjects say lack of electricity is another hindrance: "Our lives will be better after the road is built and the electricity connected. You see, everything has to be done manually. I want to learn more skills. My thoughts cannot catch up with the Han—my literacy level is low, and I have poor technological knowledge."[5] Another informant stated that: "We Miao people live in remote and backward mountain areas. Although we have had some development in these years, there is still a big gap between us and other peoples."[6]

China's economic reforms have shifted an almost uniformly poor nation into an increasingly prosperous one in the space of a mere generation. But the downfall of socialized medicine and astounding cost increases have opened a vast gap between health care in the cities and the rural areas, where the previous system of free clinics has disintegrated. The government, which under President Hu Jintao has made prioritised rural living standards in its reform agenda, has recently announced an expansion of this experiment, with increased fees and increased coverage, but the impacts on the health crisis is still to be seen. As a result, in less than a generation a rural population that once enjoyed universal, if basic coverage, is now 79% uninsured. One of the great policy changes of modern times, China has disorganized its rural communes, privatised enormous segments of the economy, and moved public health resources away from rural areas and toward the cities. Public hospitals were pushed for charging commercial rates for newly designed drugs and most procedures, and today the wages of health care workers are normally linked to the amount of money they generate for their hospitals (French, 2006).

Commercialization of High-Tech Sector

Clearly, one of the biggest changes and challenges in the professional life of Chinese scientists is the commercialization of research (Baark, 2001). The big picture of commercialization becomes more evident if one looks at the growth of contract research in universities and research institutes. This is happening even when they are not starting their own companies. As soon as Chinese firms have begun to face the challenges of market competition, they have found that productive relationships with centres of research are lucrative. This applies to all types of Chinese companies, including state-owned enterprises, TVE's, and the startup of "new technology enterprises," all of which have sought to contract universities and research institutes for research and technical services (Baark, p. 142).

Copyright © 2007, Idea Group Inc. Copying or distributing in print or electronic forms without written permission of Idea Group Inc. is prohibited.

The commercial considerations in Chinese science are also seen in the actions and strategies of foreign multinational companies (MNCs) in China. The two principal modes of MNC penetration of the system are the establishment of research centers in China and the uses of Chinese universities and research institutes as contractors for outsourcing research, development, and technical service activities. Working with MNC's is both attractive and professionally rewarding for many Chinese engineers and scientists. For these reasons, foreign firms have been able to employ some of the best and most talented from the research community. These newly discovered activities of MNCs in China have caused concerns over a new type of "internal brain drain."

In addition, the state remains the important source of funding for the nation's research activities that ensures that the influence of the bureaucratic policy culture remains strong. Chinese policymakers still have a long way in redefining the role of the state in the support of science (Baark, 2001). In terms of academics, the present age where China is and where it is further entering is an age of experts in which the relative importance of critical intellectuals to the public is declining while knowledge-based and profit-oriented professionals are becoming increasingly important (Gu & Holman, 2004). Marketization has generated fraudulent, get-rich-quick schemes among scientists. An interesting example of commercially inspired product fraud, and constructive responses to it from within the technical community, is seen in a dispute over the nutritional value of nucleic acid.[7]

Commercial involvement in genetics induces a moral environment in which blood is cherished *both* as the object of dignity *and* as the object of commercial interest. In this landscape blood has to be exchanged in nonmarket terms, with the ambition of fulfilling *both* moral hopes of better health *and* financial expectations (Hoyer, 2005). But the problem is that those material expectations may not be filled and the companies doing the research are collecting the rewards nevertheless. Specialized, for-profit firms may collect huge earnings through their access to human commodities. Access to sophisticated technologies also proves highly effective in the expansion of procurement activities, with the result that various agencies may essentially buy their way into understaffed and poorly funded labs. In short, access to advanced technologies can improve authoritative power and, eventually, generate the necessary capital to facilitate boundary expansion (Sharp, 2002). It must be stated, however, that technologies are only one of several tools that may serve capitalist interests. There is a tendency to the bureaucratization of medico-scientific knowledge and its progress to a sophisticated form of mystification. Different knowledge (be it the values assigned to fetuses or cancer medications) is thus encoded with new layers of meaning, which, ultimately, obscure their origins and transform their usefulness within medico-corporate structures (Sharp, 2002).

China and Information Systems: A Case Study of Genetic Databases

In the Chinese context, personal information systems of ethnic minorities and other genetic databases is most often nationally coordinated and governmentally monitored. Regional research divisions function as a coordinative body in a larger information system. A case example of the Chinese interlinked (bio) information system is the Chinese Biodiversity

Copyright © 2007, Idea Group Inc. Copying or distributing in print or electronic forms without written permission of Idea Group Inc. is prohibited.

Information System (CBIS), which is constructed to a National Biodiversity Information Center (NBIC). It consists of one central information system and five disciplinary division information systems, and more than 30 data source information systems. Some of the regional divisions are handling genetic information of ethnic people. The data sources include specimen collections, botanical gardens, natural reserves, field ecosystem research stations, seed banks, geneplasm banks, and research groups. The CBIS aims to.[8]

Genetic Databases and Current Issues

The concept of genetic databases is not new. For the last 30 years it has been common practice to establish registers of patients with hereditary illnesses, aimed at providing genetic services to families with these conditions. But the new generation of genetic databases are quite disparate, both in size and format. In many cases, they involve exceptionally large populations. For example, the Icelandic Health Sector Database aims to link health records with genealogical information and information about genotype. DNA samples will be collected with informed consent, whereas entry into the health records database is by presumed consent. Genomic databases are often described as population biobanks. In these biobank databases, a range of further information relating to the individuals whose genetic data are stored complements that genomic data.

There is still substantial controversy about the desirability of establishing databases and the many ambiguities regarding access and control. Concerns are engaged with individual risks which revolve around those arising from access to genetic information, both by individuals themselves and by third parties. In the latter case, these might include health insurance companies, government bodies, or the legal profession and police. The questions of confidentiality and access to these databases play an important role here. Although much effort is being put into protecting individuals, there are still possibilities for the misuse of the databases.

What has also been suggested is that genetic research based on stored (human) biosamples may have the effect of stigmatizing entire countries or particular groups of individuals, and there are concerns about commercial exploitation without adequate compensation. Also, because scientific research depends on freedom of access to samples and information, the commercial ownership of these databases may have a damaging effect on genetic research. As well as these concerns, there are a variety of socioeconomic and ethical issues advanced by this new trend in genetic science.

It is not definite whether individuals who donate DNA samples for these databases are entirely aware of the potential risks involved, and it is even less clear whether some of the arrangements that have been made with the private sector, which is becoming increasingly involved in these enterprises, are appropriately controlled. It is also not apparent how information, particularly unexpected findings, will be handled in these large population studies and how these DNA samples will be used above and beyond the stated aims of those who are establishing the databases.

One of the reasons genetic databases are being built is when health information is needed to be stored in one central location. Some developing countries, or geographical areas within developing countries, represent attractive opportunities for the development of such databases when the population is comparably genetically homogenous due to limited migration in or

Copyright © 2007, Idea Group Inc. Copying or distributing in print or electronic forms without written permission of Idea Group Inc. is prohibited.

out of the area. These databases vary and individual data are typically made nonidentifiable to users of the database. The databases are in some cases developed by public health authorities in the country, sometimes in cooperation with private corporations as in the deCODE database in Iceland, and in other cases chiefly by private corporations. These databases raise a number of ethical issues, which includes profit sharing with the community from which the data are gathered.

A second crucial informed consent issue, both for databases and for other genetic research is whether health information or genetic material can be used for other purposes beyond those for which consent was originally given without obtaining additional consent for the new uses. It has been suggested that material or information should not extend beyond those for which consent had been given. Genetic information about a specific health risk of a particular individual may imply a similar risk for other family members. In cases of comparatively isolated groups, which are unusually genetically homogenous, information about individuals may have implications not only to immediate family members, but also to the wider group.

Many of the risks in biobanking can be expected to increase in developing (and many developed) countries in the future. Responsibilities to provide proper biobanks/genetic information systems are being shifted from the public sector to the private sector in many countries, where private insurers make use of risk rating for health insurance. As a wider range of genetic tests become available and their cost continues to decline, the incentives and abilities of insurers to use this information to discriminate against individuals with risks of developing serious disease is about to increase.

Being labelled as having "bad" genes can have variety of serious social and psychological consequences for individuals, and this stigmatization may be stronger and more common where the levels of education and understanding is low. This is the case in many parts of Eastern and Southern parts of Asia.

Ethical, Legal and Social Issues (ELSI) in Genetic Research

Due to expensive medical and genetic services individuals' needs sometimes become highly variable and unpredictable, and typically if they are provided through some form of insurance. This may happen within a national health system, but increasingly in many Asian countries, at least in part, and especially in China, through private health insurance. If increasing amounts of information become available to insurers about genetic risks, many people will face large differences in their health insurance costs from genetic risks. In this way, they will be denied of health insurance, or be unable to afford it at all. Similar ethical concerns apply to the use of genetic testing by employers or potential employers.

The populations of very poor developing countries are especially vulnerable to economic exploitation by much richer developed countries or multinational corporations in genetic research or the development and use of genetic databases. Also, low education levels in some developing countries and limited familiarity with genetic medicine or research present special obstacles to obtaining truly informed consent from the population. A general feature of many developing countries is a lack of any well-developed regulatory apparatus to deal

Copyright © 2007, Idea Group Inc. Copying or distributing in print or electronic forms without written permission of Idea Group Inc. is prohibited.

with either the scientific issues in genetic research and technology, or with the ethical, legal and social issues. As genomics becomes more prominent in many developing countries, it becomes an important priority to develop necessary regulatory structures for addressing both the scientific and ethical issues. These regulatory bodies may formulate policies and action plans incorporating better utilization of electronic databases.

Electronic Data and Population Profiles

Electronic records can be accessed in combination with other databases in diverse geographic locations. This linking capacity makes it possible to compare the data to get a profile of an identifiable person or population with neither personal identifiers nor other confidential information. What are seen problematic with people related to electronic data are the privacy problems. These side effects are always difficult to deal with. Firstly, are the ownership issues. Technological advances allowing easy access to such data make it difficult to determine who is the "owner" of the computer record. Many people take it for granted that the patient owns his or her genetic record and should continue to be named as owner. But then again, one argument speaks for privacy protection when data is compiled anonymously. One important point to remember for the potential misuse of information is that the risks of fraud and abuse of individual medical information may not come from outside hackers, but mainly from those described as "authorized" users (Floya, 2001).

One practical example of a type of health record where potential misuse may take place is a record which combines lot of different kind of information and where medical and genetic information is linked through technological networks to other databases, like employment data, tax and credit records, insurance, welfare, and custody files. This could also be called as "centralization of sensitive information." The problem with the centralization is that it places too much power in a single public agency. But the decisive question is not the access to information but it is the control over the information. It would then be necessary to think of certain guidelines of restricting access to medical and research data only to those with proper authorization for providing adequate safeguards. Furthermore, even with the addition of guidelines for protecting privacy, other questions remain unanswered. It is important to know: (1) which groups should oversee enforcement of the guidelines and, (2) how effective such enforcement could be (Floya, 2001).

However, there is a growing interdependence between information communication technology (ICT) and genetic and genomic research. Some ethical issues that have traditionally been associated with ICT are now also at the center of recent ethical concerns involving genetic and genomic research. The dependence on ICT may give some insight into why many issues in the fields of ICT ethics and genetic/genomic ethics now intersect at some points and converge at others (DeCew, 2004).

Solutions to Genetic Information Management

It has been suggested that the potential harm of the genetic revolution may rather lie in the ability of technology to distribute the available resources even more unequally than is cur-

Copyright © 2007, Idea Group Inc. Copying or distributing in print or electronic forms without written permission of Idea Group Inc. is prohibited.

rently the case, and in that way enforce and strengthen the existing disparities and inequity. On the other hand it is suggested that genetics might have enormous potential in leveling the existing inequalities and providing a more just and equitable existence. There are also views that dispute the application of a benefit-sharing framework within genetics. These are mostly related to a perception that benefit-sharing actually legitimizes the attempts to commercialize and profit from (human) genome (Simm, 2005). Habitually, these lead to biopiracies.

Biopatents and Biopiracy

The appropriation of indigenous knowledge on medicinal plants or human genetic information by multinational companies or other international, national, or local agencies is known as "biopiracy," and it happens often without prior consent or compensation. Indigenous ethnic peoples rarely benefit from the financial gains of this new genetic knowledge. Pharmaceutical companies are quick to impose patents and exploit traditional knowledge, which has existed in indigenous communities for generations. The so called "TRIPS-plus"(Trade Related Intellectual Property Rights) treaties allow western countries to bypass current WTO limits on patents related to indigenous biodiversity.

The Coordinator at GRAIN, H. Hobbelink (YEAR), said in an interview: "in country after country TRIPS-plus agreements undermine national decision making processes and hijack policy options for the South, having serious consequences for farmers, research and the public interest" (p. 3). They are "manipulative" and "undemocratic" and make the debate on patenting irrelevant and outdated (BMA, 2001). In the meantime, the government of the United Kingdom has established a new commission to study how gene patenting rules can be enhanced to take account of the world's poor. The Commission on Intellectual Property Rights [CIPR] investigates the exploitation of traditional knowledge, the effects of TRIPS, human gene patenting, benefit sharing, and issues of consent (Grain, 2001).

Some of the most well known examples of the collision between traditional knowledge and genetic research are the "RiceTec" and "bintangor tree HIV/AIDS drug." The U.S. Patent and Trademark Office (USPTO) has endorsed three patents for hybrid strains of basmati rice and awarded them to a U.S. company, RiceTec, regardless of attempts by the Indian government to have all the patents that were originally granted in 1997. USPTO commanded to disclaim RiceTec from calling the rice "basmati," but allows them to label it "a superior basmati rice." This has caused some major discontent in India. The Indian Government postponed in recognizing India's claim to have basmati protected under geographical indication provisions at the WTO. India had been victorious, since RiceTec has been forbidden the use of the word "basmati" as a trade name (Devraj, 2001).

U.S. based pharmaceutical companies plans to develop a new anti-HIV/AIDS drug from Sarawak's native bintangor tree, which has evoked NGO's to criticize these schemes. M. Bujang of the Borneo Resources Institute says the East Malaysian state's natives are in danger of having their traditional knowledge of medicinal plants stolen by biopirates. He indicates that the concept of property rights is unfamiliar to them. The locals openly share benefits from traditional knowledge that have been passed down through generations. Borneo Resources Institute tries to make sure a share of any profit arising from native wisdom goes to the people of Sarawak. In the meantime, the state-led Sarawak Biodiversity Center

Copyright © 2007, Idea Group Inc. Copying or distributing in print or electronic forms without written permission of Idea Group Inc. is prohibited.

(SBC) has started a project to record, in writing, the orally transmitted knowledge of the locals. The reason for the project is found from the research finding that recognition skills are fast disappearing. Today's young people can often name only 10-20 medicinal plants and animals whereas the previous generation knew hundreds of different species. Local populations would be able to keep any written records to themselves and, therefore, guaranteeing a share in any financial benefits arising from that knowledge. The records will also help Malaysia's attempts to implement the International Convention of Biological Diversity, requiring countries to ensure benefits derived from research of native genetic resources that are shared with indigenous peoples (Chalmers, 2001). The author prefers formation of charitable trusts that may take care of these issues and evolve as a catalytic agent for economic empowerment of the indigenous communities.

The Charitable Trust

In a 2003 article, D. and R. Winickoff (2003) proposed the charitable trust as a model for genomic biobanks which is superior to commercial biobanking. A biobank organized as a charitable trust would be created by a trust agreement under which the participant in the research (or settler), "formally expresses a wish to transfer his or her property interest in the tissue to the trust" (p. 1182). By donating the tissue samples to the biobank, the donor contextually appoints the recipient as trustee of the property, who has legal fiduciary duties to keep or use the property for the benefit of the beneficiary.

Winickoff & Winickoff (2003) argue that the charitable trust presents three clear advantages, namely (1) the protection of the participants' rights, (2) the propensity to build participants' trust, and (3) the protection and maximization of the scientific value of the biological collection. Furthermore, the charitable trust model presents at least three more advantages if compared to a model based purely on contractual relationships. First, the charitable trust model favors the *separation between control and use of the collected samples*. Large collections of human tissue are often being developed as resources that enable future research projects rather than as tools to enhance pre-existing genetic investigations. Therefore, a person who stores samples and data is often not the user of the same data because that person is not carrying out genetic research directly. However , in the real world, *storage of material and of the owner are often separate*, and having an *institutional framework*—such as the charitable trust model—that builds upon this distinction shows a clear advantage (Boggio, 2005).

In practice, transparency and opportunity for ethics review are enhanced if storage and use are separate. In this scenario, third-party researchers interested in accessing the samples would always be required to file a request to access the samples—or the genetic data that are derived from the samples. By filing such requests, external researchers would make explicit the circumstances and the intended purpose of their access. This practice would certainly favor a transparent access to databases and accountability of both the third parties towards the trustees and of the trustees towards the "general public."

Second, the charitable trust model provides a governance framework that facilitates the participation of donor groups in the management of the database. Third, the charitable trust model facilitates balancing the different interests that are affected in large-scale DNA collections. The trusted biological samples can only by used to serve the interests of the beneficiary. Thus, each request for access shall be balanced against the interest of the "general

Copyright © 2007, Idea Group Inc. Copying or distributing in print or electronic forms without written permission of Idea Group Inc. is prohibited.

public" (Boggio, pp. 44-45). Now, the author would like to focus on the Chinese genetic information management system.

In China, the state still has a lot of control over the private life of individuals in the field of health and sickness. People are inclined to follow the advice of physicians because people's lives depend on them. To give blood samples for the common good is not perceived as an additional burden if the results of ignoring the genetic tests would carry some disagreeable consequences on their lives. But the decision to join genetic sampling is being done under the pressure, not free willingly by the research subjects. If there is no necessary institutional framework (as is suggested in Winickoff's model) to support subjects' rights, it becomes difficult for them to claim their share of the new genetic knowledge. Another determinant of sound research ethics in genetic sampling is the level of awareness/knowledge that research subjects have about their rights. When the population being sampled consists of ethnic minorities, communication is then, naturally, cross-cultural. Language and cultural differences should be taken into consideration when research is planned and conducted so that research participants have a full understanding of the research project.

Sometimes in Chinese academia, what is researched, to what purpose the information is used, where it is used, and who is drawing the conclusions from the research data is not agreed upon mutually. These setbacks could be avoided if the storage of material and of the owner would be separate and there would exist a separation between control and use of the collected samples as suggested in Winickoff's model. This would lead to a conclusion that the Chinese *minorities* as a research populace would be in an especially vulnerable position since they are less significant in size and power than the majority, *Han*, people. However, in the Chinese context, ethnic minorities are in many ways "strong" and dynamic agents. It is a simplified truth to claim that minorities face a vulnerable position because of restrictive obligations enforced by the government. Yet, minority privileges surpass those of the Han Chinese in the number of children permitted to a couple (generally more than one) and the special position in minority language schooling, although this has regional variation.

Minorities are not automatically voiceless, but further effort is surely needed to make their claims heard on minority matters, since minority administration is de facto in the hands of the *Han* people who make up approximately 92% of the whole population. This is true in the area of human genomics projects, for example, solely about research conducted on ethnic subjects. The existence of a "colorful" cultural variety of 54 Chinese minority people groups is one of the founding reasons for Chinese human genetic programs. But, it has to be said, the whole idea of Chinese ethnic (*minzu*) groups with clearly defined borders is a fleeting, contingent, and rather modern invention. With a history of only 50 years, the Chinese *minzu* map and theory live new renaissance. Chinese officials have adopted new DNA analysis based techniques in archeology and forensic research to prove their theory correct: that in China there exist only 55 nationalities altogether, and that regional linguistic and cultural variation is non-existent within these groups.

Copyright © 2007, Idea Group Inc. Copying or distributing in print or electronic forms without written permission of Idea Group Inc. is prohibited.

Future Issues

A medium and long-term scientific and technological development program, which was first put forward in the proposed 11th Five-Year Plan (2006-2010), will set the pace for all Chinese technological policies from 2006 to 2020. The program, on which over 2,000 experts and scholars spent more than two years, rolled out the blueprint for an innovation-oriented China. China is seen as a country in which science and technology play an enhanced role in promoting economic and social development and safeguarding national security, in which research in basic science and cutting-edge technology are strongly emphasized (Zhang, 2006, p. 24). The newly adopted scientific development program has made it clear that by 2020, scientific and technological progress should contribute about 60% to the country's economic growth with 2.5% of its GDP devoted to scientific research and development, including genetics and information systems (Zhang, 2006, pp. 24-25). In the private industry sector, Big Pharma and Western biotech companies appear to have gotten over their concerns about intellectual property protection in China, traditionally a barrier to outsourcing this type of work. They have found that the "grass is greener" for biotech development in China, where costs are much lower (Young, 2006, p. 36).

The most recent Chinese Government's White Paper[9] concerns regional autonomy of ethnic people. It says that the country's regional autonomy system for ethnic minorities adopted half a century ago has been in conformity with the country's development goals and proven to be in the common interests of all ethnic groups. After New China was established in 1949, the white paper says that the Chinese government began to introduce the system of regional autonomy for ethnic minorities to all regions where ethnic minorities lived in compact communities. By the end of 2003, China had established 155 ethnic autonomous areas. Of these, five are autonomous regions, 30 autonomous prefectures, and 120 autonomous counties (banners). According to a national census in 2000, of the 55 ethnic minorities, 44 have their own ethnic autonomous areas. The area where such regional autonomy is practiced accounts for 64% of the entire territory of China. However, not all the policies during the socialist governance have been beneficial for the minorities, and even the Chinese government acknowledges this reality. The white paper states that the economic and social development level of western China's minorities is still low compared with the more developed eastern areas. It further urges development work in remote and backward areas in Southwest China (PDO, 2005). The challenging task of implementing the technology investment and development plans for the following years is in the hands of government cadres and party leaders. It is decidedly important that the needs of the ethnic people are prioritised and their economic-regional prospects are given necessary importance.

Conclusion

In this chapter the author has tried to argue that there are a number of development needs among the ethnic people groups in East Asia, Southeast Asia, and in South Asia. However, the nature of most of the regional and economic development conditions of these ethnic minorities is transboundary. The indigenous people groups that are situated in the mountainous border

Copyright © 2007, Idea Group Inc. Copying or distributing in print or electronic forms without written permission of Idea Group Inc. is prohibited.

provinces in the states of East Asia, Southeast Asia, and South Asia, face similar difficulties due to their linguistic and cultural dissimilarity from the dominant majority populations.

It has been observed that economic reforms in China work towards finding increased access to money. However, there are a great number of hindrances that are making it more difficult for ethnic people to meet their necessities: employment (they are outside the dominant culture and language), schooling (illiteracy and limited access to information), and technological skills. In this context, genetic biobanks may pose some ethical risks for the ethnic populations, but at the same time can also be treated as a new potential source of material and health knowledge resources. They can be:

- Disease gene mapping in which profits arising from the biobanking go to the people and this may boost the local economy.

- Other plant and nature related to new genetic products based on traditional knowledge of ethnic people; any profit arising from native wisdom goes to the ethnic people.

- IPR should be part of technological training of ethnic people; this would improve the know how of genetic information system management.

- A community owned biobank (charitable trust) which could provide a financially sound solution that stands by the side of marginalized ethnic people.

There is much to be discussed on the choices that scientists and medical doctors are making while handling the data of ethnic minorities. The new information extracted from minority people is handled by bio-technicians, bio-genetic engineers and genetic laboratory personnel. But, there is no self-evident way to interpret the data of ethnic people in China. Since the beginning of the *minzu* classification system, there has been ongoing negotiation over the truth-value and existence of these groups, and questions such as what the forms of ethnic minority representation are today and what it was in the 1950s, 60s, 70s, 80s and in the 90s. Any argument over or notion of the "nationalities" characteristics' is, and must be, politically charged, since the whole existence of the *minzu* system is a calculated and systematically constructed socio-political invention.

In general, to pass on someone's genetic information to the wrong hands does not necessarily carry potential hazardous immediate consequences. But, the information becomes fundamentally sensitive if it affects the ability of minority peoples to choose where to work, what kind of position they maintain in their local community, what types of insurances are available, and so forth. Genetic databanks can open up some doors but they can also restrict available lifestyle choices. The point that the author is trying to make here is that, by considering the small numerical representation of minorities in governing bioethical bodies and their disrespected position in the nationality hierarchy, it is more difficult for them to make claims for injustices done to them. This also relates to the question that goes into the very essence of the minority debate: what, actually, is a minority to the majority; does the relationship signify weakness or strength? If and when this relation is grounded on differences, asymmetry and subject-object relations, the outcomes of human genome studies on minorities can never be purely value-free. The Han majority is the arbiter of the campaign; they thus control the conclusion drawn from the result as well.

Copyright © 2007, Idea Group Inc. Copying or distributing in print or electronic forms without written permission of Idea Group Inc. is prohibited.

References

Baark, E. (2001). The making of science and technology policy in China. *International Journal of Technology Management, 21*, 1-21.

BMA. (2001). BMA calls for debate on gene patenting. Retrieved June 28, 2006, from *http://www.ngin.org.uk/*

Boggio, A. (2005). Charitable trusts and human research genetic databases: The way forward? *Genomics, Society and Policy, 1* (2).

Brown, M. (Ed.). (1996). *Negotiating ethnicities in China and Taiwan* (China Research Monograph). Berkeley, CA: Institute of East Asian Studies, University of California.

Cavalli-Sforza et al. (1991). Call for a worldwide survey of human genetic diversity: A vanishing opportunity for the human genome project. *Genomics, 11*, 490-91.

Cavanaugh, T.A. (2000). Genetics and fair use codes for electronic information. *Ethics and Information Technology, 2*, 121-123.

Chalmers, P. (2001). Bio-pirates stalk Borneo tribe's treasure trove. Retrieved June 28, 2006, from *http://www.ngin.org.uk/*

Coleman, J.S. (1990). *Foundations of social theory*. Cambridge, MA: Harvard University Press

DeCew, J.W. (2004). Privacy and policy for genetic research. *Ethics and Information Technology, 6*, 5-14.

Devraj, R. (2001). *India still sifting grain from "Basmati" Chaff.* Norfolk Genetic Information Network (NGIN). Retrieved June 28, 2006, from *http://www.ngin.org.uk/*

Ettorre, E. (2000). Reproductive genetics, gender and the body: "Please doctor, may I have a normal baby?" *Sociology, 34*(3), 403-420.

Everett, M. (2003). The social life of genes: Privacy, property and the New Genetics. *Social Science & Medicine, 56*, 53-65.

Finkler, K. (2005). Family, kinship, memory and temporality in the age of the New Genetics. *Social Science & Medicine, 61*, 1059-1071.

Floya, A. (2001). The concept of "social division" and theorising social stratification: Looking at ethnicity and class. *Sociology, 35*(4), 835-854.

French, H. (2006, January 14). Wealth grows, but health care withers in China. *The New York Times.*

Goodman, A.H., Heath, D., & Lindee, S.M. (2003). *Genetic nature/culture—Anthropology and science beyond the two-culture divide.* Berkeley, CA.: University of California Press.

Grain. (2001). *TRIPS-plus treaties leave WTO in the dust.* Retrieved June 28, 2006, from *http://www.ngin.org.uk/*

Gu, E., & Goldman, M. (2004). *Chinese intellectuals between state and market.* London: RoutledgeGurzon Studies on China in Transition.

Copyright © 2007, Idea Group Inc. Copying or distributing in print or electronic forms without written permission of Idea Group Inc. is prohibited.

Hoeyer, K. (2005). The role of ethics in commercial genetic research: Notes on the notion of commodification. *Medical Anthropology, 24*, 45-70.

Marturano, A., & Chadwick, R. (2004). How the role of computing is driving new genetics' public policy. *Ethics and Information Technology, 6*, 43-53.

People's Daily Online (PDO). (2005, January 3). *Regional autonomy system benefits all ethnic groups in China—a white paper.* Information Office of the State Council.

Regidor, E. (2004). The use of personal data from medical records and biological materials: Ethical perspectives and the basis for legal restrictions in health research. *Social Science & Medicine, 59*, 1975-1984.

Sharp, L. (2000). The commodification of the body and its parts. *Annual Review of Anthropology, 29*, 287-328.

Sharp, L.A. (2002). Bodies, boundaries, and territorial disputes: Investigating the murky realm of scientific authority. *Medical Anthropology, 21*, 369-379.

Simm, K. (2005). Benefit-sharing: An inquiry regarding the meaning and limits of the concept in human genetic research. *Genomics, Society and Policy, 1*(2), 29-40.

Spinello, R.A. (2004). Property rights in genetic information. *Ethics and Information Technology, 6*, 29-42.

Tavani, H.T. (2004). Genomic research and data-mining technology: Implications for personal privacy and informed consent. *Ethics and Information Technology, 6*, 15-28.

Waldby, C., Rosengarten, M., Treloar, C., & Fraser, S. (2004). Blood and bioidentity: Ideas about self, boundaries and risk among blood donors and people living with hepatitis C. *Social Science & Medicine, 59*, 1461-1471.

Williams, G. (2005). Bioethics and large-scale biobanking: Individualistic ethics and collective projects. *Genomics, Society and Polity, 1*(2).

Winickoff, D.E., & Winickoff, R.N. (2003). The charitable trust as a model for genomic biobanks. *New England Journal of Medicine, 349*(12), 1182-1183.

World Health Organization. (2002). *Genomics and world health—Report of the Advisory Committee on Health Research.* Geneva: World Health Organization.

Yardley, J. (2004, March 10). Dam building threatens China's "Grand Canyon." *The New York Times*.

Young, M. (2006). Getting testy. *Beijing Review, 49*(3), 36.

Zhang, Z. (2006). Innovation renaissance. *Beijing Review, 49*(4), 24.

Endnotes

[1]   Genetic sampling of ethnic minorities primarily conducted in the Southwestern province of Yunnan, bordering Vietnam, Laos, and Myanmar. Yunnan comprehends 25 out of 55 Chinese official minorities in total. The main sampling projects are Chinese Human Genome Diversity Project (CHGDP) and International HapMap project.

Copyright © 2007, Idea Group Inc. Copying or distributing in print or electronic forms without written permission of Idea Group Inc. is prohibited.

[2]   The original idea in the nationalities' mapping endeavor was to understand the diversity of the newly founded Peoples' Republic of China. Through the decades, it has turned into a "[slapping] endeavour" where the minority label should tell it all, but in truth it does not say always as much. During the past 50 plus years, people have been using not just the official label for the nominal group, but also other ethnic signifiers—some that are altogether more important than the *minzu* name. People in rural China have found it important to define themselves according to their place of origin, to their kin, tribe, or according to blood relations. Ethnicity consists of different, varying, and multilayered factors. Put together, they make up an interlinked web of something evolving and changing and sometimes unutterable. Unutterable because the words used to describe ethnicity are in the process of change; a common vocabulary is sometimes unattainable because the linguistic differences are too great. Group names are one example of the described problem: it has usually both *emic* and *etic* versions of the same subject, consisting of the insiders' view of its world and then the versions that outsiders tend to use when referring to the group. This is still a very rough divide because ethnic groups have dozens of specific group names for those speaking different languages and following varied cultural traditions.

[3]   This article is based on a field research in Yunnan province (P.R.C). The geographical locations that the author is referring to are in the border regions of P.R.C, Laos, Vietnam, Thailand, and Myanmar.

[4]   See Brown (1996) for more information on ethnicity theories.

[5]   (Ah, 22 years/female, agricultural extension worker, Lahu minority, Lancang county, Yunnan. www.mountainvoices.org)

[6]   (Mingchun, 27 years/male, Oxfam extension worker, Miao, Weining County, Guizhou. www.mountainvoices.org)

[7]   Early in 2000, in advertisements and on the Internet, several Chinese companies claimed that nucleic acid is a nutrient that could resist ageing and prolong life. Ordinary Chinese citizens, lacking the technical knowledge to judge such claims, were attracted to the products in a kind of nucleic acid minicraze. Biochemist Fang Shimin, who has been living in the U.S. since getting his Ph.D. there, was appalled by the widespread "nucleic acid nutrient hype" and wanted to expose the "fraud in Chinese science." The matter eventually received international attention when articles on the issue and Fang's efforts appeared in both *Nature* (2001) and *Science* (2001) (Williams, 2005, p. 151).

[8]   See more information from the "Development Gateway," *The Chinagate* (www.chinagate.com.cn).

[9]   The 12,000-word document, titled "Regional Autonomy for Ethnic Minorities in China," was issued by the Information Office of the State Council on January 3, 2005.

Copyright © 2007, Idea Group Inc. Copying or distributing in print or electronic forms without written permission of Idea Group Inc. is prohibited.

About the Authors

Hakikur Rahman, PhD, is the project coordinator of SDNP Bangladesh, a global initiative of UNDP since December 1999. He is also acting as the secretary of South Asia Foundation Bangladesh. Before joining SDNP, he worked as the director, computer division, Bangladesh Open University. He has written and edited several books on computer education for the informal sector, distance education, and research. He is the founder-chairperson of Internet Society Bangladesh; editor, *Monthly Computer Bichitra*; founder-principal, ICMS Computer College; head examiner (computer), Technical Education Board; executive director, BAERIN Foundation; and involved in establishing an IT based distance education university in Bangladesh.

* * *

Copyright © 2007, Idea Group Inc. Copying or distributing in print or electronic forms without written permission of Idea Group Inc. is prohibited.

Derya Altunbas, PhD, graduated from Middle East Technical University, Department of City and Regional Planning, Turkey (1986). She worked at Uludağ University, with the Department of Public Administration and Urbanisation and Environmental Problems, Main Science Branch, for 10 years as an research assistant. She has a master's degree (1988) and a doctoral degree (1996) from the University of Uludag, Bursa, Turkey. She has been working at Canakkale Onsekiz Mart University in Turkey Biga Faculty of Economics and Administrative Science and Department of Public Administration in Urbanisation and Environmental Problems Main Science Branch as an assistant professor since 1996.

Celestino Suárez-Burguet obtained a PhD in economics from the University of Valencia, where he worked as a lecturer until 1991. He has since been a professor of economics at Universitat Jaume I, where he has also been head of the Department of Economics and Rector. He is currently the director of the Institute of International Economics. He completed postgraduate studies at the LSE and the University of Sussex (UK). His research focuses on international economics, having published on different aspects of world trade linked to new technologies, transport costs in international specialization, and economic relations between regionally integrated areas.

Tom Denison is a doctoral candidate, Denison is attached to the Centre for Community Networking Research at Monash University. With a background in library automation, he has worked on library automation projects in Vietnam and Australia and has experience in system design and specification. He co-founded INFORMIT Electronic Publishing and has consulted widely, specializing in the development of online services including online library services, the development of commercial publishing via the Internet, and the design and delivery of related educational materials. His research interests focus on the effective use of information and communications technology (ICT) by community sector organisations.

Dilip Dutta is a senior lecturer in economics and director of the South Asian Studies Group at the University of Sydney, Australia. He is the founding editor of *Internaional Journal of Development Issues*. His research interests include (1) social shaping of information and communication technology (ICT) in India and (2) endogenous growth analysis and its links with trade liberalization, environmental degradation, ICT development in Asia and other regions. Apart from his publications in journals such as *Applied Economics*, *International Journal of Social Economics*, *Journal of Interdisciplinary Economics*, *Economic Papers*, *Indian Economic Review*, *Journal of Contemporary Asia*, he has contributed chapters to several edited books.

Elizabeth Ferrier is a lecturer in communication in the Business School at the University of Queensland. She has published widely on communication and cultural theory, new media, Australian literature, film and television, and on the structure and operations of the Australian media industries. She is advisory editor and chair of the editorial board for *m/c – a journal of media and culture*. She is currently developing a major research project, linked with the Australian Creative Resources Online, investigating grassroots online content production.

Copyright © 2007, Idea Group Inc. Copying or distributing in print or electronic forms without written permission of Idea Group Inc. is prohibited.

Phil Graham is an associate professor in the UQ Business School and Canada Research Chair in Communication and Technology at the University of Waterloo. He is director of Australian Creative Resources Online, founding editor of *Critical Discourse Studies* (Taylor & Francis); and special issue editor for *Cultural Politics* (Berg). His research interests include political economy of communication, sociolinguistics, and media history. He has recently published *Hypercapitalism: Language, New Media, and Social Perceptions of Value* for Peter Lang.

Kennedy D. Gunawardana received a BSc from University of Sri Jayawardanapura, Colombo, Sri Lanka, the MBA degree from University of Colombo, Sri Lanka, and PhD degree in computer and engineering management from Assumption University, Bangkok, Thailand. Since 1985, he has worked in university education and training research at the national level. He currently is a senior lecturer in Faculty of Management Studies and Commerce, University of Sri Jayawardenepura, Sri Lanka. His current research interests are issues of information technology in developing countries, intellectual capital and artificial neural networks modeling. Dr. Kennedy is a fellow member of the Institute of Public Finance and Development Accountancy in Sri Lanka.

Ashley Jones is currently an APAI scholar undertaking his PhD through the School of Social Science at The University of Queensland. His thesis is "Mapping Communication Practice in a Master Planned Community." It is part of a broader research ARC Linkage Grant project with Delfin Lend Lease. His research interests include interpersonal communication, mass communication, new media, new technologies, and community development. Jones holds a Master of Arts in media production and has 26 years experience in the media and communication industry.

Chris Keen is a professor of information systems at the University of Tasmania. His research interests include business logistics, roles for ICTs in service industries such as tourism and hospitality, and the strategic adoption of ICTs by industry and community sectors. Keen has extensive experience in consulting activities with government agencies, and has served on a number of boards that have been concerned with the rollout of ICT solutions at the government level.

Juha Kettunen is the Rector of Turku Polytechnic, Finland. He was previously the director of the Vantaa Institute for Continuing Education, University of Helsinki and director of the Advanced Management Education Centre, University of Jyväskylä. He holds a PhD from the University of Bristol, UK, and a DSc from the University of Jyväskylä, Finland.

Jan-Eerik Leppanen was born in Finland, Helsinki. He has been involved in research and development work activities principally in the countries of East and Southeast Asia. His fields have been in rural development and in community health programmes. Leppänen has obtained academic training at the Universities of Helsinki and Amsterdam (UvA) in the fields of social sciences. In the following years, in his research project, Leppänen will be

Copyright © 2007, Idea Group Inc. Copying or distributing in print or electronic forms without written permission of Idea Group Inc. is prohibited.

exploring the cultural politics of commercial and scientific interests in biobanking activities among ethnic groups in Southwest China.

Ángela-Jo Medina possesses a master's degree in international cooperation and project management (Instituto Universitario Ortega y Gasset, Universidad Complutense de Madrid), a certificate in international public policy (Touro University), and a bachelor's degree in French and government (political science, University of Texas at Austin). She is the education coordinator at Caritas of Austin, an NGO consultant, freelance translator, workshop facilitator, and cofounder of ConcienciAcción.org, As a specialist in the analysis and management of social networks and electronic activism, she has presented the subject of e-activism and the use of ICTs for grassroots movements in national and international fora.

Laura Márquez-Ramos studied management and business administration in the Universitat Jaume I in Castellón (Spain). She obtained an Extraordinary Prize for her studies. In 2002 she joined the post graduate programme in the Department of Economics at the Universitat Jaume and started to work there as a research assistant. Since then, she has been taking part actively in several research projects within the Institute of International Economics (IEI). She became a formal member of the IEI in 2005 and is currently preparing her PhD thesis. The topic of her dissertation is globalisation, international trade, and technological innovation.

Inmaculada Martínez-Zarzoso holds a master's degree (1994) and a PhD in international economics (1998) by the University of Birmingham, UK. She is an assistant professor at the University Jaume I since 1991 and a researcher in the Institute of International Economics since 1995. Currently, she is a visiting professor in the Ibero American Institute for Economic Research at the University of Göttingen (Germany). Her fields of research include international economics, environmental economics, and transport economics. Some of the international journals in which she has been published are *Open Economies Review*, *Environmental and Resource Economics, Economic Letters,* and *Journal of Transport Economics and Policy*.

James J. Rennie is an MA candidate at Simon Fraser University, Canada, where he studies the impacts of computer technologies on public education. His research interests include the pedagogical value of multimedia technologies, critical technological training for teachers, and the use of ICTs in social justice movements. His background is in critical media studies, which he has combined with education research in order to explore creative alternatives to traditional educational practices. He has presented papers on educational technology at Canadian conferences, and plans to continue combining his passions for research, university teaching, and public education.

David Rooney is a senior lecturer in knowledge management at the University of Queensland's Business School. He has published extensively in the areas of the sociology and political economy of knowledge, knowledge management, knowledge economies, cultural industries, and history of technological change. His recent books include *Public Policy in Knowledge-*

Copyright © 2007, Idea Group Inc. Copying or distributing in print or electronic forms without written permission of Idea Group Inc. is prohibited.

Based Economies: Foundations and Frameworks and *The Handbook on the Knowledge Economy*.

Baanda A. Salim is a lecturer in the Department of Agricultural Engineering and Land Planning at the Sokoine University of Agriculture in Morogoro, Tanzania. He joined the University in 1985 and has lectured on a variety of computing courses to both undergraduate and postgraduate students. His broad area of specialization is information and electrical technologies. He holds a BSc (electrical engineering) (1985) from the University of Dar es Salaam, Tanzania; an MSc (agricultural engineering) (1987) from the University of Newcastle upon Tyne, UK; and a PhD (computer modelling) (1999) from the University of Bonn, Germany.

Martin A. Schell was born in New York City and has spent the past 22 years in Japan, Thailand, and Indonesia. He has taught English in each of those countries, rewritten Japanese-to-English translations, designed distance learning materials in Thailand, and prepared economic and security assessments in Indonesia. Now based in his wife's hometown in central Java, he serves clients on several continents as a freelance editor, workshop trainer, and writing coach specializing in the fine points of strategic communication. He is also an adjunct faculty member at NYU's Stern School of Business, where he teaches an online course in business writing.

Dean Steer has a diverse background in engineering, small business, social work, and IT administration and is currently studying for a PhD in information systems at the Launceston campus of the University of Tasmania. His primary research focus is on accessing the assumptions, attitudes, and understandings of key regional policy stakeholders with regard to ICT-facilitated regional development.

Ken Stevens is a New Zealander who is a professor of education at Memorial University of Newfoundland in Canada and an adjunct professor at Victoria University of Wellington in New Zealand. His previous academic appointments were in Australia and New Zealand, in each of which he specialized in rural education and the development of information technologies for teaching and learning. He lives in Canada and New Zealand.

Elif Karakurt Tosun graduated from Uludag University, Department of Public Administration in 1999, in Turkey. She obtained a master's degree in 2002 about "Upper Income Class Houses in Globalization Process at Bursa" and she is currently pursuing doctoral studies at the University of Uludag in Bursa, Turkey. Her doctoral dissertation is titled "Space And Social-Culture Change at City in the Globalization Process: Example of Bursa-Turkey." She has been working at Uludag University as a lecturer in the Vocational School of Social Sciences, Department of Local Administration since 2002 in Bursa/Turkey.

Paul Turner joined the School of Information Systems at the University of Tasmania in 2000 and has been active in conducting and coordinating research at basic, applied, and

Copyright © 2007, Idea Group Inc. Copying or distributing in print or electronic forms without written permission of Idea Group Inc. is prohibited.

strategic levels across a range of industry sectors with a particular focus on forensic computing, e-business, approaches to human-centred design and health informatics. Since joining the university, he has been directly involved in raising research grants, consultancies, and scholarships to value of $3.75 million and has been active in multi-disciplinary research, including with the schools of pharmacy, nursing, and medicine. Since 2001, he has published more than 70 peer reviewed papers in academic journals, books, and conferences and is the University of Tasmania's research coordinator for its involvement in the Smart Internet CRC (www.smartinternet.com.au).

Zaipuna O. Yonah holds a BSc (1985) in electrical engineering from the University of Dar es Salaam, Tanzania, a MSc (1988) and PhD (1994) in electrical engineering from the University of Saskatchewan, Saskatoon, Canada, with specialization in computer-based real-time intelligent instrumentation, control, and communications. He is a registered consulting engineer in ICTs. For 21 years, since 1985, he has taught electrical engineering and computer science at the undergraduate and graduate levels. He aggressively utilizes his information literacy and knowledge of local markets in researching and promoting innovative ICT projects for socio-economic development. He is currently one of the functional directors in Tanzania Telecom Company Limited.

Copyright © 2007, Idea Group Inc. Copying or distributing in print or electronic forms without written permission of Idea Group Inc. is prohibited.

Index

A

Asian standard English 140
active information transfer 181
adult literacy
    program 11
    training 11
advanced placement (AP) 225
affordability 311
agriculture 60
alienation 10
All Pakistan Women Association (APWA)
    254
anglophone 223
AP 225, 230
Asia-Pacific Advanced Network (APAN)
    255
Asia-Pacific Development Information
    Program (APDIP) 154
Asia-Pacific Network Information Centre
    (APNIC) 255
Asia-Pacific Program of Education for All
    (APPEAL) 201

Association for Progressive Communica-
    tions (APC) 206
Australian Creative Resources Online
    (ACRO) 160
automatic teller machine (ATM) 249

B

balanced scorecard approach 23, 24, 27,
    31, 36
Bangladesh Advanced Education Research
    & Information Network (BAERIN)
    255
Bangladesh Research and Educational
    Network (BERNET) 255
Bangladesh Telecommunications Regula-
    tory Commission (BTRC) 248
BioBanking 320, 321, 326
bio
    -patent 328
    -piracy 328
blog 64, 132, 152
bottom-up approach 197

Copyright © 2007, Idea Group Inc. Copying or distributing in print or electronic forms without written permission of Idea Group Inc. is prohibited.

Boulder Valley
    Internet Project (BVIP) 107
    School District (BVSD) 107
broadband 155
    advisory group (BAG) 169
    communication technology 175
    content 159
    infrastructure 149
    Internet 47
    network 151
    service 168
brokerage network 105, 106, 108
BSVD
    classroom 107
    network 107
bureaucracy-driven network 11
business process outsourcing (BPO) 203,
    251
Business Registration and Licensing
    Agency (BRELA) 314

C

call center 203
capability 311
carriage facilities (rainbow model layer) 5
Catholic Organization for Relief and De-
    velopment (CORDAID) 313
CEFE 115
censorship and governmental monitoring
    69
Centre for Distance Learning and Innova-
    tion (CDLI) 232, 233, 235
charitable trust 321, 329
Chinese Biodiversity Information System
    (CBIS) 324
Chinese ethnic (minzu) 330
Christian Social Services Commission
    (CSSC) 313
civil society 199
    organization (CSO) 199, 209
Clement and Shade's rainbow model 5
closed
    educational environment 232
    model 222, 224
cohesion network 105, 106, 112
colingual 140

colloquial usage 133
Colombo Stock Exchange (CSE) 275
Commission for Science and Technology
    (COSTECH) 206
Commission on Intellectual Property
    Rights (CIPR) 328
commons deed 158
communication network 2
community
    -based
        organizations (CBOs) 199
        system 198
    autonomy 11
    informatics (CI) 5, 6, 167
        researchers 177
    information center (CIC) 253
comparative advantage 197, 245
compatibility 104
competency-based economies 115
competitive
    advantage 23, 27, 35, 105, 153
    telecoms in Ireland 203
complexity 104
computer
    -mediated learning 42
    assisted learning (CAL) 263
    kiosk 2
    literacy 266, 315
    resource center (CRC) 262
    systems policy project (CSPP) 128
computing services center (CSC) 269
conflict
    cycle 57
    prevention 56, 58, 59, 70
    transformation 68
connectivity 311
contemporary globalized economy 259
content/services (rainbow model layer) 5
content management 152
contingent improvisation 104, 106, 114
cooperative method of instruction 226
copyright 152, 156, 157, 158, 159
cost efficiency 27
Council for Information Technology (CIN-
    TEC) 271
Council for Scientific and Industrial Re-
    search (CSIR) 206

Copyright © 2007, Idea Group Inc. Copying or distributing in print or electronic forms without written permission
of Idea Group Inc. is prohibited.

Creative Commons (CC) 148, 155, 157,
    158, 159, 160
Creative Content e-Platform (UNESCO)
    154
cultural
    expression 153
    innovation 151
    knowledge management system 148,
    149
    materials 149
    prefrences 136
    production 155
    tradition 153
curricular content 7
curriculum 4, 12, 45, 107
customer 23, 31, 33
    needs 35
    segments 23
cyber
    cafe 130, 277
    -cell 236
    -dissidents 64
    kiosks 43

D

data
    -base 13
    network 32
    protection law 273
    transfer rate 151
deCODE database 326
dedicated Internet connection 262
dense closed network 105
Department of Computer Science and
    Engineering (CSE) 262
developing
    countries 109, 241, 245, 283
    societies 241
development
    agencies 3
    groups 19
    of human skills 80
    project 3
DFID 208
dial-up 262

diffusion 105
    of innovation 104, 105
    of old innovations 80
    of recent innovations 80
    of technology 107
digital
    archive 149
    broadband
        environment 149
        production environment 158
    collaboration 42
    cultural production mode 149, 157
    divide 39, 46, 60, 69, 166, 168,
        183, 199, 236, 255, 261, 266,
        299
    literacy 102
    production technology 155
    subscriber line (DSL) 271
    technology 62
direct
    inward dialling (DID) 270
    outward dialling (DOD) 270
dissemination 3, 17, 123
    of information 63
    of knowledge 129
    of technology 3
    strategy 223
distance education 61
distribution-oriented strategy 309
domain name server (DNS) 270

E

e-business environment 272
e-commerce 60, 110, 111, 182, 250, 27
    2, 273, 295
    in Ireland 203
e-Europe 290
e-Europe+ 290, 292
e-Europe+ Action Plan 300
e-Europe 2005 Action Plan 291
e-ForAll 201
e-governance 61
e-government 61, 182, 250, 273, 283, 2
    88, 291, 299
e-health 67, 182, 291, 295

Copyright © 2007, Idea Group Inc. Copying or distributing in print or electronic forms without written permission
of Idea Group Inc. is prohibited.

e-knowledge 291
e-learning 41, 44, 50, 51, 141, 222,
    224, 232, 233, 234, 236, 265
e-mail 262, 272, 308
e-management 295
e-Sri Lanka 251, 273
e-student 233
e-teacher 233, 234
e-teaching 232
e-transformation 292, 294, 300, 301
    Turkey Project 294
economic
    and regional development (ERD) 123
    development 184
education 2, 182
educational institution 9
effectiveness (brokerage) network 105
electronic
    -mediated learning 44
    commerce (e-commerce) 60
    data interchange network 272
empowerment 42
English
    as a foreign language (EFL) 124
    as a second language (L2) 130, 138
enhanced communication 23
eRunway 275
ethnic
    minorities (minzu) 321, 324
    populations 321
ethno
    -political conflicts 58
    -political factors 65
European Mediterranean Partnership
    (MEDA) 292
explicit knowledge 124, 125, 126, 127
External Degree of Bachelor of Informa-
    tion Technology (BIT) 267
external
    linkages (brokerage networks) 108
    stakeholder 110
extranet 42

F

fiberoptic networks 261
finance 23, 31

Five-Year Socioeconomic Development
    Plan (SEDP) 200
focal awareness 125
formation of enterprise network 115
frame relay (FR) 270
francophone 223

G

garbage in, garbage out (GIGO) 127
General Agreement of Trade in Services
    (GATS) 253
General Education Project II 266
general information technology (GIT) 263
genetic
    biobanks 320, 321
    databases 325
    sampling 321
genomic biobank 321
genre 152, 153
genuine progress indicator (GPI) 170, 171
geographic information system (GIS)
    106, 108, 109, 110
global
    audience 132
    communication 133
    distribution networks 150
    English 122, 131, 132, 133, 135,
        139, 142
globalization 2, 5, 7, 80, 140
globalizing world 243, 244
global
    knowledge economy 2
    language 131
    market 60
    perspective 129
Global Village Energy Partnership (GVEP)
    206
governance (rainbow model layer) 5
governmental transparency 61
grassroots 150
    consultation 8, 10, 16, 17, 18
    content development 8
    creativity 150
    ICT applications 11
    interventions 58
    involvement 14

Copyright © 2007, Idea Group Inc. Copying or distributing in print or electronic forms without written permission of Idea Group Inc. is prohibited.

movements 61
    production efforts 152
    stakeholder participation 123
    support 107
gravity
    equation 86, 89, 94
    model 86
gross domestic product (GDP) 171
guard dog strategies 268
guide dog strategies 268

H

half-life of knowledge 40
Han 323, 330, 332
heterarchy 191
hierarchy 191
high-quality multimedia production 151
higher education institution (HEI)
    23, 27, 32, 36
human
    contact 68
    development index (HDI) 170
    genomics projects 330
    infrastructure 126
    resource development (HRD) 249, 250
    rights 62
    security 66
hypertext markup language (HTML)
    136, 225

I

Icelandic health sector database 325
ICT (see also *information and communica-
    tion technology*)
    -based
        education 43
        learning 39, 41, 42, 43
        mass learning 51
    -enhanced education 3
    -mediated learning 42, 44
    -related regional development
        169, 172, 174
    center 22, 23, 32, 33, 36, 266
    champion 269
    development 3, 5, 202
    implementation 201

improvement 41
    indicator 297
    infrastructure 2, 40
    initiative 200
    in learning processes 42
    networks in rural regions 15
    penetration 255
    professionals 267, 268
Ikujiro Nonaka and Hirotaka Takeuchi 123
implementation strategy 269
India's education and research network
    (ERNET-India) 255
Indian Ministry of Environment and For-
    ests (MoEF) 106, 108
indigenous
    knowledge (IK) 128
    people 321
InfoDev 206
infomediary 200
information and communication technol-
    ogy (ICT) 40, 44, 51, 56, 123,
    166, 170, 180, 181, 187, 204,
    208, 234, 242, 246, 260,
    271, 288, 299, 308, 310, 321,
    282, 283, 305, 306
Information and Communication Technol-
    ogy Agency (ICTA) 273
information
    infrastructure 203
    kiosk 8
    literacy 315
    literate person 316
    management (IM) 41, 127 265, 267
    networking 182
    society 40, 71, 292
    system 104, 106
        failure 103
    technology (IT) 126, 288
        agreement (ITA-1) 253
        education resource centre (ITERC)
            265
        intervention 108
        services (ITS) 251
infrastructure 2, 150, 155, 159
innovation 104, 105
Institute of Computer Technology (ICT)
    269

Copyright © 2007, Idea Group Inc. Copying or distributing in print or electronic forms without written permission
of Idea Group Inc. is prohibited.

instructional strategy 229
integrated
    digital services network (ISDN) 135
    library management system (ILMS)
      112
intellectual
    property (IP) 157
    property right s (IPRs) 278
inter-village connectivity and empower-
    ment initiative (Thailand) 16
interim Poverty Reduction Strategy
    (IPRSP) 204
internal
    competencies 105
    process 23, 31, 34
International Centre for Integrated Moun-
    tain Development (ICIMOD) 254
international community 2
International Institute for Communication
    and Development (IICD) 128, 313
internationalization 26, 131, 133, 137
international
    monetary fund (IMF) 204
    non-governmental organization (INGO)
      206
    private leased circuit (IPLC) 270
    public sector accounting standards
      (IPSAS) 274
    trade 80
Internet 42, 44, 58, 61, 226, 277, 288
    , 308
    -accessible creative production 160
    -based gateways 313
    leased line (ILL) 270
    service provider (ISP) 248, 262
intranet 42
IP rights framework 150
isochronal 289
ITeS 252

J

John Keells
    Computer Services (JKCS) 275
    Holdings (JKH) 275
joint venture 32

K

Kachru, Braj 139, 140, 141
kiosk 8, 61
knowledge
    -based economy 42, 43
    -economy strategy 311
    management (KM) 125,
      128, 137, 306
    object 128

L

L1 (native speaker of English) 138, 140
L2 (English as a second language) 138,
    140
labor force 23
language preservation 16
Lanka Educational Academic and Research
    Network (LEARN) 255, 262
learner-centered multimedia learning 45
learning 23, 31, 34, 42
    by doing 123
    center 61
    resource center (LRC) 112
    technologies 40
least developed countries (LDCs) 182
Liberation Tigers of Tamil Eelam (LTTE)
    260
lifelong learner 11
LISA 129, 131, 137
literacy/social facilitation (rainbow model
    layer) 5
local
    adaptation 114
    area network (LAN) 112, 224
    communities 3, 18, 23, 106, 168
    condition 110
    connection 110
    context 106
    contingency 110
    government 110
    knowledge 3, 4
    stakeholders 136
localization 122, 129, 130, 142
Looking After Children Electronic System
    (LACES) 205

Copyright © 2007, Idea Group Inc. Copying or distributing in print or electronic forms without written permission
of Idea Group Inc. is prohibited.

low-income communities 246

M

m
-teacher 233, 234
-team 234, 235
M.S. Swaminathan Research Foundation 254
mailing list 61
managed private leased circuit (MPLC) 270, 271
management for development results (MfDR) 200
marginal communities 182
mathematical network theory 191
measurement managed companies 27
media environment 152
millennium
development goal (MDG) 182
information technologies (MIT) 275
Ministry
of Economic Development (MED) 202
of Education and Vocational Training (MEVT) 312
minorities 323, 330
minzu 332
classification system 332
mobile social capital 105
modernization 6
Money Matters Institute, Inc 171
multi-national corporation (MNC) 243
multimedia super corridor (MSC) 203
multinational companies (MNCs) 324
multipurpose community telecenters (MCT) 199

N

N-Form Organization 191
NAPITSE 264
National
Biodiversity Information Center (NBIC) 325
Council for
Science and Technology (NCST) 206
Scientific Research (NCSR) 206
Development Strategy (NDS) 204
Examination Council of Tanzania 314
Growth and Poverty Eradication Strategy (NGPES) 200
ICT policy 306
Institute of Education (NIE) 265
Policy on Information Technology in School Education (NAPITSE) 262, 263
Poverty Eradication Strategy (NPES) 307
Science Foundation (NSF) 107
Strategy for Socioeconomic Development (NSSED) 204
Telecommunication Corporation (NTC) 249
native speaker 131
network
analysis 104
closure 105
linkage 106, 110
project 23
new ICTs (nICTs) 56, 59, 64, 69, 70
New Partnership for Africa's Development (NEPAD) 205
Nielsen 134, 135, 136, 137
non-governmental organizations (NGOs) 61, 106, 115, 123, 204, 210, 300
Nonaka, Ikujiro 124, 125, 126, 127
nonnative speaker 131
nonprofit organization 60

O

observability (attribute of innovation) 104
ocalization 130
ODA 203
OEMs 272
Okinawa Charter on Global Information Society 206
one-stop-shop (OSS) 200
open
-source software licensing 157
copyright arrangements 156
educational environment 232
model 224
of teaching and learning 222

Copyright © 2007, Idea Group Inc. Copying or distributing in print or electronic forms without written permission of Idea Group Inc. is prohibited.

schools 237
source software 251
Open University of Sri Lanka (OUSL) 263
optical fiber network 261
Organization for Economic Coop-
    eration and Development (OECD)
    183, 206, 244
outlocation service 252
outsourcing service 252

P

Pakistan
    Educational Research Network (PERN)
    255
    Telecommunication Company Limited
    (PTCL) 249
Pan Asia networking (PAN) 255
Parliamentary Online Information System
    (POLIS) 314
participatory design model 107
passive information transfer 181
peacebuilding 68
pedagogical
    functions 235
    practices 4
peer-to-peer linkage 108
people-track approach 134
personal digital aid (PDA) 242
physical infrastructure 243
pluricentricity 140
points-of-presence (POP) 270
post-secondary education 41
poverty 309
    monitoring master plan (PMMP) 309
    reduction (PR) 181, 185, 201
    reduction strategy article (PRSP) 200
    reduction strategy paper (PSRP) 309
primary
    and secondary school 14
    public education 11
private sector 285, 315
    entrepreneurs 300
problem-based activities 32
production-oriented growth strategy 309
project management perspective 103
Prometeus 40

public
    education 11
    infrastructure 9
    television networks 152
pull principle 153
push principle 153

R

radio frequency identification technology
    (RFID) 243
reconciliation 66, 67, 68
reconstruction 65, 66, 68
regional
    area 167
    communities 181
    development (RD) 185
    grouping 105
    partnership program (RPP) 202
    planning 283
relative advantage 104
remote communities 18
rights and empowerment strategy 310
rural
    areas 61, 270, 306, 307
    centers 18
    community 8, 222
    sector 268

S

SAARC Agricultural Information Centre
    (SAIC) 254
safety
    network 105
    driver 105, 108
Sarawak Biodiversity Center (SBC) 328
Sarvodaya Shramadana movement 254
scanner 22, 39, 102, 336
school
    district digital
        Intranet 231
        intranet 223
SchoolNet 224
science parks 32
service/access provision (rainbow model
    layer) 5

Copyright © 2007, Idea Group Inc. Copying or distributing in print or electronic forms without written permission
of Idea Group Inc. is prohibited.

Sharing with Other People Network
    (SWOPNet) 312
short-term milestones 35
Singlish 140
small and medium enterprise (SME) 200,
    208, 249, 268, 272, 315
Small Island Developing States Network
    (SIDSNet) 205
social
    , technical, economic, environmental,
        and political (STEEP) 314
    capital 182, 198
    content 198
    development 184
    network analysis 104, 105
societal development strategies 254
socio
    -demographic factors 168
    -economic development 42, 180, 201,
        205, 253, 261
socioeconomic 59, 140, 168, 201
    development 42, 180, 201, 205, 253,
        261
    factors 285
    gains 201
    transformation 282
software tools (rainbow model layer) 5
South Asian
    Association for Regional Cooperation
        (SAARC) 254
    Network Operators Group (SANOG)
        255
South Asia on the Human Development
    Index 250
Sri Lanka
    Institute of Information Technology
        (SLIIT) 263
    Telecom (SLT) 261, 270, 271, 277
    Telecommunications Authority (SLTA)
        271
stakeholder 23, 106, 268, 276
    assessment model (SAM) 116
    group 131
    network 116
State Planning Organization (SPO) 284
state wide area network (SWAN) 253
stationary social capital 105

STEM~Net 224, 225
strategic
    initiative 35
    management 26
    path 35
    planning 24
    success 35
    theme 28
strategy map 23, 33, 34, 36
strong ties 105
structural holes 105
subsidiary awareness 125
Sudan Virtual Engineering Library – Sus-
    tainability Network (SudVEL-SKN)
    13
support
    network 106, 112
    infrastructure 112
sustainable
    development
        initiatives 14
        networking program (SDNP) 254
    livelihoods approach 309
Sveiby, Karl-Erik 124
synergies 32

T

tacit knowledge 124, 125, 142, 245
Takeuchi, Hirotaka 124, 125, 126, 127
Tanzania Global Development Learning
    Center (TGDLC) 315
technical
    infrastructure 295
    literacy 2
techno-fetishism 7
technological
    differences 91
    innovation 79, 80, 94
    knowledge 182
technology diffusion program 106, 108
techspeak 131
tele-learning (e-learning) 222
telecenter 1, 8, 15, 43, 199, 249, 260
telecommunication 168, 260, 261, 271
    bandwidth 274
    infrastructure 277

Copyright © 2007, Idea Group Inc. Copying or distributing in print or electronic forms without written permission
of Idea Group Inc. is prohibited.

Telecommunications Regulatory Commis-
    sion of Sri Lanka (TRCSL) 262
telemedicine 67
tertiary educational sector 15
traditional
    learning method 61
    method
        of instruction 226
        of communications and teaching 10
    school 237
    teaching 222
trainer-of-trainers model 107
transparent governance 57
transport infrastructure 94
trialability 104
trunk telecommunications network 261
Turkish
    National Information Main Plan (TU-
        ENA) 294
    Scientific Research Institute (TUBI-
        TAK) 292
TZ-MDGs 307

U

U.N. Millennium Development Goals
    (MDGs) 306
U.S. Agency for International Develop-
    ment (USAID) 108
U.S. Patent and Trademark Office (USP-
    TO) 328
Uganda Business Information Network
    (UBIN) 200
UN-MDGs 307
underdeveloped countries 283
UNDP 203, 204
unemployment 322
UNESCO 206
United Nations Development Program
    (UNDP) 170
United Nations Educational, Scientific and
    Cultural Organisation (UNESCO)
    205, 244
United Nations Institute for Training and
    Research (UNITAR) 154
university education 14

UN Millennium Development Goals
    (MDGs) 305
urban area 307

V

VEEM (Victorian E-Commerce Early
    Movers) 110
very small aperture terminal (VSAT) 248
village information kiosk 8
virtual
    classroom 42, 51
    organization 23, 31
    private network (VPNs) 270
    Souk 128
    teaching 222
Vista School District digital intranet
    225, 230, 232, 233, 237
voice over IP (VoIP) 310

W

weak ties 105
Wealth of Nations Triangle Index 171
Web 272
    -based
        course 230
        knowledge dissemination 136
        learning 42
        magazines 64
        site 277, 288
WebCT 230
wiki 152
wireless application protocol (WAP) 273
World Summit on Sustainable Develop-
    ment (WSSD) 206
World Trade Organization (WTO) 253
World Wide Web (WWW) 44

Copyright © 2007, Idea Group Inc. Copying or distributing in print or electronic forms without written permission
of Idea Group Inc. is prohibited.

Looking for a way to make information science and technology research easy?
Idea Group Inc. Electronic Resources are designed to keep your institution
up-to-date on the latest information science technology trends and research.

Information Technology Research at the Click of a Mouse!

InfoSci-Online

⇨ Instant access to thousands of information technology book chapters, journal articles, teaching cases, and conference proceedings

⇨ Multiple search functions

⇨ Full-text entries and complete citation information

⇨ Upgrade to **InfoSci-Online Premium** and add thousands of authoritative entries from Idea Group Reference's handbooks of research and encyclopedias!

IGI Full-Text Online Journal Collection

⇨ Instant access to thousands of scholarly journal articles

⇨ Full-text entries and complete citation information

IGI Teaching Case Collection

⇨ Instant access to hundreds of comprehensive teaching cases

⇨ Password-protected access to case instructor files

IGI E-Access

⇨ Online, full-text access to IGI individual journals, encyclopedias, or handbooks of research

Additional E-Resources

⇨ E-Books

⇨ Individual Electronic Journal Articles

⇨ Individual Electronic Teaching Cases

IGI Electronic Resources have flexible pricing to help meet the needs of any institution.

www.igi-online.com

Sign Up for a Free Trial of IGI Databases!